THE
Biodiversity
Gardener

Establishing a Legacy for the Natural World

Paul Sterry

WILD
NATURE
PRESS

PRINCETON

Published by Princeton University Press
41 William Street, Princeton, New Jersey 08540
99 Banbury Road, Oxford OX2 6JX
press.princeton.edu

British Library Cataloging-in-Publication Data is available

Library of Congress Control Number 2023930184
ISBN 978-0-691-24555-3
Ebook ISBN 978-0-691-24556-0

Series Publisher Julie Dando,
WILDNATUREPRESS Ltd., Plymouth

Printed in Slovakia

10 9 8 7 6 5 4 3 2 1

Hampshire Record Office (HRO) are custodians of the following documents,
images of which are reproduced with their permission:
1827 Enclosure Map for the parish of Pamber, reference HRO Q23/2/108,
1827 Enclosure Award, reference HRO Q23/1/2 pp. 634–723,
1838 Tithe Map for the parish of Pamber, reference HRO 21M65/F7/185/2,
1838 Tithe Apportionment for the parish of Pamber, reference HRO 21M65/F7/185/1,
Pamber Overseers of Poor 1795–1814, reference HRO 15M70/PO1,
Little Fields Indenture, reference HRO 33A12/1,
Beaurepaire Annual Accounts for the financial year 1 April 1680 to 31 March 1681
compiled by Thomas Brocas, reference HRO 48M50/9.

Cover image: Pedunculate Oak
Back cover: Common Toad, Bramble, Sparrowhawk, Yellow-necked Mouse, Cockchafer and Marsh Tit
Title page: Gatekeeper caterpillar
all by Paul Sterry

Contents

To see a World in a Grain of Sand
And a Heaven in a Wild Flower
Hold Infinity in the palm of your hand
And Eternity in an hour
From *Auguries of Innocence* by William Blake (1757–1827)

Acknowledgements

I would like to thank the following people who have helped with encouragement and support for the project: Julia Cady and Mic Cady, Andrew Cleave, Julie Dando and Marc Dando, and Robert Kirk. In addition, I would also like to thank my copy editor Annie Gottlieb for her meticulous attention to detail and insightful comments.

Others who have provided help, ranging from invaluable background information and constructive comment to advice on identification, include: Stephanie Albery and Alan Albery, Mark Avery, Paul Beevers, Jenna Burlingham, Andy Clements, Tom Cullum and Jackie Cullum, Jonty Denton, Dave Gibbs, Sue Gordon, Heather Halls, Karl Hughes and Nicola Hughes, Evan Jones, Ben Kite, Belinda Lugg and Keith Lugg, Adrian Moss, Adam Rattray, David Rymill of the Hampshire Record Office, Graham Vick, and David Wolfe QC.

Lastly, I would like to thank my neighbours who inspired me to embark on my biodiversity project and motivated me to write this book.

Introduction

The Biodiversity Gardener is a tale of the decline of nature on the one hand, and the potential for reversing the trend at the local level on the other. It is not a book about rewilding as such and it is certainly not about conventional gardening. Rather, it encourages people to understand the ecological complexity of the man-influenced environment around them, their impact on it, and their potential to do good. The story reminds us of how our ancestors altered and shaped the English countryside. As a consequence of rural economics and the way the land was used through the ages, inadvertently our forebears gave rise to the biodiversity richness that still flourished until the mid-twentieth century: rural history and natural history are inextricably linked.

The Biodiversity Gardener allows the reader to grasp just how catastrophic the decline in wildlife has been since that time and to recognise the role played in that ruination by modern rural economics. I am not the first to say this, but the UK is now one of the most nature-depleted countries on the planet. During my lifetime – nearly seven decades – erosion and degradation of native wildlife in the British countryside has reached such a level that there is an urgent ecological imperative to safeguard pockets of biodiversity for the future. A living equivalent of Kew's Millennium Seed Bank, if you like, and a habitat-driven approach that anyone who owns land can adopt, benefiting not just plants but all forms of native wildlife. From my experiences, no plot is too small, and anyone who cares about wildlife should consider using at least part of their land for genuine biodiversity enhancement. The only other ingredients required are an enquiring mind and an environmental conscience.

The story is told through the prism of a north Hampshire cottage, in the context of its half-acre plot as well as its place in the surrounding countryside. The background spans four hundred years or so from the cottage's construction in the late sixteenth century to the current day and illustrates how rural history and land use helped shape the area's natural history. Fast-forward to the present day: with recent environmental loss in the surrounding countryside, we discover the role the cottage and garden might serve in the long-term recovery of local natural history. It is a story that will be played out elsewhere in lowland Britain, and offers food for thought for others.

The bigger picture

Stepping back a pace, in the wake of the last Ice Age, settlement of the British Isles by humans followed one step behind colonisation by wildlife. Geology and altitude notwithstanding, in the absence of man much of the landscape would have become and remained forested in some shape or form. However, from the outset, colonising humans began altering the landscape, shaping the land to make it more habitable for people and influencing natural history as a consequence. For Britain's plants and animals, the impact of forest clearance, and the subsequent use and management of the cleared land and remaining woodland, were profound.

In the millennia that followed the retreat of the last ice sheet, low-impact land exploitation and a relatively slow pace of change meant that, by and large, wildlife was able to adapt in step with the changing environment. The unintended consequence of the resulting mosaic of habitats would have been greater wildlife variety – what, today, we call biodiversity – than would have been present in the absence of human intervention. This rather begs the question of whether increased

In the part of north Hampshire where I live, there are no areas of genuine wilderness left, and the entire landscape, woodland included, has been altered by man over the millennia. However, woodland management that was unintentionally sympathetic to wildlife contributed to the rich biodiversity many of us value today, by accident rather than design.

numerical biodiversity per se is always the best outcome for wildlife species that would occur naturally in the absence of man. However, since we cannot turn back the clock, that discussion in the context of Britain is largely academic. Apart from a few now-extinct large mammals (including apex predators) and species that were subsequently domesticated, biodiversity gain was the consequence of man's influence on, and use of, the British countryside in that formative era. Evidence for the ancient ancestry of 'working the land' can be found across Britain, including in my native north Hampshire. Here, the Romans occupied Silchester, near where I live, and farmed the land between there and Basingstoke for 400 years before the advent of the Anglo-Saxons in circa 450 CE. This relatively low-impact use of the land continued until and throughout the medieval period.

● A GOOD READ

The Biodiversity Gardener is a personal tale. For a wide-ranging account of human impact on the environment, a compelling overview is provided in Trevor Beebee's book *Impacts of Human Population on Wildlife*. It covers some of the same ground as I do, explores different avenues, and provides wide-ranging evidence-based detail. It makes for an alarming but compelling read. In addition, anyone interested in the environment in general, and biodiversity loss and advice about reversing the trend in particular, then good reads would include anything and everything written by Dave Goulson and George Monbiot. See the References section for suggestions.

Recent times

Over the centuries that followed the appearance on the scene of Anglo-Saxons, agricultural advances gradually made commercial exploitation of the land more profitable and achievable. Despite this, the diversity and abundance of wildlife that accords with most people's notion of the bucolic British countryside would have remained intact. It was not until the dawn of fully mechanised and industrialised agriculture, ushered in after the end of the Second World War, that things started to go badly wrong. This led to what we see today: non-stop exploitation of the land, and unprecedented chemical abuse inflicted by industrial-scale application of fertilisers (both synthetic and organic in origin), pesticides and herbicides.

Based on personal observation, many modern-day country dwellers are oblivious to, or ignorant of, the wildlife that the countryside harboured just 70 years ago. They know no better and, using birds as an example, for many of them a landscape without Grey Partridges and Turtle Doves is the new normal, the void being filled by Pheasants and Woodpigeons, species whose presence and abundance is a direct and negative consequence of contemporary human land use.

Formerly widespread, the Turtle Dove is now to all intents extinct at the local level where I live in north Hampshire, as a result of changes in farming practices.

At the heart of this book is a garden that, for at least four centuries, provided the needs of residents of the dwelling that sits at its centre. Today its role has been flipped: it has become a haven for wildlife in an increasingly sterile farming landscape, one from which the ecological needs of the countryside might be drawn by future generations.

The fight back

Fortunately, however, there are members of my generation who are painfully aware of the demise of British wildlife. They are not willing to sit by and let the native plants and animals they grew up with sixty years ago slide towards extinction without pushing back; I am among their number. It is unrealistic to expect attitudes among the farming community or aspirational land developers to change at a fast enough pace to make a difference. Consequently, it requires others to step up to the plate, people willing and able to place conservation before self-interest. This is where rural gardens and small plots of land have a vital role to play.

Landscape-scale rewilding projects are to be applauded, but it is worth remembering their limitations; planting trees and scattering wildflower seeds is just the beginning. You cannot buy or plant the web of life that constitutes a native habitat: it takes time – years – to develop, and colonisation has to come from somewhere. Gardens and relatively small plots of land can help in that regard and serve as reservoirs for these future endeavours. *The Biodiversity Gardener* illustrates one example of how this might be achieved, and highlights the potential difference that just a small plot of land could make.

Managing land for native wildlife

Conventional wildlife gardening tends to be slanted towards human interest, typically with as much emphasis placed on benefits to gardeners as to the particular wildlife in question – and sometimes more so. As an indication of this predictable bias, taxa in the spotlight are often iconic, or showy and eye-catching. While this approach may benefit a select band of species, it typically does little to promote overall native biodiversity, and advice on the subject sometimes comes across as feel-good gardening adorned with a whiff of environmental virtue signalling and tokenism. It is also a reminder that, in most situations, conventional gardening is about control, specifically the notion that we can and should organise nature.

The Biodiversity Gardener aims to turn the conventional gardening mindset on its head, in an attempt to ease our controlling grip on our immediate environment, and to let things follow their natural course, albeit with

Orange-tip butterflies are a welcome sight in spring. If I adopted a tidy-minded, conventional approach to gardening, and 'weeded' out Garlic Mustard – the larval foodplant – they would not breed in my garden and any adults seen would be ones that were passing through, not resident. On the left is an adult male while on the right is a superbly camouflaged, counter-shaded caterpillar aligned with its foodplant's seed pod.

a purpose and in a direction of our choosing. There may well be collateral benefits for the gardener as well as for biodiversity: in my experience meaningful fulfilment is more likely to be achieved by genuinely helping the environment rather than by the nebulous pursuit of happiness through horticultural self-gratification. For me, creating a biodiversity garden has been, and still is, a process rather than an event. Instrumental in the progression has been a growing awareness of the creeping ecological degradation going on around me, and I have been informed as much by local history as natural history. The book aims to open the eyes of readers to similar environmental trends where they live and, through example, inspire them to do something practical to help reverse the trend. One person's actions may not make a significant difference, but collectively and connectively biodiversity gardening surely has a role to play.

Why is biodiversity important?

Firstly, we need to answer the question *what is biodiversity?* On the grand scale it is a measure of the variety of life on earth. For me in the context of my garden, it is the number of native species that it harbours. Some species are generalists and will occur in a wide range of habitats. Others are more specialist and restricted – butterfly species whose larvae feed on a single habitat-specific foodplant, for example, will only occur where that plant grows. It therefore follows that the greater the habitat diversity in a given area – in this instance my garden – the more biodiversity it will harbour.

My reasons for supporting biodiversity are fundamentally ethical and moral: with the privilege of living on planet Earth comes the responsibility of taking care of what is, after all, our home. However, if self-interest is more of a consideration, then a practical argument presents itself. The greater the biodiversity in a given area, the greater the complexity of its ecosystems. With complexity comes a degree of stability and an ability to withstand short-term environmental variations – a buffer if you like – and the possibility of habitats and their inhabitants adapting to longer-term trends. Addressing the blight of biodiversity loss head-on and as a matter of urgency might just buy us enough time to save what we can of dwindling nature in the hope that the self-inflicted existential threat of global warming and its underlying causes are addressed and resolved in time. The goal: to ensure lasting, globally stable ecosystems – and hence a stable planet – for future generations of plants and animals, humans included.

Putting wildlife first

At its core *The Biodiversity Gardener* encourages the reader to reflect, in the context of the garden and further afield, on the following advice: 'Ask not what nature can do for you, ask what you can do for nature'. It invites the garden owner to develop a better understanding of the complexity of their environment, to hone identification skills in order to measure their success or otherwise, and to acquire an informed resilience when it comes to defending and promoting the approach. Successful and fulfilling biodiversity gardening requires an appreciation of the innate and inherent beauty and complexity of biological systems rather than simply adhering to perceived values of what natural beauty means. By following this route, you will be abandoning the mantle of 'gardener' in the conventional sense in favour of becoming warden of your own private nature reserve.

Using insight garnered from a passion for British natural history spanning more than six decades, *The Biodiversity Gardener* offers advice for anyone who wants to help native biodiversity. It is not a practical guide to gardening as such. Instead, it charts my own experiences, those that inspired me to embark on the project and that continue to motivate me. Underpinning the book is a personal journey from reluctant traditional gardener to enthusiastic biodiversity garden custodian. The genesis for this transformation was partly a love of nature but more a sense of desperation at the destruction of biodiversity I was witnessing. It was also

I take heart from the fact that, in most years, one or two pairs of Chiffchaffs take up residence in and on the margins of my garden in spring. As they feed on invertebrates, I assume their presence is a reflection of the abundance and diversity of their food in the vicinity.

a response to frustration at the failure of government (at the borough council, county council and national level) and conservation bodies to halt this loss, and indeed in some instances their compliance and complicity in the destructive process.

When it comes to conservation in the UK, I am definitely a glass-half-empty person, a pessimist in some people's eyes but a realist in my own. With day-to-day exposure to biodiversity decline all around me I find it hard to be anything else. Certainly, in the Hampshire borough of Basingstoke where I live there are few genuinely good-news stories when it comes to wildlife. At the national and international level, with a handful of exceptions, what I read and hear in the media only contributes to my overall disillusionment. This includes existential environmental matters trivialised to a level that would be an insult to a ten-year-old, and a public spoon-fed with a rose-tinted view of the world that seldom encourages environmental reflection, let alone action. I have lost track of the number of times local news outlets have trumpeted some new rewilding project or other, while never once mentioning housing- and agriculture-driven 'dewilding' losses going on alongside; losses so egregious that they greatly outstrip any meagre rewilding gains. I am also underwhelmed by some of our celebrated natural world pundits, who know

what is going on and could and should do more to open people's eyes by dint of their public profile. Still, we would not want gloomy prognoses to encourage people to switch off literally or figuratively, or anyone's social media fan base to be affected, would we? Meanwhile the rape of the natural world continues apace.

As if that were not enough, in the autumn of 2022 we began to hear rumours of government intentions to sweep away environmental red tape. First there was The Retained EU Law (Revocation and Reform) Bill that was introduced to Parliament on 22nd September 2022 with the aim of reviewing or abandoning all post-Brexit laws (around a quarter of which relate to the environment) by the end of 2023. The inference was that these would be replaced by something better. But better for whom? That was always going to be question. Then there were proposals to set up new 'investment zones' and 'streamline' the planning process, which in political speak may well mean removing environmental obstacles that stand in the way of development. Predictably, given a sense of betrayal and with past experiences in mind, alarm bells went off in the conservation world. Hardly surprising since the legal frameworks surrounding protected species legislation, habitat directives and new Environmental Land Management Schemes were all in the firing line.

Different approaches

Rewilding is a welcome conservation response to biodiversity loss in the UK. However, context is important, and there will be instances where the approach is not necessarily in the best interest of native biodiversity. An example might be the planting of trees in a wildlife-rich meadow with the goal of creating woodland. Put simply, by design the result will be the destruction of one wildlife-rich habitat with its own suite of habitat-specific creatures in the hope of replacing it with another. What is needed is an understanding of natural history at the local level, an ability to recognise good habitats and their significance when you see them, and an informed ability to balance the costs of environmental change against any perceived biodiversity benefits.

My quest has been to recreate in my garden a microcosm of those wildlife-rich habitats that occur in my local area, and are typical of the garden's soil type: these are hedgerows and scrub, woodlands, meadows and ponds. All are under threat in the vicinity and many fine examples have been lost already. It was never the intention for my garden to simply be a refuge for wildlife. The hope, which has been realised, was that

My garden's role transcends its current biological significance. It has become, in essence, a Noah's Ark in miniature, from which re-colonisation of species currently extirpated from what remains of the surrounding countryside might just occur, should future landowners nearby have a change of environmental heart and a Damascene conversion to ecological enlightenment. By adopting and adapting this approach to suit their own plots, other gardeners and landowners are encouraged to do their best for native wildlife and create their own wildlife oases.

Common Toads lived in my garden in low numbers before a pond was created and are one of five species of amphibians whose populations have benefitted from this new breeding site. Future generations of toads will disperse and colonise new locations. As an aside, in his essay *Some Thoughts on the Common Toad* George Orwell (born Eric Arthur Blair, 1903–1950) comments on the unique beauty of a Common Toad's eye.

by fostering these habitats, species appropriate to them would colonise and flourish; at its simplest, the long-term aim was and is to maximise native biodiversity. However, the situation is more subtly nuanced than that, and I do have priorities: I give preferential treatment to species that the evidence of my eyes tells me are particularly vulnerable in the area, and try not to encourage or benefit the few that already prosper in the twenty-first-century British landscape.

Biodiversity gardening does not mean neglect or a descent into chaos, and along with other like-minded souls I too make concessions to conventional gardening. I retain areas of mown lawn, a fruit cage, a small vegetable plot, a few herbaceous beds, that sort of thing, all of which also contribute in various ways to biodiversity enhancement. However, I do have an evolving strategic plan, a managed retreat from conventional gardening, informed by knowledge of the local area and a long-term vision of what I want to achieve. Prospective bodiversity gardeners would benefit from this approach, along with a means of measuring success. This is where raising your ecological awareness and honing your identification skills come in useful.

Common Hawthorn is a component of scrub and hedgerows in my garden, connecting with the wider local landscape, literally and biologically. It is a great plant for native wildlife: its flowers are nectar sources for insects in spring; the leaves are food for an array of invertebrates; its dense, spiny structure is ideal for certain species of nesting birds; and its berries are eaten by birds, while the seeds they contain are food for small mammals. Many of the Hawthorn-dominated hedgerows in the parish where I live would have been planted as a consequence of the 1827 Pamber Enclosure Act (see p. 96).

Does size matter?

In terms of size, my biodiversity garden is nothing to shout about. It might be considered large by urban standards but it is on the small side of average in the rural context. And on a farming scale it is positively minute. However, its relatively modest size only serves to emphasise just what nature can achieve in terms of biodiversity enrichment in a small space and in a short period of time. That is especially true if you are fortunate enough to live in an area that historically was rich in wildlife.

● EVOLUTION IN ACTION

If cared for appropriately, even a small plot of land can make a difference for biodiversity recovery. What is equally remarkable is that tiny areas, particularly ones that are isolated geographically, can be all it takes to drive the process of evolution. Take the Galápagos Islands, for example: naturalists will be familiar with the consequences of evolution-in-action on an archipelago's fauna, and how island individuality helped Charles Darwin shape the concept of natural selection. All the more surprising then to find that isolation encouraged the same process on our own doorstep. The case in point is a plant called Lundy Cabbage. First brought to the attention of botanists by GP Dr Elliston Wright in 1936, it grows on the eponymous island in the Bristol Channel and nowhere else in the world, restricted to the southern half of the perilously sloping east side. Judging by its current habitat preference, it is a plant that has evolved – most likely since the end of the last Ice Age – to colonise unstable ground, specifically the scree slopes and landslides that are a feature of that part of Lundy. Few competing plants can tolerate this instability. The evolution of a new and unique species occurred in an area no greater than perhaps 80 acres (32 hectares), and in reality just a fraction of that because of the limited extent of its favoured unstable habitat. For a detailed picture of Lundy Cabbage, a scholarly article by S. G. Compton and R. S. Key in the Journal of Ecology provides further background (see the References section for details).

Not only is Lundy Cabbage unique, but two beetles – Lundy Cabbage Flea Beetle (shown here) and Lundy Cabbage Weevil – feed on it and also occur nowhere else in the world.

There is an irony to the fact that in some instances actions that contribute to biodiversity loss are undertaken in the name of combatting climate change. Taking wind turbines as an example, there is a finite risk that flying birds, such as these Swifts, will be killed by collision with the rotating blades. Solar Parks also have their drawbacks: being fenced in, they impact wildlife connectivity, and if the vegetation beneath the panels is sprayed with herbicides any meaningful benefits for native biodiversity will be minimal.

A work in progress

My biodiversity garden did not appear overnight. It is the culmination of a series of projects that complement one another and work *with* the surrounding environment, the result being ecological synergy. The project is still a work in progress, but even today I would wager that there is more native biodiversity, and far more wildlife abundance per square metre, in my half-acre garden than on land nearby that either is farmed intensively, or has been industrialised. That would not have been the case when I first encountered my cottage some fifty years ago, and not even when I moved here around twenty-five years ago. But in the intervening half century, changes in the way the land around me is used now means my garden is an island of biodiversity in a sea of increasing ecological impoverishment.

The superficial end of the wildlife gardening spectrum might be described as *sapiens*-centric, and there are parallels with the debate about climate change, where responses to it are primarily framed in terms of the impact it will have on us as individuals and for future generations of people. All well and good, but the approach allows us (and more importantly decision-makers supposedly acting on our behalf) to sideline, overlook or ignore the catastrophic destruction of biodiversity caused by the human race in my lifetime, a decline that continues apace alongside the warming of the planet.

Why bother, you might ask? When life is so short, some might say just get on with it and enjoy yourself. For my part, having experienced environmental degradation first-hand, I cannot in all conscience sit back and do nothing, and I return to the notion that with privilege comes responsibility. The aim of *The Biodiversity Gardener* is to encourage other people to open their eyes to what is going on around them and to inspire them to do something about it. We can all do something. Shame on us if we do nothing at all.

What does the future hold?

Based on experiences close to home in north Hampshire, I don't see informed environmental awareness manifesting itself among enough of the population to make a difference in my lifetime. And I suspect the situation at the local level is reflected nationwide. Born in the wake of the Second World War and raised during the post-war austerity years, many equate success with material wealth and see it as something to aspire to and achieve by whatever means available, without ever questioning the impact of their economic growth on the environment. Added to that is a population many of whom are shockingly wasteful and do not care about the environmental cost or consequences of the food they eat, only its price. Statistics abound but according to figures quoted in a 2021 House of Lords report entitled *Food Waste in the UK*, the UK produced around 9.5 million tonnes of food waste in 2019. If the current population were to cast its collective mind back a generation to the Second World War, there might be lessons to be learned: in August 1940 it became an offence, punishable by imprisonment, to waste food.

The only slim hope for UK wildlife and indeed planet Earth lies with the next generation, so let us hope they do not take after their parents. Bequeathing them pockets of genuine native biodiversity with which they can build back Britain biologically is probably the best legacy that any individual can leave. In this regard I am encouraged by the vision of the handful of like-minded souls I have come across, including some farming landowners, who have acted on their environmental consciences and benefited native biodiversity as a result.

Without pockets of native biodiversity such as my garden, where is future recolonisation by native wildlife going to come from? You can buy the seeds of Greater Bird's-foot-trefoil, seen here in my garden, but you cannot purchase and sow the eggs of Common Blue butterflies whose larvae feed on the leaves of the plant.

Understanding habitat requirements is vital for nuanced conservation in our human-influenced countryside. In the context of the UK, the Stone-curlew's fate is inextricably linked to farming, specifically the way in which land is managed. They nest on bare ground in areas where these nervous and largely nocturnal birds have an uninterrupted view of potential threats. Plant early and the vegetation will be too high by the time they nest in spring, plough the field at the wrong time and eggs and young chicks will be destroyed, and spray molluscicides and insecticides on the land and there will be nothing for them to eat. Although the land around my cottage would never have suited the species, in my youth they bred within cycling distance of Basingstoke where I was born.

The Biodiversity Gardener is not a polemic against farmers, nor an attempt to persuade them to farm in different ways. For that argument, and for an overview of the environmental impacts of farming at the national and international level, Dieter Helm's *Green and Prosperous Land* is a must-read book (see the References section for details). It explains the environmental consequences and economic folly of the present industrialised approach to farming. In evidence-based detail, it discusses the concept of natural capital, and covers subjects including soil sequestration of carbon and the disproportionate contribution that industrial agriculture makes to the release of this element. The pessimist in me cannot see the book's suggestions being adopted in a time frame that will halt both climate change and biodiversity loss. In that regard, *The Biodiversity Gardener* provides a lifeline for individuals frustrated by the current state of affairs, those who want to leave a biodiversity endowment policy for future generations but currently lack direction.

At its best modern farming can produce worthwhile food and benefit certain species of wildlife. However, tinkering with farming methods alone is never going to halt the overall decline in wildlife. Stating the obvious, by intent an arable field can never provide the right environment for ancient woodland species or unimproved grassland specialists.

For anyone so obsessed with the accumulation of wealth that every scrap of land they own must earn its keep, this is not the book for you. Nor is it a book for anyone who sees the role of their garden or plot of land as something to provide them with a route to happiness. Biodiversity gardening demands a commitment and in some senses a sacrifice: only by compromising some of our aspirational wealth and desire for personal gratification will meaningful benefits for wildlife be achieved. By way of a bonus, though, it is a route to genuine fulfilment in life.

Once widespread, Grey Partridges are in decline and to all intents extinct where I live. In spring and summer, adults and chicks feed largely on invertebrates. Spray these out of existence and there is nothing for the birds to eat. Well-intentioned it may be, but just as damaging to the prospects of both these open country specialists is any notion of planting trees in arable fields where these species still occur: Stone-curlews and Grey Partridges do not and cannot live in woodland.

Like many other towns in southern England, Basingstoke has sprawled and spread since the end of the Second World War. This photograph was taken in 2008. In the decade or more that has followed, many of the fields in the distance have disappeared, replaced by more concrete, bricks and mortar.

Setting the Scene

Humble beginnings

As I began to expand my horizons in my teens, there was a time when the worst question I could be asked was 'Where were you born?' I would squirm and try to change the subject, but if pressed I had to answer 'Basingstoke', and in my formative years this was a source of deep embarrassment. The town can number among its luminaries the novelist Jane Austen (1775–1817), who was born and grew up in nearby Steventon in the late eighteenth century. In addition, the writer and cricket commentator John Arlott (1914–1991) was born and educated there; and the naturalist Gilbert White (1720–1793) also received an education in the town. However, despite its illustrious associations, mention of the town's name in the big, wide world when I was growing up invariably produced eyebrow-raising reactions ranging from sneering pity to scorn and derision. Contemporary alumni of the school I attended include conservationist Mark Carwardine and gardening royalty's Monty Don, both of whom have since gone on to accomplish great things. I cannot bask in the glow of their achievements, however, and remain stigmatised by my place of birth.

Less-than-flattering references to Basingstoke can be found in Gilbert and Sullivan's *Ruddigore*, and (with echoes of John Betjeman's view of Slough) at one time *Country Life* readers apparently voted the modern town centre the sixth 'most hated eyesore' in the country; it could not even rise to the challenge and be *the* most hated. It turns out that contempt for the town can be traced back even further. In the 1821 translation of the *Travels Of Cosmo the Third, Grand Duke of Tuscany, through England, during the Reign of Charles the Second (1669)*, we learn: 'His highness having arrived early at Basingstoke, walked on foot through the town, which is wretched, both in regard to the buildings, the greater part of which are of wood, and the total absence of trade; so that the gratification of his curiosity did not compensate for the fatigue of walking even a few paces'. We also learn that on being approached by the Mayor and two other officers who wished to wait on him that '... his highness civilly declined this public demonstration of respect'.

While I agree with the Duke's verdict on the town, our reasons differ. Unlike him, I rather like the sound of 'wretched' wooden Basingstoke, not to mention its 'absence of trade'. What a pity most of its historic half-timbered buildings were destroyed and replaced by the soulless sea of concrete that is the modern town centre. As you can probably gather, I have a rather jaundiced view of Basingstoke, having witnessed its character, environment and wildlife being wilfully destroyed and degraded in my youth.

So, why stick with the place, you might ask? Despite Basingstoke the town being anathema to anyone, like me, for whom natural history is their passion, the surrounding countryside was at the time I was growing up rich in wildlife. Even though we are talking about the 1960s and '70s, the full impact of mechanised, industrial farming had yet to be felt everywhere, and pockets of real biodiversity lingered on. Just how significant the borough of Basingstoke was in wildlife terms I did not realise at the time: it was all I knew. It took another two decades for me to fully appreciate this reality, by which time considerable damage had been done and much of the biodiversity I knew while I was growing up had been destroyed.

Notwithstanding a few pockets of biodiversity richness in the vicinity, twenty-first-century Basingstoke is essentially an environmental blot on the landscape, and the surrounding farmland has been largely stripped of its native biodiversity. However, it was not always the case, and to put things in historical perspective, as recently as the late 1930s its rural society and landscape probably had more in common with the era of Jane Austen than twenty-first-century Britain, such has been the pace of change.

At this point it is probably worth setting the scene regarding Basingstoke's relatively recent past. At the end of the Second World War, it remained a modest-size market town whose population growth rate over the previous 150 years mirrored much of southern England: 2,589 in 1801; 4,263 in 1851; 13,000 in 1945. Prior to the Second World War it was surrounded by agricultural land that was probably as good for certain types of wildlife as farmland can ever be. Arguably, the richest period for open countryside biodiversity came during the 1930s agricultural depression when many fields remained untilled and hedgerows uncut, and toxic industrial chemicals had not yet appeared on the farmer's palette.

The onset of war in 1939 saw the start of change: productivity understandably became paramount, and as much land as possible was turned over to agriculture, including areas that historically had never been ploughed. In the era that followed, agriculture and urbanisation altered the environmental landscape forever, and it would be a mistake to see the two as anything other than inextricably linked.

As far as Basingstoke is concerned the environmental effects of the Second World War began to be felt before the last German bomb fell on English soil. In 1944, a Greater London Plan was prepared by Sir Patrick Abercrombie to implement recommendations in the 1939/1940 Barlow Commission that aimed to 'disperse' one million people from metropolitan London to outlying towns. As one of these 'beneficiaries' it was proposed that Basingstoke could receive 20,000 people. Discussions were held between the London County Council (LCC), Hampshire County Council (HCC) and Basingstoke Borough Council (BBC). The presence of existing industry and a mainline railway station were features in favour of the town as a resettlement site.

Partly as a trip down memory lane, but also to check that my recollections were correct, a while ago I decided to leaf through the pages of a now-defunct broadsheet called the *Hants and Berks Gazette*. In the knowledge that Basingstoke Library (now a Discovery Centre) held it on microfiche I paid a visit.

In its day the *Gazette* was a weekly production and the main media source of information for the community of the time. The births, deaths and announcements pages were the Facebook of their day, with extensive adverts fulfilling the roles of eBay and Google. But it was the 'Letters to the Editor' columns that I found most illuminating. With distinct parallels to Twitter, personal spats were played out, albeit at a weekly snail's pace. And disgruntled missives were printed, quite often from titled dignitaries or landowners.

My research started with the year 1955, the year of my birth but also the time when concerns and objections about the expansion of Basingstoke became most vocal. As I continued my read, the language and tone of letters changed subtly, with thinly disguised snobbery and xenophobia increasingly obvious through reference to, for example, fears about introducing so many 'council houses' into the social mix, and the effects that 'clearance of the slums of London' would have on the community. There were letters from concerned farmers about the prospect of throngs of 'newcomers', unfamiliar with country ways, blocking the streets and preventing the steady flow of animals from the station to

A copy of the defunct broadsheet newspaper the Hants and Berks Gazette, published on 2nd July 1937.

the market and slaughterhouse. And even one letter that expressed fears that new residents would dilute the rural Basingstoke accent. Some of the sentiments expressed sound rather familiar, don't you think?

Reading the pages of the *Gazette* confirmed my suspicions that as far as the environmental downfall of Basingstoke was concerned, the effects of farming, urbanisation and self-interest were inseparable. On 11 February 1955 it devoted two thirds of a broadsheet page to reporting on the Basingstoke Branch of the National Farmers Union Annual Dinner under the banner headline 'Basingstoke Over-balanced with Council Houses'. A speech was given by the then Deputy Mayor of the Borough in which a couple of sections caught my eye. On the subject of Basingstoke expansion, he was reported as saying: 'I want you to impress upon everybody you know to oppose the proposed development tooth and nail.' He also said: 'Already Basingstoke – and not only our town but many other towns like it – are overbalanced with council houses owing to the war condition.' In an aside, another principal speaker, a Brigadier and Commandant of the Police College, offered advice to farmers when dealing with Civil Servants. He said his personal motto was 'It was only worth talking to them if they were two things – civil and a servant. Some people seemed to forget that when they are vested with a little power, they had to be both civil and a servant and not dictators.' As tempting as it might sound, try adopting that attitude today and see where it gets you.

A week later another half page was devoted to the National Farmers Union (NFU) under the heading 'Farmers Attack L.C.C Project,' and the *Gazette* printed the following: 'The Basingstoke Branch of the National Farmers Union – a body to which 320 local farmers belong – have adopted a resolution expressing strong opposition to the proposed development of Basingstoke to house London's overspill.' Interestingly, one of the resolution's proposers farmed land immediately to the west of 'old' Basingstoke and had previously written to the *Gazette*'s 'Letters' pages expressing his opposition to the expansion. However, not long after that he applied to Basingstoke Borough Council for permission to develop 64 acres of his land for housing purposes, which evoked a spiky response from a Councillor. Reported in the 'Town Council' pages in the *Gazette* the Councillor said he was '... surprised at the activity in local building and especially in the case of the 64 acres ... it was made by

the gentleman who, he understood, had been writing in the local press for a considerable length of time against the taking over of valuable agricultural land for building purposes'. Perhaps with a hint of sarcasm he added: 'I do not know how he can console himself now that he is taking the land himself with the idea of building houses for private enterprise. I just don't know how this kind of thing makes sense.' A spat in the Letters pages ensued, the land was eventually sold for housing and the rest is environmental history.

While the aforementioned '64 acres' was still farmland it supported breeding Lapwings, seen here, along with Skylarks. Long since destroyed, the former farm is now replaced by the bricks, mortar and tarmac of the Berg Estate in Basingstoke.

On 25 February 1955 the *Gazette* reported on a meeting of the Basingstoke Rural District Council where it was noted they had received a letter from the NFU in which they 'strongly opposed the proposed development of Basingstoke by the London County Council' and also expressed a fear that the development would not stop at the (then) Borough boundary. Various councillors attempted to assuage these fears with assertions that it would 'never happen'. With hindsight it looks like the NFU's fears were grounded.

The first agreement with London County Council was signed in 1959 to build 3,500 houses, and after that Basingstoke never looked back, with relentless development being the clarion call. Private as well as Council housing got the green light and where compliant landowners did not meet the need, then compulsory land purchase was a tactic employed by Basingstoke Borough Council. I was intrigued to find that some did not give up without a fight, and in 1966, stable owner Alfie Cole – a local celebrity of the day – drove a pony and trap (containing manure) to Downing Street along with a petition protesting against the compulsory purchase of his 10 acres. However, on further reading it turned out his motives were financial rather than environmental: he was offered £10,000 for the land whereas he claimed it was worth £120,000, or so it was reported.

Pamber: a country parish

Despite environmental erosion, Pamber is still exceptional in terms of biodiversity; and in statutory terms it is the most important one for wildlife in the whole of the Basingstoke and Deane Borough Council (BDBC) area. Roughly 25 percent of parish land has Site of Special Scientific Interest (SSSI) status because of its wildlife; and in terms of area, it accounts for roughly 37 percent of land with SSSI designation for which BDBC is the Local Planning Authority. In addition, the parish harbours seven ancient woodlands designated Sites of Importance for Nature Conservation (SINC) plus UK Biodiversity Action Plan (UK BAP) Priority Habitat Inventory sites. Unsurprisingly, it also hosts a generous suite of notable and protected species. The parish is undeniably rich in biodiversity but its relative significance in terms of designation is in part a testament to the destruction of wildlife-rich habitats elsewhere in the borough that predated SSSI designation, which began in the 1950s.

● DESIGNATIONS

In statutory terms, land in England is organised and defined by a hierarchy of divisions, some ancient, others more modern, all complicated by the occasionally overlapping statuses of administrative districts. The largest subdivision with which most people are familiar is the County, of which currently there are 48 non-administrative units in England. Taking the county of Hampshire as an example, it is divided into, for administrative purposes, 11 boroughs, districts or cities, one of which is the Borough of Basingstoke and Deane, administered by Basingstoke and Deane Borough Council (BDBC). The borough is sub-divided into parishes, one of which is Pamber, in which my cottage and garden are located. Although tinkered with over the years, the system of parishes in England can trace its origins back through the centuries, with many current parish boundaries reflecting, or defined by, amongst other things, manor land ownership in the medieval period and even further back in time. In recent times, a few new parishes have been created, usually to reflect urban sprawl and development. Country parishes typically contain a number of settlements, which for electoral purposes are divided into *wards*.

Dominating the north of the parish, Pamber Forest is an area of semi-natural ancient woodland with Site of Special Scientific Interest status.

The Water Vole is one of several UK BAP priority species in the parish of Pamber. Once widespread, it has declined in range and numbers, and is now extinct on several of the waterways – streams and ditches – where it once occurred.

is agriculturally poor, and for centuries it was fit for little more than growing trees, cutting hay, low-yield arable production and grazing a few animals. Land ownership and tenancy regimes meant much of the working population scratched a living and in terms of food, subsisted from working relatively small plots: one man with an axe, a scythe and a shovel, and perhaps not much more. This historically small-scale, English-style subsistence farming resulted in a mosaic of land use and habitats that persisted more or less intact in Pamber until a few decades or so ago. My cottage and garden provide an intact example of this that stretches back through the centuries.

Not to belittle it, but Pamber's good fortunes in the biodiversity department are down to chance. Underpinning everything is a complex geological mosaic comprising predominant Bagshot Beds of clay and sand, studded with areas of Bracklesham Bed clay, marl and sand topped with plateau gravel; the parish is fringed to the east and south by London Clay. The consequence of the underlying geology is land that

Looking at old maps and reading the landscape's archaeology and ancient hedgerows means you can trace the history of land use in the parish back to the days of Roman occupation – the adjacent parish of Silchester hosts the Roman settlement of Calleva Atrebatum, and within 500 metres of my cottage are the remains of a Roman brick kiln. To use rather flowery language, the landscape of the parish is like a palimpsest – an ancient parchment manuscript, used and reused over time with previous text and boundaries scraped away and overwritten but not entirely obscured. Hints of the past can be discerned by those with a keen and informed eye.

Nearby Silchester is a well-studied archaeological site, and the Roman walls give visitors an idea of the scale of the settlement known as Calleva Atrebatum. For more information about Roman Britain a suggested read is *The Agrarian History of England and Wales, Volume I-II, A.D. 43–1042* (General Editor H.P.R. Finberg), specifically the chapter on Roman Britain by S. Applebaum. See the References section for details.

Fragments of Roman pottery and tiles can be found here and there in the parish.

In the past, the parish of Pamber was more wooded than it is today. The 1838 Tithe* Map seen here (HRO reference 21M65/F7/185/2) and the accompanying Tithe Apportionment (HRO reference 21M65/F7/185/1), show large swathes of forested land, contiguous with, and extending south from, the existing boundary of what today is known as Pamber Forest. In addition to woodland, the mosaic of land uses in Pamber, as listed in the Tithe Apportionment, includes pasture, meadow, arable, heath, orchard and hop garden. Since that time, almost all the enclosed areas of woodland lying outside sites that now have conservation status have had their forest cover removed, replaced either by agricultural land or grassland of varying quality in terms of biodiversity.

* Tithes were originally a tax where one tenth of a person's annual produce was paid to support the Church; the produce was often stored in a Tithe Barn. As a result of the 1836 Tithe Commutation Act, by the time of Pamber's 1838 Tithe Apportionment things had changed: tithes were given monetary value (assessed by land use and acreage) and were no longer payment in kind, and the amount due was paid to the landowner. Tithes were finally abolished by The Tithe Act, 1936.

Land use listed in the 1838 Tithe Apportionment for the parish of Pamber	Acreage
Heath	76.25 acres
Heath and arable	6.87 acres
Arable	641.10 acres
Pasture	143.85 acres
Meadow	169.30 acres
Wood	860.60 acres
Plantation	85 acres
Water	2.57 acres
Wood and water	1.35 acres
Furze	1.66 acres
Combined dwellings and gardens	79.62 acres
Pasture and wood	0.90 acres
Orchard	8 acres
Waste, roads and lanes	59.01 acres
Public House, Arms and gardens	2.10 acres
Hop gardens	8.75 acres
Industrial (Brick Kiln Yard)	3.15 acres
Public Gravel Pit	2 acres
TOTAL	2,150.08 acres

The original measurements of area were recorded in the 1838 Tithe Apportionment (HRO reference 21M65/F7/185/1) as acres, roods and perches. For ease of comparison with modern acreages, the original measurements have been decimalised. For more information about the original document, see p. 49. Where land is described as being 'arable,' this does not necessarily translate to many people's perception of the word in the twenty-first century. Arable meant land suitable for growing crops, not necessarily cereals. Unlike today, where non-stop, year-round exploitation of the land is the norm, back then arable fields would have been 'rested' every three or four years. This might have meant leaving the land fallow for a year when it would be colonised by nature, or planted with a gap-filling 'catch crop', and subsequently grazed by a few animals before being ploughed in preparation for sowing the next arable crop.

The rich biodiversity found in Pamber Forest, the parish's SSSI-designated meadows and its SINC-designated woodlands is a consequence of centuries of varied land management, largely dictated by changes in agricultural economics and, in historical terms, the

The main reason for Pamber Forest's SSSI designation was not its woodland as such but its invertebrate communities. Notable species include a number of hover-flies whose larvae feed on sap runs on tree trunks, and Pamber Forest is also home to one of Britain's rarest insects: a caddisfly that goes by the rather uninspiring English name of Scarce Brown Sedge. In recent years, it is known from just two locations: woodland streams in Pamber Forest 500m to the north of my cottage and a recently discovered site in Norfolk. Formerly it occurred at a couple of locations in Berkshire, but it has not been seen there in recent years.

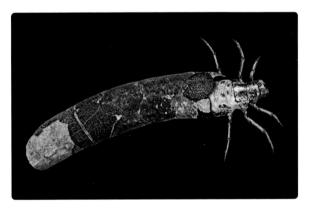

The Scarce Brown Sedge has an unusual life history for a representative of a group whose larvae live in water. In this instance, to call this caddis' larval stage aquatic is to oversimplify matters. It spends the winter months submerged in flowing woodland streams, but come the spring and early summer, the water gradually dries up and the larvae become semi-terrestrial and live in damp leaf litter. They pupate on land and emerge as next-generation adults come the first damp, cool conditions of autumn.

limited physical resources available to affect change at speed. Designated land does not exist in isolation, and there is good reason to suppose that, in the past, much of Pamber had biodiversity comparable to that found in currently designated areas.

LOCAL HISTORY
AND THE RURAL ECONOMY

The boundary of the ancient byway that abuts my garden is defined by a hedge and bank that demonstrates its ancient pedigree. Integral to its structure these days are the gnarled roots of veteran Field Maples and Pedunculate Oaks, with a few lines of Wild Service-trees elevating its notable status.

The previous importance for wildlife of Pamber's lost woodland heritage is hinted at by looking at hedgerows in the parish, in locations where these are the last remnants of earlier tree cover. In some locations the species composition suggests that their heritage as boundary banks dates back at least five hundred years, and map evidence lends weight to the contention about ancestry.

Historical land use in its many, evolving forms is the force that shaped the rural landscape of the parish of Pamber, and an unintended consequence was the creation of its rich biodiversity heritage. There is an irony to the fact that contemporary rural land use – industrial farming practices and urbanisation – are the forces that are destroying the same landscape and degrading its biodiversity.

When it comes to the day-to-day existence of centuries-past inhabitants of my cottage, no information appears to exist, nor is it likely to. I imagine pressing needs to stay warm and fed would have taken priority over keeping records or diaries, always assuming those who lived here in the seventeenth century would have been able to read and write in the first place. However, anecdotally a picture can be painted of the lives of ordinary folk by interpreting accounts, which still exist, for grander establishments in neighbouring parishes. The accounts themselves provide insight

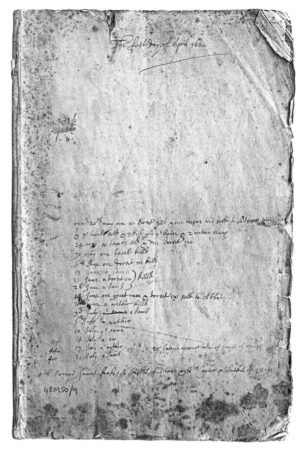

The financial transactions of the Beaurepaire Estate were recorded in extraordinary detail by Thomas Brocas in his accounts book entitled rather unassumingly 'The first day of April 1680'. The financial year is the same one that we use today, 1st April to 31st March, and Mr Brocas was clearly a good book-keeper: I have done a few spot checks using a financial spreadsheet and calculator, and he was accurate to the penny.

The 1680/1681 Beaurepaire accounts are set out in a clear and straightforward manner with the income for a given week, or weeks, on the left page and the expenditure for the corresponding period on the right page. This particular entry, for late November, makes fascinating reading. Subtle differences from modern-day spelling do not need an explanation. For clarification and for a younger generation, the following information might be useful: the financial system of the day was pounds (£), shillings (s) and pence (d); Lady Day and Michaelmas Day were half-yearly junctures between tax periods and contractual ties, the former being 5th April, the latter being 29th September; 'discompt' is an archaic word meaning to discount; a 'quire' is 25 sheets of paper; 'Redding' in the context of the accounts is presumably the town of Reading; 'gte' is shorthand for guarantee; and 'peers' is a phonetic spelling of structural piers.

into the workings of landowning estates and reveal the two-way relationship between landowner and those who worked the land.

The Beaurepaire Estate lies roughly 1.5km from my cottage, and the personal account book of the then-owner Thomas Brocas for the financial year 1 April 1680 to 31 March 1681 is located in the Hampshire Record Office (HRO reference 48M50/9). I would like to thank Alan Albery for alerting me to its existence and helping me interpret the information it contains. The boundary of Beaurepaire Estate abuts that of the parish of Pamber. At the time of the accounts, this relatively small manor also owned land elsewhere, including in Pamber, which gave it 'right of common'; this allowed the estate to collect timber and depasture pigs. The estate exists to this day although the original house was destroyed by fire at the time of the Second World War.

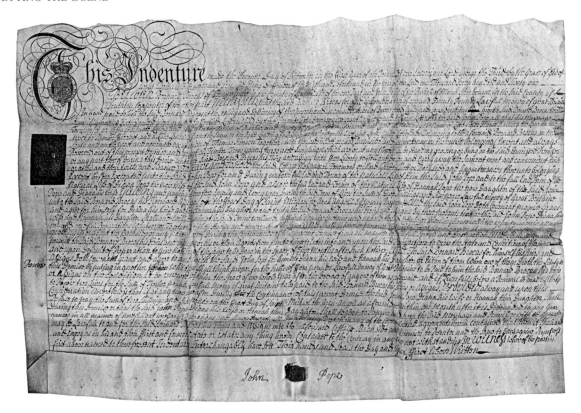

Held in the archives of the Hampshire Record Office (reference HRO 33A12/1), this 1761 Indenture relates to a property referred to as Little Fields House, which based on the description of its location is my cottage. The landlord was Bernard Brocas of Beaurepaire, presumably a descendent of Thomas, the architect of the 1680/1681 financial accounts. The tenant was called John Pope, a resident of the neighbouring parish of Monk Sherborne, and the annual rent was £21. Using the National Archives currency converter, that equates to roughly £2,150 in today's money. I would like to thank Alan Albery for alerting me to the existence of this lease and helping me interpret the information it contains. According to the 1838 Tithe Award for Pamber, the cottage and garden was owned at the time by another Bernard Brocas (possibly a descendant) and rented by one George Stamp. When combined with a nearby allotment that George Stamp also rented from Bernard Brocas, a tithe of 2s 4d was due, roughly £7.90 in today's money.

Left Stepping back several centuries, another example of a local building on a grand scale presents itself in the form of what is known today as Pamber Priory, sometimes referred to as Pamber Priory Church. In reality, it is located not in its namesake parish but a stone's throw away in Monk Sherborne. Construction began in the wake of the Norman Conquest, and the priory itself was founded around 1110 A.D. Once one of the wealthiest priories in England, it owned land in the area, including in the parish of Pamber. Although much of the site has been plundered over the centuries for its stone, the church remains intact, along with the churchyard in which residents of my cottage would have been buried.

WOODLAND MANAGEMENT, PAST AND PRESENT

First, we should perhaps ask a fundamental question. Why did any woodland survive the post-glacial spread of mankind across the British Isles instead of being cleared for settlement or the production of crops? Put in simple terms, the answer is that it had a value. Underpinning this is rural economics and basic common sense: woodlands made money for their owners – timber could be sold – but more significantly trees were vital for everyday survival, their timber used for heating and construction.

In the part of north Hampshire where I live, around 300 years ago there was a switch from rather ad hoc woodland management to a method referred to today as coppice-with-standards; in part this would have been achieved by clearance of previous unwanted trees and shrubs and selective planting. Coppice is a woodland practice that involves a rotational cycle of cutting shrubs and small trees almost down to ground level. Get the timing right and, in the hands of skilled practitioners, multiple pole-like stems grow; the tree or shrub in question can live for hundreds of years if sympathetically managed. Only a few species respond well to coppicing, and in the local area Hazel and non-native Sweet Chestnut were the species of choice. The standard trees were usually evenly spaced and the typical species near me was Pedunculate Oak, with the occasional Sessile Oak adding to the mix.

The standard trees were a woodland's medium- to long-term assets, to be cut and felled when a local need demanded it or when external market forces and prices dictated their time had come. Arguably of more significance, coppice products provided the short-term financial benefits that underpinned the economics of the approach. For a couple of centuries, the production of beer was the primary influence: Hazel provided a regular supply of fuel for drying Hops and malted

Right Woodland management and entomological plusses and minuses. On the plus side, unmanaged coppice provides precisely the shady environment that suits the growth of straggly plants of Honeysuckle, a requirement for White Admirals. And Speckled Woods and their primary foodplant False-brome also benefit from benign neglect. By contrast, shady coppice does not suit the Silver-washed Fritillary, the larval foodplant for which is Common Dog-violet in Pamber. The plant does best in open, sunny spots in the early stages of the rotational cycle of coppice regrowth, and full-grown caterpillars love to sunbathe on the woodland floor.

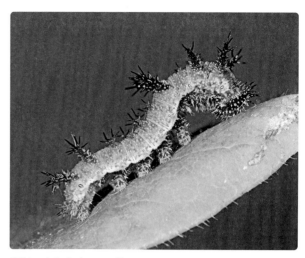

White Admiral caterpillar.

Speckled Wood egg.

Silver-washed Fritillary caterpillar.

THE ENVIRONMENTAL CONSEQUENCES OF BEER PRODUCTION

Beer has been an important part of our heritage for centuries, and its origins stretch back beyond medieval times to the era of Roman occupation of Britain. The brewing process obviously creates an alcoholic drink, but its recreational use notwithstanding, beer served a far more practical purpose. It was a way of creating safe and storable water, something that we take for granted today. For yeast to ferment and for brewing to work, a carbohydrate source – sugar or starch, for example – is a basic ingredient. In Roman times, the fruits of the Wild Service-tree are said to have been used for this purpose, and the name 'service' may be a phonetic corruption of the Latin word *cervisia*, meaning beer.

The Hop is a dioecious species, with male and female flowers borne on separate plants. The Hops that are used in brewing are the fruits that form from female flowers, dried for storage and ease of transport.

The Romans are credited with bringing with them, and planting, Wild Service-trees, and my local area is a stronghold for the species. Several hundred are reckoned to grow in Pamber Forest, twelve veteran trees grace the boundary of the ancient byway that runs beside my cottage, and one grows in the garden.

In more recent times, malted Barley has been the carbohydrate source of choice. Malting is the process where Barley grains are germinated and, once sprouted, they are dried in a kiln. For the last few centuries, if not longer, an additional and traditional ingredient in

the beer maker's toolkit has been Hops. Although our ancestors were unaware of the plant's antibacterial qualities, they recognised that its use prolonged the storage of so-called small beer (the second brew from the mash) in particular.

Hops were being cultivated in Holland as early as the thirteenth century, and at the time imports satisfied most of the market demand in England. Over time, however, homegrown Hops became profitable and former arable land, orchards and meadows were converted to this crop in many parts of southern England, including Pamber.

Hops are still grown commercially today in parts of Britain. However, where the plant appears in hedgerows in Pamber, it is most likely a naturalised relic of former cultivation. Those that grow in my garden and that persist in nearby hedgerows are a sign of the past importance of the plant in the rural economy of the area.

The larvae of a few moth species that are generalist feeders will eat Hop leaves, among them the Pale Tussock, whose caterpillars were known as 'hop dogs' in times past. However, one moth whose larvae feed exclusively on the Hops is the Buttoned Snout (shown here). At the local level the species has become scarce, in line with the decline of Hop-growing in north Hampshire.

Barley, while Sweet Chestnut (and to a lesser degree Hazel) poles were the frameworks up which the Hops grew. The amount of woodland required to produce the products needed for beer production was far greater than that needed for growing the Hops themselves. In terms of ecological impact, the influence of Hop-growing was out of all proportion to the size of the crop.

By the end of the nineteenth century, the need for timber related to Hop production had dwindled to the point where it was not viable in north Hampshire. For a relatively brief period, coppice products such as hurdles filled the gap but eventually the practice fell out of favour in my part of the world. However, the collateral biodiversity benefits that this rural industry unintentionally created linger on, and can still be seen by those with the eyes and the imagination to interpret the wildlife and habitats around them. If coppice neglect continues, the significance for the wildlife adapted to thrive in the open, managed woodland that coppicing creates will diminish. However, it is not necessarily all bad news, and a different suite of creatures stand a chance of benefitting.

A selection of woodland products past and present.

The cottage and garden

I first encountered the cottage and garden where I now live when I was five or six years old. The then owner was a friend of my father with a shared interest: they were Radio Hams, anachronistic today but seen as a pioneering, if slightly eccentric, hobby in its day.

In my formative years natural history was the only thing on my mind and I was captivated by the cottage's enchanting rural setting, which was a far cry from the desolation of Basingstoke. Consequently, I would tag along on visits and pester my father to continue on natural history forays after notes had been compared about exotic CQ call signs and the finer points of radio valves had been discussed.

Summer forays would often take the form of fruitless searches for Purple Emperors, which were rumoured to live in nearby Pamber Forest although I could never find them. It was not until I moved to the cottage years later that I succeeded in seeing this legendary insect in Hampshire, fittingly a female that appeared in my garden. As a child, however, failure did not stop me trying, and I had more success with the local Purple Hairstreaks and Silver-studded Blues. In those days I collected butterflies because, guided by the literature of the time, I knew no other way of marking my progress and achievements. The parallels with trainspotting, stamp collecting and the listing end of the birding spectrum were lost on me at that age; and it took me until maturity to realise the inherent

My cottage is oak-framed, the timber most likely having been locally sourced at the time of its construction.

Assuming the date to be correct, this watercolour of my cottage (left) was painted in 1949. The dwelling had changed very little when I first encountered it in the 1960s and the image on the right shows it today, complete with a different style of thatch and a couple of extensions. All reasonable efforts were made to trace and contact the artist C.F.K. Smith and their family.

In my schoolboy days, Purple Emperors were the stuff of myth and legend and I had to content myself with finding the butterfly's slightly less impressive Pamber Forest companion, the Purple Hairstreak. These images are contemporary, the former (left) was photographed locally and the latter (right) in my garden.

contradiction in my actions – killing the very things I claimed to be passionate about.

In its day my cottage would have been a humble dwelling, originally most likely a single room, with a mezzanine sleeping area. The original part of the building has an oak timber frame whose style and method of construction suggests it was built towards the end of the sixteenth century. A few of the panels in the oak frame are still filled with rendered wattle and daub but most are brick-lined, which I assume are later modifications. The original part of the cottage has a thatched roof and, inside the roof space, what I presume to be original roof supports can be seen. Over the centuries, the cottage has been altered and added to, with varying degrees of sympathy.

When I moved to the cottage around 25 years ago it retained most of its charm and the rural setting that I remembered from my childhood. On all sides there were hedgerows and grassland in the form of old hay meadows and fields used to graze horses. At that time the countryside surrounding the cottage was as rich, in wildlife terms, as the garden itself and I took it for granted. Little did I know this was set to change, and today much of the native biodiversity richness of the surrounding land has been lost or degraded by changes in land use. As a result of intensive agriculture and creeping urbanisation and industrialisation, the garden has become a tiny island of biodiversity richness in a rising sea of environmental degradation. The story of nature's fight-back is the next chapter in the story of the cottage and garden.

British-made clay tobacco pipes can be dated reasonably accurately by style. In this example, found in my garden, the pipe maker's name appears on the stem as J. Chamberlain. The company was based in the Littleport district of Portsmouth and was in business from around 1850 to 1870. Along with many other Portsmouth pipe makers, J. Chamberlain are likely to have used clay from the Isle of Wight, and the shield, seen in relief on the bowl, is one of their trademarks. Fortunately, this example is also marked by a significant date: 1856 on one side of the bowl and Peace on the other, to mark the end of the Crimean War (1853–1856). I was able to glean background information from a booklet entitled *The Clay Tobacco Pipes of the Portsmouth Harbour Region 1680–1932* (see References for details). Yes, there really is a book on the subject. The fact that a pipe made in Portsmouth ended up in a garden at the other end of Hampshire is an indication of how much toing and froing went on in times past.

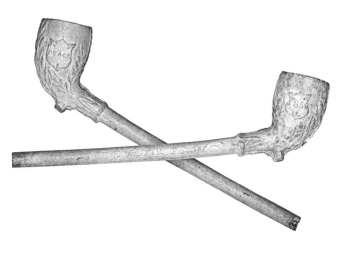

Environmental Decline and Fall

Overview

No self-respecting naturalist would contest that in the space of a generation the UK has seen a catastrophic decline in biodiversity and wholesale destruction of wildlife-rich and wildlife-friendly habitats. To back up anecdotal observation with evidence, the *State of Nature 2019* report found that 40 percent of UK species have declined since 1970 and that, in England, of the 7,615 species assessed, more than 1 in 10 is threatened with extinction in Great Britain. (See the References section for more information.) Thanks to modernised, increasingly intensive agriculture and urbanisation (housing and industrialisation) we now live in a land where self-inflicted biodiversity impoverishment is the new normal.

Sociological and demographic changes alongside technological advances in our ability to exploit the land for profit and food have been driving forces, underpinned obviously by an increase in the UK population: depending on your sources, 16 million in 1841; 50 million in 1948; 66 million in 2017. However, perhaps population growth and 'progress' alone are not enough to explain the devastation, and maybe human nature is part of the equation.

In case anyone thinks the decline in British wildlife is a new phenomenon, Brian Vesey-Fitzgerald (1905–1981) – author, and editor of *The Field* magazine from 1938–1946 – was bemoaning the destruction of the English countryside as far back as 1969 in his book *The Vanishing Wild Life of Britain*. It was written in the wake of Rachel Carson's seminal work *Silent Spring*, which brought to public attention the effects of toxic agricultural chemicals on the environment. See the References section for details of both books. In his book Vesey-Fitzgerald discusses not only pesticides and industrial farming but man's changing and increasingly distant relationship with the natural world. In the preface, on the subject of disappearing wildlife he puts it most succinctly: '… there is nothing new about it. Wild life has always been vanishing from Britain. It has been doing so from the moment that Man began to colonize the island.'

Fifty years on from the publication of *The Vanishing Wild Life of Britain*, things have only got worse, and here is where human nature perhaps plays its part. Recently, Peter Kahn and Thea Weiss formulated the concept of environmental generational amnesia (see the References section for details). It is a phrase that describes how each generation views the world into which it is born, no matter how degraded, as normal and its environmental baseline. It is a depressingly familiar mindset to any seasoned natural historian who has lived through the destruction of the last half century. However, in my experience the mentality only applies to people who are aware of, or give a damn about, the environment in the first place. Sadly, many people I encounter on a day-to-day basis display environmental ignorance or indifference as standard; and environmental contempt is depressingly widespread. Continuing with medical metaphors, perhaps a better description would be 'ecopathy'. If such a condition were recognised, its definition might be a pathological inability to empathise with the natural world or care about the environmental consequences of your actions.

Since the end of the Second World War the greatest impact on wildlife and biodiversity in the part of the UK I know best – north Hampshire – has come from agriculture, with urbanisation a close second. That urbanisation destroys or diminishes biodiversity is self-evident when open countryside is built upon or concreted over. But the impact of agriculture can be equally profound, more so today than in the past. This bold statement needs some qualification and an explanation of why, historically, some farmland could legitimately have been described as having been good for certain types of wildlife; why today a few pockets of farmed land continue to support excellent biodiversity; and why other extensive tracts of agricultural land are in essence sites of native biodiversity desolation, albeit green ones.

Farming intentionally replaces what would otherwise be a natural habitat and the fact that the process may have begun hundreds, sometimes thousands, of years ago does not alter this fact. Compared to the land it replaces, by design farmland inevitably supports altered biodiversity. In general, the agricultural aim when growing a crop is to maximise yield from typically one species in a given area, and to minimise or marginalise

competition. Notwithstanding these qualifications, prior to the Second World War what might be called traditional farming did inadvertently benefit a select range of wildlife species. And land use in the broadest sense helped create some of the habitats that naturalists value so much today: flower-rich hay meadows and coppiced woodland are two examples. Our farming and land-managing forebears were not conservationists, of course, but the unintended consequence of their aspirations and limited ability to affect the land meant, for example, that native floral diversity flourished in un-ploughed and un-sprayed hay meadows, winter food for seed-eating birds was provided in the form of spilled grain and arable 'weed' seeds in stubble fields, and Bluebells thrived in coppiced woodland.

● A SIGN OF THE TIMES

Brian Vesey-Fitzgerald's environmentally aware and prescient words in *The Vanishing Wild Life of Britain* might come as a surprise to anyone familiar with some of his other writing. He was an establishment figure of his time, and lived in an era when, with faintly Biblical undertones, everything in nature needed a reason to exist; and had a role to play in the lives of men, with the good a species provided and evil it wrought weighed on the scales of judgement.

Members of my generation who grew up with an interest in natural history will probably remember 'Lady-bird' books, for which Vesey-Fitzgerald was the author of titles on birds in Series 536. By contemporary standards, his 1950s text may seem a bit 'off-message', especially the helpful hints he provides about finding the nests and eggs of each species described. However, if you factor in prevailing attitudes, some of his words could be seen as an attempt to influence the thinking of the time for the better. Bear in mind the books were written for young readers and open with a welcoming 'Hullo, children!' from the author.

In the text of 'A Second Book of British Birds and Their Nests – A Ladybird Senior' we discover that: Jackdaws 'are easy to tame and can be taught to talk'; the Great Tit 'does a great deal of harm to spring buds and autumn fruit' but on the positive side it 'destroys vast numbers of insects throughout the summer'; fortunately for Nuthatches we read that they 'do no damage in gardens' and that Fieldfares 'do much more good than harm on farms'; we are told that the Great Spotted Woodpecker 'is a very useful

bird'; and on the subject of Barn Owls that 'No one should ever kill Owls, they are much too useful.'

In the next title in the series 'A Third Book of British Birds and Their Nests – A Ladybird Senior' we learn that: 'Many people dislike the Little Owl intensely, but it undoubtedly does more good than harm'; that Coal Tits 'eat a lot of insects, so they are useful to man'; that in winter Corn Buntings 'gather into big flocks and raid the farmyards'; that despite the Blackcap being fond of strawberries and currants it 'does not really do a great deal of harm in a garden'; that 'a few people eat Curlews'; and, to lighten the mood, if you were to put a Goldcrest into an ordinary matchbox 'there would be plenty of room all round, although its tail might protrude.'

Vesey-Fitzgerald's 'Ladybird' texts shed light on prevailing attitudes of the time, and even if there was an attempt to provide an upbeat message, the words still seem out of place in the twenty-first century. But are things today so very different? Certainly, attitudes are more open-minded with regard to birds among far more of the population than 70 years ago. However, when it comes to other forms of native wildlife, I don't think enlightenment has reached the point where aphids, wasps, cockchafers and slugs are universally welcomed by conventional gardeners and the farming community. An acceptance that all forms of life, humans included, are inter-related and inter-dependent underpins biodiversity gardening. Consequently, it will be interesting to see if the attitudes of any readers are influenced and changed by reading this book and adopting the approaches it describes. I hope so.

While much of our wildlife has suffered as a result of industrial agriculture and urbanisation, the Woodpigeon is one of the few species to have benefited. Sustained through the winter months by winter crops such as Oilseed Rape, and fed in gardens, its numbers and range have not been adversely affected. The fact that an already common and widespread species benefits from industrial farming is not a positive environmental outcome to be celebrated: the Woodpigeon's gain is the Turtle Dove's, Skylark's and Corn Bunting's loss.

With echoes of John Betjeman's 1969 poem 'Harvest Hymn', this field in the parish of Pamber was sprayed with herbicides and plant life expunged for months on end while the land was up for sale. The sight is not an uncommon one as you drive the lanes of north Hampshire and adjoining Berkshire. More recently, the land has been sold and become the subject of two planning applications: the first to build a house in open countryside, which was refused; the second a change of land use for part of the field to be used as a fenced-in dog-walking enclosure.

Stepping back a pace, it is useful to set these farming changes in context. The 1947 Agriculture Act probably signalled the beginning of the end for (unintended) wildlife-friendly farming, in the Borough of Basingstoke as elsewhere in the UK. In an era of austerity and an atmosphere of aspirational growth the government's aim was to ensure that wartime high levels of agricultural production were maintained. Guaranteed prices were negotiated annually by the Ministry of Agriculture and the National Farmers Union, with previously agreed subsidies taking care of shortfalls between market prices and the aspirational income 'requirements' of farmers. Farmed products were promoted through marketing boards, which had been set up before the war.

The introduction of subsidised farming and price stability coincided with more mechanised techniques (which allowed more rapid and much deeper ploughing, for example) and the onset of widespread use of chemicals: this included the infamous DDT and then lethally toxic cyclodiene organochlorines, such as aldrin and dieldrin, which literally poisoned the landscape and killed seed-eating birds outright along with their predators. In a short space of time the English countryside was changed literally and metaphorically, along with a bucolic way of life. Nowadays the damage continues, of course, but rather than poison farmland birds outright we simply starve them out of existence through, for example, the use of ever-more 'efficient' herbicides and insecticides, and non-stop exploitation of the soil.

Basingstoke

I grew up on the western outskirts of 'old' Basingstoke and in the late 1960s cut my natural history teeth as I walked and cycled lanes and farmland byways. The memory can play tricks, of course, but I recall that singing Skylarks and calling Lapwings were constant companions in spring and early summer, my wanderings unwittingly taking me from one territory to the next. Later in the season,

I can picture arable fields that supported abundant 'weeds' including what I now know to be Corn Marigold and Pheasant's-eye; and 'unimproved' grassland that resonated with grasshopper song and thronged with meadow-breeding butterflies. In winter, every mile or so I would bump into a sizeable mixed songbird flock feeding on spilled grain in a stubble field.

Pheasant's-eye, a former arable 'weed' but nowadays to all intents a thing of the past on farmland around Basingstoke.

These days it is a cause for celebration to hear a singing Skylark in the borough of Basingstoke.

Today of course the birds of traditional farmland and the arable weeds are mostly gone; and the skies are empty of birdsong, their former haunts either destroyed by urbanisation or rendered worthless to their kind by modern farming practices. Nowadays, much of the farmland that immediately surrounded the pre-Second World War market town of Basingstoke has long-since gone, destroyed by urban expansion. That which remains in the borough has lost most of the value it once had for wildlife: despite being green to the eye much of it is little better than concrete, bricks and mortar in terms of the biodiversity it supports. Consequently, I rejoice on the rare occasions I hear a singing Skylark or grasshopper in the borough, or come across a host of summer butterflies.

An indication of the urbanisation and expansion of Basingstoke over the last couple of centuries is provided by population figures, which are: 1801 – 2,589 (the first census); 1851 – 4,263; 1861 – 4,654; 1945 – 13,000; 1959 – 30,130; 2019 – in excess of 113,776.

The parish of Pamber

In sociological terms, over the last two centuries the parish of Pamber has transformed itself from a feudal peasant-and-squire rural economy in which most of the population had close ties to the land into one largely comprising, amongst the working population, an aspirational tradesperson majority and a professional minority. In the main, all are well-off by comparison with previous generations. The former group are largely reliant on the economic pillars of house-building, and day-to-day property upkeep and maintenance. The parish has much in common with contiguous Tadley, and the social mix contrasts with the predominantly and defiantly middle-class neighbouring parishes of Silchester and Monk Sherborne. These have dodged the bullet of urbanisation and industrialisation probably because, collectively, their residents can afford to value the aesthetics of their surroundings more than the money they might make from developing the land. For now, at least ...

Predictably, the parish's human population has grown in line with the rest of the world. The 1841 Census for Pamber reports a population of 484 (263 male and 221 female); according to a more recent Census, Basingstoke and Deane Borough Council revealed that 2,631 souls were resident in 2011. The relationship between Pamber's human population and the land has also changed over time. Scrutinise the 1838 Tithe Map (HRO reference 21M65/F7/185/2) and Tithe Apportionment (HRO reference 21M65/F7/185/1) for the Parish and almost every scrap of land that was not wooded was exploited directly or indirectly in the production of food. Although much of this production benefited landowners, those who actually worked the land would have been reliant upon it for sustenance.

In an era that predated supermarkets and home deliveries, at the time of the 1841 census it is easy to imagine that smallholders, tenants and agricultural labourers had no option but to grow or raise what they

Photographed in July, three months after it had been sprayed with herbicides, this field in Pamber remained essentially devoid of plant life, indeed almost all life save for the occasional withering annual, destined to die. Neither producing food to feed the nation nor benefiting wildlife, it was in a state of intentional sterile limbo.

ate in order to survive, barter or buy what they could not produce, and if the opportunity arose glean, poach or steal. Today, offhand I can only think of a couple of Pamber residents who are largely dependent on parish land for the food they eat. And given the way that national food supply chains work, opportunities to buy and consume anything wholly parish-produced are extremely limited. Furthermore, the amount of land in Pamber devoted to food production in its varied forms has changed over the last two centuries. In 1838 (using Tithe records) around 800 acres were used in the direct or indirect production of food: roughly 680 acres of arable, gardens and allotments; and 320 acres used more indirectly, for example hop fields used in beer production, and pasture and hay for animals. In 2022 (using Google Maps area counter and field observations) around 615 acres were used in the direct or indirect production of food: 445 acres of arable land; 60 acres for hay and winter grazing; and 110 acres of mixed farming, including dairy. Excluded from the figures was land that had been sprayed into sterile limbo and fields devoted to supporting recreational 'hobby' horses.

For most twenty-first-century Pamber residents, the countryside, if accessed at all, is used as a human and canine recreational playground, an outdoor gym or for the pursuit of 'getting in touch with nature' well-being. The disappearance of an existential hands-on dependency on the land has shaped attitudes towards, and an ignorance of, both the land and its wildlife. Scratch the surface and apparent concerns about the local environment usually turn out to be superficial at best and more to do with the vista than any informed and meaningful understanding of conservation.

Financial wealth may reside in the adjacent parishes of Silchester and Monk Sherborne but the irony is that in biodiversity terms, poor old Pamber is still infinitely richer than its neighbours. Sadly, however, its biological assets are fast disappearing thanks in part to those of its landowners and residents who are indifferent to the environmental tides of change that sweep across the land. Their attitudes are emboldened, aided and abetted by the planning process. By my reckoning, the last five years saw applications to build around 80 houses (typically 4- or 5-bedroom homes) in open countryside in rural parts

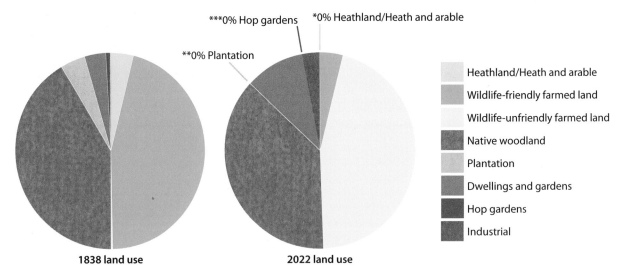

The parish of Pamber covers roughly 2,100 acres and these charts show the major land uses as proportions of the total in 1838 and 2022. The figures for the former were derived using the 1838 Tithe Map and Tithe Apportionment for the parish of Pamber (see p. 2 for both details of both documents). Modern land use areas were estimated using Google maps and field observations. The assumption has been made that, by dint of history, in the absence of intensive agricultural methods most land farmed in 1838 would have been as friendly towards wildlife as farmland can ever be. Defining farmed land as being wildlife-unfriendly is subjective and in a contemporary context that would include seeding with vigorous grass cultivars, spraying with agrochemicals and year-round land-use. Between the two dates, the following changes occurred including those relating to land uses too small in terms of acreage to register on the charts. *All 83 acres of heath/heath and arable were lost to housing development. **All 85 acres of plantation were replaced by arable. ***All 9 acres of Hop gardens were replaced by arable or pasture. Roughly 870 acres of farmed land switched from wildlife-friendly to wildlife-unfriendly land use. Dwellings and gardens increased from roughly 80 acres to more than 190 acres and Industrial land use rose from 3 acres to 57 acres.

Question: When is green not a good environmental colour? Answer – when it is an intensively farmed arable field, or seeded and sprayed 'grassland' depleted of its natural biodiversity. The one saving grace of industrial farmland is that it is still *land* and could in theory be restored to have some semblance of value to wildlife. Once urbanised and covered by bricks, mortar and tarmac it is lost forever.

of the parish of Pamber, with additional proposals as replacements for agricultural buildings. Prior to that, I can only think of a handful of new-build houses being permitted in open countryside during the previous two decades, often new houses built to replace older dwellings. The planning floodgates appear to be open.

Away from land that has statutory protection, nominal or otherwise, Pamber's natural environment is under threat like everywhere else. Apart from a few enlightened or selfless souls whose motives are not financial, most landowners in the parish use the countryside for profit or pleasure and retain ownership or purchase land as an investment, with short-term exploitation or longer-term gain in mind. At one end of the spectrum is a medium- to long-term commercial approach (farming and equestrian activities); at the other extreme is get-rich-quick exploitation, typically in the form of creeping industrialisation, the lure of developing land for housing or that latest agricultural cash crop, solar farms. Being of no commercial value, biodiversity is only grudgingly included in the planning equation; it is simply an annoyance to be dealt with via

the planning process, using the services of compliant ecologists.

In the parish of Pamber, low-impact land use was what shaped the landscape and created the mosaic of habitats that underpin the parish's once-rich but now-dwindling biodiversity. What might loosely be termed 'farming' helped create the parish's wildlife diversity, so there is an irony to the fact that 'farming' (or more precisely the use of open countryside) is the underlying cause of its destruction. Farming refers to itself as an industry and indeed in recent decades the approach to agricultural land use has been just that – industrial. Seemingly non-stop use of the land and application of everything from synthetic chemicals to human sewage sludge have all taken their toll on native wildlife. As a consequence, nowadays there is more biodiversity and wildlife abundance per square metre in my garden than on intensively farmed land in the parish of any sort – by an order of magnitude. The dispiriting trend continues, and as aspirational economic growth is pursued the parish is entering a new phase in its rural history: the transition of countryside into a more overtly urban and industrialised landscape.

Pamber is still nominally a rural parish populated in part by twenty-first-century 'country folk'. However, despite its apparently pastoral setting, many of its inhabitants have a rather sketchy and selective appreciation of the wildlife on their doorsteps. A consequence of a lack of natural history awareness is that for many residents the environment around becomes just a 'view' or somewhere to walk and empty their dogs; and most live in blissful ignorance of the impact they have, directly or indirectly, on biodiversity around them and its decline. And there are a few for whom environmental contempt would seem to be a fair representation of their attitude towards the natural world.

The cottage and garden

Within walking distance of my house, even today I can still find every widespread British reptile and amphibian species and almost all the butterfly species you could reasonably expect in lowland England on neutral and acid soils, not to mention birdlife ranging from Dartford Warbler to Woodcock. A Wild Service-tree grows in the hedge bordering my garden with more in nearby hedgerows. In spring, I hear the occasional Skylark singing overhead, and each year I receive visits from wandering Purple Emperors and see the occasional Kingfisher patrolling my stream.

Sounds idyllic, doesn't it? But the reality of living in this part of north Hampshire is slightly different. Until a decade or so ago, the ecological blight affecting the countryside around me seemed small scale, piecemeal

This Woodlark was photographed on nearby Silchester Common, within walking distance of my cottage. On three occasions in the last decade, the species has graced my garden, on two occasions singing from the top of a Pedunculate Oak tree.

and something that in the grand scheme of things was having only marginal impact. With hindsight I was being naïve and deluding myself that all was well. The reality of the situation dawned on me with the loss of a nearby hay meadow. In previous years I had been the privileged beneficiary of clouds of Meadow Brown butterflies, plus all manner of other refugee species including Harvest Mice, that descended on my garden from this particular meadow at hay-cutting time. Now that is all gone.

That nearby habitat destruction was the trigger for me to stop mowing a significant part of my lawn in an attempt to create my own meadow in miniature. At the time my expectations were low given that I planned to do nothing other than cut the grass once a year; in some ways my meadow started life as little more than a memorial to the fallen wildlife of the parish. However, the evolution of this grassland habitat has been as inspirational as it has been surprising and provided the impetus for me to embark on other biodiversity gardening projects.

As a footnote, the fate of Pamber's former hay meadows continues to evolve now that a much more reliably lucrative cash crop has appeared on the farming landscape: solar panels. Solar parks are without doubt eyesores, and their appearance in the neighbourhood has eroded further the illusion of living in the countryside. However, their presence presents the environmentalist in me with a dilemma. How can I object to the production of so-called green energy and not be accused of nimbyism?

Elsewhere, most objections to solar parks are argued on the basis that, when sited on farmland, they are destroying the British countryside. However, in intensively farmed locations where solar parks are proposed or have been built, the case may be more nuanced. The chances are that what matters to me about the countryside – its native biodiversity – will already have been degraded by modern farming practices and what remains will be an illusion of good health. Fields may look green but they are virtually sterile in terms of native biodiversity. Consequently, looking at the issue dispassionately, anything that replaces the chemical and physical abuse to which intensively farmed land has been subjected could in theory benefit some forms of native wildlife. And who knows, any decades-long solar park lease might just give the land and its native biodiversity breathing space to recover. Always assuming this part of the planet Earth is still habitable for future generations by that time.

That's the theory. The flaws in the plan are, of course, in the detail. There are instances near me when those responsible for managing the land on which solar parks sit spray the vegetation with herbicides, thereby rendering meaningless any aspirational biodiversity merits peddled as part of the planning process associated with their installation. A specific case in point was reported in the *Basingstoke & North Hampshire Gazette* on 5 May 2022, under the frontpage headline 'Anger

as energy firm kills flowers'. The solar farm in question is owned by the Octopus Energy Group, and is sited on 18 acres of land at Hill End Farm, a mile or so to the south of me. The publicly voiced 'anger' was that of the landowner James Bromhead, frustrated at his inability to ensure wildlife-friendly land management by reasoned argument and gentle persuasion. Unless by prior arrangement, once an agreement for a solar park has been signed the landowner relinquishes control over management of the land for the lifetime of the lease.

As a further twist, despite their overtly industrial appearance, solar parks are classed as agricultural in terms of land use and the planning process. There is a requirement that the land be returned to its previous agricultural state at the end of the project. A return to chemically abused, intensively farmed land would destroy at a stroke any biodiversity net gain and environmental enhancement achieved during the intervening years and render the aspirational greenwash start-up credentials of the project meaningless. For anything meaningful to come out of solar parks in the long term, these environmental flaws need to be acknowledged and addressed.

Sprayed with herbicide at the start of the floral season, the land beneath these solar panels provides few benefits for native biodiversity.

The Common Spotted-orchid occurs near where I live in good numbers in some fields but is completely absent from other apparently suitable and botanically rich sites nearby. There is obviously something not quite suitable about the locations from which it is absent – it might be previous land use, drainage or a subtle difference in the soil's fungal component on which orchids are dependent.

Practical Biodiversity Gardening

Basic principles

What I have attempted to do in my garden, and the approach I invite others to consider adopting, is to create or encourage a microcosm of wildlife-rich habitats that occur in the local area. A lifetime of interest in, and spent searching for, British wildlife has taught me that we live in a landscape that comprises a patchwork of subtly different habitats-within-habitats, each component part having its own unique combination of plants and animals. This variety and lack of uniformity is what has driven the evolution of the rich diversity of British wildlife over the millennia.

The factors influencing the diversity of species, and their abundance and distribution across the British Isles, are varied and include underlying geology and soil type, topography, climate and historical land use. Taking plants as indicators, it can be puzzling why a given species is present in one location but absent from another apparently suitable site nearby. Sometimes the puzzle is too complex to fathom. Better to accept that complexity and variety exist even at the local level, and factor this into your expectations when managing your biodiversity plot and assessing the success or otherwise of your endeavours.

A consequence of this biological complexity for the prospective biodiversity gardener is that the ambitions for one garden will never be quite the same as those for another. There is no magic formula, just an approach; an underlying understanding of your local natural history is both crucial and empowering as a basic tenet. In terms of knowing what you want to achieve, a starting point is to locate wildlife-rich habitats in the vicinity and identify and record the species of locally appropriate plants and animals they host. With the notion of complexity and variety in mind, it is always a good idea to visit a number of sites to get a better overall 'feel' for the environment around you. Although it may sound superficial, another essential ingredient is to appreciate *visually* what decent habitats look like throughout the year. You may need to abandon some of your preconceptions and you will certainly need to raise your awareness of seasonal ecological complexity.

DO YOUR HOMEWORK

It can also be invaluable to understand the role that historical land management will have played in the evolution of biodiversity in your local area. No one location will be the same as another, and it can be a useful exercise to do a spot of historical research. A considerable amount of information is available online but a more hands-on approach might be to access your county archives. If Hampshire, where I live, is anything to go by, then tucked away somewhere in the vaults you will find local Enclosure Awards and Maps dating back hundreds of years, equally informative estate accounts, and Tithe Awards, Apportionments and Maps. In the case of Hampshire, the latter documents can also be purchased online from their Record Office for each parish, and provide field-by-field detail about land use. The level of detail extends to the use of fields as arable, pasture, or for growing Hops; whether plots of land were homesteads and gardens or orchards; and insights into the nature of wooded land. Enclosure maps give an indication of the location of extant and lost hedgerow field boundaries.

The phrase 'abandon preconceptions' is a fitting slogan for prospective biodiversity gardeners to keep in mind. Another bit of advice is to acquire a healthy dose of scepticism when it comes to what you are told or read about native component species and the ways

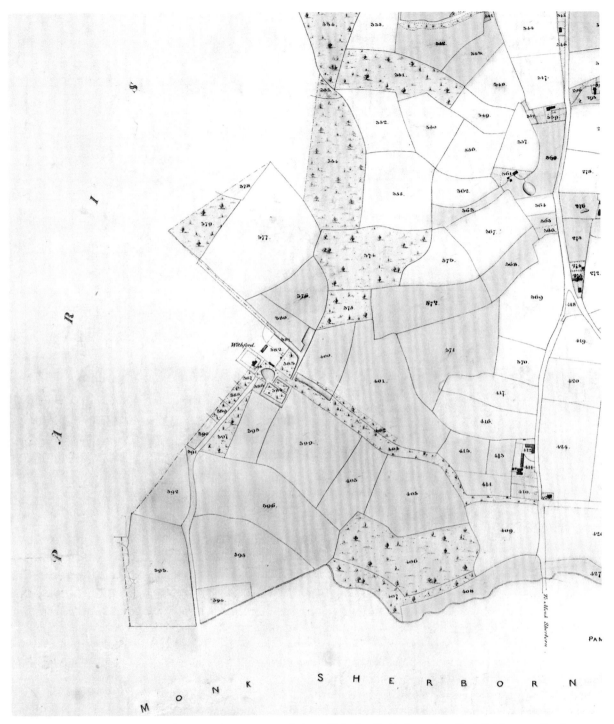

Pamber's 1838 Tithe Map and Tithe Apportionment contain incredibly detailed information. Each field or woodland plot on the map is given a number that corresponds to its appearance in the ledger, organised by owner alongside a precise measurement of the land area, its agricultural use, and the tithe due. Areas were specified in the ledger as acres (A), roods (R) and perches (P). An acre is a unit of land area measured as one furlong (660 feet) by one chain (66 feet). There are 4 roods in an acre, and 40 perches in a rood. A sample page from the Tithe Apportionment (opposite) and an enlargement of the relevant part of the Tithe Map (above) provides an idea of the detail that the documents contain.

No. 4.——LONDON: Sold (by Authority) by ROUTLEDGE, 11, Ryder's Court, Leicester Square.

LANDOWNERS.	OCCUPIERS.	Numbers referring to the Plan.	NAME AND DESCRIPTION of LANDS AND PREMISES.	STATE of CULTIVATION.	QUANTITIES in STATUTE MEASURE.			Amount of Rent-Charge apportioned upon the several Lands, and Payable to the Rectors.			REMARKS.
					a.	r.	p.	£	s.	d.	
Beach William Hicks Esqr.	Himself	13	Common Piece	Heath	27	3	39				
		49	Allotment in Black Lane	Arable	12	1	22				
		59	Allotment in Bentley Green	Arable	14	1	3				
					54	2	24	5	2	-	
		371	Upper Hazells	Pasture	10	2	16				
		372	Mallards Meadow	Meadow	5	3	26				
		374	Prince's Grove Coppice	Wood	8	3	36				
		375	Prince's Grove Riddle	Wood	2	1	4				
		376	Little Chalgrove	Pasture	2	3	17				
		377	Great Do.	Arable	14	2	16				
		379	Part of Hog Park	Wood	3	0	22				
		380	Orchard	Pasture	2	0	12				
		381		Water		2	20				
		382	Yard and Rickyard			3	25				
		383	Pasture and Withys	Wood		2	5				
		384	House and part of Garden				36				
		385		Wood & Water		3	24				
		386		Meadow			27				
		387	Part of Old Orchard	Wood		1	1				
		388	Part of Little Hop Garden	Furze		1	24				
		389	Part of the Pits	Wood		1	16				
		390	Part of Black Close	Pasture		2	-				
		391	West Heath Lane & Waste		1	1	20				
		392	Part of Yew Tree Piece	Meadow	3	0	16				
		393	West Heath	Arable	10	3	35				
		394	Graffage Piece	Arable	1	3	30				
		395	Chamberlain's Close	Meadow	11	1	10				
		396	Chamberlains Meadow	Meadow	14	3	22				
		397	Corner Piece	Wood	1	2	25				
		398	Drive Riddle	Meadow	3	1	12				
		399	Butcher's Close	Pasture	10	2	36				
		400	Four Acres	Pasture	3	3	16				
		401	Lower Hazells	Pasture	10	1	10				
		402	Hazells Row	Wood		2	36				
		403	Little Clapper Hill	Pasture	5	1	20				
		404	Wyford Lane		5	1	22				
		405	Gt. Clapper Hill	Pasture	9	1	36				
		406	Clapper Hill Coppice	Wood	11	2	10				
					161	2	11	24	17	-	

in which you might manage your plot for wildlife. Keep an open mind when it comes to advice from single-interest conservation sources who may, for example, focus on what is best for their favoured animal group at the expense of others. Don't assume that wildlife and conservation bodies necessarily know best when it comes to the management of your land, in particular regarding grassland management. In addition, where natural history is concerned it is always dangerous to make generalisations and to decide on your habitat priorities and component species based on extrapolating from other geographically distant locations. And lastly, it seldom hurts to ignore advice that comes from those who manage land commercially, pundits with a conventional gardening mindset, and those who stand to benefit financially from you accepting what they have to say.

So, the moral of the story is decide for yourself, and for that you need to be informed at the local level and have honed your identification skills and broadened your understanding of the complexity and inter-relatedness of all aspects of British wildlife. As one last tip, it cannot hurt to cancel subscriptions to gardening magazines in favour of signing up to the likes of *British Wildlife* magazine; to consign gardening books – specifically ones about garden makeovers – to dark cupboards in favour of field guides and books about natural history and ecology; and shun garden centres as purveyors of all things horticulturally generic and mass-produced in favour of specialist nurseries and seed catalogues of responsibly produced native species.

Although driven to biodiversity gardening as a response to environmental degradation going on around me, I was lucky in one sense. My tiny parcel of land still retained latent biodiversity and for the most part all I did was unlock its potential as I retreated from conventional gardening into a world of biodiversity and habitat enhancement. Not everyone is so fortunate, and some plots of land will have had the disadvantage of having been farmed industrially in a previous life.

However, no plot of land is beyond environmental redemption. Based on local evidence and observation, the speed of recovery will depend on the degree of agricultural chemical and physical abuse to which the land had been subjected prior to it becoming a garden – that includes the application of herbicides, fungicides, pesticides, fertilisers, and deep ploughing. Gardens that came into existence prior to the 1940s are unlikely to have been exposed to industrial agrochemicals. Those built on more recently farmed land are likely to need more time to recover.

TIPS FOR CREATION

Conventional gardening wisdom for new occupants of a plot is to do nothing to the garden for a year and see what appears: unless or until you know what in horticultural terms you've got, you won't know how to plan for the future without undoing the past. The principle of environmental benign neglect can also be an informative approach for budding biodiversity gardeners at the outset of their personal journeys. For example, when I began to encourage meadow habitat in my garden, I just left the grass uncut to see what appeared. The same light-touch, hands-off approach also serves the biodiversity gardener well when it comes to overall guardianship of the land. Generally speaking, as regards managing land for wildlife, my experience is that less is more and inaction will often provide a better outcome than over-action. Test the water when it comes to changing your management regime and do not undertake wholesale changes unless you are absolutely certain you are not doing more harm than good.

By considering my local area and the limitations of my plot of land, elements of the following wildlife-rich habitats are ones I chose to represent in my garden: soil; grassland; ponds; hedgerows; and woodland in a general sense. With the proviso that no one place is exactly the same as another, those habitats might be starting points for other prospective biodiversity gardeners. However, if your garden sits on chalk or on land that might have been heathland in a past life, then your ambitions would be different.

Soil

It may seem odd to begin a section on 'practical biodiversity gardening' with the subject of soil, or include it at all. However, this part of the equation is crucial to the success of any project and needs to be treated with the same respect as any other component of a healthy biodiversity garden. It is the soil that unifies the whole plot, and indeed healthy natural habitats everywhere. Skin is the largest organ of the human body and the one most often overlooked or taken for granted; it might help to think of soil as its ecological equivalent. The treatment of soil as nothing more than a growing medium for agriculture and cultivation, rather than as a habitat, is a contributory factor in the decline of native biodiversity.

Sooner or later, anyone with a plot of land, time to spare and a concern for native biodiversity will be faced with a dilemma. One approach to minimising your environmental impact and reducing carbon consumption is to grow your own food. If native biodiversity is at the forefront of your ambitions, then managing your space in terms of natural habitats instead of agricultural output will be the goal. There is a hybrid approach, of course, one that I adopt. I supplement my diet with a few vegetables grown without chemical input, and allocate as much as possible of the garden space – including soil – for the benefit of native wildlife.

WHAT IS SOIL?

In the context of biodiversity gardening and the history of land use it is perhaps helpful to go back to basics. Soil is the top layer of ground, usually several inches (occasionally feet) deep, that sits on top of a layer called subsoil, which in turn resides on the underlying bedrock. Subsoil is a relatively inert layer in biological terms, composed mainly of leached material – minerals, clay and humus fragments – that have filtered down from above, with a component of fragmented bedrock at its lowest level. It lacks most of the essential ingredients for plant growth. Soil (sometimes referred to as topsoil) is the interesting layer from the perspective of the biodiversity gardener and the one where all the biological action takes place.

PLANT BIOLOGY

Following on from this, a spot of plant biology may help the prospective biodiversity gardener understand the needs of plants. It will also provide insight into what has driven humans through the ages to want to alter the soil for their own benefit.

There are four main building blocks when it comes to the growth of plants, and indeed their very existence: these are the elements carbon (C), hydrogen (H), oxygen (O) and nitrogen (N). Plants obtain carbon and oxygen by absorbing carbon dioxide (CO_2) from the atmosphere via their leaves, and they obtain hydrogen from water (H_2O) via their roots. These are the ingredients needed for photosynthesis, the process by which sugars (the building blocks of carbohydrates) are created using sunlight energy, captured by the green pigment chlorophyll, to fuel the reaction. Oxygen is liberated as a by-product of this chemical reaction. Plants also need to respire and during the daytime the requirement for oxygen is satisfied by photosynthesis. After dark, oxygen is absorbed from the atmosphere through the leaves. In addition, uptake also occurs via the roots.

Despite its comprising 78 percent of our atmosphere, most of a plant's nitrogen requirements are obtained not from the air but by root absorption of dissolved salts called nitrates. In natural circumstances nitrates result from the decomposition of organic matter, be that plant remains or animal remains and waste, the process being undertaken by soil bacteria. This nitrogen-fixing reaction is vital to all life on earth, nitrogen being a crucial component of amino acids and proteins, without which life cannot function. In nature, nitrates are relatively hard to come by and some plants – members of the pea family for example – have harnessed nitrogen-fixing bacterial power by hosting colonies that live in root nodules.

In addition to these building blocks, a number of other elements are essential for plant growth. The main ones are calcium (Ca), iron (Fe), magnesium (Mg), phosphorus (P), potassium (K) and sulphur (S). As examples of their importance, magnesium is a constituent of chlorophyll, without which photosynthesis cannot function and plants cannot live; phosphorus is a key component of chemicals that control and regulate cellular-level energy storage, release and transfer; its significance is obvious. There are other trace elements whose presence, as the name suggests, is only necessary in minute amounts, some of which are not necessarily a requirement in all plant groups. These include manganese, boron, zinc, copper and molybdenum.

SOIL STABILITY

Left to its own devices, soil is a complex web of life, one that builds up year on year and depends on stability to function properly. It is the layer from which plant roots gain most of their nutrition and water. Soil is a mix of mineral components (eroded rocks, in essence) and organic matter, sometimes referred to as humus; the latter comprises the organic remains of plants and animals. There is huge variation, however, in the precise make-up of any given patch of soil, influenced by a range of factors including soil acidity or alkalinity (pH), the nature of the mineral component, geological past, organic input and of course any history of land use. Binding the organic and inorganic elements of soil together, literally and metaphorically, is a framework of organisms that call the soil home. At the microscopic level there are bacteria and thread-like webs of fungal mycelium that among their decomposing and recycling virtues include making nitrogen available to plants. Earthworms, nematodes and a myriad of other invertebrates circulate organic matter through the soil, help aerate it, and affect water retention and drainage. This latter function is vital for all forms of life in the soil, including plants, which need air spaces, albeit minute ones, in order to take up oxygen and 'breathe'.

That is the stable side of the story of the soil. Plough soil and you not only disturb or destroy the web of life that comprises the soil layer, but you also mix what remains with subsoil, the layer that has little value in terms of plant growth. Why do it then? The cultivation of soil provides an opportunity to favour individual species: seeds of a specific plant can be sown which produce a crop to feed people or livestock. It is a practice that post-glacial colonisers of Britain probably brought with them and it is steeped in history. Without intervention, consequences are impoverishment of the soil and the need to fertilise the land if you want to continue the process of producing viable harvests. Long before the concepts of elements and the Periodic Table became known, those working the land were aware that the addition of organic matter – be it rotting vegetation, manure or other animal matter such as bone meal – often had a beneficial effect on plant growth. The realisation that the beneficial agents – nutrients – had to be dissolved in water for plant uptake to be achieved came later. It was followed by an appreciation that soil pH affected the solubility of some 'salts' and hence their availability to plants.

Put at its simplest, a good soil for native biodiversity is stable, undisturbed soil. Disturbance, be it digging at the small-scale end of the spectrum or ploughing at the other end, at best interferes with the fragile web of life the soil harbours and at worst has the potential to destroy it. This web of life and the soil structure that stability helps create and support is more than just a curiosity. It is essential for the cycle of life and death, with decomposition and the recycling of nutrients at its core. Soil stability also plays a key role in that other buzzword phrase of our time, carbon sequestration. Dieter Helm's *Green and Prosperous Land* is a must-read for anyone wanting to know more about the subject.

However, if your garden or plot of land has been disturbed in the past, do not despair. I have no doubt that over the centuries mine has served as a garden for the cottage's inhabitants, and every scrap of soil will have been disturbed, dug or even ploughed at some time. And garden manure – animal and probably human in origin – and compost will have been added to the mix. Despite this (and maybe in part because of this), when I embarked on the project it turned out that my garden still harboured native biodiversity in abundance, in part dormant and just waiting to be unlocked by a change in management. Two details may have had a bearing on its pace of recovery: ploughing, if that occurred in times past, is likely to have been far shallower than mechanisation permits today, hence soil and subsoil mix is likely to have been less drastic; and modern era agrochemicals have never been used as far as I am aware, and so the seed bank and soil fauna are less affected.

As an aside, in earlier agricultural times, ploughing powered by horse or ox was rarely deeper than six inches. Seeds buried deeper than that would have survived for decades until brought to the surface inadvertently; some species only germinate on exposure to light. The disadvantage of this method to the farmer was that in some soils it created a hardpan leading potentially to water-logged ground. This was eventually solved by the invention of the semi-digger plough pulled by a tractor or traction engine, which broke the pan and allowed deeper cultivation. The greater depth of disturbance had an adverse effect on the survival of the soil's seed bank.

Commercial farming is another matter. The dawn of manufactured fertilisers began in earnest with the Industrial Revolution in the early nineteenth century, underpinned by advances in our understanding of chemistry, and plant composition and requirements. This led inevitably to the dominance of, and farming's reliance on, manufactured chemicals, including fertilisers. As an example, the application of ammonium nitrate provides the crop with an artificial source of nitrogen. A consequence of disrupted soil structure is enhanced run-off into waterways, bringing with it elevated levels of nitrogen, along with phosphorus. This leads to a process called 'eutrophication' that results in excessive growth of algae and plants inappropriate to the water body in question – that is, pollution by another name – and phosphorus is especially implicated as a significant culprit.

SOIL WATER RETENTION

A stable soil structure serves another function, the significance of which is increasingly recognised. Grassland with a long-established and healthy layer of soil (as opposed to a disturbed soil/subsoil mix) and a blanket of vegetation is likely to retain water to a greater degree than ploughed farmland. From an environmental perspective the benefit is a soil that acts like a sponge during periods of heavy rainfall, slowly releasing water over time, rather than as a waterboard that speeds up the process of surface run-off. The implications for flooding are obvious. As a responsible landowner, the biodiversity gardener should consider the consequence of their actions on the wider environment and perhaps factor the soil's water retention into their personalised conservation equation.

Grassland

In the context of southern England at least, grassland is a man-made habitat that requires regular intervention for it to remain in that state and for the land not to transition to scrub and eventually woodland. Historically, grassland biodiversity was an unintended consequence of a farming regime that, near where I live, would have involved cutting a hay crop and subsequent winter grazing of the sward by livestock. In more recent times – particularly in the last half century – the industrialisation of grassland management has caused a severe decline in the very biodiversity that the original farming practices inadvertently encouraged.

NO ROOM FOR IMPROVEMENT

To an untutored eye, one bit of grassland looks superficially much like another, but in terms of biodiversity and its significance for native wildlife this is an illusion. Perhaps counter-intuitively as far as the layperson is concerned, ecologists refer to good-quality grassland that is rich in wildlife as 'unimproved' where it has not been ploughed, artificially seeded or treated with agricultural chemicals. I will return to the ploughing side of things later, because in certain circumstances historical ploughing may not necessarily be as damaging as it might first appear.

Unimproved grasslands rich in native biodiversity are a rare commodity these days in my part of the world. Most of what we see today in southern England is so-called 'improved' grassland, which is unfriendly to wildlife, having been seeded by farmers with vigorous grass cultivars and treated with agrochemicals to promote selective growth and kill any plants that might compete; predictably the knock-on effect is significantly depleted biodiversity across the spectrum. Near where I live, this sort of grassland typically hosts just a handful of flowering plant species. In the main these are either aliens, or the born-survivor 'weeds' of agricultural land. Invertebrate life is greatly impoverished as well. The scale of the loss of unimproved grassland is as staggering as it is depressing. As far back as 1987, a review by R. M. Fuller alerted the conservation world to the fact that 97 percent of wildlife-rich unimproved grassland in England and Wales had been lost between 1930 and 1984; see Further Reading section for details. Things

have only got worse since that time, if where I live is anything to go by.

Before embarking on a meadow restoration project, it is a good idea to get an idea of what a really good unimproved meadow looks like, both in terms of overall appearance and species composition – and not just its plants but other forms of wildlife too. Bear in mind that no one meadow will be quite like another. Even in your local area, its floral (and hence biological) composition is influenced by a range of factors such as soil type and pH, drainage and the regime of historical land use. Therefore, try to get an idea of what several good unimproved meadows in your neighbourhood look like during

Yorkshire-fog growing in unimproved and hence botanically complex grassland.

In my meadow, floral interest begins in April with the appearance, from left to right, of Field Wood-rush (also known as Good Friday Grass), Sweet Vernal-grass and Glaucous Sedge.

the summer months. Sadly, in most parts of lowland Britain, it will be a challenge to find even one nearby. Nevertheless, that is your task. One aspect of grassland management where you might want to keep an open mind is the cutting regime – both timing and technique. That even applies to locations that are nominally managed for wildlife, for reasons I will come to later.

Good quality meadows will not have appeared overnight, but will have acquired their species diversity over time, in some instances over centuries. This knowledge tells us that it is unrealistic to expect to be able to simply plant some flowers and create a mature meadow. A meadow is a habitat, and so much more than its floral component species. You might be able to buy some of the seeds, but you cannot purchase the myriad other species that constitute the web of life of a mature meadow. All you can do is prepare the ground and give nature the time it needs to complete the task of creating a habitat.

Study good meadows close up and you will discover that they are seldom uniform in terms of

floral composition. Even within a single field or field complex, subtle variations in soil structure and topography can, for example, result in underlying pockets of damp ground, with adjacent drier areas. A good example of this range can be found, not too far from my cottage, at Ashford Hill Meadows National Nature Reserve. Here, varied topography and historical land use means that at one extreme there are hollows wet enough to support Water-violet; elsewhere there is inundated grassland with Marsh Stitchwort, Ragged-robin and Southern Marsh-orchid; and there are dry slopes with anthills adorned by Dyer's Greenweed and Mouse-ear Hawkweed, that's when the grazing regime is managed correctly. All of this is set against an expansive backdrop of commercially cut hay meadows adorned with Bulbous Buttercup and Yellow-rattle. This mosaic of habitats-within-a-habitat jostle side by side.

Even within my tiny garden meadow there is variety. The garden slopes south and at the meadow's lowest point, closest to the stream that defines the boundary, the ground is damp. This is where species such as Cuckooflower and Greater Bird's-foot Trefoil thrive best. Towards the upper end of the slope, where the soil is drier, Common Toadflax and Hedge Bedstraw flourish.

INSPIRATION AND ROLE MODELS

Inspiration for meadow restoration came in part from visiting SSSI-designated fields in the parish, roughly 1.7km from my garden. These were the subject of an article in *British Wildlife* magazine by Alan Albery entitled 'Agriculture and wildlife conservation: accident or design?' (see References for more information). It turns out that as recently as the 1950s, some of these were arable fields that were ploughed occasionally and farmed in a non-intensive manner. Their 'restoration' occurred naturally without any intervention other than a sympathetic vegetation-cutting regime. The most significant factors aiding meadow recovery at this site were that agricultural sprays and artificial fertilisers had never been used (hence the soil seed bank remained intact), and a rotation of land use meant there had always been fallow pockets of land to act as reservoirs of biodiversity, allowing recolonisation to occur elsewhere subsequently.

These fields received their SSSI designation *after* the restoration process had begun, a measure of just how rich in biodiversity they had become and the success of the project. At the last count they harboured more than 250 species of flowering plants, plus all the associated invertebrate life you could expect, not to mention thriving populations of Adder, Grass Snake, Slow-worm and Common Lizard and a suite of mammals that includes Harvest Mouse. I was encouraged – it seemed that by doing nothing, or very little, there was a chance I really could create a positive outcome for biodiversity. In terms of management, I also had a vision of what I wanted to avoid. Specifically, an approach where hay production was the primary goal; and where the timing and method of haymaking literally cut short floral diversity and wrecked the life cycles of grassland creatures, specifically meadow-breeding butterflies. From the outset I knew I wanted to adopt a more nuanced approach to managing my small meadow, one that maximised biodiversity rather than a commercial hay crop.

When I embarked on my do-little approach to grassland management, what I didn't know for sure was

Germander Speedwell puts on a colourful show in my meadow in late spring, favouring drier parts of the plot.

the history of land use of my patch of meadow. I knew that I had never sprayed it with anything, and historical mapping evidence seemed to suggest that it had never been anything other than a garden in the past. However, in the back of my mind, I knew from local examples that I would have to take a longer-term approach if the land had been subjected to past agrochemical abuse. Only time would tell if it harboured environmental riches or an impoverished flora.

Here are some interesting comparisons, which are personal and anecdotal observations that are not backed up by rigorous science. This proviso notwithstanding, they do provide insight into the consequences of land management, past and present, for wildlife. Apart from the SSSI grassland, the figures were determined by 'field walk' counts across or alongside the fields in question, on public footpaths in May and August 2021.

1. SSSI grassland, 1.7km from my garden (see article in *British Wildlife* magazine by Alan Albery entitled 'Agriculture and wildlife conservation: accident or design?', volume 11, no.1, 1999).

Land-use history	A network of meadows where, until the 1950s, low-impact non-intensive farming took place.
Management regime	Managed for wildlife.
Agrochemical history	The land has never been sprayed with agrochemicals; meadow restoration has occurred through intentional relative inaction and without any introductions.
Botanical outcome	250 native species of flowering plant at the last count.
Grassland butterflies (as invertebrate indicators of biodiversity)	10 species.

2. Meadow, 500m from my cottage.

Land-use history	Former intensively farmed land, seeded with a bizarre mix of species in 2003, almost all of which failed to reappear in subsequent years.
Management regime	Cut commercially for hay, usually in July, then grazed by sheep for varying periods from autumn to late winter.
Agrochemical history	Sprayed with agrochemicals until 2003, currently not sprayed.
Botanical outcome	31 native species of flowering plant nearly 20 years later.
Grassland butterflies (as invertebrate indicators of biodiversity)	6 species, only 3 of which occur in good numbers.

3. Meadow, 100m from my cottage.

Land-use history	Shown as woodland on the 1827 Pamber Enclosure Map and replaced by grassland since that time.
Management regime	Cut commercially for hay, usually in July
Agrochemical history	Unknown.
Botanical outcome	47 native species of flowering plant.
Grassland butterflies (as invertebrate indicators of biodiversity)	6 species, 4 of which occur in good numbers.

4. Grassland, 500m from my cottage.

Land-use history	Shown as 'arable' on the 1838 Pamber Tithe Apportionment and Map, now replaced by seeded grassland.
Management regime	Cut for silage, usually in May.
Agrochemical history	Sprayed with herbicides, fertilisers and fungicides.
Botanical outcome	Seeded grass cultivar dominates. 11 other flowering plant species present in low numbers.
Grassland butterflies (as invertebrate indicators of biodiversity)	0 species.

This meadow, on land that was intensively farmed in the past, puts on a colourful show of dandelions in spring but contains far fewer species overall than are found in genuinely unimproved grassland in the area.

A BIODIVERSITY WORK IN PROGRESS

When it came to my meadow, by the end of the first year I had my answer. More than 40 species of flowering plant and grasses had appeared along with meadow butterflies that I suspected might be breeding and not just visiting. As the years have passed the numbers have risen in terms of floral composition. The tally exceeded 100 flower species at the last count, and new ones appear now and then. In addition to anticipated arrivals, strange and surprising additions (given the soil type) have included Wild Basil and Pyramidal Orchid both of which persist; and in 2022, three plants of Corky-fruited Water-dropwort. On the invertebrate front I have had confirmation that ten species of grassland butterfly actually breed in this tiny pocket of grassland, and they contribute to the more than 450 species of Lepidoptera (both butterflies and moths) that have been recorded in my garden over the last two decades.

In terms of what might be expected from good-quality lowland unimproved grassland on neutral loamy soil in southern England, I would say there are strong indications that my garden's meadow-restoration project is on its way to being a success. Rather than slavishly mowing the grass once a week from spring to autumn, I now cut what was previously lawn once a year with the satisfaction of having a wonderful grassy meadow in miniature as my view in the summer months.

A few years ago, Grass Vetchling made its first appearance and is now positively rampant.

STARTING FROM SCRATCH

If there is any possibility that the site of your prospective meadow might have been grassland in a former life, or is currently a lawn, my advice would be to do what I did: let nature take its course, and let the grass grow literally and metaphorically with only light intervention and see what appears. However, although I suggest you do not let impatience get the better of you, there will always be situations where positive intervention is needed to kick-start the genesis of a meadow. These might include areas where tarmac or concrete has been removed to reveal bare earth, or gardens located on land that was previously intensively farmed, or indeed farmland itself where the landowner wants to restore the environment to something that intentionally encourages wildlife.

There is plenty of advice available in print and online – a bewildering array of options, actually. As a starting point for scrutiny one example might be guidance offered by Warwickshire County Council, a link to which is listed in the References section. Ultimately, however, you alone should make the decision about how to manage your own prospective biodiversity garden, having considered all the options and weighed up what's best in your situation. Bear in mind, however, that many of the examples and outcomes cited use floral diversity as their marker, and intensively farmed land as a starting point. If your preference is to look at the bigger picture, beyond the scope of just flowers, then you need to consider what might be the desired outcome if, for example, there was chance that Harvest Mice might take up residence in your plot.

First of all, it is useful to picture the desired end result, which should be a stable, undisturbed soil structure protected by a modest blanket of decomposing vegetation and a carpet of mosses; and a seasonal floral diversity that comprises native species appropriate to the soil type and geographical location. When you

● ASSET STRIPPING

The term 'soil fertility' is used to describe levels in the soil of nutrients needed to support plant growth. Farmers and conventional gardeners who want to encourage particular crops or flowers usually go to great lengths to enhance soil fertility, often with the aid of chemicals or organic matter. When it comes to meadow restoration or creation, however, conventional wisdom has it that soil fertility is the enemy. The reasoning behind this is that most native component meadow species are adapted to nutrient-poor soils and cannot compete with the few vigorous 'botanical thugs' that benefit from enrichment. As a consequence, wholesale soil-stripping is sometimes advocated as a way of removing fertility (especially with fertiliser-saturated farmed land) to create a blank canvas for sowing. It is saying something when, in essence, the advice is that the soil is too polluted for nature to thrive so let's remove it. However, it also feeds into the line of thinking that says instant meadow makeovers should be the goal. I wonder whether the main beneficiaries are the businesses advocating such an approach and wholesale suppliers of seeds. Personally, I would avoid anything as drastic, in the main because my aim would be not just to maximise floral diversity but to benefit biodiversity as a whole; in that regard I see the residents of the soil as having a say in the matter. Besides, if your environmental thinking is joined up, you need to consider where the stripped soil would go and what the environmental consequences would be for the recipient land. No, if I was giving advice to myself, I would suggest, at most, light scarification and seed scattering. The same advice might work for you, perhaps employing alternate strips of scarified and undisturbed soil if you think there is chance the soil's seed bank retains plant species of interest.

have created your own Field of Dreams in floral terms, with the phrase 'build it and they will come' in mind, the associated invertebrate life will appear or colonise over time.

It is human nature to want to feel you are doing something and, influenced in part by a conventional gardening mindset, there is often a sense that meadows need to be created rather than being left to create themselves. The truth is that there is no shortcut to producing a meaningfully biodiversity-rich grassland: it has to develop over time. However, in some situations, there may be an ecological imperative to kick-start the process, albeit with as light a touch approach as possible.

If you do decide you want to catalyse your meadow creation or restoration project, then I would suggest the absolute 'nos' are: don't spray and don't plough. And yes, I have come across instances where landowners wanting to 'create' a meadow have sprayed the ground with herbicides and deep-ploughed the soil; their aim had been to produce what they saw as a blank canvas to work with, little realising they had all but destroyed any remaining native biodiversity and soil health that would have been their allies in the recovery process.

SOWING THE SEEDS

Although by and large I leave my meadow to do its own thing, I have been known to scatter a few seeds from elsewhere. Examples include Yellow-rattle, which I wanted to encourage to spread, and the occasional handfuls of seeds from end-of-season meadows nearby. However, in all instances I have had the landowner's permission to collect, and to do otherwise would constitute botanical theft. It goes without saying that under no circumstances should seeds be collected from nature reserves, sites where wildlife is prioritised; or private land without the owner's permission.

The main route taken by prospective meadow restorers is to buy commercially produced seeds, which are widely available. The choice and range can be bewildering. General advice would be to avoid companies for which so-called 'wildflower seed mixes' are a minor part of their commercial profile, and a token nod to the aspirations of conventional wildlife gardeners. There are specialists out there who supply the seeds of individual species, which will allow you to customise your choice, and who offer mixes tailored to suit reasonably specific soil types. There are danger signs

BOTANICAL SCAR TISSUE

An inevitable consequence of soil disturbance, be that ploughing or scarification, will be the appearance of a range of plants, notably thistle species, that thrive on the resulting topographical chaos. Rather than throw your hands up in horror, an alternative approach is to view them as appropriate elements in the evolution and development of stable grassland communities. If you take the long view, you will find that those species that depend on disturbance will be ephemeral and diminish over time. Thistles, and other disturbed ground specialists, are in a sense botanical scar tissue, species that are a natural response to the wounds of disturbance, part of the healing process, and ones whose significance will diminish as soil and grassland recovery takes hold. While you have thistles in abundance, learn to enjoy them for their place in the ecology of the British Isles. They are wonderful sources of nectar and foodplants for insects, with seeds that are a natural mainstay for birds such as Goldfinches and Linnets.

Marsh Thistle, one of several species that thrive on disturbance and whose importance for native wildlife is often overlooked.

to watch out for, however, in the choice of descriptions and the sometimes misleading and inaccurate use of words such as 'wild', 'native', and 'natural'. It never hurts to scrutinise the claims made by commercial outlets with a sceptical eye.

Personally, I have slight misgivings when it comes to wildflower mixes in general, and in particular an almost pathological dislike of those mixes that describe themselves as colourful. More often than not they comprise alien species and former agricultural 'weeds' which have no place in a stable grassland habitat. Generally speaking, they offer a botanical conjuring trick, an illusory fix to convince the unwary that they have created something worthwhile for nature. Good quality chalk downland and hay meadows in the Yorkshire Dales can be visually stunning. However, the reality for prime unimproved grassland on neutral soil in the part of southern England where I live is that it is seldom going to be like the spectacle of colour depicted on seed mix packets. An acceptance of that fact, and an appreciation of native plants for their own sake, is part of the learning curve associated with embarking on meadow management.

I have come across rather odd examples of wildflower mixes marketed as appropriate to a meadow in the part of England where I live. Many are short-fix annuals associated with the disturbed ground of historical arable farmland, species that hark back to the days when agrochemicals had not obliterated them from the

If you go down the route of creating your own mix, arguably the best approach is to put conventional flowers to the back of your mind and concentrate on the botanical backbone of any meadow: its grasses. And if grassland-breeding butterflies are a priority, then favour their larval foodplants above promoted nectar sources.

It may be tempting to sow the seeds of colourful flowers such as Corn Marigold. However, like other former arable 'weeds', the species thrives only where the ground is routinely disturbed and has no place, and will not persist, in the stable soil structure of a meadow where the aim is to provide meaningful long-term benefits to native wildlife.

landscape. Others have dubious native status and a few are exotic aliens. From the perspective of someone who wants to promote native biodiversity appropriate to my particular location, inappropriate species mixes often include: Common Poppy, Cornflower, Corn Marigold, Corn Chamomile, California Poppy and Phacelia.

As a prospective seed buyer you would do well to adopt a degree of scepticism regarding any mix that calls itself 'local'. Do your homework and check the species composition against what grasses and other wildflowers grow near you on verges and nearby grassland nature reserves. 'Locally sourced' is another sales description to be scrutinised carefully, and bear in mind that just because a species is native to the UK it does not mean it is necessarily appropriate for your area or particular soil type. Almost all the plants we grow in our gardens grow 'wild' somewhere in the world. Using the word in the context of 'wildflower' can mislead people into equating the term 'wildflower' with something that is native, appropriate or indeed desirable.

Having shattered some of the illusions of prospective seed buyers it is worth mentioning that there are some good mixes available. As a starting point, those that lack a gaudy, disturbed-ground annual-species component are the ones to consider. A few reliable outlets adopt a more nuanced approach and sell mixes tailored for particular soil types. This is still a slightly scattergun approach to seeding the land, and not all species will 'take' in the long term. I have tried sowing mixtures designed for my soil type (neutral loam, which is fertile clay and sand containing humus) in an abandoned vegetable plot; roughly 60 percent of the species in the mixes flourished, initially at least, while the others failed. If you opt for surveying nearby verges and good quality meadows and choosing the species yourself, some seed sellers offer a range sufficient to cover most eventualities in terms of basic species.

Species that do well in my meadow include the following, in no particular order: Yorkshire Fog; Creeping Soft-grass; Cock's-foot, Crested Dog's-tail; Red Fescue; Common Bent; Smooth-stalked Meadow-grass; Meadow Foxtail; Tufted Vetch; Common Vetch; Meadow Buttercup; Goat's-beard; Common Knapweed; Hedge Bedstraw; Rough Hawkbit; Meadow Vetchling; Oxeye Daisy; Selfheal; Bugle; Common Sorrel; Wild Carrot; Hogweed; Yarrow; and Yellow-rattle. Some are species that benefit from residual fertility in the soil and their significance will diminish in time, I suspect.

Caterpillars of the Grass Rivulet moth feed on the seeds of Yellow-rattle and spend their brief lives inside the seed capsules. If you cut a field too soon, before the caterpillars are fully grown and have left their seed-capsule home to pupate in the soil, you will destroy the moth's life cycle. The consequence is depleted biodiversity and an overall erosion of complexity in the natural world.

ON THE VERGE OF EXTINCTION

Stepping outside the boundaries of my garden for a moment, it is an interesting aside to return to the subject of roadside verges. Having driven past a gaudily planted verge in a north Hampshire town I was reminded of a visit to a Yellow Book garden, an occasion where I overhead an uncharitable critic describe the garden in question as 'an eyesore in purple, pink and orange'. And I was also reminded of a link someone sent me concerning a roadside wildflower scheme in Rotherham.

The article appeared in the *Rotherham Advertiser*, and was entitled 'The story behind Rotherham's bloomin' lovely River of Colour', a link to which can be found in the References section. It concerned a seemingly laudable aim to grow 'wildflowers' beside an otherwise uninteresting eight-mile stretch of road. What could be wrong with that? Gaudy colour combinations notwithstanding, the photograph used to illustrate the article showed a predictably strange mix of former arable 'weeds' – just the sort of thing that intensive

Yellow-rattle is a great component of, or addition to, any meadow. As well as being attractive, it has a semi-parasitic lifestyle and takes nutrients from the roots of its grass hosts, inhibiting the growth of rank species.

A ghastly mix of colourful former arable 'weeds' and alien species on a north Hampshire verge. The sight may be pleasing to untutored human eyes, but from the point of view of all but a few native wildlife species the display is essentially worthless.

charm the eyes of passing motorists. To me that seemed like a victory for those producing and selling seeds and herbicides to councils, and a loss for native biodiversity. The article revealed another factor in the appeal of the planting scheme: a cost saving to the local council when it came to roadside verge cutting.

Returning to the subject of that north Hampshire town's verges, judging by the species mix on show, the wildflower verge-planting scheme had taken a leaf out of Rotherham's book and used the same or a similar source of seeds. However, less than a mile further down the road, on the same day I came across another verge (well, a roundabout actually) that was just as colourful. There was a difference, however: this one consisted of naturally colonising native species appropriate to the soil type.

The beauty of this natural verge was that, to promote genuine and meaningful biodiversity, the council need do nothing other than mow the vegetation once a year, in autumn when the plants had set seed. Those tasked by local councils to manage roadside verges would be well advised to read a document produced by the charity **Plantlife** entitled *Roadside Verge Best Practice*, a link to which can be found in the References section.

Because the underlying ground on the previously mentioned roundabout is chalk, downland plant species such a Marjoram and Kidney Vetch were thriving. If managed in an intelligent and informed manner, roadside verges have the potential to be good for native wildlife. In this instance, the insect fauna included the Small Blue butterfly, whose larval food is Kidney Vetch.

arable farmers want to be rid of – and a scattering of alien species and dubious natives. From what I could make out, the main components comprised a cultivated form of poppy, California Poppy, Cornflower and Corn Marigold. How would they maintain this mix of peculiar annual plants, I wondered? All was revealed when I read on to the section where an official stated, 'Hopefully in late March 2015 we will weed-kill all of the eight miles and reseed it again in April'.

So, if the report was accurate and I understood it correctly, the reality was that native verge wildflowers along with the sown species were destined to be sprayed to death so the cycle could continue and inappropriate and sometimes alien (but colourful) species could

A roundabout in the same north Hampshire town as that with the planting scheme, boasting an abundance of native chalk flora including Marjoram, Kidney Vetch, Perforate St John's-wort, Small Scabious, Goat's-beard and much, more, plus all the native biodiversity that goes with it.

A PLEA FOR RAGWORT

A few years ago, a neighbour knocked on my door and asked if I knew I had Ragwort growing in my garden and what I was going to do about it. My replies were 'yes' and 'nothing' in that order, to which he responded in a slightly tongue-in-cheek tone that it was a 'notifiable' weed and that he would have to report me. This was not the first time I had faced the subject, so, as the clenched-teeth polite conversation continued, I told him that as far as I was aware there was no such thing in English law as a 'notifiable' weed and perhaps he meant one of the five plant species classed as 'injurious' in the Weeds Act of 1959.

Anyway, all five so-called 'injurious' weeds are great for invertebrates and I am proud to say I have them all in my garden – in moderation. When I asked my neighbour to point out the offenders, I was able to

tell him that the plants in question were not in any case Common Ragwort but Hoary Ragwort (a forgivable mistake) and Common Fleabane (less so), neither of which have a whiff of illegality associated with them.

Search the internet on the subject of Ragwort and you will find some wildly inaccurate information, bordering on scaremongering. There are, however, two excellent websites, details of which can be found in the References section. These are 'Ragwort Facts' and a **Buglife** document entitled 'Ragwort: Noxious weed or precious wildflower?'

If you like to check things for yourself then read the Weeds Act of 1959. It is easily accessible online and states that where the Minister (then MAFF – Agriculture, Fisheries and Food) 'is satisfied that where there are injurious weeds to which this Act applies growing upon any land he may serve upon the occupier of the land a notice in writing requiring him, within

Spear Thistle.

Creeping Thistle.

Curled Dock.

Broad-leaved Dock.

Ragwort.

Rogue's Gallery: the plants named in the Weeds Act of 1959 are Spear Thistle *Cirsium vulgare*; Creeping Thistle *Cirsium arvense*; Curled Dock *Rumex crispus*; Broad-leaved Dock *Rumex obtusifolius*; and Ragwort *Senecio jacobaea*. As an aside, since the Act was created, a progression in botanical classification means the latter species is now known as Common Ragwort *Jacobaea vulgaris*. Several other species of ragwort, not specified in the Act, also grow in the UK.

the time specified in the notice, to take such action as may be necessary to prevent the weeds from spreading.' Bear in mind that 'injurious' does not mean poisonous; rather, it relates to plants that might have an economic impact on farming. And it is all about the potential for 'spreading' rather than merely having them on your land. As far as I can see you can grow as much of the five as you like and there's no legal requirement to remove them unless the Secretary of State, or an authority specifically appointed to act on his or her behalf, asks you to do so.

The other bit of legislation that relates to Common Ragwort is the Ragwort Control Act 2003, and it is also worth a read. It is available online (see the References section), is brief and to the point, and enabled a Code of Practice to be laid down. The Code itself is introduced by the then Minister of State for Rural Affairs and Local Environment Quality, who refers to himself as 'Minister for the Horse'; perhaps this indicates his leanings in the debate about the evils and merits of ragwort, who knows? Anyway, the document strikes me as oddly contradictory: at one turn it conjures up nightmare visions of dead and dying horses – hundreds of them – dropping like flies through Ragwort poisoning; and at the other extreme it extols the virtues and value to wildlife of Common Ragwort. To me it has the hallmarks of a document written by a committee, but one whose polarised members could not agree.

Despite the dystopian world, littered with dead horses, that the Code of Practice depicts, it states: 'The scale and extent of illness and death in animals through ragwort poisoning is difficult to determine, as an autopsy would be required in every case to confirm the exact cause of death. There is no current test available to diagnose accurately whether an animal is suffering from ragwort poisoning, and certainly no test to help determine whether any such poisoning relates to ingestion of conserved or live ragwort.' To my mind, that is another way of saying the 'evidence' is unfounded.

I have nothing against horses, but if you accept the above statement and choose to believe the facts as presented on the websites mentioned above, then the risks to horse health are hugely exaggerated, as is the attributed number of deaths. That Common Ragwort contains toxins is not in dispute, but so do any number of other native wildflowers – in many cases, the same

The flowers of Common Ragwort are an important source of nectar for insects, especially hover-flies.

toxins as occur in Common Ragwort. And in the context of horses and other livestock perhaps the living plant is better described as distasteful rather than poisonous. The evidence of my own eyes tells me that horses avoid it, and where I live an abundance of the plant is usually a clear indication of over-grazing. It is only a potential danger when inadvertently cut and dried as a constituent of a hay crop and only if subsequently consumed by animals as winter feed in vast quantities.

For those with concerns about the floral makeup of the English countryside, maybe Common Ragwort should not be top of the list. A better contender might be Hemlock Water-dropwort. I have heard this umbellifer described as the most poisonous plant in the UK. It is a welcome natural component of wet meadows near me, and the flowers are a valuable source of nectar for insects in summer. However, in the last decade it has begun to proliferate in eutrophic ditches (beside which horses trot) enriched by fertiliser run-off from intensively farmed fields. In the grand scheme of things, I would suggest that intensive farming and eutrophication are subjects really worth worrying about.

Stepping back from the issue of toxicity and live-stock, Common Ragwort is a hugely important native wildflower and an integral component in meadows. It is a wonderful source of nectar for insects, and according to Buglife there are 30 invertebrates that are confined to it; this number includes of course the Cinnabar moth, whose caterpillars feed on nothing else.

In some specific circumstances there may be a case for controlling Common Ragwort in the context of its 'injurious' status – the potential for spreading leading to an economic impact on adjacent farmland

The Cinnabar moth's aposematic colours (red and black in adults, orange and black banding in caterpillars) warn potential predators of their distasteful nature. Quite literally they are what they eat, and accumulate toxins present in their larval foodplant.

– and perhaps even regarding livestock. Fine, so long as the perceived 'need' for control is based on real evidence and the Secretary of State, or an appointed representative, has reviewed the evidence and had his or her say on the matter. But whatever the rights and wrongs of Common Ragwort, it is undeniably the only species of *Senecio* (now *Jacobaea*), or yellow composite, that is specified in the Weeds Act of 1959. Nevertheless, I have a feeling that my neighbour may not be alone when it comes to mistaken identity. I have come across formal complaints about a perceived lack of 'Ragwort control' beside motorways and dual carriageways. For a start, unless the adverse consequences of 'injurious' spreading can be demonstrated, I cannot see there is a legal requirement to 'control' it unless a minister deems it necessary. But more significantly, the species in question is more likely to be Oxford Ragwort than Common Ragwort. I am not aware of any legal requirement for the former species to be 'controlled', despite the strange claim in the Code of Practice that other species of ragwort 'may need to be controlled'.

ALIEN INVADERS

The Botanical Society of Britain and Ireland has produced a new atlas covering the 3,500 or so vascular plant species that grow wild in Britain and Ireland, including the Isle of Man and the Channel Islands. The ratio of native plants (ones that clung on during the last Ice Age or colonised under their own steam subsequently) to those considered to have been introduced by humans by accident or design is now 49:51. Alien plant species now outnumber natives in Britain and Ireland.

Although many non-native plant species appear to have little impact on native UK biodiversity, some provide genuine cause for conservation concern. Looking at the bigger picture, of course all of them have a legitimate place in the environment, but only in the parts of the world where they originate. Problems arise when they are introduced by man to other locations: in the absence of the biological checks and balances of their native ranges, vigorous species can smother native plants and in the process wreck formerly thriving ecosystems. In the UK, examples include Japanese Knotweed, a botanical thug that, if left unchecked, rampages along hedgerows and woodland margins. Himalayan Balsam is an unwelcome discovery along any riverbank, while New Zealand Pigmyweed is every UK freshwater enthusiast's worst nightmare, smothering and blanketing entire ponds in a season.

In case anyone thinks this alien invasion is a one way process, the UK has done its fair share of exporting unwelcome visitors, and has contributed to the spread of invasive species worldwide. In North America, Purple Loosestrife, introduced accidentally and intentionally, is a major invasive problem in wetlands and the subject of eradication programmes. And my copy editor, Annie Gottlieb, informs me that Oxeye Daisy (a welcome resident in my garden) is considered an invasive weed in the US state of Minnesota. In Australia, Sea Spurge (seeds of which are thought to have arrived with ships' ballast) is classed as an invasive weed. While Pennyroyal, a mint that is revered for its rarity in the UK, was inadvertently introduced to New Zealand by settlers and is now classed as an agricultural pest.

Purple Loosestrife.

MEADOW MANAGEMENT

Historically, meadows did not exist for their aesthetic appeal nor for the biodiversity they supported. Instead, they were an agricultural land use that produced a crop. Referred to as hay, this crop is cut vegetation that includes a significant grass component, and is dried and stored as animal feed for the winter months. The practice continues to this day, although the botanical composition varies greatly, from hay derived from species-rich unimproved meadows to the utilitarian, agro-industrial crop derived from agriculturally improved grassland. Hay differs from straw, which is the stalk by-product of an arable crop such as wheat; among the uses of straw are animal bedding, and thatching. Hay also differs from silage, where grass and other plant material is cut 'green' and preserved by the acidification that results from fermentation.

Meadows that are promoted today with native biodiversity in mind still need some form of management if the intention is to preserve the habitat and prevent an otherwise natural progression towards scrub development and eventual woodland succession. Like many others, I see the value of scrub for wildlife, but since in my part of the world unimproved meadows appear to be more threatened than scrub, I make the distinction between the two in the context of my garden. The aim with my tiny patch of grassland is to maintain it as a meadow, fixed in time ecologically in terms of the vegetative succession that would otherwise follow. I encourage the development of scrub elsewhere in the garden.

Conventional wisdom has it that seasonal cutting is the way to approach meadow management for biodiversity, with the removal of cut material an essential stage in the process. The aim, particularly when it comes to restoration or creation of meadows on fertiliser-laden farmed land, is to impoverish the soil and hence hinder the growth of vigorous species, giving more delicate plants a fighting chance. The depletion of soil levels of potassium is seen as especially crucial in reducing the growth of vigorous species and encouraging diversity among less-competitive plants. One way in which that is achieved is by the removal of cut grass. That's the method I employ in my garden, not so much because I feel the need to reduce fertility per se, but more because it tallies with the original way of managing the land that helped create and maintain local grassland biodiversity in the first place.

I can also see the merits of leaving areas of rank grassland to flourish. Stepping back in time, it is hard to imagine that men with scythes achieved the same manicured results when cutting as we see with the mechanised process today. Furthermore, historically, I can also picture neglected areas of 'waste', marked on Tithe Maps as such but now incorporated into farmed land, being periodically colonised with rank grassland. On larger meadow-restoration plots near me, I have seen the advantages of benign neglect, where landowners cut part of their grassland every other year in a rotation pattern or not at all.

The end results are meadows that would probably fail to meet Natural England's 'favourable status' standards in terms of botanical make-up and visual appearance. However, the resulting knee-deep matted sward has its own beneficiaries, notably small mammals such as Harvest Mice and armies of Short-tailed Voles, plus a suite of predators. Nowadays, I see Weasels and Stoats in my garden once in a blue moon, the last sighting being of the former, four years ago; these overgrown fields are the only places near me where I stand a reliable chance of seeing them today. In my youth, my recollection is of regular encounters of both, almost every time I went out for a bike ride, as they dashed across the road, or more regularly as roadkill victims or grisly trophies on gamekeepers' gibbets. Today, these specialist small-mammal predators appear to have vanished from large swathes of north Hampshire's countryside, one conclusion being there is nothing for them to eat and they have been starved out of existence.

TIMING IS ALL

Based on experience with my patch of meadow, and by observing what I perceive to be management successes and failures on other sites, I would say that timing is all when it comes to cutting. In my garden I adopt a flexible approach because each season is different. I generally wait until everything has set seed (typically late August or early September), and I am happy to leave patches of late flowerers (Musk-mallow and Betony, for example) uncut until much later in the season.

Many people will have come across bad examples of how to manage grassland without necessarily realising it. Taking roadside verges as examples of linear meadows I have lost count of the number of times I have seen council verge-cutters or contractors decapitating

● MEADOW MANAGEMENT: A CASE STUDY

Photographed in early June, this area of open countryside, not far from where I live, provides a graphic example of the restorative power of nature. It also sheds light on the ways that alternative methods of land management can either help or hinder the speed of biodiversity recovery. Until 2011, the land in this image was part of a larger field that had been heavily grazed by horses for many years. It changed hands and, tasked by its new multiple owners, a contractor grew arable crops for two years, using agrochemicals as part of his strategy. Thereafter, three of the field's owners adopted different approaches to management of the parcels of land that they owned. Bearing in mind that the observations, interpretation and speculation on my part are subjective, it is nevertheless interesting to consider the following:

Plot A

Management regime Regular cutting; the plot had just been cut.

Floral makeup in early June Viewed from the margin, perhaps 11 species of flowering plant (including grasses and rushes) in low numbers. Much of the ground was blanketed by cut vegetation.

Meadow butterflies as indicators I would rate the chances of meadow butterflies breeding in the plot as slim, or at least the completion of their life cycles as unlikely. In early June, life-cycle stages of many of the 'brown' butterfly species would be using tall, standing grasses, either as caterpillars or, depending on the species, adult butterflies about to emerge from their chrysalises. Cut the grass and remove it and you stand a good chance of killing them. Cut the grass and leave it where it fell, as happened here, and the smothering blanket will most likely destroy them.

General wildlife Little obvious wildlife on show. Had ground-nesting birds, such as Skylarks, been attempting to nest, the likelihood is that cutting the grass at this strategically important time would have resulted in nest failure.

Plot B

Management regime Grassland recovery has been allowed to take place naturally. Winding paths and meadow 'clearings' are cut but otherwise the vegetation is left untouched.

Floral makeup in early June On my visit, I noticed 41 species of flowering plants (including grasses and rushes).

Meadow butterflies as indicators Based on observations in previous years, 8 species of butterfly whose caterpillars feed on meadow plants breed in Plot B. Three species were on the wing in early June, which is what I would have expected for the time of year.

General wildlife The dense vegetation supports a thriving population of small mammals, especially Short-tailed Voles and Wood Mice. These in turn attract the attentions of predators that include Kestrel, Buzzard, Red Kite, Barn Owl and Tawny Owl. Slow-worms and Grass Snakes are present too, and a recently created pond in the field has breeding populations of Common Toads and Palmate Newts. Skylarks breed in Plot B. Outside the nesting season flocks of Linnets and Goldfinches are attracted by the seeds of meadow plants, while passage and wintering Stonechats include invertebrates such as spiders in their diet.

Above *A Barn Owl photographed in the parish of Pamber on vole-rich grassland that is being restored on previously farmed land (Plot B in the image on p. 68).*

Left *The contents of a couple of passes with a sweep net on Plot B reveals an abundance of life, mostly insects.*

Plot C

Management regime Regularly grazed by sheep. A newly planted hedge defines the boundary between this plot and Plot B.

Floral makeup in early June The close-cropped sward appeared to support a community of grazing-tolerant species, with 16 species in evidence by scrutiny from the margin.

Meadow butterflies as indicators Given their reliance on tall, dense grassland, it is most unlikely that any meadow butterfly species are able to breed in Plot C, except perhaps in the hedge-fringed margins.

General wildlife Little obvious wildlife on show. If present, small mammals are likely to be restricted to the margins, and the field offers no opportunities for ground-nesting birds.

Photographed in mid-August, these images show my uncut garden meadow (left) and nearby grassland that had been cut for hay six weeks earlier. My meadow retained its three-dimensional structure and was alive with butterflies, grasshoppers and other insects plus late-flowering nectar sources such as thistle species and Common Fleabane. The commercially cut grassland was devoid of any obvious signs of life.

orchid spikes in their prime in May, and witnessed the manicuring they employ in summer. It comes as no surprise then that the reason why Grass Vetchling thrives in my garden but has been driven to extinction on the local roadside verges is down to timing. The species is an annual that relies on hot dry weather to blacken its pods to the point where they explode and release their seeds. Cut the plant before it has had a chance to release its seeds, which happens on verges where it used to thrive, and it soon disappears from the scene.

Visibility and safety are clearly reasonable reasons for cutting certain stretches of roadside, but I suspect that the timing of verge-cutting might on occasion have more to do with occupying a workforce during an otherwise slack period. Dig a little deeper and in some instances verge-cutting is done in response to complaints from taxpayers and their elected representatives about the 'untidy' (i.e., flowering nicely and biodiversity-rich) appearance of their roadside verges. This is further indication of the disconnect between society and nature, and a measure of the level of environmental ignorance among some in the community.

AN ANTIDOTE TO BOTANICAL BUZZ CUTS AND AGRICULTURAL MANICURE, THE UNKINDEST CUTS OF ALL FOR WILDLIFE

Personal experience has influenced the method and approach I use to manage my tiny meadow. Informative was a visit a few years ago to a hay meadow whose status is that of a nature reserve. When I first visited the site in question, four decades in the past and long before it acquired SSSI status, it was cut in late summer in a rough and ready manner, hay was then harvested and a few head of cattle spent the winter months grazing the land. A situation not dissimilar, I imagine, to what would have happened four centuries earlier. However, on my most recent visit, which was in June, I discovered that the vegetation had already been cut to within an inch of its life, nothing was in flower and there was precious little evidence of invertebrate life. When I questioned the timing and degree of manicuring, I was told words to the effect that '... this is the way hay has always been cut.' This may be accepted contemporary practice among commercially minded land managers and sub-contractors, but I would question the use of the word 'always', for reasons I will explain. However, regardless of arguments for and against, I knew that this buzz-cut approach to meadow management was not for me.

This brush with contemporary meadow management prompted recollections of schoolboy summer holidays spent observing and pursuing wildlife in waist-high grassland near where I grew up. Haymaking timing is ingrained on my memory because it coincided with the point where seasonal happiness – exploration of the countryside throughout the month of August – ended and a return to the misery that school represented began. In addition to the timing, I also recall the end result of haymaking: not the manicured designer stubble of the twenty-first century but a landscape that was far more unkempt and varied in appearance. I also knew from the evidence of my own eyes that my favourite meadows, which were cut late in the season and in a slapdash way, harboured more wildlife across the board than those subjected to a more regimented approach. Not only in that particular year but equally significantly in the year that followed.

Even though those schoolboy recollections of unintentionally wildlife-rich hay meadows stretch back more than 50 years, the methods used then were still mechanised. Step back further in time and manual labour would have been the driving force. As anyone who has attempted to cut a hay field by scythe will testify, the outcome is never the manicured 'lawn' that results from twenty-first-century cutting-edge technology. Plus, even with a small army of men and women at work, it would have taken much, much longer.

My meadow in early September with drifts of grasses in seed, and late-season insects including egg-laying grasshoppers. Adult meadow butterfly species have died off by now, but their life cycles continue with, depending on species, their eggs or larvae in readiness for the autumn and winter ahead.

I have a nagging feeling that the perception of what a 'good' hay meadow should look like after cutting is informed in part by agricultural or horticultural mindsets where the desired outcome is seen as being neat, tidy and controlled, with nature put back in its place until the following spring. So, here's is a plea to budding biodiversity gardeners with meadows among their charges: ignore any tidy-minded advice about what a winterised meadow should look like and imagine the variety of life that will be encouraged by giving your grassland a 'trim' rather than a buzz cut.

TOOLS OF THE TRADE

From personal experience, the tools of the trade used to cut a hay meadow can also have an impact on species diversity and abundance. In the first year of creating a meadow I was daunted by the task and the volume of grass that needed to be tackled. I tried hand-cutting using a large scythe, but a lack of dexterity and experience meant I was a danger to myself. As a result, I resorted to using a strimmer, only to abandon that when I inadvertently cut a young Grass Snake in half.

Nowadays, I cut the grass by hand using shears. This may sound preposterous, but I treat the process both as exercise and an opportunity to observe the grassland community at close quarters. Not wanting to turn a pleasure into a chore, I spread the activity over a period of 7–10 days. This allows me to manicure around my ever-increasing anthills and to cater selectively for the larval foodplant needs of my grassland-breeding butterflies. A further advantage of this slow-paced approach is that I reduce the chances of chopping the legs off a fleeing frog or killing other forms of wildlife – they have a chance to hop away. That sort of environmental collateral damage is an inevitable consequence of speedy, mechanised cutting.

I appreciate that this method of grassland management may not be appropriate for others and a more mechanised approach may be called for, not least in situations where the meadow in question is greater in area. Before you cut, however, consider what you want to achieve. If the intention is more than just a hay crop, and is as varied an outcome for wildlife as possible, you should consider your options. You could, for example, set the cutter at least a foot off the ground; you could consider cutting in rotation, perhaps dividing a meadow area into halves, each cut in alternate years;

or you could cut on a rotational strip basis, and set aside one area that you never cut. If wholesale cutting is what you want, then a tip to reduce the carnage caused to wildlife by mechanised cutting comes from conservation management advice regarding Corncrakes and the cutting of Hebridean machair grassland. Start the operation from the middle of the field and work outwards. Do it the other way round, working towards the centre, and wildlife is concentrated with nowhere to run, with fatal consequences.

Unless there is a pressing need to provide someone with fresh vegetation, following tradition I leave the cut grass lying for a few days before raking into piles. This allows the material to dry and become hay, but the process serves an additional, biodiversity-related function: it allows a little bit of extra time for meadow flower seeds to mature and fall, and any insects or other invertebrates to make their escape. I leave clumps of Cock's-foot uncut until after the first frosts, allowing time for Large Skipper caterpillars to find sanctuary and hibernate in the heart of the tussock.

A STACK OF HAY

Hay originated as crop that was stored and used to feed animals during the winter months. Since I don't keep livestock, I had to decide what to do with the grass I cut from my meadow. Nowadays I absorb a fair amount into grass piles and compost mounds that fringe my garden, and as a testament to the power of decomposition it always amazes me how quicky its volume diminishes. Some grass piles are specifically and strategically placed to serve as nesting mounds for Grass Snakes.

Now and then, I supply some of the cut vegetation as a source of supplementary food to a neighbour who keeps a small flock of conservation-grazing sheep. In this instance, with Common Ragwort in mind and as a 'just in case' courtesy to my sheep-owning neighbour, before I cut the grass I 'pull' the ragwort stems. I also pull the stems of thistles that have set seed and stack them, tucked away somewhere in my hedgerow boundary. The reason for this is that they will have already been used by various bush-cricket species, females of which use their dagger-like ovipositors to lay eggs inside stems. Destroy the stems or feed them to animals and you kill the next generation of bush-crickets.

Grazing my meadow was suggested to me as a way of 'tidying up' the appearance of the land and resolving the issue of excess hay. And it is often advocated as a way of enhancing floral diversity when restoring meadows. However, on balance I rejected the idea partly because it would be completely inappropriate for the size of my plot, but also because it would not achieve the outcome I wanted. I want to benefit as great an array of biodiversity – especially invertebrates – as possible and not just flowers. A close-cropped sward, nibbled to within an inch of its life, was the last thing I wanted.

MANAGING EXPECTATIONS

My heart sank the other day while chatting to a neighbour who had embarked on a small-scale meadow project the previous year. At the start, I had tried to explain that if benefitting native wildlife rather than horticultural self-gratification was his aim, then grassland should be the goal, not a gaudy mix of annual former arable weeds. He ignored my advice, scarified the soil, and scattered seeds of the usual suspects – flowers that appeal to the human eye but which are largely meaningless in terms of long-term benefits. In year two, his 'meadow' lacked the previous year's garish floral component, which was no surprise to me. However, he was disappointed that what he called 'weeds' (i.e. native grassland species) had replaced his seeded annuals. Rather than celebrating the natural grassland restoration that was in progress, he was contemplating either abandoning the project or repeating the pointless seeding process. The dismay I felt was obvious when I tried to persuade him of the folly of this course of action but I doubt I will have changed his thinking. Sadly, an inability to understand the role that grass species play in meadow ecology meant that what should have been regarded as a success was to him a failure.

Although ecological role is more important than visual appearance in the biodiversity garden, there is intrinsic beauty to be found in grasses in their own right, if you have the eyes to appreciate it.

FOCUS OF ATTENTION

One advantage of managing a small meadow like mine is that I can adopt a nuanced approach and encourage particular favourites; by so doing I hope that the resulting mosaic has collateral benefits for others. Here are a few examples of groups in which I take a particular interest when it comes to cutting regimes and the support of their botanical allies. In some ways these groups are more than just favourites, and I think of them as indicators and a means by which I can gauge success or otherwise. The grassland butterflies are a sign that the meadow hosts a sufficient range of larval foodplants and that I am creating enough variety in my cutting regime. Anthills and grassland-specialist fungi are a sign that stability and structure in the underlying soil are becoming properly established.

Grassland butterflies and nuanced management

My interest in butterflies can be traced back to my childhood, a time when meadows and grassland featured prominently in my school summer holidays. Consequently, it is both a pleasure and a privilege to be able to help beleaguered grassland butterflies in my garden. If you want to maximize the benefits then you need both an appreciation of, and an ability to recognise, the larval foodplants of your residents, and an understanding of their ecological requirements. None of the grassland-breeding species in my garden would benefit from a close-cropped approach to meadow management. Most overwinter as caterpillars, usually in some form of cocoon or shelter, the location of which depends on circumstances and the species involved. Some hide away at ground level, others find protection inside clumps of grasses or construct protective tents from leaves, and a few hibernate inside the leaf sheaths of grasses. Cut the vegetation down to ground level and you will stand a good chance of unwittingly destroying entire generations of butterflies; subsequent intensive grazing of the cut meadow is only likely to make matters worse. For the life-cycle images that illustrate this section, I have included the date on which they were photographed. This demonstrates the importance of not disturbing a meadow during spring and summer; do so and you risk damaging the chances of butterfly life cycles being completed. For the sake of clarity, the words larva and caterpillar, and pupa and chrysalis, are one and the same.

On the whole, meadow butterflies are relatively easy to identify. They show a range of life-cycle needs, with some species being generalists and others having more specific requirements for survival. As such they make an excellent group for the purposes of monitoring, and the biodiversity gardener could do a lot worse than follow procedures adopted by the United Kingdom Butterfly Monitoring Scheme (UKBMS). Through the use of techniques such as defined transects, timed counts and seasonal monitoring, the approach has the potential to create reliably accurate data for a given plot of land that can be compared month to month, and year to year, thus revealing trends. However, the UKBMS only concerns itself with adult butterflies, not other stages in the life cycle.

A freshly emerged Ringlet, photographed in my meadow on 26 June.

THE MEADOW BROWN: a useful indicator of habitat loss and degradation

The Meadow Brown is an undemanding butterfly that tolerates a wide range of natural grasslands and is quick to colonise new habitats. As such, it makes a good indicator subject for the study of environmental health. In locations where it does occur, UKBMS data would seem to indicate it is not in peril. However, where I live the evidence of my own eyes suggests a far less rosy status if you identify locations where, in theory, it should occur and most likely did occur historically, and compare these with sites where it actually occurs today. Using presence or absence rather than numerical transect-counting, and stepping back in time a century or more before the industrialisation of agriculture, a bleaker anecdotal picture emerges for the Meadow Brown, at least where I live.

Using detail provided about land use by the 1838 Tithe Map and Tithe Apportionment (see p. 27), at that time there were 313 acres or so in the parish of Pamber where land use is listed as either meadow or pasture. Simply by virtue of date, these would have been 'unimproved' in the accepted modern sense because it was more than a century before artificial agrochemicals made an appearance on the farming scene. Furthermore, it is likely that stock and hence grazing levels on pasture would have been less than today, and seasonal land use more varied. Therefore, the assumption I am making is that all 313 acres would have been suitable, in varying degrees, for Meadow Browns. This supposition ties in with anecdotal evidence, the reminder coming from a passage in Jeremy Thomas's book *The Butterflies of Britain and Ireland*. He quotes Victorian entomologist Charles Golding Barrett who, on the subject of the Meadow Brown, said there was 'hardly a grassy field in the United Kingdom from which it is wholly absent'. Jeremy Thomas compares that statement with the start of the twenty-first century when he was writing his book, and makes the point that this was no longer the case then, thanks to agricultural 'improvement'. See the References section for book details.

I cannot claim to have undertaken detailed surveys of every corner of every grassy field in the parish of Pamber. However, I have looked at a considerable number from footpaths and gateways, and observed the nature of the grassland on the ground and using Google terrain searches. The majority of grassland in the parish is now 'improved' for agricultural yield, and dominated by seeded grass cultivars whose vigour is chemically assisted, with competition from other plant species virtually eliminated in the same manner. Consequently, I estimate that there are now just 75 acres in the parish of Pamber where Meadow Browns are present or might occur. In the period from 1838 to the current day that represents a 76 percent

loss in habitat suitable for this most generalist of insects. Unsurprisingly, those 'improved' fields I have looked at lack other insect indicators such as grasshoppers and harbour minimal floral diversity.

On the plus side, the fact that Meadow Browns colonised my garden after I stopped mowing the lawn and allowed meadow habitat to develop is a testament to the butterfly's amazing ability to colonise and its environmental resilience. It is also a reminder that there is hope, for some species at least. Furthermore, it demonstrates the crying need to create pockets of biodiversity from which future colonisation by wildlife might occur elsewhere if times change for the better.

A newly emerged Meadow Brown, photographed on 12 June.

As a cautionary note for would-be butterfly surveyors, it helps to understand the natural history of individual species before drawing conclusions about abundance or relative abundance. Individual adult Meadow Browns live for little more than a week, and the species' staggered emergence means they are on the wing from the middle of June until the end of August. On the other hand, Gatekeeper and Large Skipper adult emergence is more synchronised; individuals of the former emerge in mid- to late July and live for 3–4 weeks, while the latter appears in mid-June and an individual's lifespan is 6–7 weeks. If you undertake a 'snapshot' butterfly survey on a single day in mid-July, you will encounter a relatively small proportion of the site's true Meadow Brown population (early emergers will be dead, late emergers yet to appear), while almost the entire population of Gatekeepers and Large Skippers will be on the wing.

My garden meadow butterflies: their dietary needs and ecological requirements

Meadow Brown

Gatekeeper

Ringlet

Marbled White

Small Skipper

Large Skipper

male

Small Copper

female

Common Blue

A Meadow Brown caterpillar, photographed on 23 April.

A Meadow Brown chrysalis, photographed on 18 May.

Meadow Brown

Larval foodplants in my meadow Bents *Agrostis* spp., Downy Oat-grass, False-brome, fescues *Festuca* spp., meadow-grasses *Poa* spp. and Cock's-foot.

Other larval foodplants eaten elsewhere A wide range of grasses are mostly likely consumed, but relatively fine-leaved species appear to be favoured when adults are egg-laying.

Ecology Eggs are laid on grass stems and leaves in summer, and young larvae hibernate low in the vegetation. The caterpillar stage lasts from July to the following May. Growing caterpillars feed in spring, mainly after dark, on grass leaves in the meadow 'canopy' and pupate nearer to the base. Cut the grass too short and, depending on time of year, you run the risk of destroying eggs or killing the caterpillars.

A Gatekeeper caterpillar, photographed on 8 June.

A Gatekeeper chrysalis, photographed on 13 June.

Gatekeeper

Larval foodplants in my meadow A wide range of grasses including bents *Agrostis* spp., fescues *Festuca* spp., Common Couch and meadow-grasses *Poa* spp.

Other larval foodplants eaten elsewhere A wide range of grass species are included in the species' larval diet.

Ecology Location appears to be more important than component species; classic sites include grasses growing in hedge-rows and alongside and amongst scrub patches. Eggs are laid on grass leaves, and the caterpillars hibernate in these locations; the caterpillar stage in the life cycle lasts from August to the following May. In spring, growing caterpillars feed on grass leaves and pupate among the tangle of vegetation lower down. Avoid being overzealous when 'tidying' the garden in autumn, and specifically, leave any grassy margins to hedgerows and scrub undisturbed.

*A Ringlet caterpillar,
photographed on 18 April.*

*A Ringlet chrysalis,
photographed on 18 May.*

Ringlet

Larval foodplants in my meadow Cock's-foot and False-brome.

Other larval foodplants eaten elsewhere Cock's-foot and False-brome are reckoned to be the most important foodplant grasses in most locations; other species may include Common Couch, meadow-grasses *Poa* spp. and Tufted Hair-grass.

Ecology Eggs are mostly scattered indiscriminately and the caterpillar stage lasts from September to the following May. Young caterpillars hibernate in low meadow vegetation, so avoid an unduly tidy approach when cutting the grass. In spring, growing caterpillars feed on grass leaves and pupate among the tangle of vegetation lower down.

Marbled White

Larval foodplants in my meadow Cock's-foot, Red Fescue, Sheep's-fescue, Timothy and Yorkshire-fog.

Other larval foodplants eaten elsewhere Tor-grass.

Ecology Eggs are generally scattered indiscriminately. Young caterpillars hibernate in low meadow vegetation and the caterpillar stage in the life cycle lasts from September to the following May. In spring, growing caterpillars feed on grass leaves and pupate among the tangle of vegetation lower down. Avoid an unduly tidy approach when cutting the grass and do not cut it too short.

Small Skipper

Larval foodplants in my meadow Yorkshire-fog.

Other larval foodplants eaten elsewhere Yorkshire-fog is reckoned to be by far the most important grass for this butterfly but occasionally Creeping Soft-grass, False-brome, Meadow Foxtail and Timothy may be eaten.

Ecology Large clumps of grasses are favoured for egg-laying and the tiny caterpillars remain there, side by side, from August until the following spring in cocoons constructed inside a leaf sheath. In spring, growing caterpillars construct a 'tent' by drawing together the sides of a grass leaf with silk strands. They pupate in a loose cocoon in a similar place. Cut the grass too short at any time during this period and you stand a good chance of killing the life-cycle stages. Make sure you leave clumps of the larval foodplant mostly intact when you do decide to cut the grass.

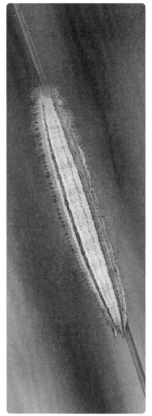

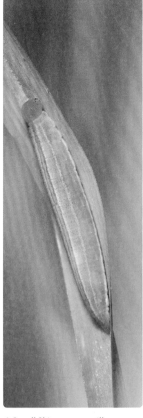

*A Marbled White caterpillar,
photographed on 2 June.*

*A Small Skipper caterpillar,
photographed on 6 June.*

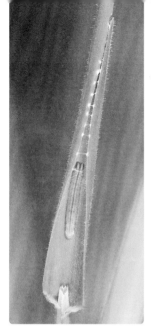

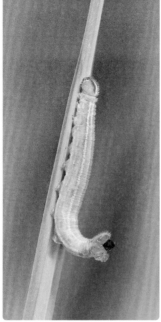

In spring, the growing Essex Skipper caterpillar constructs a 'tent' by tying the sides of grass leaf together with silk strands; it hides inside this during the daytime and pupates in a loose cocoon in a similar place. Photographed on 11 May.

Essex Skipper caterpillars have an unusual way of keeping their immediate environment clean: when they are about to defecate, they extend their abdomen like an elephant's trunk, flare the tip and shake the dropping clear. Photographed on 6 June.

An Essex Skipper chrysalis, photographed on 16 June. The chrysalis is attached to a grass leaf, low down in the vegetation, within a loose shroud of other leaves bound together with silk.

Essex Skipper

Larval foodplants in my meadow Cock's-foot.

Other larval foodplants eaten elsewhere Creeping Soft-grass, occasionally False-brome or Common Couch.

Ecology Clumps of Cock's-foot are favoured for egg-laying. Strings of eggs are laid in leaf sheaths and they remain in this state from July until the following March. The caterpillar stage lasts from early April to early June. Cut the grass too short at any time during this period and you stand a good chance of killing the life-cycle stages. Make sure you leave clumps of the larval foodplant mostly intact when you do eventually cut the grass or you will certainly kill the eggs.

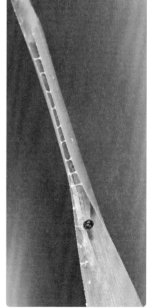

A newly-emerged Large Skipper resting beneath a grass leaf, photographed on 7 June.

A Large Skipper egg, laid on the underside of a grass leaf, photographed on 13 July.

A newly-hatched Large Skipper caterpillar, photographed on 22 July.

A young Large Skipper caterpillar binding and drawing grass leaf margins together with silk to create a protective tent, photographed on 25 July.

Large Skipper

Larval foodplants in my meadow Cock's-foot.

Other larval foodplants eaten elsewhere Purple Moor-grass on acid soils.

Ecology Large clumps of grasses are favoured for egg-laying and the caterpillar hibernates inside a shelter constructed deep in the grass clump. The caterpillar stage lasts from July until the following May. Cut the grass hard at any point during this period and you stand a good chance of killing caterpillars. Make sure you leave clumps of the larval foodplant largely intact when you do cut the grass.

A mating pair of Common Blues, photographed on 27 May.

A Common Blue egg laid on a leaf of Common Bird's-foot-trefoil, photographed on 5 June.

Common Blue

Larval foodplants in my meadow Common Bird's-foot-trefoil and Greater Bird's-foot-trefoil.

Other larval foodplants eaten elsewhere Black Medick, Common Restharrow and Lesser Trefoil.

Ecology Hibernates as a caterpillar, at the base of its foodplant. Leave patches of the larval foodplants intact when cutting the grass.

A basking Small Copper, photographed on 21 July.

Small Copper

Larval foodplants in my meadow Common Sorrel.

Other larval foodplants eaten elsewhere Sheep's Sorrel and very occasionally Broad-leaved Dock.

Ecology Hibernates as a caterpillar at ground level, so don't be too vigorous in your cutting regime in the vicinity of larval foodplants.

Most grassland butterfly caterpillars hide in low vegetation during the day. They are active mainly after dark and are easiest to find using a strong LED torch, feeding among stems and leaves. This particular individual is a Meadow Brown, photographed on 20 April.

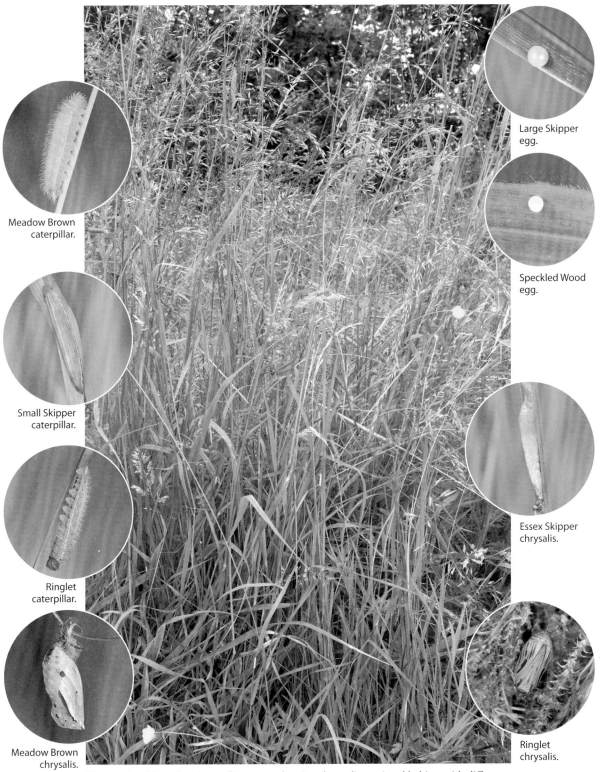

Meadow Brown
caterpillar.

Large Skipper
egg.

Speckled Wood
egg.

Small Skipper
caterpillar.

Essex Skipper
chrysalis.

Ringlet
caterpillar.

Meadow Brown
chrysalis.

Ringlet
chrysalis.

For grassland-breeding butterflies, a meadow is a three-dimensional habitat with different niches and locations important at different life-cycle stages and times of year.

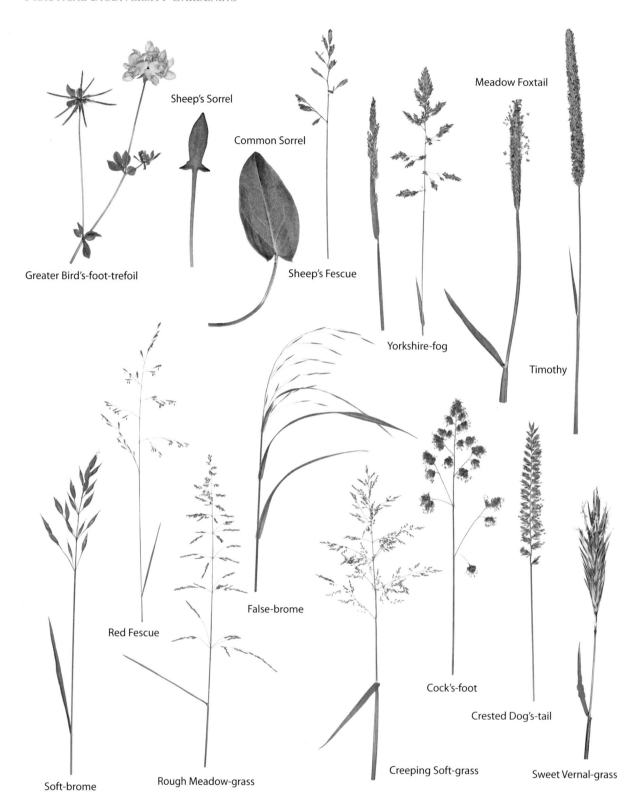

Sheep's Sorrel

Common Sorrel

Meadow Foxtail

Greater Bird's-foot-trefoil

Sheep's Fescue

Yorkshire-fog

Timothy

False-brome

Red Fescue

Cock's-foot

Crested Dog's-tail

Soft-brome

Rough Meadow-grass

Creeping Soft-grass

Sweet Vernal-grass

A selection of meadow plants in my garden that are important larval food for my grassland butterflies.

MEADOW BUTTERFLY WISH LIST – SMALL HEATH

In my youth I don't recall having any trouble finding Small Heaths as I travelled around north Hampshire. True, the species was distinctly patchy in occurrence, even in a given meadow, because of its seeming dislike of lush vegetation and a predilection for naturally sparse grass cover. Chalk downs and heath margins were prime locations. However, it also occurred in the wider meadow landscape because most sites invariably had areas of short grass – for example, margins to well-used tracks, Rabbit-grazed areas or naturally poor patches of soil created by some hidden underlying geological influence. Today, the situation for the Small Heath is bleaker, and I can only think of a couple of sites within a mile radius of my garden where it occurs. Nevertheless, a wanderer usually turns up each year, and I live in hope that by my varied and rather haphazard approach to meadow management I will have created a suitable spot for the species to colonise.

Grassland moths

It is no surprise that the caterpillars of grassland moths feed on meadow plants. However, even to the experienced observer, it is hard to discover the presence of the caterpillars of species you know to be present through observation of adults. Many have caterpillars that nestle in the base of plants during the daytime, sometimes throughout the winter months, and only emerge to feed on leaves after dark. A few small species have caterpillars that live inside seedheads and even pupate there, rendering their presence to our eyes invisible without a search. A select group of caterpillars spend their entire lives underground, feeding on plant roots; members of the swift family of moths are

Ghost Moth.

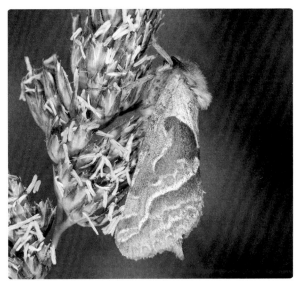

Orange Swift.

A Large Yellow Underwing caterpillar, unseen and tucked away during the hours of daylight, emerges to feed under cover of darkness.

classic examples: Orange Swift, Common Swift and Ghost Moth have all been recorded as adults in my garden and yet I have never found their caterpillars. The caterpillar stage of some species spans two years, further emphasising the importance of undisturbed soil and a stable soil structure. The likelihood is that all moth species that are associated with grassland in my garden will pupate in the soil or amongst the ground-level sward.

The Dark Arches caterpillar lives a partly subterranean life, eating the roots and basal stems of meadow plants.

Grasshoppers and bush-crickets

Spotting grasshoppers in my garden also takes me back to my childhood summers, to an age when I could still hear even the shrillest and most high-pitched of chirps. At the time I took them for granted because they were everywhere. Today, however, grasshoppers are a group of insects that has suffered badly in north Hampshire, intolerant of inappropriate grassland management and slow to spread and recolonise. Consequently, it was a thrill to discover I had three species in my tiny meadow, whereas when the ground was lawn, I assumed I had none.

The appearance of grasshoppers in my meadow presumably meant that colonisation from nearby grassland had taken place, just in the nick of time before native biodiversity sterility was imposed; or that they were present in the garden in small numbers already and I had overlooked them. Grasshoppers appear to have modest requirements when it comes to grassland management, other than to be left undisturbed as much as possible. In my experience, cutting the main area of grass as late in the season as possible clearly benefits the group, allowing females sufficient time to mature and lay their eggs in the soil. I do, however, keep a winding path mown throughout the summer because males seem to like sunny patches and arenas from which to sing.

A female Meadow Grasshopper, sunning herself on a sheltered stem in my meadow.

A female Long-winged Conehead egg-laying in a Bramble stem on the margins of my garden meadow. This illustrates the environmental consequences and folly of burning or in other ways destroying plants that are sometimes perceived as scrub. Almost every native species has a role to play in maintaining the web of life that underpins biodiversity.

Long-winged forms of Roesel's Bush-cricket, such as this individual, occur occasionally in the population and are responsible for the species' progress north. This one is a female, recognised as such by her sickle-shaped ovipositor, a feature that she uses to insert eggs into the stems of meadow plants.

Grasshoppers are sensitive to agricultural disturbance. In my experience the presence or absence of the three species of grasshoppers that live in my garden can be used as an indication of the native biodiversity health or sickness, specifically regarding invertebrates, of farmed countryside; where they are present, a good mix of other invertebrates is likely to be present as well. Grasshoppers are now extinct in all the intensively farmed fields in the parish of Pamber that I have looked at, along with those bird species historically associated with farmland whose diet during the breeding season depends on invertebrates – Grey Partridge and Skylark are good examples.

Grasshoppers are members of a group of insects called Orthoptera, and bush-crickets are among their related cousins. When I first became seriously interested in the group nearly 50 years ago there were two species – Long-winged Conehead and Roesel's Bush-cricket – that were major rarities, each with just a handful of colonies to their name, and most within sight of the sea. Since then, they have had a major upturn in their fortunes and – I still have to pinch myself – both now live in my meadow. However, although I welcome them in my garden, I do not regard their appearance as a conservation success story. In my youth, both were at the climate-limited northern edge of their European ranges on the south coast of England. A warming climate has allowed them to survive winters further north, the progress of Roesel's aided by the occasional appearance of long-winged forms that can fly as well as hop.

Meadow Orthoptera – grasshoppers and bush-crickets

At first glance, these insects can be tricky to distinguish from one another. However, there are a few key pointers that allow certain identification. Male grasshoppers are always appreciably smaller than females of the same species. The markings and angles that separate the dorsal and lateral surfaces of the pronotum (the saddle-like structure that covers and protects the rest of the thorax) are diagnostic in grasshoppers. Female bush-crickets have dagger-like ovipositors that are used for laying eggs, often in plant stems. Colour is not an especially useful feature for separating superficially similar orthoptera because some species are variable.

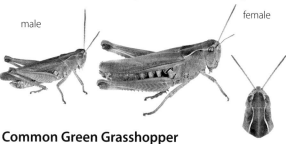

Common Green Grasshopper

This species is almost always bright green, and that includes the wings. The pronotum markings are more noticeably in-curved than those of a Meadow Grasshopper. The eggs are laid in the base of clumps of grasses.

Meadow Grasshopper

Males are long-winged while females are short-winged and cannot fly. Body colour is typically either green or straw-brown, but occasionally bright pink forms occur. The pronotum markings are gently curved and almost parallel-sided. The eggs are laid in the soil.

Common Field Grasshopper

Typical forms are straw-brown but some have tinges of green, generally on the body and not on the wings. Mature males develop a red tinge to the tip of the abdomen. The pronotum markings are sharply angled and defined by a striking white line. The eggs are laid in the soil.

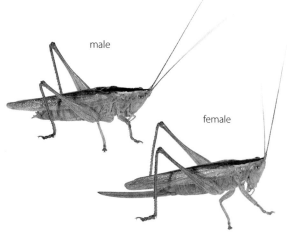

Long-winged Conehead

Note this bush-cricket's slender, bright-green body and pointed angle to the head. The dorsal surface to the body is dark in both sexes, and females have a long, straight ovipositor, used for laying eggs in the stems of plants, including Bramble and thistles.

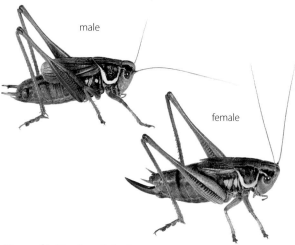

Roesel's Bush-cricket

The pale margin to the side of the pronotum is a good pointer to identification. Most males have relatively short wings; others are long-winged. Females have a slightly curved, dagger-like ovipositor, used for laying eggs in the stems of meadow plants and rushes.

An anthill in my meadow that has been investigated and probed by a Green Woodpecker.

Ants

I realised I had ants in the garden from the outset but had no idea about their abundance or significance until I stopped mowing the lawn and meadow restoration began. Ten years on, colony mounds of Yellow Meadow Ant dot the small meadow and grow in stature each year; fancifully, it's rather like termite mounds in miniature dotting the African savannah. Today, the most impressive are 30cm tall. The colonies contribute to the ecology of the grassland, the insects' diet said to include root-dwelling aphids and other insects. Together with other insect species in the garden, the ants are food for foraging Green Woodpeckers; and Slow-worms are also extremely partial to their kind, the reptile's largely subterranean lifestyle presumably an adaptation to this component of their diet.

An anthill is just the tip of an entomological iceberg and a network of tunnels and chambers will exist underground, hidden from view, expanding and developing over time and entirely dependent on stable, undisturbed soil. Ants are great redistributors of biological wealth, with all manner of organic matter finding its way underground, from seeds to other insects. In addition to circulating life from surface to soil, they are aerators of the soil in the same way as earthworms and Moles.

Across the globe it is well known that ants of many species have evolved intimate and largely symbiotic relationships with members of a family of butterflies called Lycaenidae, better known as blues, hairstreaks and coppers. Depending on species, ants provide a degree of protection for the caterpillars and chrysalises of the group in return for secreted, sugary 'honeydew'. Species found in the UK are no exception, and the Large Blue – not a garden species I know – represents the apogee of this relationship: the caterpillars only survive living inside the nests of a specific ant species, feeding not on plants but the larvae of their hosts.

In the context of my garden, it is thought that Common Blue caterpillars also have some sort of relationship with ants, although evidence for this is patchy. The caterpillars certainly produce 'honeydew', and I have read that they are capable of producing shrill chirps, inaudible to our ears but thought to be attractive to ants. Lycaenid butterfly chrysalises are also attractive to ants. No coincidence perhaps that I once found a Purple Hairstreak chrysalis in an ants' nest in my garden.

● THE ANT WOODLOUSE

Ants have also evolved some unusual associations with other wildlife. Occasionally you may have turned over a garden stone or slab and inadvertently revealed an ants' nest. Look closely the next time this happens and you may spot tiny white woodlice living happily among the ants: this is the Ant Woodlouse whose mouthful of a scientific name is *Platyarthrus hoffmannseggii*. The presence of this terrestrial crustacean is tolerated by the ants and the relationship is reputed to be symbiotic. The benefit to the ants is presumed to be the 'cleaning' function the woodlice perform, since their diet comprises detritus derived from ant prey and other organic leftovers.

If you have an area of chalk downland near you that hosts Horseshoe Vetch, it may be worth a visit on a summer's evening. Study the turf closely after the sun has set and you stand a chance of seeing the caterpillars of Chalkhill Blue butterflies being 'milked' by ants.

Grassland fungi

Grasslands have their own suite of associated fungi, the precise mix as varied as meadow habitats are diverse; for a full account of the subject the New Naturalist title Fungi is informative. Several species of fungi thrive in my meadow and on my remaining lawn. Not as many as I would like, but perhaps the numbers will grow with time. Grassland-specific fungi are among the groups of wildlife hardest hit by agricultural land-use changes and the loss of unimproved grassland. So, I take some comfort from knowing that I have a few representatives of that most iconic of meadow groups, the waxcaps.

Some fungal species favour the decaying layer of dead plant matter and moss that develops over time at ground level. Perhaps more significant in terms of grassland ecology are those with mycorrhizal threads permeating the soil. They contribute to the cycle of life, breaking down organic matter and in turn distributing nutrients. Few if any will survive the disturbance of ploughing. However, many rely on a seasonally shortened sward, the result of cutting, for spore dispersal – to raise spore-releasing mushrooms and toadstools clear enough of the ground to catch the breeze. It is important to remember that a toadstool or mushroom is just the ephemeral, reproductive structure of the fungus, the main body comprising a network of soil-permeating threads termed the mycelium. Most fungi produce their spore bodies from late September to early November, and so as not to damage them, I try to ensure I have cut and raked the grass before then. Some species prefer,

or perhaps are more visible in, short grass, and appear alongside the margins of the meadow or remaining lawn. For information about fungi, see p. 288.

A plea for lawns

Waxcaps (including members of the genus *Hygrocybe*) are indicators of good quality grassland, and lawns have great potential in that regard, given that many species of these colourful toadstools benefit from close-cut mowing. What they can't survive is unwarranted soil disturbance, the application of chemicals and the removal of moss. If you want to keep a lawn and yet benefit native wildlife, including waxcaps, then never apply chemicals of any sort, and learn to love the layer of moss and decaying vegetation that develops. See it as an ecological ally not an enemy, one that harbours a rich array of invertebrates as well as fungi.

I know of a few gardens nearby whose lawns are graced with a diminutive, short-grass-specialist orchid called Autumn Lady's-tresses. It does not grow in my garden but I live in hope. If you think there is a chance it might grow in your garden, leave suitable areas of lawn uncut throughout August – the species is the latest-flowering orchid in the UK, and often not in bloom until early September.

Woodland

Like those of my generation with an interest in natural woodland, I have George Peterken and the late Oliver Rackham to thank for helping me see the wood for the trees, as it were. Following their insights, this personal overview of the history and environmental significance of north Hampshire woodlands will hopefully help inform those biodiversity gardeners who also have an interest in trees and shrubs.

Where I live, deciduous woodland is the natural forested default. Although evergreen Holly trees are scattered here and there, the dominant trees are species that shed their leaves in autumn and appear dormant during the winter months. The term 'deciduous woodland' is an all-embracing generalisation: look closely and there are as many habitat subdivisions as there are native tree species in the area. There are woodlands that comprise mature oaks with an understorey of coppiced Hazel; in other places Ash dominates (or did until the arrival of die-back); there are groves of Alder on waterlogged soils (the resulting habitat goes by the name of carr) that are often coppiced, sometimes pollarded; and White Willow stands that are grown for cricket bats. The list goes on.

WOODLAND HISTORY AND NATURAL HISTORY

Remaining pockets of deciduous woodland in north Hampshire serve as reminders of the ancient 'wildwood' that would have colonised and cloaked the landscape as the ice sheet retreated. However, almost without exception those that remain today are managed habitats, altered over the centuries by man to produce commercial crops. Economic history underpins their very existence, appearance and the reason why they have remained wooded. However, the fact that some of the best wildlife-rich wooded areas (for example many Bluebell woods in southern England) are classified by ecologists as 'semi-natural ancient woodland' is in no

The structural frame of my cottage is Pedunculate Oak and those original floorboards that remain are a mix of oak and elm.

⬤ WOODLAND DEFINITIONS

Deciduous – trees whose leaves are shed in autumn and regrow in spring.

Evergreen – trees whose leaves are not shed each autumn but persist throughout the year, being replaced periodically.

Conifer – a tree that reproduces by means of cones and which has needles not broad leaves.

Broad-leaved – a generalised, catch-all term (sometimes spelt broadleaf) relating to trees whose leaves are broad, not needles. They reproduce by means of flowers, and produce fruits.

Coppicing – the woodland practice of cutting shrubs almost to ground level, periodically and on a rotational basis, the aim being to create regrowth of long, straight poles.

Pollarding – the woodland practice of pruning and cutting trees at head height or above (beyond the reach of grazing animals) to produce regrowth of stout branches.

Pamber Forest owes its existence to the role it played in historic rural economics.

way derogatory. From a wildlife perspective, it is the legacy of millennia of woodland cover in one form or another, and the history of traditional, relatively slow-paced land use, that created Britain's varied ancient woodland heritage. Our ancestors were not conservationists. What remains of our rich woodland biodiversity is an unintended consequence of historic woodland exploitation.

In Pamber, timber from Pedunculate Oak was favoured in the construction of timber-framed houses (such as my cottage) and barns; plantings of Sessile Oak produced long, straight trunks for beams. In addition, in the late sixteenth and early seventeenth centuries both oak species from Pamber were used in naval ship construction. Stately elms (now gone from the landscape) provided planks, and because of the timber's durability in water, piles and boarding fashioned from elm, known as camp-shot, was used for shoring up river banks; whole trunks may have been bored and used as sewage pipes for wealthy households, and it was the favoured wood for coffins. Coppiced Hazel served a range of purposes, from poles used in hop-growing to

baskets, hurdles and barrel hoops. Birches were used to make besom brooms. At the non-specialist end of the spectrum, fuel was by far the greatest consumer of wood (much of it destined to be used by landowners), followed by its use in fencing and dead-hedging. Tree

It is the continuity of wooded cover that is the secret to Pamber Forest's biodiversity success: its invertebrates, not its trees, were significant in its designation, in 1951, as a Site of Special Scientific Interest SSSI. The Cow-wheat Shieldbug is just one of many notable insects found there.

species favoured and management regimes adopted were dictated by rural economics – what was going to yield the best income from the land at any given time.

Although natural regeneration is part of the picture, many of the mature trees we see today will have been planted, sometimes centuries ago. As an example, just to the north of my cottage, take Pamber Forest Nature Reserve which is classified as ancient semi-natural woodland. Although the history of near-continuous wooded cover dates back millennia, almost none of the trees it harbours are ancient. Estate records suggest that a massive restructuring took place in the late seventeenth and early eighteenth century, converting the former wood-pasture to coppice-with-standards woodland. To my eyes most are not much older than 150 years, a select few might be 250–300 years old (a fine age but still not ancient), and many will have been planted. The age structure reflects the commercial uses to which the woodland has been subjected over the centuries.

WOODLAND MANAGEMENT AND EXPLOITATION THROUGH THE AGES

The fate of woodland throughout the ages has always been subject to the vagaries of rural economic forces. On a financial whim, trees and entire woodlands have been grubbed out. Historically, that has happened near me. If you compare the 1838 Tithe Map (HRO reference 21M65/F7/185/2) and Tithe Apportionment (HRO reference 21M65/F7/185/1) with the situation at the turn of the twentieth century, then more than 24 acres (10 hectares) of woodland to the south of my cottage had been removed and replaced by arable and grassland, and approximately 110 acres (45 hectares) of woodland that connected my cottage with Pamber Forest had also gone. Alongside this woodland destruction, commercial planting of trees (most likely conifers) also occurred during the period. However, if you look at the ecological balance sheet comparing the extent of native deciduous woodland from start to finish, there was an overall decline in acreage during the nineteenth century, particularly with regard to native tree species.

The era following the Second World War was probably when things started to go badly wrong for woodland in the part of north Hampshire where I live, and no doubt elsewhere in southern England. The timing ran in parallel with the industrialisation of farming, and some of the underlying factors driving the changes were the same: economic forces underpinned ultimately by a rise in the human population, the perceived need for growth and productivity in all its guises, and technological advances. An increasingly mechanised approach to forestry ushered in habitat alteration on a far grander, and speedier, scale than historically had ever happened.

A few miles down the road there's a poignant reminder of attitudes at the time towards the plight of woodland in the post-War era. It concerns an ancient woodland called Bramley Frith whose boundary has remained unchanged since the Domesday Book. Historically, its primary role would have been as a source of wood fuel for its owners, and in medieval times the predominant species would have been Pedunculate Oak and Ash. One coppiced Ash stool was more than 20 feet across, and its age is likely to have exceeded 700 years; this was just one of many truly ancient trees in Bramley Frith. Around three centuries ago, land use and management of part of the woodland switched to oak standards with coppiced Hazel, the latter providing the short-term commercial benefits, being used as fuel for drying Hops. The unplanned and unintentional benefits to the wildlife of north Hampshire were significant. A rich ground flora developed, including a carpet of Bluebells. The fruiting Hazel, mature Pedunculate Oaks and Honeysuckle (where not removed by foresters) were perfect for the Hazel Dormouse. After wildlife-sympathetic woodland management resumed in the 1990s, Bramley Frith became a nationally important stronghold for the species.

One of Bramley Frith's genuinely ancient coppiced Ash stools.

Ecological disaster struck in the late 1960s when the Central Electricity Generating Board (a forerunner of National Grid) bought the woodland. It was then gutted, not for commercial timber exploitation but to locate and screen an industrial electrical substation complex and presumably avoid accusations of 'ruining the appearance of the English countryside'. As a result, 21 acres (8.5 hectares) of wonderful ancient woodland at the heart of Bramley Frith were destroyed and replaced by gravel, concrete and electrical installations, from a total area of 110 acres (44.5 hectares) just to assuage the anticipated sensibilities of the public. That's a loss of roughly 20 percent. As far as I am aware, there was no outcry from the public at the time about the *destruction* of ancient woodland, and there would have been precious few routes by which it could have been prevented.

A WAKE-UP CALL
THAT SHOULD HAVE BEEN HEEDED

A decade later, those with the eyes to see had become aware that something was going badly wrong with British woodlands. In 1980 the Nature Conservancy Council (a previous incarnation of what is now Natural England and its devolved equivalents) embarked on an inventory of ancient woodland because by that time Britain had already lost half the ancient woodland it possessed in 1945. It culminated in, amongst other things, a trilogy of books including one by Charles Watkins entitled *Britain's Ancient Woodland: Woodland Management and Conservation* (see the References section for details). In it, it is interesting to note that the Forestry Commission stated it had 'decided that all ancient woodland on the NCC inventory should be managed with due regard to its intrinsic conservation and historical interest'. Hmm ... I am not convinced that aspiration ever turned into reality. Regardless, the book sets out to provide advice about appropriate ancient woodland management, and the text is as relevant today as it was then.

In common with farming's strengthening impact on the environment, things have gone from bad to worse for native woodlands in my lifetime. Their degradation takes many forms. At one extreme there is the modern, industrialised approach to woodland management – chainsaw gangs rather than a few men with saws, axes and billhooks; at the other there's disturbance and misuse by members of the public. Wholesale destruction is also entirely achievable – lawfully – thanks to the

granting of felling licences obtained from reincarnations of the Forestry Commission – Forestry England and its devolved counterparts. Licence applications rely on the honesty and environmental awareness of the applicant and, when it comes to the potential for impact on wildlife, a fairly sophisticated level of knowledge of natural history and a conscience.

THE FUTURE FOR WOODLANDS

Woodland economics continues to be among the most significant factors influencing the appearance and fate of privately owned British woodland.

Modern-day threats mean that it is all the more important to protect what is left, but also to enhance woodland habitats where we have some control. It is not just the woodlands themselves that need help, it is their surroundings and settings too. Surviving woodlands are fast becoming islands in oceans of imposed biodiversity sterility, sitting isolated in farmland and disconnected from neighbouring woodland by the removal of hedgerows. The inter-connectivity between woodlands provided by hedgerows and scrub are vital if degraded woodlands are ever to recover.

To maintain the woodland structure that today's casual observer perceives as being 'good', and the biodiversity that informed naturalists cherish, some form of management needs to continue. Gardening on a grand scale if you like, and our generation has the benefit of hindsight and the ability (some might say responsibility) to do the right thing. Countless books have been written on the subject of managing woodland with wildlife in mind and Charles Watkins's book is both a useful reference and a good starting point.

In the twenty-first century you could be forgiven for thinking that attitudes towards woodlands have changed. Everywhere you look we are entreated to plant trees, and councils the country over proudly display their green credentials by planting token trees while at the same time permitting development that impinges on or destroys existing woodland. On the face of it there appears to be a groundswell of public opinion opposed in principle to ancient woodland destruction associated with the likes of HS2. However, 'over-riding public interest' often trumps any efforts to combat these losses. I have a sneaking suspicion that governments of whatever persuasion would not impose these rulings if they felt they would lose votes, and will have taken the temperatures of voters in that regard. A reasonable conclusion is that collectively public indifference to wildlife loss is an underlying contributory factor in the fate of woodlands. An eavesdropped conversation about the tax benefits of buying woodland – see below – reinforced my feeling that 'over-riding self-interest' has a role to play.

PLANTING TREES

Despite what you might read to the contrary, you cannot plant a woodland. You can plant trees, of course, but a woodland is a community of plants, animals, fungi and the rest, and an ecosystem that takes centuries to evolve and establish. It reaches from the tips of the roots and their fungal partners to the leaves at the ends of twigs. It embraces the invertebrates associated with the roots, bark, timber, leaves and flowers; the life that

lives amongst its epiphytic dependents; and larger animals that rely on this web of life for survival. And the community extends to the woodland's ground flora and associated wildlife. The progress and evolution of a woodland is measured in years, decades and centuries, not days, weeks or months. As a result, woodland 'creation', management and enhancement, where biodiversity is the priority needs to take the long view, one stretching well beyond the lifespans of anyone planting the trees or reading this book.

If you plant trees on land that historically had tree cover or reinstate a hedgerow (things you can discover from Tithe and Enclosure maps, for example) then the chances are you will have a head start in the process of turning tree-planting into meaningful woodland creation. The germs of woodland life – seeds and essential fungal partners, for example – are more likely to be lying dormant and awaiting resurrection than if

● WOODLANDS FOR SALE – Financial net gain vs biodiversity net loss

I was at a funeral recently and eavesdropped on a conversation about tax. Given the circumstances, unsurprisingly the initial subject under discussion was death duties and ways of avoiding them. However, the topic expanded to cover tax avoidance generally and the subject of woodland ownership came up. In the manner of barrack-room financial advisors everywhere, I suspect the advice on offer contained a few inaccuracies and elements of financial wishful thinking. However, it did shed light on contemporary reasons why people consider buying woodland in the current economic climate, and how human nature and self-interest continue to play a role in woodland well-being.

A primary reason suggested for buying woodland was that you could then simply fell the trees and not pay tax on the profit. With the caveat that I am not a tax expert, I would say there are elements of truth to that, but it is not the whole truth. As far as I can make out, profit generated from a growing timber crop is exempt from Capital Gains Tax, but only where the woodland has been and continues to be managed as a commercial investment; the exemption does not apply to the land the trees are growing on. Income from the sale of timber extracted from commercial woodlands is exempt from both Income and Corporation taxes, but again it must be demonstrated to HMRC that the operation is commercial.

As far as I can see, tax relief would not apply were somebody to buy an ancient semi-natural woodland that had been neglected for half a century, clear-fell the site and sell the timber. Or at least I sincerely hope so.

Those are some of the commercial considerations that influence people who want to profit from woodland exploitation. On the conservation side of the equation, the government has introduced what it calls a 'Conditional Exemption Tax Incentive Scheme' that offers owners of woodland sites conditional exemption from Inheritance Tax and Capital Gains Tax in return for not felling trees. The exemption applies only if it can be demonstrated to HMRC that the site has scientific, scenic or historic significance; an example would be an ancient semi-natural woodland that featured on either Natural England's or Scottish Natural Heritage's Ancient Woodland inventories. There are other reasons and criteria why a woodland might qualify for exemption – as a Site of Special Scientific Interest, for example, and it might be argued that Site of Importance for Nature Conservation status was also sufficient. Who knows what the situation will be once the dust has settled on the small print of the new Environment Act? However, the cynic in me suspects that the route to obtaining financial advantages by *protecting* woodland will always be more challenging than the road to exploitation.

the site, in a former life, was industrialised, sprayed farmland. Woodland regeneration on land that was previously farmed intensively is entirely possible, of course; it is just that the process of establishment is likely to take longer to show signs of meaningful woodland biodiversity developing.

THE CASE FOR *NOT* PLANTING TREES

Mention in passing has been made already of the ecological concept of succession of vegetation, a process whereby vegetative colonisation of bare ground follows a natural progression from herbaceous plants including grasses, through scrub and eventually to woodland. This would have happened on a grand scale at the end of the last Ice Age, in parts of Britain formerly covered by the glacial icesheet. It also happens all around us today if we have the eyes to see. Speak to any seasoned naturalist or anyone who has managed land for any length of time and they will confirm this. Left to its own devices, vegetative colonisation will follow this trajectory and within the space of 20 years woodland will have formed of its own accord on open ground, at

A CAUTIONARY NOTE

Nobody with an environmental conscience can object to the planting of trees in principle. It is often presented as a way of mitigating the pace of change of global warming, the idea being that carbon is removed from the atmosphere via the trees' leaves, with photosynthesis sequestering it in the plants' cells. This is, of course, a process common to all plants and not unique to trees. All well and good if your only concern is climate change. However, if promoting, safeguarding and encouraging native biodiversity is an outcome that you hope to achieve by planting trees, there is a danger the result will be the exact opposite. For example, if trees are planted in an unimproved meadow rich in grassland wildlife, attempts to create a woodland will, by design as well as in practice, ruin a perfectly good habitat and potentially destroy the native wildlife adapted to open grassland. The moral of the story is to undertake extensive surveys of any land where tree-planting is planned, and balance the consequences for existing wildlife against any perceived future benefits.

no cost to the landowner and almost by definition with minimal likelihood that non-native and inappropriate species will have found their way into the mix. What is lacking when it comes to adopting this approach is often patience, with an inability to comprehend that the span of a human life is but the blink of an eye when it comes to the recovery or establishment of healthy, biologically complex habitats.

MATURE TREES

There are just five mature native trees in my garden, which hardly constitutes a woodland. However, I live in a generally wooded area, one that was much more wooded in recent history and which still retains ancient woodland remnants in its hedgerows and tree belts. By nuanced management and planting, I have cultivated representative elements in miniature of almost all the significant woodland niches. These span the divide between scrub, woodland edge and hedgerow, factor in dead wood, include a scattering of woodland flowers and place great emphasis on soil and fallen leaves. The garden benefits from connectivity with tree belts and ancient hedgerows in the vicinity. In conventional gardening terms there is a concept referred to as 'borrowed landscape' where the gardener works with countryside features that they do not own in order to enhance the visual appeal of their garden. In my garden, the ambition is more of a 'biologically connected landscape', not for my benefit but to integrate my miniature woodland habitats with the surrounding landscape.

It might be hard to accept that a tiny patch of tree cover is anything more than a nod in the direction of woodland conservation. However, perhaps a snapshot of the garden's invertebrate life provides an indication that it is more than just a token gesture, and has significance in the context of landscape with a history of woodland cover and hedgerow remnants. In my modest-sized garden (just half an acre) I have recorded over 400 species of moths, the majority of which are associated with woodland and scrub in some shape or form. To put this in perspective, it is interesting to compare this number with nearby Pamber Forest, a nature reserve given SSSI status primarily on account of its invertebrate fauna. Since records began, this 500-acre site has recorded around 800 species of moths. The moth list for the whole of the UK, including migrant rarities, is around 2,500 species.

HEDGEROWS, HISTORY AND NATURAL HISTORY

Hedgerows are important for wildlife in a broad sense, and part of their significance lies in their origins. They are an integral part of the north Hampshire landscape and across the British countryside as a whole. However, 'hedgerow' is broad-church term and they vary in style and construction considerably from place to place. Even locally, a hedgerow on chalk soil just five miles away will be different in terms of species and structure from one in the parish of Pamber; and further afield, a Cornish 'hedge' is in essence a stone wall. This diversity highlights the dangers of making generalisations.

My interest in hedgerows, particularly in the context of biodiversity gardening, lies in their value to wildlife, not their historical origins. However, their history and natural history are so inextricably linked that without an appreciation of the role they played in shaping the countryside it is hard to make a case for conserving their value for wildlife. By way of a disclaimer, the following observations relate just to the part of lowland England where I live and do not represent a definitive account. They do, however, indicate the extraordinary complexity of social, agricultural and natural history through the ages.

The aesthetically pleasing appearance of hedgerows belies their original, more practical function: that of defining boundaries and containing or excluding livestock. Some hedgerows are in essence tree-belt remnant borders of lost woodland, sites where historically it might have existed for centuries before being cut down and replaced by another land use. Others mark ancient byways, and many we see today would have been planted historically to define boundaries. There is a strong correlation between hedge-planting and Enclosure, the statutory process of consolidating land and enlarging farms that began in the medieval period and picked up pace from the seventeenth century onwards. For the sake of clarity, Inclosure is the archaic spelling of Enclosure.

There are some extant hedgerows near me that predate Parliamentary intervention and a few whose origins, not their current shrubs of course, might date back to the days of Roman occupation. However, prior to formal Enclosure and widespread planting of hedgerows, containment or exclusion of livestock would have been achieved in part by the deployment of fences and dead-hedges, the latter by their very nature temporary structures. Dead-hedging relies on the use of stakes hammered into to the ground to provide a framework. An appreciation that some of these stakes took root, and that during their lifetime dead-hedges served as protective nurseries for natural sapling colonisation, may have helped inform the subsequent approach to the planting of living hedges.

Lurking in the historical background to the subject of hedgerows is the question of who owns what. Land disputes are nothing new; they have been going on for as long as humans have staked a claim to land on which they have settled. The historical story of defining ownership of England's pleasant land is an unpleasantly complex one involving disputed land rights, boundary disputes, annual transhumance associated with scattered land use, dubious claims of ownership, and

Common Hawthorn is an important component of Pamber's hedgerows, and significant for native wildlife. The fruits, which are a such a feature of autumn, are a source of food for birds.

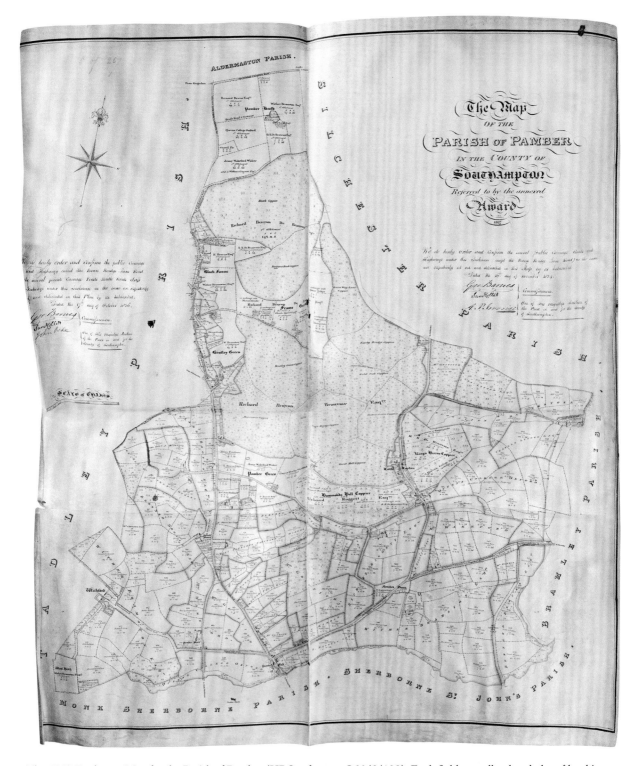

The 1827 Enclosure Map for the Parish of Pamber (HRO reference Q23/2/108). Each field, woodland and plot of land is assigned a number, ownership and acreage with a detailed account being found in the accompanying document, the 1827 Enclosure Award (HRO reference Q23/1/2 pp 634–723).

of course outright deception; in recent centuries, Enclosure Awards often enshrined the end results.

As a huge generalisation, until the seventeenth century, by and large an arrangement referred to as the open field system was in place across England. Communal farming, for want of a better expression, meant that at a basic level each settlement would have had parcels of land that were divided into specific uses for its inhabitants: houses and gardens; meadows for hay production and winter livestock grazing, with animals excluded prior to hay cutting, and thereafter enclosed by dead-hedges during winter; land for common grazing, which might have included heathland, woodland or marshes; and arable. To illustrate the point that all parishes are different, the underlying soils of Pamber are agriculturally poor, and among the crops of wheat, oats, beans, and hay, heavy horses (used in timber extraction) and horses for riding would have been consumers of the latter three. The situation would not necessarily have been the same, for example, where more fertile soils and historical land use had led to a less wooded, more open landscape.

A further ingredient in the land mix were areas referred to as 'waste'. These plots lacked measurable economic value and as agricultural 'offcuts' would most likely have been used unofficially by peasants, amongst other things to collect fuel or cultivate. No one settlement would have been the same as another, and the situation in Pamber, where I live, is complicated by the fact that its namesake forest was historically a Royal Hunting Ground; this placed constraints on residents, particularly with regard to deer, and muddied the waters when it came to subsequent claims of land ownership.

Enclosure was a process not an event, one that began in the medieval period but became particularly popular in the eighteenth and nineteenth centuries, enabled by Acts of Parliament known as Enclosure Acts. Motivated by economic forces, notably agricultural productivity, and underpinned by agricultural advances, Enclosure allowed landowners to enshrine ownership and create legal property rights to parcels of land previously thought of as 'common' and accessible to the peasant population. It thereby extinguished 'common rights'. Enclosure subsequently allowed small parcels of land to be consolidated into larger farms through exchange and sale, and was driven by, and benefited, landowners, and in some cases wealthier tenants.

Until the start of the nineteenth century, the means by which Enclosure was achieved was piecemeal landowner-driven parish-by-parish petitions to Parliament that resulted in Enclosure Acts and Awards being passed, with Commissioners appointed to interpret the outcomes on the ground. Thereafter, to streamline the process and bypass the need for Parliamentary scrutiny, a series of General Enclosure Acts established a body of Enclosure Commissioners to oversee the procedure.

Enclosure Acts and Awards often came with strings attached, in the form of legally binding obligations placed on landowners, and sometimes tenants, to plant hedges to demarcate boundaries, those boundaries having been decided by appointed Commissioners. Instructions were sometimes rather precise and included the requirement for ditch-and-bank planting, protection of hedges during establishment, and the need for maintenance. A small industry developed to cater for the vast numbers of saplings required, with the term 'quicks' creeping into common parlance regarding fast-growing shrubs.

Nowadays hedgerows are rightly perceived as being important for wildlife in their own right. If maintained sympathetically they are havens for nesting birds, hedgerow flowers and insects, and they also serve as corridors connecting larger areas of biological interest and, in particular, otherwise-isolated pockets of native woodland. In ecological terms, hedgerows function in the same way as woodland edge, the woodland zone that in my experience supports the greatest biodiversity.

The benefits of Enclosure to landowners, and sometimes tenants too, are obvious. For landless peasants and the rural poor the consequences were equally profound, and the cumulative effects of Enclosure had implications for society as a whole. An inability to pay the rent or put food on the table contributed to depopulation of the countryside, and an increasingly urbanised workforce that underpinned the Industrial Revolution.

In recent decades, hedgerows across Britain have had a troubled existence, with many having been grubbed out to create larger farmed fields. Increased agricultural efficiency was often used to justify Enclosure and the planting of hedgerows in previous centuries. It is perhaps ironic that twentieth-century agricultural efficiency was a reason for grubbing them out: in the 1960s the Ministry of Agriculture, Fisheries and Food provided grants to encourage farmers to embark on this destruction.

● HOOPER'S LAW − A rule-of-thumb way of ageing hedgerows

The number of tree and shrub species present in an established native hedgerow increases with time, through natural colonisation. In the 1960s Dr Max Hooper devised a method of estimating the age of a hedgerow by counting the number of woody species in a given length. This is referred to in ecological circles as 'Hooper's Law', the simplest version of which is: the age of a hedgerow (in years) = the number of woody plant species in a 30-yard section x 100. This 'law' needs to be taken with a pinch of salt, however, and treated not as definitive but as an indication of a hedgerow of interest and worthy of further investigation.

In decades past, a few well-meaning landowners near here planted hedgerows that included most of the locally appropriate species that you could expect; on the face of it they now appear to be many hundreds of years old when their true age is nearer to 30 years. At the other extreme, there are several hedgerows in the vicinity whose heritage from historical records dates back hundreds of years, yet they contain just a couple of species.

The dangers of drawing wider conclusions from specific observations notwithstanding, anecdotal evidence suggests that narrow hedges of Blackthorn and Hawthorn, a familiar sight in the parish of Pamber today, are likely to have been planted in response to the 1827 Enclosure Award. In the part of north Hampshire where I live, a more reliable way of spotting a truly ancient hedgerow is to look for bank-and-ditch tree growth, and gnarled old Field Maples which were a favoured hedgerow species around here in the medieval period.

The moral of the story is that when attempting to place hedgerows in historical context an informed approach and questioning mind are assets, with subsequent reference to historical maps and records proving invaluable. Using a combination of approaches, many of the surviving hedgerows near me are likely to have been planted around two hundred years ago to define boundaries; a typical count along a 30-metre stretch might be 5–6 species. In addition, there are much older hedgerows and tree belts – with a heritage dating back five hundred years or more – that mark the boundaries of ancient byways and the former Royal Forest of Pamber; a typical count for these might be 10–15 species.

When on the hunt for ancient hedgerows, it is also worth paying attention to ground flora: the presence of Wood Anemone (seen here), Wood-sorrel or Goldilocks Buttercup would set botanical pulses racing in my part of the world.

MY GARDEN'S HEDGEROWS

Historical and mapping information indicates that the current boundaries of my half-acre garden have been associated with the cottage since it was constructed in the early sixteenth century. Evidence also points to a much earlier enclosure of the land, my cottage perhaps sitting on the footprint of a previous, much more rudimentary dwelling. Almost certainly, from that point onwards the garden would have been defined and protected by some form of barrier, be that fencing, dead-hedging or a living hedgerow. The eastern side of the garden is bounded by a truly ancient byway, whose borders are marked by classic indications of age: a complex mix of shrub and tree species including Wild Service-trees, growing on banks flanked by ditches, and an associated ground flora comprising several ancient woodland botanical indicator species such as Pignut, Wood Anemone and Goldilocks Buttercup.

The historical significance of hedgerows is also hinted at in my cottage's title deeds, specifically a clause in a 1960 conveyance that states: '... the purchasers and their successors in title will at all times hereafter maintain and keep in good condition on the western boundary of the premises hereby conveyed a good and substantial hedge row ... with cattle proof chestnut cleft fencing throughout the hedge row or such other good and sufficient cattle proof fence and hedge'. Interestingly, among the names on the conveyance were The Right Honourable Thomas Baron Glentanar, K.B.E. and Sir Ian Frederick Cheney Bolton K.B.E. LL.D, acting as trustees for the vendor. I doubt very much that trustees of such lofty standing, or the vendor or the purchasers (whose address was Elm Park Mansions, Chelsea), would have ever visited my humble cottage. It is more likely that it formed part of part of a property portfolio that provided rental income.

When I took occupancy of the cottage, the western boundary was rather neglected, although the remains of a well-maintained and veteran hedgerow could still be discerned. It contained a few gnarled, multistemmed Hazels, but had developed sizeable gaps and was no longer an impenetrable barrier. A derelict hedge of gradually disintegrating Monterey Cypress marked the eastern side of the garden, the northern boundary was open to the road and a stream defined the southern limits.

Over the period of my occupancy, I have altered things. Partly for privacy, I have installed a fence on the western side, keeping the remaining natural hedgerow shrubs intact and adding to their number with species appropriate to the area. I have removed the conifer hedging and installed a fence on the north and eastern flanks of the garden, planting inside the fence an infant and developing hedgerow of native shrub species. The fences have gaps at ground level that allow safe passage for creatures such as amphibians. Today, the augmented hedge on the western side of the garden has thickened up nicely, to the point where Dunnocks, Wrens and Blackbirds regularly nest in it and Blackcaps now and then. The other hedgerows are still works in progress. My ambition is that, long after my lifetime, the planted and augmented hedgerows will have become fully established by the time the fencing starts to decay.

MUCH-MALIGNED SCRUB

Left to its own devices, bare ground is colonised by a succession of increasingly robust plant communities that ultimately lead to the formation of woodland. Scrub is a general catch-all term used to describe a stage in the process, a transition phase where open habitats have been colonised by species robust and woody, but not quite trees. Scrub continues to be viewed with disdain by many, including some conservationists, seen as a stage that 'destroys' previously fragile phases in vegetative succession that are deemed to be of more importance for wildlife.

There are indeed circumstances and situations where colonising scrub is bad news. For example, if your aim is to protect a community of fragile dune plants, or chalk downland flora, then judicious scrub-clearance may be necessary. However, there is a danger that by referring to scrub universally in a pejorative way we demonise the habitat as a whole, and overlook its virtues. It may be this mindset that continues to drive, for example, overzealous 'scrub-bashing' clearance of gorse in an attempt to recreate an arguably inaccurate and generalised vision of what heathland looked like in the past.

In historical terms, periodic scrub encroachment would have been the outcome on many areas of neglected 'waste' land in the countryside. If we acknowledge the role that the history of human land use has played in shaping our natural history, then scrub will have made

The flowers of Bramble are an extremely important nectar source for insects throughout the summer months.

Long-tailed Tits are scrub specialists that feed on invertebrates, notably insects and spiders.

just as much of a contribution to biodiversity as any other habitat. In that context, it should be seen as a habitat worth factoring into the conservation equation, and part of the remit of any prospective biodiversity gardener.

In the absence of 'wildwood', I regard impenetrable scrub as the next best thing, in the main because it is a habitat where creatures can, by and large, live their lives without suffering the consequences of interacting with humans. I have little difficulty promoting scrub in my garden, my aim being to create as complex and three-dimensionally dense a mass of vegetation as possible.

Scrub is more than just a safe haven for wildlife and protective nursery for sapling trees, and its component plants and shrubs provide an invaluable source of food for a range of animals. Using scrub in and around my garden as an example, a succession of nectar sources for all manner of insects begins with Blackthorn in spring and ends with Bramble in late summer; and fruits of all kinds provide food for insects and birds from early autumn to winter.

Scrub is a colonising habitat. In recognition of its ability to encroach, and the small size of my garden, I do contain its spread. One approach to scrub creation has been to allow previous conventionally gardened areas of shrubs to 'go wild' under their own steam, not replacing alien species when they die off. I have also planted small areas of infant scrub; this requires almost no effort on my part other than planting a selection of

bare-root Blackthorns and Common Hawthorns, and letting Brambles and Common Nettles do the rest. By definition, my patches of scrub are largely inaccessible to me, so as marks of success I use the presence of breeding Long-tailed Tits, Blackcaps and Chiffchaffs as indicators, their nesting preferences ranging from head-high dense cover to ground vegetation.

TREE AND SHRUB SPECIES TO PLANT

If you want to plant trees and shrubs with the aim of benefitting your local native biodiversity in a meaningful way then the best advice that I can offer is to do your homework. Only by understanding the species composition of long-established, wildlife-rich mature hedgerows and woodlands near you will you know what your ambitions should be and which species to plant. Presuming you are not planning a large-scale woodland, in the context of a garden it is best to aim to replicate woodland edge and hedgerow.

Unless you live in a particularly wildlife-rich area, the task should not be too daunting and you will have just a dozen species to contend with. These will inevitably include alien species which, by and large, I would suggest you avoid. However, do your research and survey properly and you will have not only a species list, but a rough idea of the proportions of each species from which you can prepare your own planting plan, tailored to the biodiversity needs of your

SPINDLE, APHIDS AND A CHANGE IN DIRECTION

I went to university to study Zoology, more specifically Entomology and Applied Entomology; in the main that was because I liked insects. Perhaps surprisingly, therefore, during that period of my education I switched from entomology to parasitology. Not because I had abandoned my interest in insects – far from it – but because I became disillusioned by the mindset of many of those teaching me, specifically when it came to the 'applied' aspect of the course. Bear in mind those were different times, but it seemed like all my tutors wanted to do was kill insects, not marvel at them. Put simply, I chose parasitology because I had fewer compunctions about killing parasitic worms than insects as part of my studies. It turned out that did not work either. I soon developed a grudging respect for my subjects' abilities to control the world around them and survive: it seemed that everything from the cestode worms that I studied to fungal parasites routinely manipulated the physiology and behaviour of their hosts – their environment in other words – for their own benefit. As part of the bigger story, it was an illustration that when it comes to the instinct for survival through environmental management, there is little difference between these lowly creatures and humans.

Returning to my entomological education, I recall attending a lecture, given by someone who was a landowning farmer as well as an academic. The assembled students were given an example of how, from the lecturer's world view, practical entomology had done a great service to agriculture and to feeding the country. The example cited was the unravelling of the life cycle of the Black Bean Aphid and empirical evidence that a widespread and relatively common hedgerow shrub, Spindle *Euonymus europaeus*, was the major overwintering host for eggs of this species; in spring hatchlings soon turn their sap-sucking attentions to Broad Beans if the crop presents itself, impacting crop yield. The answer, the lecturer told us, was to grub out Spindle from as much of the farmed landscape as possible, something that he announced with glee he was more than happy to do.

I saw it rather differently and wondered, for example, what role overwintering aphids might play in the bigger ecological picture, as food for birds and as hosts for an array of parasitic wasps. However, those sorts of thoughts had no place at the time. Today of course the environmental landscape has shifted and, in the context of insects, academic emphasis is as likely to be directed towards conservation as control.

Nowadays, with biodiversity in mind, and an appreciation of how little we know collectively about the complexity of natural systems, I would happily plant Spindle in my garden even though I am partial to Broad Beans. The trouble is it does not thrive on my soil type, favouring calcareous or more free-draining ground than mine. For a thorough account of the ecological importance of Spindle, an article in the *Journal of Ecology* by P. A. Thomas, M. El-Barghathi, A. Polwart is a good start; for more details, see the References section.

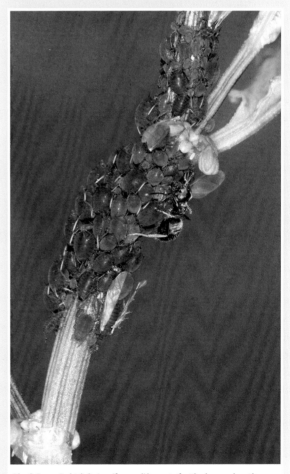

Black Bean Aphids being 'farmed' by ants for the honeydew they produce. In return for their sugary treat, the ants defend the aphids against predators.

immediate surroundings. You may not need to act alone, of course, and if you are lucky, you may have like-minded neighbours with a concern for hedgerow wildlife with whom you can compare notes. In some instances, others will have done the homework for you. A shining example comes from another location in north Hampshire in the form of the Overton Biodiversity Society's informative 'A Study of Local Hedgerows' (see the Reference section for details). No doubt there will be similar examples across the country.

Some native tree and shrub species host more invertebrates than others, and occasionally you may come across their supposed relative merits presented like a biodiversity League Table. Prospective tree planters should beware because it is a mistake to equate numerical invertebrate associations with overall ecological significance. Better to take the view that all native shrubs and trees are favoured by different arrays of native wildlife, not just invertebrates, and are part of the bigger picture. All make invaluable contributions to the complexity of native biodiversity. In terms of their value to wildlife, native trees and shrub species are different from one another, not better or worse. For more information, read an article by Keith Alexander, Ted Green, and Jill Butler in *British Wildlife* magazine entitled 'The value of different tree and shrub species to wildlife' (see the References section for details).

Numbers quoted often hark back to a study that appeared in the *Journal of Animal Ecology* in the early 1960s. As it happens its author was an old teacher of mine, the late Professor Sir Richard Southwood. Read the original paper, and you will discover that any League Table interpretation misrepresents both the data and intention of the study. Without going into detail, the biodiversity gardener's best approach is to ignore any supposed numerical importance placed on a given tree species, focus on what's appropriate and proportionate to where you live, and let nature do the rest.

THE CHOICE IS YOURS

When you embark on a hedgerow or woodland scheme you have two options: grow the trees and shrubs yourself, or buy them. There are all manner of specialist outfits willing to sell you almost any native species you care to mention. If you go down the purchase route then the range of species you buy should be determined by your own local knowledge. However, you will still be faced

by a number of options: the size (and hence age) of the specimen; and whether it has been grown in a pot or comes as a bare root plant. The choice depends partly on your budget but also on your botanical impatience. Pot-grown plants are more expensive than bare root; older, larger specimens are not only more expensive than their younger, smaller cousins but will be faster to produce the impression of a hedgerow or woodland taking hold.

I have relatively limited experience of alternatives or outcomes, but on balance I usually opt for bare root trees and shrubs of short to medium height (it depends on what is available) to be planted in a damp, mild spell in late winter. If I am feeling particularly enthusiastic, I put cardboard collars around their bases to temporarily inhibit the growth of neighbouring plants in the first few weeks of establishment. However, I find it useful to take a leaf from nature's book when it comes to subsequent husbandry. In my experience, those seedling trees and shrubs that most successfully make it to maturity in the wild grew in the protective embrace of rank vegetation and light scrub. In their formative years most are species that do best with the shade of woodland cover rather than exposure on bare ground. Consequently, by the time spring has arrived I welcome the cover that nettles and Cock's-foot provide saplings, as protection from direct midday sun, the subtle humidity they encourage, and the reduced likelihood of the soil baking dry. I do, however, water newly planted tree and shrub species during their first year of growth, irrespective of weather, and I am particularly attentive in that regard during dry spells.

I also grow from seed, in the sense that if I have a bumper crop of acorns I scatter them in the hedgerows, and bury some if I can be bothered. The same applies to Hazel nuts and the fruits of shrubs like Guelder-rose and Blackthorn. If I come across an infant oak growing where I don't want it – in the meadow for example – I will move it; thanks to the Jays in my garden that is a frequent occurrence. And borrowing from an old gardening habit, if I like something and have to prune it, I invariably push some of the twigs into the ground. In my experience I get a success rate of 1 in 10 with Hazel, Common Hawthorn and Blackthorn, and 1 in 5 with any species of willow I care to try; and that's factoring in a degree of subsequent neglect on my part. The realisation that twigs of certain shrubs take root when stuck in the ground may have informed the historic transformation from dead-hedging to the planting of living hedgerows.

DENSITY OF PLANTING AND MAINTENANCE

Like many biodiversity gardeners I am a bit impatient and probably plant more densely than needed. Still, as far as I am concerned a dense hedge is a good hedge, the only proviso being I do not want to compromise the growth of all of its component species in the initial stages, and overplanting risks that outcome. Typically, I plant alternately or in sequence depending on what species I am planting, in a staggered, vaguely two-row system, each bare root whip 30–50cm apart. If I am feeling energetic, I alternate or vary between planting vertically and at 45 degrees. I find the latter approach encourages the whips to thicken up low down, and gives me the chance to weave and intertwine the stems. Sometimes I protect my hedge with my own version of a dead-hedge. Using stems cut from a pollarded willow I impale stakes vertically in the ground every 50cm or so, then impale others at 45 degrees, weaving their stems together through the vertical 'poles'. The reality is that in many situations this 'dead hedge' takes root and over time becomes part of the living component of the new hedge. As a word of warning, however, be careful where you stick your willow wands. Imagine that they will look like in 10 years' time: some locations may not be appropriate.

Typical hedgerows in the part of north Hampshire where I live, even those that are 'managed' unsympathetically, often host large, mature trees spaced out along their length. Around here Pedunculate Oak is a typical species, with others, such as Wild Cherry, Ash and Silver Birch being seen more occasionally. Sadly, the majestic hedgerow elms that I remember from my childhood are a thing of the past, having long since

The stately elms may have vanished from Pamber's hedgerows but Small-leaved Elms live on as small shrubs, spreading by means of suckers. The leaves are food for the caterpillars of the Lunar-spotted Pinion moth, which makes an occasional appearance in my moth trap.

In the context of English woodlands, Hazel is the species that is most associated with regular maintenance, and indeed exploitation, by cutting – known as coppicing. Stems are cut down close to ground level, which encourages regrowth of pliable stems in the years that follow.

succumbed to Dutch Elm Disease. In some situations, even hedging species, such as Hazel and Common Hawthorn – usually regarded as multi-stemmed shrubs – appear as single-stemmed trees now and then. The presence of mature Field Maples is an indication of a truly ancient lineage.

If you want to replicate the 'feel' of local hedgerows in your garden, like me you might want to plant two or three individual trees perhaps 50 metres apart with the intention that they become mature trees for the next generation. If you have the space to plant trees with a future woodland in mind, try to think 20 years into the future and imagine what they will look like, and the space they will fill and require. Visit a nearby mature semi-natural woodland to get an idea of the structure of a wildlife-rich woodland: depending on your space, your goal may not be an achievable one. If you want to maximise the flowering and fruiting potential of a tree or shrub, and have the space to accommodate it, then you could follow the orchard model and plant trees in the open, unencumbered by neighbours.

I prune my lengths of hedgerow now and then, but with no real attempt to keep them looking conventionally neat. Wherever possible, I try to weave unruly stem growth into the main body of the hedgerow and to enable this I sometimes cut the stem partly through on the side facing away from the direction I want to bend it, thereby increasing the chances of it bending rather than snapping. As long as a reasonable part of the stem

Within a five-kilometre radius of my cottage (with soils ranging from chalk to neutral clay/loam and acid sand), native and naturalised tree and shrub hedgerow components include the species shown in this visual short-cut identification guide using leaves.

Yew Native, mainly on chalk but planted elsewhere in churchyards.

Small-leaved Elm Native, sometimes locally dominant in hedgerows, spreading by suckers, but seldom reaching a mature girth due to Dutch Elm Disease.

Wych Elm Native and local; larval foodplant for the White-letter Hairstreak.

Pedunculate Oak Native, and the commonest and most widespread oak species in north Hampshire. A significant species for native woodland biodiversity.

Sessile Oak Native to the UK but probably mainly planted and naturalised in Pamber.

Sweet Chestnut Long-established introduction, planted for coppice.

Downy Birch Native, doing best on wetter ground than Silver Birch.

Silver Birch Native, favouring free-draining, usually acid soils.

Alder Native, favouring wet ground beside rivers and in damp hollows; widely planted.

Aspen Native, favouring clay and sandy soils. Quick to colonise suitable ground.

Goat Willow Native and scattered. The larval foodplant of the Purple Emperor butterfly.

Grey Willow Native and widespread, forming thickets on damp ground and beside ditches and streams.

Crack Willow Native and widespread in damp ground.

Hazel Native but also widely planted in the past for coppice. The nuts are eaten by Hazel Dormice.

Crab Apple Native and occasional in woodland and hedgerows.

Common Hawthorn Native, widespread and a common hedgerow species. Good at all stages for wildlife.

Midland Hawthorn Native and naturalised. An indicator of ancient woodland but also widely planted for ornament and hedging.

Wild Cherry Widespread and scattered in hedgerows and woodland.

Cherry Plum Introduced and widespread in hedgerows, flowering appreciably earlier than similar Blackthorn.

Blackthorn Native and common as a hedgerow species; also forms dense thickets.

Bullace Introduced, naturalised and occasional in hedgerows.

Horse-chestnut Introduced and planted for ornament; of little value to native wildlife.

Field Maple Native and a locally common component of hedgerows and ancient boundary tree lines.

Sycamore Introduced and planted, often spreading by self-seeding.

104

Beech Native to the UK but probably mainly planted in Pamber.

Hornbeam Native but also widely planted for ornament and hedging, and in times past for coppice.

Spindle Native, widespread on chalk and alkaline soils, and planted elsewhere.

Dogwood Native, widespread and common in hedgerows and widely planted.

Wild Privet Native, widespread and locally common on calcareous soils. Planted elsewhere but not to be confused with ornamental privet species.

Black-poplar Native and rather rare. Its timber is larval food for the Hornet Moth.

Hybrid Black-poplar Introduced and planted.

Buckthorn Native and widespread, mainly on neutral and acid soils.

Alder Buckthorn Native and widespread, mainly on alkaline soils.

Wild Pear Native, scattered and much confused with Common Pear, naturalised from discarded cores.

Rowan Native, favouring acid soils. The berries are eaten by birds, particularly thrush species.

Small-leaved Lime Native, local in woodland and also widely planted.

Lime Introduced and planted.

Cherry Laurel Introduced, widely planted for screening, and of little value to native wildlife.

Rhododendron An invasive alien to be avoided at all costs, and removed where it appears; fortunately, it only thrives on acid soils.

Wild Service-tree Native and naturalised, having been spread and planted by the Romans.

Elder Native, widespread and a common shrub of hedgerows and woodland edges.

Norway Maple Introduced and planted.

Ash Native, widespread in woodland and hedgerows and also widely planted. Large trees are disappearing due to Ash Dieback Disease, caused by the fungus *Hymenoscyphus fraxineus*.

Holly Native and a widespread shrub in woodland and hedgerows.

Guelder-rose Native and widespread on soils ranging from neutral to calcareous. Natural range is confused by widespread planting for ornament and as a hedgerow component.

Wayfaring-tree Native and widespread on calcareous soils, but widely planted elsewhere for ornament and becomes naturalised in hedgerows.

remains uncut, it will survive. In a very amateurish way, I also try to replicate elements used in 'hedge-laying': this traditional way of maintaining hedgerows involves cutting a proportion of any large, vertical stems partly through close to ground level and bending and weaving them into a neat framework.

As with most forms of maintenance for wildlife, when it comes to hedgerows the best advice is don't overdo it. Some shrub species respond better than others to cutting, and from a wildlife perspective work should only be undertaken in the winter, ideally after berries and fruits have been consumed by birds and mammals.

Undertaken in a regular and informed way, Hazel management by coppicing prolongs the natural life of the shrub. However, a cautionary note needs to be sounded, one that underlines the need for an informed and sensitive approach to managing hedgerows, especially given that Hazel is a common component species in north Hampshire. Having talked to seasoned woodsmen and people with coppicing experience, the approach is only recommended with relatively young growth – stems under 10 years old. If the Hazel in question hasn't been coppiced for more than, say, forty years (stems more than 15cm diameter perhaps) then if you cut them all down you are likely to kill the shrub. Cut perhaps a third of the stems and the chances of the tree surviving are greatly improved. That's food for thought when it comes to looking after your own hedgerow.

FALLEN LEAVES AND COMPOST

A deciduous woodland is nothing without its fallen leaves. Because of the pejorative undertones I try to avoid the expression 'leaf litter': unlike plastic, for example, leaves are natural and welcome, not polluting and antisocial litter. They are part of the annual cycle of life, layer upon layer adding structure and integrity to the soil each autumn. They feed an army of invertebrates and untold networks of fungi, all playing their recycling part in the web of life that makes up a healthy woodland. Granted, not everyone can see the appeal in a layer of fallen leaves. However, I find the sight of an autumnal blanket a delight to behold and a comforting reminder of the passage of the seasons in temperate England.

As a consequence, I place great store in the leaves that fall in my garden and despair of the mindset that drives tidy-minded neighbours to use leaf blowers, as part of their attempts to rid themselves of these natural gifts. And I weep at the sight of sodden leaves heaped on bonfires. For me they are akin to funeral pyres to biodiversity loss, tears being the appropriate response to this tragic waste of organic matter and its removal from the ecosystems on which we all depend; in short, the sheer mindlessness of the operation. Then of course there's the contribution that bonfires make to the fire starter's carbon footprint.

Fallen leaves are more than just sources of nutrients to be recycled into the soil. The blanket they create is a layer cake of different habitats, with fungi permeating

The Miller spends the winter months as an unobtrusive chrysalis hidden inside a fallen leaf. The adult moth emerges the following spring and is on the wing in May and June.

Would you stamp on or set fire to a Holly Blue butterfly? Assuming the answer is 'no' then by composting or shredding fallen leaves in summer, or heaven forbid putting them on a bonfire, the effect will be the same. This individual had pupated beneath a fallen Holly leaf in early June.

A covering of fallen leaves, spread like a blanket on a herbaceous bed in the dead of winter.

and breaking down the lower strata, and myriad invertebrates permeating and aerating the whole. Even fresh-fall leaves have an ecological role to play. It is well known that most moth species pupate in the soil but a fair number of species, in my garden at least, use freshly fallen leaves as refugia for pupation, spun silk helping to secure their protective case. Bury them deep in compost and you reduce the chances of adult moths being able to emerge the following spring. Burn the leaves and you will kill them outright, along with every other creature that calls fallen leaves home.

A herbaceous bed in early February: already the first shoots of spring are appearing through the blanket of fallen leaves spread a few months earlier.

silken cocoon   chrysalis exposed

newly emerged adult

Having spent spring and early summer feeding as a caterpillar (see p. 169), this Red Underwing pupated in mid-June, in a silken cocoon woven among fallen willow leaves. The adult emerged on 27 July. If I had raked and composted leaves on the ground, there is a good chance I would have damaged the chrysalis; and if the leaves had gone on a bonfire I would have killed the moth.

What do I do to ensure a balance between the needs of inhabitants of fallen leaves and the desire to keep my remaining areas of cut grass and gravel reasonably free of leaves? Unsurprisingly, I rake the leaves and create leaf piles around the garden, some in amongst my infant hedgerows. However, I reserve the bulk of my autumn fallen leaves to serve as winter blankets for my remaining herbaceous beds. By early spring, when Snowdrops have finished flowering and the herbaceous perennials are making tentative appearances, the blanket of leaves will have all but disappeared, such is the pace of natural recycling; by spring, there is no sign at all that the beds had a winter blanket of leaves. As for any leaves that linger on my lawn, I leave them to the army of earthworms that call my garden soil home; before you know it, they have dragged the leaves underground.

DEAD WOOD

Dead wood is an important element in woodland ecology and its presence there, and in the garden, should be viewed with a positive outlook. At its simplest level it is a source of nutrients that, thanks to the action of fungi and a myriad of invertebrates, in time are returned to the soil. However, more than that dead wood is a niche, if not a habitat, in itself harbouring an array of invertebrates and fungi that live nowhere else. There are species of insect, such as the Lesser Stag Beetle, whose larvae only live inside dead wood. Adopting a tidy-minded approach to woodland management of trees and dead wood in the context of the garden is one of the worst things you can do for native wildlife.

In recognition of the relatively small size of my garden, and perhaps with a nod to the remnants of conventional gardener that still lurk in me, my approach is to stack dead wood in strategic gaps in my hedges and out-of-the-way corners. I don't add logs and branches to piles of compost or smother them in grass cuttings, but rather I create wood-only piles that decay with time. Over the years, a few of the trees in my garden have died. Where safe to do so I have left them to decay where they stand.

One of the standing dead trees in the garden is home to a thriving colony of Rhinoceros Beetle larvae that is diminishing as the tree itself begins to disintegrate. I don't plan to move the tree until it falls. It goes without saying that if you value native wildlife, you should never burn fallen and decaying dead wood.

Great Spotted Woodpeckers find plenty of wood-boring insect food in the standing dead and dying timber in my garden.

FUNGAL ASSOCIATIONS

It is hard to overemphasise the importance of fungi in the context of woodland, including their role in a wooded garden setting. Mushrooms, toadstools and brackets are the reproductive spore-producing manifestations of a fungus. Their ephemeral appearance, mainly in autumn, is a visible reminder of fungal diversity, the long-lasting main bodies of which will be hidden from view and permeating their growing medium. Depending on the species, the mycelium may permeate the soil, colonise dead wood or fallen leaves, cause galls on flowers and fruits, penetrate living plant tissue, and even parasitise animals. In the context of woodlands, the ecological significance of fungi goes far beyond decomposition and recycling, and perhaps the most important role played is by those species that act in partnership with the trees themselves.

In some cases, intimate symbiotic relationships have evolved between fungus and tree, often ones that are highly species-specific. In such cases the fungus sheathes the tree's roots, and *hyphae* (the thread-like framework of the fungal body) extend into the soil and also penetrate cells in the tree's roots. This association is known as a mycorrhiza, which literally translates as

'fungus root'. The benefits to the fungus are that it is able to derive most of its energy requirements from the products of photosynthesis in the tree's leaves. In return, the tree obtains nitrogen and phosphorus, which are otherwise in short supply, from fungal action in the soil. In many instances healthy tree growth is only possible if a mycorrhizal relationship has developed. Many of the UK's native trees, and some shrubs, have evolved these relationships; those with fewest or no mycorrhizal associations include Ash, hawthorns, Field Maple, elms and Holly.

Fungal mycelium permeating fallen leaves and the soil.

Freshwater

The clay component of the soil and subsoil in Pamber, the north Hampshire parish in which I live, has directly and indirectly influenced the freshwater habitats around me. In addition, almost every aquatic location near the cottage was either created by humans, or has been modified and influenced by people through the centuries. The environmental history of freshwater has influenced the area's aquatic biodiversity and continues to have an effect. Gaining an appreciation of the historical significance of water in Pamber has helped inform my approach to managing freshwater in my garden.

PAMBER'S FRESHWATER

Historically, the nature of Pamber's soil would probably have meant that often there was too much standing water in winter, with some near-permanently waterlogged ground here and there, and sometimes not enough in summer when crops, livestock and humans needed it most. With varying degrees of success, water has always been 'managed' in the parish to mitigate this variability. At one end of the spectrum there are historical records of a few moated farmsteads in the general area; these were not grand affairs but ones where the function of the moat probably had more to do with food – stew ponds for fish – than security. In all likelihood most farmsteads of a reasonable size would have had ponds, used as water supplies for livestock; in some instances, their function might have been, not exclusively, what are called in planning parlance today 'balancing ponds', ones whose role was to accommodate and collect excess run-off water during periods of sudden flooding. Water would have been a precious commodity. A few streams criss-cross the parish too, and a network of ditches have eased drainage of land used for agriculture and forestry.

Wells would have satisfied the drinking and sanitary requirements of many of the parish's human inhabitants. However, the significance of beer should not be overlooked. Not for recreational use, but as a means of sterilising and storing 'safe' drinking water, something of particular importance during the relatively dry summer months. This in part explains the scattered presence in the parish of Hops, an ingredient in brewing, one valued for its preservative properties long before people were aware of the existence of bacteria or the concept of anything 'antibacterial'. For further discussion of the significance of Hops, see p. 32.

Elements of the historical freshwater framework of the parish still exist today. Unfortunately, as meaningful aquatic habitats, many of the moats have disappeared, their fate to be drained, and sometimes infilled and erased from memory. A few of the farm ponds remain, but several have been infilled and forgotten, if the 1838 Tithe Map (HRO reference 21M65/F7/185/2) is compared to the situation today. Ditches are still present but their importance to agriculture, and hence their maintenance, has diminished with the rise in popularity of land drains. Streams still flow through the parish. Although they may appear to follow a natural course, referring to historical maps, since the middle of the nineteenth century many have had their courses tinkered with – generally straightened to ease flow through a particular landowner's plot. There is no reason to suppose that modification of watercourses did not happen in earlier times although, of course, people's ability to make dramatic changes would have been limited. The difference between the past and the present lies in our mechanised ability to gouge out watercourses at pace with a digger, rather than employing the services of men with spades. Work that would have taken weeks or months a century ago can now be achieved in the space of a few hours. This has had a profound and negative impact on native wildlife because of its inability to cope with the speed at which subtly different freshwater niches can be destroyed.

EXISTING FRESHWATER IN MY GARDEN

When I moved to my cottage there were two elements of the parish's freshwater network present in the garden: a well and a stream that defines the southern boundary of the plot. The story of the well is slightly more complicated than first appears. In common with many in the parish, its fate at the hands of previous owners was to be filled with rubble and rubbish, topped with soil then grassed over. When I moved to the cottage, I knew there was a well somewhere in the garden but had no idea of its location. I persuaded a water diviner friend of mine to survey the garden and, armed with a pair of bent coat hangers, sure enough he discovered its

The brick-lined well in my garden, containing water whose level is just below that of the ground.

essence a seasonal, surface-water winterbourne that dries up in summer. By contrast, today, as in the past, the underlying water table ensures the well contains water throughout the year. The well itself has no particular value for native biodiversity in my garden. It does, however, shine an interesting historical light on the history of human occupation of my garden.

The stream that runs at the bottom of my garden is typical of many in the parish, with a width of about 2 metres and its bed from 1–1.5 metres below the level of adjacent land. In hot summers it dries to a trickle, the resilient populations of Three-spined Sticklebacks confined to dwindling pools. By contrast, during periods of heavy rain it becomes a raging torrent and regularly bursts its bank. The highest peak in a period of spate usually comes two or three hours after the heaviest rains have finished, an indication of the extent of the catchment area upstream and the speed of run-off from the land; at such times the silt-laden water, run-off from farmland, is the colour of milky coffee.

whereabouts. Clearing the well was a challenge, but the result revealed a beautiful brick-lined column stretching down into depths it would have been unwise to explore. The extraordinary effort it must have taken to dig and line the well emphasises the fact that the stream is in

The stream at the bottom of my garden, in spring after a rather dry spell.

Although I cannot imagine the stream's course in relation to my garden will have changed much over time, it has been altered downstream. Looking at the 1838 Tithe Map (HRO reference 21M65/F7/185/2) it took a meandering detour to the south before returning to its current route downstream. It has been straightened since, running through what on the Tithe Map is marked as a large pond; the purpose of this pond is unknown but the role of a 'balancing pond' would seem to suggest itself, given the proximity of farm buildings at the time, perhaps doubling as a fish pond.

When it comes to 'managing' the stream I try to minimise my intervention. With a neighbourly nod to residents downstream, I regularly remove large branches that would otherwise cause log-jams but other than that I try to do as little as possible. I am wary of being overzealous for a number of reasons. The debris – silt, leaves and twigs – that lines the bottom of the stream is home to an array of aquatic invertebrates. Among my favourites are the demoiselle damselflies, and both Banded Demoiselle and Beautiful Demoiselle occur.

Egg masses laid by the Mottled Sedge caddisfly on leaves overhanging the bed of my stream in late summer, at a time when the watercourse was dry.

Their larvae reside in the silt and gravel from autumn to spring while the gorgeous adults dance above the stream on sunny days in the summer months. If I cleared out the debris too enthusiastically, I would run the risk of killing the life cycle.

A range of caddisflies also call the stream home, their case-building larvae trundling along the stream bed and adults furtively loitering in streamside vegetation – generally speaking, caddises are a shy and retiring group of insects. An interesting example called the Mottled Sedge is among their number. I occasionally catch adults in my moth trap and observe larvae in the stream. It is their eggs, or rather their egg masses, however, that are far more visible reminders of the species' presence. In late August and early September females lay blobs of eggs – the size of the end of your little finger – on leaves that overhang the stream bed. They never lay away from the stream, even when it is dry, so presumably localised humidity caused by residual moisture is their cue. Over a period of a couple of weeks larvae develop inside the egg masses, and with the arrival of the first heavy rains of autumn these deliquesce and 'drip' larvae into the water. If I adopted too heavy-handed an approach to the management of streamside vegetation, too early in the season, the chances are I would kill the egg masses. This is another reminder that, unless you are certain of the consequences of your actions, a light touch is always best.

POND CREATION

When I moved to my cottage I inherited another water feature – a swimming pool. Not a grand affair, but a rather shoddily built construction sited, unhelpfully, beneath an oak tree. I persevered with it for a few years but became gradually more and more disgusted by the amount of ghastly chemicals I had to pour into it to prevent the water stagnating. Eventually I gave up and it remained dormant until I plucked up courage to do something about it.

Biting the bullet, I removed the liner, imploded and landscaped the sides, covered the debris with a protective layer of sand and then lined the result with butyl sheeting. By so doing, I was able to rid myself of something I had come to hate and to replace it with a feature that became a biodiversity asset to the garden and source of great pleasure. The pond's dimensions are roughly 7 x 5 metres; at it deepest it is roughly 1.5

metres and it shelves towards the margins. With a bit of low-tech engineering, I was able to run a pipe from the guttering of an adjacent garage roof to top up the pond with rainwater. I stocked the pond with a few strands of pondweed species, native to the UK but not necessarily to north Hampshire – Water-starwort, Rigid Hornwort, Opposite-leaved Pondweed and a couple of White Water-lilies obtained from friends; these were quarantined first to be sure I was not introducing New Zealand Pigmyweed. Ivy-leaved Duckweed appeared without an invitation along with a few other welcome species but, overall, I did not obsess about the botany of the pond.

There is no real precedent that I know of to determine what a small pond in north Hampshire should harbour in terms of native plant species. Many of the 'village' ponds in my area are adorned with conspicuous introductions, and quickly become choked if these no doubt well-intentioned additions include the likes of Yellow Iris; this species is a bit of a botanical 'thug' in the context of a small pond. My advice would be to look at any examples in your area and consider your approach

My pond, photographed in the summer of 2022.

carefully. The ambition with my pond is to prioritise the aquatic environment primarily for its freshwater animal inhabitants, rather than favouring eye-pleasing flowery margins for my personal gratification. So personally, if I spotted a plant that appeared to be doing well in a nearby village pond, I would avoid introducing it into mine.

Within a couple of years of starting the pond project, the pondweeds had flourished, creating the three-dimensional underwater world I had hoped to achieve. Their colonisation has now reached the stage where I am considering thinning out the vegetation a bit – ponds are transitional habitats that left to their own devices would be the agents of their own destruction, turning from freshwater to dry land over time. To illustrate this point, I turned a bit of a blind eye to this aspect of pond life for a couple of years only to discover that a Grey Willow had taken root in the middle of the pond, presumably the result of a snapped-off twig falling into the water – willows are notoriously good at that. Anyway, I removed the willow and planted it in my hedge because I want my pond to stay a pond.

When I constructed the pond, I had no particular aims other than to create an aquatic habitat for invertebrates and whatever other creatures happened to come upon it. I assumed, correctly as it turned out, that dragonflies and damselflies, being the wanderers that they are, would find their own way. And I had high hopes for amphibians, since I routinely came across Common Toads and Common Frogs in the garden. With amphibians in mind, I knew that I never wanted to stock the pond with fish.

I constructed the pond in late autumn and to my delight, despite its being sparsely vegetated, Common Frogs, Common Toads and Smooth Newts appeared the following spring. In February the following year, I saw my first Great Crested Newt in the pond – a magnificent male. More surprising was the observation, a day or so later, of a large larval Great Crested adorned with characteristic frilly gills. It was far too early in the season for the current year's young and this was an example of neoteny – one of the previous year's offspring that had not metamorphosed into an adult.

The significance of the observation of a neotenous larva was that Great Crested Newts had colonised the pond in its *first* year of existence. The nearest Great Crested breeding pond that I know of is roughly 1.5km away. I find it hard to believe that on completion of my

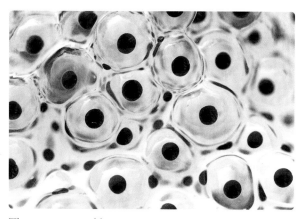

The appearance of frogspawn was a sign that my newly created pond was serving the purpose for which it was created, namely enhancing the prospects for biodiversity.

This neotenous Palmate Newt was spotted in January and would have been spawned 10 months earlier. Although it resembles a small adult it retains larval gills.

pond newts from this other pond sniffed the air and immediately made a beeline in my direction. More likely they were in the area already, and this reinforces the important point with UK amphibians that they should be seen as *terrestrial* animals that are obliged to return to water to breed. Most of their adult life is spent on land, and terrestrial habitats should be factored into their conservation.

My pond now hosts all five native amphibian species you could expect to find in this part of southern England. It is now well vegetated, and a surface view

is all that is really possible. Observations are biased towards males of all species, which have a habit of lurking in the shallow margins awaiting the appearance of females; these tend to disappear into the depths on arrival. With the aid of a powerful LED torch, here's a snapshot indication of numbers from 2021: Great Crested Newt – a maximum single-evening count of 7 males with at least 2 additional noticeably different males seen on other evenings; Smooth/Common Newt – a maximum single-evening count of 72 males; Palmate Newt – a maximum single-evening count of

A typical torchlight view of a Great Crested Newt in my pond.

My garden pond in the dead of winter, covered in a blanket of ice.

17 males; Common Frog – a maximum single-evening count of 12 hopeful males around the margins and 5 amplexus pairs, with 21 clumps of spawn, subsequently mostly consumed by the newts; Common Toad – a maximum single-evening count of 15 males but lots of comings and goings judging by the colour forms noted on different days.

If I had not been making use of an existing hole in the ground, I would have sited my pond elsewhere in the garden. And if I had had the time and the resources I might have opted for a different approach to its creation, namely 'puddling'. Given that most of the remaining historical ponds in the vicinity were created in an era that predates the advent of butyl liners by decades if not centuries, this is the method that would have been used. In essence you dig a hole in the ground, line it with clay (not in short supply around here) if the ground does not already include this medium and 'puddle' it – using footwork, to drive out all pockets of air to create an impermeable layer that retains water.

POND MAINTENANCE

My pond is a freshwater habitat, not a drinking pool, and so intentionally I have encouraged natural vegetation to colonise the margins and fill the underwater space, thereby creating a three-dimensional submerged world. If you do the same then sooner or later you will need to do a bit of clearance to avoid the pond becoming too overcrowded with vegetation. What constitutes

SOME TOP TIPS TO ASSIST WOULD-BE POND CREATORS

- Locate a new pond away from mature trees; there is a danger roots might puncture the liner and, more significantly, fallen leaves may choke the pond.
- Make use of any existing hole in the ground – the root-space left from a fallen tree, for example – rather than dig a new hole.
- Ensure a depth of at least one metre in the middle of the pond.
- Profile the pond to ensure gently shelving margins.
- Allow the margins to 'soften' with natural vegetation.
- Use the heaviest-duty butyl liner possible.
- Butyl liner degrades through exposure to sunlight, so encourage plant growth and a light covering of debris, algae and diatoms.

- Do not introduce fish into a small pond if you want to encourage native freshwater invertebrates and amphibians.
- Quarantine any aquatic 'gifts' from friends for a few weeks in case they harbour undesirable alien species such as New Zealand Pigmyweed.
- When it comes to maintenance, little and often is usually the best way.
- If you feel you need to remove debris or thin out the vegetation, place the removed material on a board that slopes back to the water's edge and leave it for a few hours; entirely aquatic creatures such as dragonfly larvae will then stand a chance of returning to the pond, rather than dying due to prolonged exposure to air.

'overcrowding', and the level of clearance, is for you to decide given your particular circumstances.

With my pond I adopt a 'little and often' approach and – only in early winter – I remove small areas of weed and decomposing water-lily leaves, plus any accumulations of fallen leaves. Inevitably this contains large numbers of aquatic creatures that I want to return to the pond. Consequently, I place the removed weed and debris on a board, propped up so it slopes back into the water. I then sift through the weed for invertebrates and leave it for the rest of the day in the hope that anything I have missed gradually makes its own way to the water, guided by gravity.

An important thing to bear in mind is that the accumulated organic debris at the bottom of the pond will itself be full of life. What we might call 'debris' will constitute 'home' for many invertebrate species, such as the larvae of the Broad-bodied Chaser dragonfly. Do not be overzealous and adopt too tidy-minded an approach when it comes to the silt and debris that lines your pond.

Useful organisations include the **Freshwater Habitats Trust**, a charity that offers advice and a wealth of information about all things freshwater. Visit freshwaterhabitats.org.uk to find out more.

The cottage as a habitat

Given its age and relatively rural setting it is not surprising that my cottage is regarded by local wildlife as part of the environmental landscape, and by some as a niche to colonise. It is used as a retreat from inclement weather in winter, although snowfall has become a rare event in recent years.

Old Lady (left) and Svensson's Copper Underwing (right).

Svensson's Copper Underwing.

In mammalian terms the most welcome tenants of my cottage and garage are bats, which use it both for daytime roosting in summer and for winter hibernation. There are plenty of bat-sized gaps between the base of the thatch and the building structure as well as opportunities to access loft spaces in both house and garage. In addition, I have bat boxes strategically placed on the side of the cottage.

Some of my other small mammal visitors are not quite so welcome. I don't mind the occasional Bank Vole or Pygmy Shrew when it scurries across the floor although, unsurprisingly, I do live-trap them and liberate them in the garden. It is more of an uphill struggle with Wood Mice and Yellow-necked Mice, particularly after the first heavy rains of autumn when their numbers build up. I live-trap these as well, but experience has taught me that I have to let them go a considerable distance from the cottage to prevent them returning straight away, such are their homing abilities. I do not tolerate incursions into the house by Brown Rats and Grey Squirrels and I take more drastic action with regard to both species.

It is not often a house owner gets to utter the phrase 'I found an uninvited Old Lady in my bedroom last night' but such is the case with my cottage in summer. The Old Lady in question is, of course, the eponymous moth which, along with a species called Svensson's Copper Underwing, often seeks refuge indoors for a daytime sojourn in summer, only to wake up at dusk and fly insanely around the nearest bedside lamp. Later in the season, Peacock butterflies often find their way through an open window in search of somewhere to hibernate during the winter months.

I read somewhere that 'if you live in a thatched house, you never live alone'. The old part of my cottage

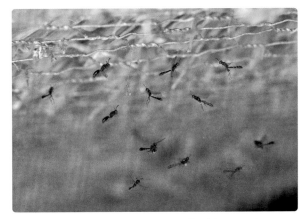

In late spring and summer, the cut ends of the straw in my thatched roof are alive with insects, in the main an array of what I take to be more than one species of tiny solitary wasp, plus attendant parasitoid wasps (see p. 179). All are minute and do not damage the thatch – in the manner of leaf-cutter bees, they use the cut ends of straw as nesting tubes. Provisioning items I have seen the various species carrying back to their homes include minute flies and what looks like pollen.

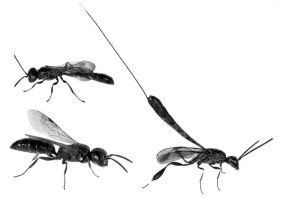

A selection of the solitary and parasitoid wasps that frequent my thatched roof. The latter, with its slender ovipositor, may be a species of *Gasteruption*. However, precise identification of the insects involved is not something I have attempted.

A Peacock butterfly roosting indoors in my cottage.

consolidated and compacted material at the bottom of the thatch and Common Wasps sometimes find a way through the straw to the roof space, where they construct their football-sized paper nests. A recent addition to the list has been that new arrival on the UK scene, the Tree Bumblebee. The species' presence is slightly alarming because workers act aggressively towards anyone moving in the vicinity. However, usually I do not have to concern myself for long: on every occasion they have attempted to nest they have failed by midsummer thanks to relentless predation by Hornets that also use the thatch to nest. I treat these intimidating insects with the caution and respect they deserve, having been stung on a couple of occasions. From my limited experience their sting is more intense than that of a wasp but does not last as long. I value both species for the predatory role they play in the garden's web of life and when I get stung it is usually because I have carelessly or inadvertently intruded into their world without thinking about the consequences.

has a thatched roof, and having spent more than 25 years living here I have to agree. In some senses, it is a giant 'bee hotel' catering for the nesting needs of a range of species. Leaf-cutter bees occasionally use the

Managed retreat from conventional gardening

The truth is I was never a good gardener in the conventional sense. I lacked the enthusiasm and ruthless, single-minded drive needed to stamp my vision of the world on the plot of land where I live. And I did not really have a vision of my own: much of my approach stemmed from books on the subject I had been given and television programmes I had watched – advice from others. From the outset I was aware how much the direction in which I was being steered was at odds with the true love of my life, natural history. And the other truth was, like many other gardeners, I suspect, I was never really satisfied with the results. Consequently, conventional gardening gave me only occasional and transitory pleasure at best and never long-lasting satisfaction.

My disconnect with conventional gardening grew over time, and with increasing years I found it more and more difficult to align myself with people whose near-obsessive tendency was to regard as enemies those plants and animals I knew as friends. Put simply, the concept of pests and weeds began to sicken me.

Not even when I had fallen most deeply under the conventional gardening spell could I regard earthworms or Moles as the enemy: as far as I was concerned anyone who considered worm casts or molehills as unwelcome needed environmental enlightenment rather than advice about pest control. For most of my time as a failing conventional gardener, I never lost the sense that, from the perspective of my garden wildlife, it was me that was the unwelcome guest.

Abandoning the conventional gardening mindset was a huge relief. I no longer had to care what anyone else thought about my untidy borders and neglected, Daisy-studded lawns. My only concern became how well I was benefiting local native biodiversity and my reward was the knowledge that I was no longer fighting nature but acting on its behalf.

The switch from conventional gardening to managing my plot for the benefit of native biodiversity has been a gradual and evolving process. For one thing, I did not have the time, resources or inclination to change the whole garden in one fell swoop. For another,

Blurring the distinction between conventional garden and meadow.

Some of my remaining traditional garden plants are not without merit, of course, and Dusky Crane's-bill is a magnet for insects such as this Early Bumblebee in spring.

I also value a cultivated loosestrife called *Lysimachia clethroides* whose arching sprays provide feeding platforms for a surprising array of my meadow butterflies; on a couple of occasions, the flowers have even been graced by a Dark Green Fritillary, an unusual wanderer that does not breed anywhere near where I live. Taking advantage of the insect bounty, the well-camouflaged crab spider *Misumena vatia* regularly lurks on the flower heads and this one has caught an unwary Meadow Brown.

I intentionally wanted the process to be gradual, so that I could read the natural signs as things developed to gauge my approach's success or failure. Furthermore, it would have been arrogant in the extreme to think I had all the answers before I even embarked on the project. Look and learn has been a useful axiom.

This gradual approach has meant that I have not entirely abandoned all aspects of traditional gardening, and indeed many of the features and plants, non-native though they may be, provide a valuable contribution to my garden's wildlife. My approach is perhaps best described as managed retreat: I no longer dig or 'weed' my remaining herbaceous beds and borders and instead let natural succession take over. I keep disturbance to a minimum, allowing soil wildlife and stability to develop. Those moth species whose caterpillars feed on plants in these herbaceous beds are likely to pupate in the soil, along with others whose caterpillars have wandered there for the same purpose. I certainly don't want to disturb or kill them. The borders' cascades of Tufted Vetch and Greater Bird's-foot Trefoil have equal rights in these horticultural outposts to those remaining cultivated plants.

BUTTERFLY-BUSH

Despite the name, I confess to having a morbid dislike for Butterfly-bush. Perhaps it suffers from a bit of guilt by association in my eyes: tainted by a reminder of housing estate front gardens in the Basingstoke of my youth, developments that had destroyed the countryside I valued more than houses. However, there is a more rational side to my misgivings about the plant. Yes, it is it is a good nectar source for a few relatively long-proboscis, nettle-feeding butterflies such as Peacocks and Red Admirals. However, there is a danger that by portraying it as universally 'good for butterflies', and not qualifying that statement, the illusion is perpetuated that it is a cure-all for everything that ails butterfly species across the spectrum. It is not. In the grand scheme of things, larval foodplants are the key to helping beleaguered butterfly species, most of which will not and cannot use Butterfly-bush as a nectar source. More important, however, are its invasive properties. Native to the Far East and not the UK, on areas of chalk and in other free-draining locations the plant is a rampant invader that crowds out more delicate native species. The environmental scar that is the M3 cutting adjacent to Winchester in Hampshire provides a dispiriting example of how Butterfly-bush takes over when left unchecked. Despite what I have said, I still have a solitary Butterfly-bush in my garden, a relic of a previous horticultural life but one that I won't replace when it dies. I do, however, cut it after flowering to prevent it ever setting seed.

Butterfly-bush with attendant Peacock butterfly.

PESTS

I came across a book on my shelves the other day on the subject of aphids. Written by Roger Blackman and published in 1974, it reminded me that, in the context of farming, pests are an entirely man-made phenomenon. They are just what you would expect if you replace a natural, biodiverse environment with a single-species crop. Hardly any species will benefit from this cataclysmic change, but for those that do, they have just been provided with unlimited food and minimal competition. Furthermore, if you disrupt the web of life and kill off predators, you remove the natural checks and balances that control pest species populations.

No surprise then that in the agricultural world aphids are usually seen as the enemy, these days killed by chemicals but with the alarming prospect of genetic engineering playing a future role, with unknown but perhaps predictable consequences long-term for the natural world. In the context of my garden, however, I do not think of aphids in that light. They are fascinating creatures in their own right: of the more than 600 species in the UK most have complex life cycles, often involving seasonally different hosts, usually a woody shrub in winter and more succulent options in spring and summer; seemingly endless generations with some morphs winged, others wingless; and of course, they are for most of their lives parthenogenetic. In my garden I think of aphids not as pests but as a crop in themselves. They provide 'honeydew' and are 'farmed' by ants in my meadow and are food for insects as diverse as ladybirds and hoverfly larvae in summer to Chiffchaffs and Goldcrests in autumn.

I still have roses in my garden and although I adore their blooms, I appreciate the appearance of aphids in spring when, for a brief period, they smother my rosebuds. Look closely and their role in the garden's web of life will become clear, with another reason for keeping roses becoming evident in summer when neatly circular holes appear in the leaves. These are the work of my leaf-cutter bees, who use the leaf portions to construct nest chambers in burrows; these are sited in timber, sometimes in the densest, oldest parts of my thatched roof, in homemade bee-homes, or occasionally in a bank. Each completed and sealed chamber is stocked with honey and pollen and contains a single egg. For more information about leaf-cutter bees, see p. 181.

A PLEA FOR IVY

Despite what you might have read, Ivy is not a parasite. It gains no nutrition from the plants over which it clambers and instead is best thought of as an epiphytic climber. Although I undertake a bit of judicious pruning now and again, if it is becoming particularly rampant across a doorway, for example, I generally try to leave it alone as much as possible. Its natural history merits are many. Its flowers provide late-season nectar for a whole range of insects from bees to butterflies during the daytime and moths after dark, and its maturing berries are food for birds in late autumn and early winter. It is the main larval foodplant for the summer brood of Holly Blue butterflies: females lay their eggs on flower buds in August, then caterpillars feed on them before pupating, often in the dense foliage. This same dense cover offers sanctuary and shelter for roosting birds in winter and nesting species in spring.

Ivy, rampant on a side entrance to the cottage. A succession of birds nested here in the spring of 2018: two pairs of Blackbirds, a Song Thrush and a Robin.

Small Dusty Wave, a moth whose caterpillars feed on Ivy.

A Red Admiral feeding on a bank of Ivy flowers.

Ivy berries provide a winter feast for birds, especially thrushes.

Don't confine the exploration of your garden to the hours of daylight. Armed with a powerful torch, make your acquaintance with the night shift of slugs, snails, insects, amphibians, bats and much more.

The New Naturalist –
A Biodiversity Gardener's Wildlife Overview

Biodiversity gardening should not be seen as self-sacrifice or a chore but rather as a delight. It provides an opportunity to create meaningful benefits for the environment while revealing the wonders of nature on your doorstep. It allows you to get the most from the wildlife in your garden while making the most of your plot of land *for* wildlife.

For many committed naturalists, part of the satisfaction of adopting the biodiversity gardening approach will derive from knowing what has been achieved. An enquiring mind and sense of curiosity are the basic tools of the trade, and allow the budding naturalist to progress in their understanding of the world around them and appreciate environmental advancement on their doorsteps. Being able to recognise what you see aids this understanding. The process is a bit like learning a new language and can seem like a daunting task at first. However, the more species you can identify the easier subsequent recognition becomes; and the more you become of aware of the gaps in your knowledge.

If you are a beginner, there is no need to feel inadequate when it comes your knowledge of the natural world. If you want some reassurance, just watch a few episodes of University Challenge: the best minds in Britain may be able to answer questions on Greek mythology and particle physics, but most have a woefully poor understanding of even basic natural history. And universally challenged ignorance is not confined to those answering the questions. 'Name the common British parasitic plant whose scientific name is *Hedera helix*' was one question that I recall. At the risk of sounding pernickety, Ivy is an epiphyte not a parasite.

The Biodiversity Gardener is not a field identification guide. However, given that proviso it may help to provide some pointers and guidance for the twenty-first-century new naturalist. Basic biology and a brief summary of classification helps set the scene and fosters an understanding of the relationships between the various plant and animal species in your garden. Plus, it will help you to recognise pointers to those groups that merit special attention, in part because they are relatively easy to identify and quantify and act as indicators of progress.

Garden wildlife classification

Scientists and naturalists divide living things into groups, members of which have characters in common, and the father of this approach was the eighteenth-century Swedish scientist, Carl Linnaeus. Under the system he devised, life on earth is classified using a hierarchical system based on external similarities and biology. For the novice biodiversity gardener, getting to grips with classification may seem like an esoteric exercise. It is not. Developing an understanding of how the living world is ordered is invaluable when it comes to managing the land over which you are custodian: it underpins our ability to identify species and helps us understand their inter-relatedness. It also sheds light on the complexity of the world around us, allows us to better engage and communicate with like-minded people and helps the aspiring biodiversity gardener to grasp the needs of their charges. In hierarchical order of decreasing magnitude, here is the running order of living things:

Kingdom ➤ Phylum (plural Phyla) ➤ Subphylum (plural Subphyla) ➤ Class ➤ Order ➤ Family ➤ Genus ➤ Species

Outmoded in some circles, perhaps, but for the purposes of *The Biodiversity Gardener* the simplest way of arranging classification is to divide living things into five Kingdoms: Plants; Animals; Fungi; Protists (diverse and mainly single-celled organisms); and Prokaryotes (organisms such as bacteria that lack a nucleus and internal cell membranes). The biodiversity gardener will be concerned mainly with the three groups that are visible to the naked eye: Plants, Animals and Fungi, and this book concerns itself only with representatives found in terrestrial and freshwater habitats.

PLANTS

Plants are living organisms that photosynthesise, using the green pigment chlorophyll to capture sunlight energy. This is used to fuel the chemical process *photosynthesis* whereby carbon dioxide from the air, and water absorbed via a plant's roots, are converted to sugar and oxygen. Growth notwithstanding, most plants we come across are anchored in one spot by roots and grow in soil. Looking at the bigger picture, the plant kingdom is divided into a number of phyla, and those of relevance to the biodiversity gardener are:

Mosses (phylum Bryophyta) which do not have an internal vascular system, lack a proper cuticle and are prone to desiccation. Some tolerate drying out, but most thrive only in damp situations. Reproduction involves a process called 'alternation of generations': one stage produces male sex cells that swim in the surface film of water and fertilise female sex cells; the resulting fertilised embryo grows attached to the parent plant and produces capsules from which airborne spores are liberated and disperse.

Liverworts (phylum Hepatophyta) which also lack an internal vascular system, requiring damp conditions for survival and reproduction. They reproduce in a similar way to mosses. Some liverworts are flat and almost seaweed-like while others are leafy. Root-like outgrowths underneath the plant anchor it to the substrate on which it grows. Liverworts lack a proper cuticle, making them prone to desiccation; hence they favour damp and humid situations.

Horsetails (phylum Equisetophyta) have recognisable roots and a vascular system. They overwinter and spread thanks in part to the presence of a swollen, food-storing underground stem called a rhizome. Upright, jointed aerial stems appear in spring and bear whorls of radiating branches. Spore-producing structures are arranged in cones, and spores grow into small, single-sex plants; for fertilisation to take place, male cells must swim in a film of water to find female cells on another plant.

Ferns (phylum Pteridophyta) also have recognisable roots and a vascular system and reproduce by means of spores. Ferns are relatively large and robust plants, some species forming sizeable clumps while others spread extensively by vegetative growth. As with mosses and liverworts, fern reproduction involves alternation of generations. The stage in the life cycle that most people regard as typically fern-like is the spore-producing stage, the spores themselves being produced in structures on the fronds. Liberated spores give rise eventually to a tiny, liverwort-like plant that produces sex cells, males of which must swim in a film of water to reach the anchored female cells.

Conifers (phylum Coniferophyta) typically grow to sizeable shrubs or trees, and have needle-like leaves. Their naked seeds are unprotected by an ovary or fruits and typically are produced in cones. Conifer flowers lack petals. Male flowers are short-lived, falling off after they have released clouds of pollen. By contrast, female flowers persist after being fertilised by pollen and develop into cones containing the seeds. Most rely on the wind for pollination and also for seed dispersal. A few close relatives of the conifers, such as the Yews, produce cones that are fleshy, fruit-like and known as arils.

Flowering Plants (Angiospermophyta or angiosperms) are a large and diverse group of vascular plants that range from small and relatively delicate annuals to robust and towering trees. What they have in common is that their seeds are protected by fruits. An almost infinite variety of flower design helps define the group, each containing specialised organs designed to facilitate reproduction. Find out more about flowering plants on p. 126.

ANIMALS

Characters that are used to define an animal include organisms that feed on organic matter, respire oxygen, respond to stimuli via specialised sense organs and are capable of movement. These definitions are not entirely helpful, since plants are also capable of responses to stimuli and movement, albeit at a much, much slower pace; and they respire. Another characteristic might be an organism that cannot manufacture its own food.

As a broad-brush approach to classification of the animal kingdom, the most profound division is between invertebrates (animals without backbones) and vertebrates (animals with backbones). Vertebrates belong to the phylum Chordata; all other animal phyla listed below can be defined under the umbrella term 'Invertebrates'.

Sponges (phylum Porifera) a mainly marine group with a couple of fresh-water representatives.

Jellyfish and allies (phylum Cnidaria) a mainly marine group represented by *Hydra* in freshwater ponds.

Flatworms (phylum Platyhelminthes) a group of mainly parasitic species with a few free-living representatives in freshwater.

Roundworms (phylum Nematoda) a group that contains some notorious mammalian parasites, but a vast and largely unseen array of often microscopic soil-dwelling representatives.

Earthworms, leeches and allies (phylum Annelida) a group of segmented worms that includes soil-dwelling earthworms and predatory freshwater leeches.

Molluscs (phylum Mollusca) this group includes familiar slugs and snails.

Arthropods (phylum Arthropoda) a large and diverse group that, in the context of the garden, includes crustaceans (terrestrial woodlice and freshwater crustaceans), millipedes, centipedes, arachnids and insects.

Vertebrates (phylum Chordata) a group that includes Amphibians, Reptiles, Birds and Mammals. Fish are also vertebrates but are not considered further in the context of the biodiversity garden.

FUNGI

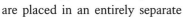

Until relatively recently, fungi were thought of as plants, albeit rather unusual ones. Today, however, they are placed in an entirely separate kingdom from either plants or animals, or come to that the kingdoms to which Bacteria and Protista belong. They differ from plants by having chitin in their cell walls (a feature they share with certain animals) but they do not photosynthesise. Instead, they acquire the energy and nutrients required for growth by a range

of means, including decomposition of organic matter, symbiotic mycorrhizal relationships with the roots of plants, notably trees, by parasitism, and in a few instances predatory behaviour. The bulk of a fungus comprises a web of tiny threads called hyphae that permeate their growing medium. They reproduce and disperse by means of spores, liberated by fruiting bodies that include familiar toadstools, mushrooms and brackets.

Flowering plant life histories, structure and tips for identification

It is helpful for the aspiring conservation botanist to have at least a basic understanding of the structure, biology and life cycles of flowers and plants. Interesting in its own right, an insight into the flowering plants that grow in your garden or on your land will help you better understand their needs. Furthermore, an ability to identify what you are looking at will allow you to refine your approach to managing the land for the benefit of native wildflowers overall. Although *The Biodiversity Gardener* is not a field guide, what follows is some background information and a few pointers to aid and improve the identification process.

GENERAL DISTINCTIONS: MONOCOTY-LEDONS AND DICOTYLEDONS

Flowering plants enclose and protect their seeds in fruits. Without getting too technical, they can be further divided and classified according to the biology of germination into what botanists call monocotyledons and dicotyledons. Monocotyledons include grasses, sedges, rushes, orchids and lily relatives and have one so-called seed leaf, which feeds the germinating seedling, either through photosynthesis or directly from stored food; their main leaves are typically narrow and have parallel veins. The remaining familiar flowering plants are known as dicotyledons and have a pair of seed leaves and main leaves that have a network of veins.

HERBACEOUS AND WOODY PLANTS

Many wildflowers are relatively flimsy and modest in size. Those that lack woody stems, and die back in winter, are called herbaceous plants. By contrast, a few (from a wide range of plant families) are more substantial, their size supported by their robust internal structure; trees and shrubs are familiar examples.

By counting the annual growth rings in this cross-section through the trunk of a Pedunculate Oak, its age on being cut was around 185 years. It was planted in the reign of George III, was the subject of nine British monarchs and witnessed two world wars.

A tree is often defined as having a single main stem of five metres or more with a branching crown above this; shrubs usually have numerous stems arising at ground level and normally do not reach the height of a tree. Unlike herbaceous plants, trees produce woody tissue; this serves to conduct materials around the plant, and leads to the production of permanent shoots that do not die back in winter. Just below the surface of a tree's trunk is a layer called cambium that is constantly producing new cells. Those that grow on the inside develop into woody tissue called xylem that conducts water from the roots to the shoots, buds and leaves. A new layer of woody tissue is laid down each year, and xylem eventually forms the bulk of the trunk and branches; in a cut trunk these annual layers of woody tissue are evident as 'rings', which can be counted as a way of ageing a tree. Cells that grow outside the cambium layer form conductive tissue, known as phloem, which carries sugars from the leaves down to the roots.

LIFE CYCLES

Most flowering plants have life cycles that can be categorised as either annual, biennial or perennial. Annual plants are ones where the entire life cycle – germination, growth, flowering and seed production – takes place in a single season. With biennials, the life cycle is spread over two years, most growth taking place in the first year, and flowering and seed production in the second year. Perennial plants are longer-lived and produce flowers and seeds every year once they have reached maturity; trees and shrubs are perennial plants. Depending on the species, trees, shrubs and smaller perennial plants may be evergreen (their leaves are a permanent feature and not shed) or deciduous. With the latter, the plant is devoid of leaves during the winter months, fresh ones appear in spring and these are shed again in the autumn.

In addition to creating new generations by the production of seeds, some plants spread by means of

Mistletoe, which grows on a range of trees, is an example of a semi-parasite. Although it can photosynthesise, it cannot survive if its roots do not tap in, literally, to the tissues and vessels of its host for water and nutrients. Yellow-rattle, that distinctive meadow plant, is semi-parasitic on the roots of grasses and cannot survive in their absence; see p. 61 for more information on Yellow-rattle.

vegetative growth. Examples are so-called 'runners', and rhizomes and stolons, which are underground stems that produce new plants along their length. The majority of plants found in the garden are free-living for want of a better expression, having leaves that photosynthesise and gain water and nutrients from the soil via their roots. Outside the scope of most biodiversity gardens there are species that are saprophytes, do not photosynthesise, and gain their nutrition from decaying organic matter through an intimate association with soil fungi; and then there are parasites. Within the scope of biodiversity gardens are a few plants that are semi-parasites, species that photosynthesise but rely on others to provide for some of their needs.

FLOWER STRUCTURE AND FUNCTION

Flowers may delight the human eye, but their role is strictly functional. They are the plant's reproductive organs and they have evolved to maximise the chances of successful fertilisation taking place. In a few species of wildflowers, male and female sex cells appear in separate flowers, or even on different plants. However, in most species both sexes are present in the same flower. Male sex cells are contained within pollen, tiny grains that are produced by structures called anthers and borne on slender stems referred to as filaments;

collectively, anthers and filaments are referred to as stamens. The female part of a typical flower comprises the ovary, containing the female sex cells, above which is the stigma; this structure receives the pollen and is carried on a stem called the style.

For a new generation of plants to be created, a flower's male sex cells must fertilise female cells of the same species. This process is called pollination. Some plants are able to pollinate themselves, but most go to great lengths to avoid this and ensure that cross-pollination takes place. With some plants, such as grasses and catkin-bearing shrubs, their pollen is carried by the wind to others of the same species; a vast quantity of pollen is required to achieve a successful outcome with such a game of chance. Most other species adopt a more targeted approach and employ the services of animals – insects in almost all cases – to carry out the role of pollen transfer. In exchange for a meal, in the form of nectar, insects unwittingly carry pollen on their bodies to the next flowers they visit; with luck, a neighbouring plant of the same species will be visited by the insect while it still retains some pollen on its body. In almost all species, flower structure has evolved to avoid self-pollination and to maximise the chances of cross-pollination – pollen being transferred to visiting insect pollinators and received from other plants by the same agents.

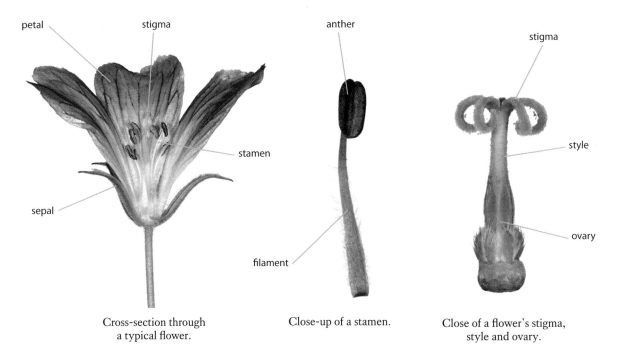

Cross-section through a typical flower.

Close-up of a stamen.

Close of a flower's stigma, style and ovary.

Grasses, such as Cock's-foot, rely on the wind for cross-fertilisation and produce vast quantities of dust-like airborne pollen that is carried on the breeze.

When it comes to the pollinating relationship between insects and some flower species, plants do not have everything their own way. For example, this tiny solitary bee provisions its nest with pollen to feed its larvae. It has evolved special hairs (called 'scopa') on the underside of the abdomen that help transport the cargo. Cross-fertilisation of flowers may inadvertently occur, but from the bee's perspective pollen is merely a source of food.

● 'MICROSPECIES'

In most plants, sexual reproduction involves fertilisation of a female egg by male genetic material carried by pollen, typically from another plant. Both male and female elements contain half the genetic complement of their parent plants. The resulting fertilised embryo has a full complement but will be slightly different in genetic terms from both its parents. This is what drives natural selection – some offspring will be more suited to the environment where they find themselves germinating than others and are more likely to survive and reproduce themselves.

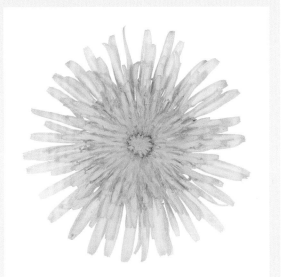

Leafing through field guides to wildflowers you may have wondered why some groups, such as dandelions and brambles, are often broken down into 'microspecies'. Indeed, more than 250 of the former group are recognised in the UK.

This puzzle concerning 'microspecies' has to do with their biology and life-history, and a process known as 'apomixis'. In these groups of plants, seeds are not produced as a result of pollination. The egg has a full complement of genetic material from the outset, identical to its parent, and develops directly into a seed. Almost every offspring plant is identical to its parent; differences, which then may go on to become new 'microspecies', arise only through genetic mutations, not the combination of genetic material from two different parents.

In return for nectar, insects such as this Tree Bumblebee unwittingly transfer pollen – a plant's male sex cells – to another of the same species, thereby increasing the chances of cross-fertilisation.

THE POLLEN RECORD

Under the microscope, the structure and appearance of plant pollen is distinctive enough for reasonably accurate and consistent identification to be achieved. Expert eyes are needed, and archaeologists use the information about species presence and relative abundance to interpret the historic and prehistoric landscape: if you can date a layer of soil and identify the pollen to genus or species level, this can shed light on the habitat at the time, and by inference human activity. For example, it might tell you the types of crops used in cultivation; or the relative abundance of Greater and Ribwort Plantains, plants associated with disturbance, might indicate the level of human activity.

If Hazel pollen features heavily in a sample, it might suggest the shrub's significance in past woodland composition and management on the land in question. But as a cautionary note, taking Hazel as an example, if it is coppiced to produce regenerating wands these are often not mature enough to flower before being cut, hence no pollen is produced. If that were the case, absence of Hazel pollen in a sample would not be evidence that Hazel was unimportant in the rural economy of the time. It also illustrates how scientific disciplines benefit from cooperation and how, for example, a failure to factor in plant natural history and woodland management could lead to the wrong conclusions being drawn from pollen analyses.

Looking at the bigger picture, pollen analysis has also confirmed that scrub and woodland colonisation of post-glacial Europe followed a natural and anticipated progression and succession: conifers were first to appear, their dominance waning as other species better-suited to the slowly warming climate appeared on the scene and spread northwards.

Hazel is wind-pollinated and each catkin (the male flower) produces countless millions of dust-like pollen grains, which contain the plant's male sex cells. The pollen of wind-pollinated plants, and that includes grasses and many tree species, is more likely to feature in quantity in soil samples than that produced by flowers which use targeted pollination by insects.

FLOWERS AS AIDS TO IDENTIFICATION

Flowering time of year can provide a useful clue to identification, but it is not infallible; features such as structure, colour and size are more reliable. With regards to colour, bear in mind that certain hues – the gradation between pink and magenta, and shades of blue for example – are impossible to print on the book page (due to the inking process) but can be portrayed accurately on computer, tablet and phone screens. Some flowers show radial symmetry, and the number of petals (or what look like petals), their colour, shape and texture all are important. Others exhibit bilateral symmetry or have unusual and distinctive shapes.

To follow are a range of alternatives:

3-petalled flower

4-petalled flower

5-petalled flower

Trumpet-shaped flower

Bell-shaped flower

Tubular flower

Multi-flowered heads

Clustered heads

Out of the ordinary

FRUITS, SEEDS
AND THEIR USE IN IDENTIFICATION

Fruits are the structures within which a flowering plant's seeds form and are protected, and their shape and design often provide useful clues in identification. From the plant's perspective, fruit structure and function are closely related, their role in life being to ensure dispersal of the next generation of plants. Some are carried on the wind assisted by wings or parachutes; others are transported by animals, attached to fur and hair; a few employ the services of birds to disperse in return for the reward of a juicy fruit. Some fruits can even float and are dispersed by water, and a few explode to liberate their seeds.

Although the seeds of some species are quick to germinate, many are capable of dormancy and will usually only germinate if conditions are suitable and appropriate stimuli – temperature, humidity and light

– trigger them. Not every seed will germinate at the same time, or in the same year, which is an advantage in evolutionary terms. In normal circumstances, seeds have a finite life expectancy – perhaps five to ten years in the wild. Many remain dormant in the soil and this seed bank is a way by which plant growth appears, as if by magic, when soil is disturbed or turned over. If subject to controlled artificial drying they may last longer, but under certain conditions seeds' 'shelf life' can be extended almost indefinitely if they are kept in the deep freeze; Kew's Millennium Seed Bank project stores its seeds at $-20°C$. There is some speculation that natural deep freeze conditions may have allowed the seeds of some species to endure the last Ice Age.

Plants have evolved an intriguing array of strategies and fruit structures to ensure dispersal of seeds as far from the parent plant as possible. Their appearance can be useful in plant identification and to follow are a few examples:

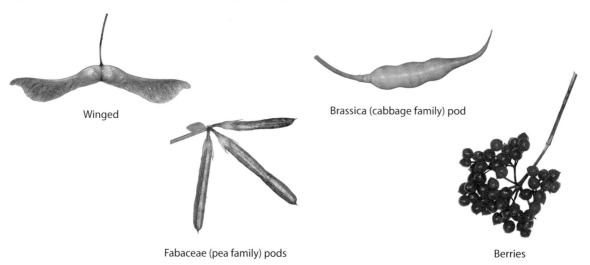

Winged

Brassica (cabbage family) pod

Fabaceae (pea family) pods

Berries

Parachutes

Hooked spines or hairs

Capsules

LEAVES

Leaves are vital to a plant's existence, being responsible for photosynthesis and the formation of sugars. Their size, shape and number will have evolved to suit the growing habits and habitat of the species in question, and broadly speaking leaves of one individual will be similar to those of other members of the same species. It is worth bearing in mind, however, that with some plants a degree of variability exists, and in some species basal leaves will be an entirely different shape from those carried on the stem. Furthermore, there are instances where unrelated plants have superficially similar leaves. These provisos notwithstanding, leaves are your allies when it comes to identification. Apart from flowers themselves, they offer some of the best clues to the identity of any given plant.

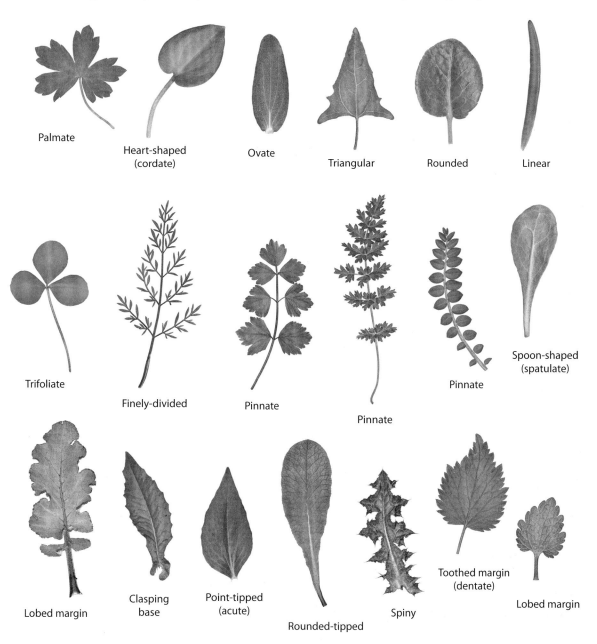

Palmate

Heart-shaped (cordate)

Ovate

Triangular

Rounded

Linear

Trifoliate

Finely-divided

Pinnate

Pinnate

Pinnate

Spoon-shaped (spatulate)

Lobed margin

Clasping base

Point-tipped (acute)

Rounded-tipped

Spiny

Toothed margin (dentate)

Lobed margin

OTHER FEATURES AND FACTORS THAT AID WILDFLOWER IDENTIFICATION

In the past a beginner's approach to identification might have been to flick through a book, find a picture of something that looked vaguely right and hope for the best. Nowadays, modern technology allows you to take a photograph on a mobile phone with an app identifying the plant for you. This simplistic route means you run a risk of misidentification, especially if you concentrate on just one feature, such as the flower. But more importantly you will not gain knowledge or any insight into plant species and family relationships. Successful and informed wildflower identification relies on using a combination of plant features including growing height; habitat, soil preferences and distribution; the presence of special features such as hairs; stem shape; leaf size and shape; flower structure, colour and size; and fruit structure. Although it can seem pedestrian, it really is worth doing things 'the hard way' using keys that gradually narrow down the alternatives. Not only are you more likely to end up with a correct identification, but more importantly, slowly but surely you will build up an informed overview of the botanical world around you. Before long, you will be able to say at a glance, for example, 'I know that's a forget-me-not'.

Flower size and colour, and the plant's hairs, help identify Early Forget-me-not.

GROWING HEIGHT

Many annual plant species don't carry on growing indefinitely but reach a point where growth ceases – a standard maximum height – often when they begin to flower; their height will be dictated by their life cycle, internal structural integrity and the growing season. The same applies to herbaceous perennials. Even woody species, which continue to grow after they have reached maturity, reach a point where they don't gain in overall height any more. Plant size can, therefore, be a useful indicator in the process of identification, and even the fact that some species are prostrate and grow flat to the ground is informative.

HABITAT, SOIL PREFERENCES AND DISTRIBUTION

Some plant species are widespread geographically and not fussy about where they grow, while others are much more restricted or particular. Some will only grow in woodland shade; others might be meadow species. Some favour acid, free-draining soils while others will only grow with their 'feet' in water or on chalky soils. In terms of range, many familiar plants are widespread throughout the UK, but some have either a northerly or southerly bias to their distribution. All these factors have a bearing on where precisely a plant grows and are useful aids to identification.

SPECIAL FEATURES

When attempting to identify a mystery plant it is always useful to cast a quizzical eye over the specimen and, in the role of nature detective, look for interesting and unusual features. These might include hairs that, depending on the species, could be downy and felty, stiff and bristly, glandular and sticky, or capable of inflicting a painful sting. Or perhaps the plant or just the leaves give off a distinctive aroma when rubbed or bruised.

STEM SHAPE

When viewed or imagined in cross section, the appearance of the stem can be informative, sometimes suggesting family ties and on occasion separating superficially similar species. Variations on the stem shape include cross sections that are round, square, or angular with flanges or rows of hairs.

Terrestrial Invertebrate classification and identification

Invertebrates are classified into a number of subdivisions, each one of which is called a phylum (plural phyla). Some phyla are associated mainly or exclusively with water and are dealt with later in the book. Terrestrial representatives are discussed here, and for simplicity's sake, phyla that contain animals that are tiny, hard to find, or both are ignored; instead, those that are easily found and of greater interest to the amateur naturalist are featured. Terrestrial invertebrates found in the garden are represented by three main phyla: Annelida (segmented worms); Mollusca (snails and slugs); and Arthropoda (a large and complex group that includes most other terrestrial invertebrates).

ANNELID WORMS (PHYLUM ANNELIDA)

Annelid worms have soft, segmented bodies and often bear bristles to aid movement. Most terrestrial annelid worms live in burrows in the soil, or among leaf litter. Leeches, which in the UK are mainly associated with freshwater habitats, have smooth muscular bodies that can be contracted or lengthened, and suckers that provide grip. For more information about annelid worms see p. 221.

MOLLUSCS (PHYLUM MOLLUSCA)

Molluscs are soft-bodied animals with their bodies divided into three main regions: an obvious head, the main body mass containing the organs, and a foot for movement. The group contains many freshwater and marine representatives (the former discussed on p. 239), but in terrestrial habitats the group is represented by slugs and snails (the latter of which have a hard shell to protect the body). For more information about terrestrial molluscs see p. 223.

ARTHROPODS (PHYLUM ARTHROPODA)

Arthropods have an external skeleton that is given rigidity by a substance called chitin. They have paired, jointed legs, and movement is achieved by internal muscles which are attached to the inside wall of the exoskeleton. Members of the phylum found in terrestrial and freshwater habitats include the following: centipedes; millipedes; crustaceans; spiders and allies; and insects. The arthropod classification system used by the National Biodiversity Network has been adopted.

Introducing Arthropods

In most biodiversity gardens arthropods are likely to be the best represented and most conspicuous group of invertebrates. Plus, they are also likely to be the most abundant animals in any given plot. Consequently, they deserve special attention and a more detailed breakdown of their classification.

CENTIPEDES AND MILLIPEDES (SUBPHYLUM MYRIAPODA)

Centipedes (class Chilopoda) are elongated, segmented arthropods and each body segment has a pair of legs. They are predators, as might be guessed from looking at the pair of sharp poison claws at the head end. Millipedes (class Diplopoda) are similar to centipedes but the elongate, segmented body has two pairs of legs per segment. They feed on plant tissue and detritus and are relatively slow-moving.

Millipede

Centipede

CRUSTACEANS (SUBPHYLUM CRUSTACEA)

Most crustaceans are found in water – both marine and freshwater – and a few species can be found in ponds and streams. They are also well-represented in terrestrial habitats by woodlice. These are tied to damp environments and have segmented bodies with a hard dorsal carapace and seven pairs of walking legs.

SPIDERS AND ALLIES (SUBPHYLUM CHELICERATA, CLASS ARACHNIDA)

This varied group of arthropods has four pairs of walking legs – this distinguishes them from insects, adults of which have three pairs. Arachnid bodies are divided into two obvious regions. In addition to spiders, the group also includes false scorpions, ticks, mites and harvestmen.

INSECTS (SUBPHYLUM HEXAPODA, CLASS INSECTA)

Given their diversity and abundance in the British countryside and their significance to the biodiversity garden, insects deserve special consideration. Extraordinary facts and figures abound for the group: they are among the most numerous organisms on the planet and also the most diverse, the million-plus species known worldwide being found in almost all terrestrial and freshwater habitats; even in Britain and Ireland there are around 25,000 documented species with many others yet to be described.

Insects are also extremely diverse in terms of appearance. As adults they are characterised by having three pairs of walking legs and a body that is divided into three obvious regions: the head, which supports many sensory organs as well as the mouthparts; the thorax, to which the legs and wings, if present, are attached; and the segmented abdomen within which many of the main body organs are contained. The dietary habits of insects range from strictly vegetarian to voraciously predatory.

Important orders of larger insects for the biodiversity gardener:

Butterflies and moths (order Lepidoptera) are striking insects, adults of which have wings covered in scales, allowing extraordinary colours and patterns to be displayed; their mouthparts are modified to form a long, sucking proboscis. There are four distinct stages in the life cycle and their larvae are often referred to as caterpillars.

Grasshoppers and bush-crickets (order Orthoptera) are characterised by the adults' ability to hop or jump. Their bodies are generally rather cylindrical and the life cycle involves a series of increasingly adult-like nymphal stages.

Dragonflies and damselflies (order Odonata) have slender bodies and mainly transparent paired wings. Adults are terrestrial while their nymphs are aquatic; both stages in the life cycle are predatory.

True bugs (order Hemiptera) comprise an extremely varied group of insects (ranging from aphids to shieldbugs) with sucking mouthparts; adults of many species are winged, these either folded flat over the body at rest, or held tent-wise. The life cycle involves a series of increasingly adult-like nymphal stages.

Earwigs (order Dermaptera) are flattened-bodied insects with pincer-like appendages at the tail end; forewings are modified to form protective plates while hindwings are either reduced or absent.

Lacewings and allies (order Neuroptera) are slender-bodied insects with proportionately large wings as adults, held in a tent-wise manner when at rest. Lacewing adults and larvae are predatory.

Scorpionflies (order Mecoptera) are distinctive insects with a long beak-like structure on the head used for feeding; they feed mainly by scavenging dead insects. Males have a curved and swollen 'tail' from which the common name derives. The larvae are soil-dwelling.

Caddisflies (order Trichoptera) are associated with freshwater. Adults bear a passing resemblance to smaller moth species; their wings are coated in hairs and held in a tent-like manner at rest. The larvae are all aquatic and construct and live inside cases made from leaf fragments, debris and sand grains depending on the species.

True flies (order Diptera) are a varied and diverse group, adults of which have one pair of wings (hind wings are reduced to tiny, club-shaped stabilising organs). Adults have sucking or piercing mouthparts.

Bees, wasps, ants and sawflies (order Hymenoptera) are an extremely variable group, adults of which have two pairs of membranous wings; some species live communal lives and females of a few species have powerful stings (modified ovipositors).

Beetles (order Coleoptera) are a diverse group, adults of which have biting mouthparts and the front pair of wings modified to form protective plates called 'elytra'; hind wings, when present, allow flight and are often folded beneath the elytra at rest.

Insect wings and flight

Insects are the only invertebrate group to have evolved wings and mastered the power of flight. Not all insects have wings, of course, but of those that do, most have two pairs of wings. Insect wings are membranous and they are lent support by a network of rigid veins. In some insect groups, the wings are transparent, while those of butterflies and moths are cloaked with scales and extremely colourful.

A Large Yellow Underwing – moths and butterflies use two pairs of wings for flight.

With true flies, such as these hover-flies, the front pair of wings power flight while the hind wings are reduced to tiny stabilising organs.

Insect life cycles

Life for a typical insect starts with an egg laid by a female. The growing stage (larva) hatches and its rigid skin is moulted several times as it grows. Each successive step is called an instar and with some insects (true bugs, for example) the insect becomes more adult-like with each moult. With others, the larva just gets bigger with each instar; when fully grown, it metamorphoses into a pupa, from which the adult emerges.

An adult female Green-veined White.

A Green-veined White egg.

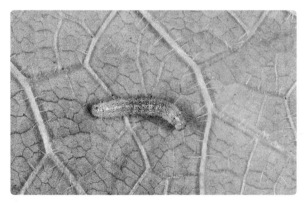

A Green-veined White caterpillar or larva.

A Green-veined White chrysalis or pupa.

● BUTTERFLY AND MOTH LIFE CYCLE TERMINOLOGY

Butterfly life cycles follow a sequence that is similar to many other insect groups: a fertilised female lays eggs, which hatch into larvae (singular larva), that metamorphose into pupae (singular pupa) and emerge as the next generation of adults. To confuse the situation slightly, butterfly and moth larvae are popularly known as caterpillars and the pupa is often called a chrysalis. The process of metamorphosis that involves the transformation of a caterpillar to a chrysalis is still called pupation.

The New Naturalist –
A Closer Look at Garden Wildlife

A thriving biodiversity garden will harbour hundreds, possibly thousands of species, each of which will have an ecological role to play. You will inevitably have your own favourites, but try to take a balanced view and resist the temptation to assign league table merits and failings to too many. With an eye to overall biodiversity in the garden, this chapter deals with the main wildlife groups and explains their role in garden ecology and their requirements for survival.

Not all wildlife in the garden is immediately obvious, and there are techniques and approaches that aid the study of natural history generally, and specific groups in particular. Employing these approaches will enhance your appreciation of the world around you and your sense of achievement and hence fulfilment. These rewards run hand in hand with the need to monitor progress and an obligation to record your findings for your own benefit and for posterity. Study techniques available to the biodiversity gardener range from tried and tested old favourites to state-of-the-art twenty-first-century innovations.

Butterflies

Butterflies are an iconic group of insects, and just over 60 species have been recorded in the UK, 50 or more of these being seen on a reasonably regular basis. As a general rule, the more urban the setting the fewer species will be observed, but in an average garden in a rural location or a suburban plot with wild habitats in the vicinity, 20 or so of the UK's species are likely to wander in. With some, there is a chance they breed already in your garden, and with the rest there is the potential for them do so by appropriate management of habitats and the plants that caterpillars eat in your garden. The way to encourage them is not to focus on the role of nectar in their adult lives but to understand and prioritise their life-cycle requirements: not just caterpillar foodplants and egg-laying locations but, depending on the species, provision for caterpillar overwintering, and sites of pupation and adult hibernation.

For the biodiversity gardener keen to chart their progress, butterflies have another advantage: all the species that occur regularly in the garden can be identified easily with a just a little bit of practice and experience. Butterflies are worthy of support in their own right but their significance in a biodiversity garden transcends their own presence. By helping butterflies through appropriate management, you will be assisting other invertebrates without necessarily realising it. The range of butterfly species, and their numbers, are ideal indicators of the overall natural health of your garden; and they allow you to monitor your progress and impact as you introduce wildlife-friendly habitat management.

The Orange-tip is a welcome addition to any biodiversity garden. Whether the species is a transient visitor or a breeding resident is entirely dependent on how the plot's vegetation is managed.

STUDYING BUTTERFLIES

As with many aspects of natural history, the study of butterflies has been transformed since my youth. Thankfully, these days a camera and pair of close-focussing binoculars are the tools of the trade, rather than a net and a killing jar. Observing and studying adult butterflies is the straightforward part. Getting to grips with the various life-cycle stages is more of a challenge, but a necessary one if you want to make a meaningful difference to the survival of butterflies in the garden, and not just a superficial attempt to provide sources of nectar for a few pleasing-to-the-eye species.

Butterflies are relatively easy to observe when feeding on nectar, although typically they are extremely active and encounters will be fleeting. If you are keen for more prolonged observations then think about alternative approaches.

Overcast days when there is the occasional glimmer of sunshine can offer equally good opportunities for observation, the insects often spreading their wings in anticipation of receiving warmth from the sun's rays while not inclined to become active enough to take flight. At either end of the day can also be good. In the early mornings, before the sun has risen high above the horizon, butterflies will emerge from their nighttime retreats and bask on leaves. At the end of the day, the same often happens in reverse. Members of the 'blue' family of butterflies typically spend the night clinging on to a grass stem and take up position an hour or so before sunset, at which time they can be observed extremely closely.

ASSESSING BREEDING

One of the most satisfying outcomes of enlightened, biodiversity-friendly management is the discovery that butterflies are actually breeding in your garden and not just visiting. One way to demonstrate this is by finding stages in the life cycle other than adults: eggs, caterpillars, or chrysalises. Although this is easier said than done, it is not an impossible task. If you can recognise the caterpillar foodplant of the butterfly in question then that is a good starting point. At appropriate times of the year, you will be able to look for caterpillars, as well as eggs; if you know where precisely a butterfly is likely to lay its eggs, you even stand a chance of watching the process happen. Finding chrysalises is more of a challenge because, being vulnerable, most species conceal themselves in dense cover. However, the chrysalises of a few species hide in plain sight, and once you know what to look

On dull days, some butterflies such as this Large Skipper are often inactive and if you search carefully and find one you are almost certain to be able to watch it closely, albeit most likely with its wings closed.

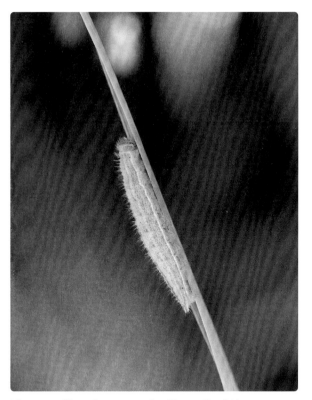

The Dingy Skipper is an occasional visitor to my garden in spring and I live in hope that one day it might colonise. In theory the garden provides the right ingredients for a colony to become established: clumps of its caterpillar foodplants Common and Greater Bird's-foot-trefoils and adjacent patches of sunny, open ground. Biodiversity gardeners elsewhere may be more fortunate than me.

The caterpillars of many grassland butterflies hide away during the daytime to avoid predators and emerge to feed after dark. Use a bright LED torch to find caterpillars such as this Ringlet, photographed in my meadow on 12 April.

for and where, your chances of discovery are greatly improved.

With parallels to the recording of breeding in birds, with butterflies you can also look for *evidence* of breeding. An example of this might be the observation of a newly emerged individual drying its wings on vegetation, although bear in mind this often happens very early in the morning, and mostly in cover. Another approach is the discovery of a mating pair of butterflies, which indicates the likelihood that they originated nearby in the garden, with egg-laying following on shortly afterwards. Mating also typically happens early in the morning, often within minutes of a female having emerged from her chrysalis.

To allow butterflies to make the most of your plot of land, to follow are some insights into the lives and life-cycle requirements of species that occur in my garden. They are potential residents of other plots in lowland southern Britain. The special requirements of meadow butterflies are discussed on p. 74.

A mating pair of Gatekeepers.

TREE AND HEDGEROW BUTTERFLIES

Purple Hairstreak p. 143.

Holly Blue p. 143.

Speckled Wood p. 144.

Comma p. 145.

Brimstone p. 146.

Peacock p. 147.

Small Tortoiseshell p. 148.

Red Admiral p. 148.

Orange-tip p. 150.

Green-veined White p. 150.

Small White p. 151.

Large White p. 151.

Purple Hairstreak – a life on oak ▼ ▶

In the main this species is rightly considered to be a woodland butterfly, one specifically associated with oaks and forming faithful colonies. In the context of my garden the tree in question is a mature Pedunculate Oak, and although separated from its nearest neighbours by 50 metres or so, it hosts a colony of this delightful butterfly. Adults are on the wing in July and August and spend most of their time high in the canopy. They are only occasionally seen in flight, mainly in the early evenings, but individuals can sometimes be discovered in eye-level foliage on damp, drizzly days. A favourite food is 'honeydew' (aphids' sugary excretion) that collects on leaf surfaces. Eggs are laid at the base of next year's leaf buds; if you want to see one for yourself, wait until winter when the leaves have fallen and look for tiny white pinheads. The caterpillars hatch in April and feed on oak buds, at first burrowing inside. In June they pupate, so it seems always on or in the ground beneath their host tree, and I can only assume the caterpillars 'drop' from the tree rather than crawl down, but who knows. One chrysalis I came across was in an ants' nest, accidentally exposed by turning a stone, sited beneath the outermost branches of the tree. If you want to do your best for Purple Hairstreaks, avoid unnecessary tree pruning and, assuming this is undertaken in winter, inspect the cuttings for eggs and rear them through; and avoid unduly disturbing the soil beneath the tree.

A fully-grown Purple Hair-streak caterpillar on 2 May.

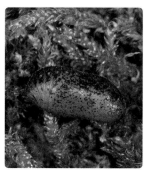

A Purple Hairstreak chrysalis amongst moss on the ground.

An adult male Purple Hairstreak basking on a Pedunculate Oak leaf.

Holly Blue ▼

For a successful colony of Holly Blues to thrive in the garden, both Holly and Ivy need to be present because the butterfly's life cycle relies on both plant species. There are two broods of Holly Blue each year. The spring generation, on the wing in April and May, lays eggs on Holly flower buds, while the summer generation, which flies in July and August, lays on Ivy flower buds. In the case of both generations, the caterpillars eat the flowers, then pupate beneath a leaf or at the base of the plant – pupation lasts through June with the first generation and from September to April with the second brood. If you have to prune or cut back Ivy then the least harmful time of year from a Holly Blue perspective would be in spring (when Holly Blues are flying). However, bear in mind that its dense cover may harbour nesting birds which must not be disturbed. If you have to prune Holly then the least harmful time of year from the point of view of this butterfly would be

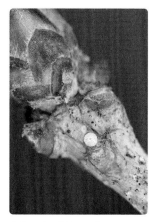

A Purple Hairstreak egg, discovered by searching twigs that had fallen to the ground after a winter gale. They resemble shining white pinheads against otherwise dull buds.

A young Purple Hairstreak caterpillar that hatched on 3 April. The tiny larva bears a striking resemblance to the bristly brown scales that surround the leaf buds of Pedunculate Oak.

winter, after any berries have been consumed by birds. There is a conservation dilemma for you to ponder. The Holly Blue caterpillar is often parasitised by the ichneumon wasp *Listrodromus nycthemerus*; see p. 179 for more information.

An adult female Holly Blue basking.

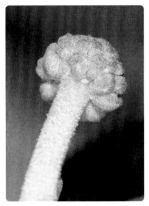

A Holly Blue egg, at the base of an Ivy flower.

A caterpillar feeding on a Holly berry.

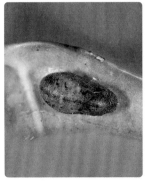

A chrysalis, attached by silk to the underside of a Holly leaf.

A resting adult Holly Blue with its wings closed.

Speckled Wood ▼ ▶

In terms of studying its life cycle this is the most enigmatic butterfly in my garden. I see adults in reasonable numbers, off and on, from early spring to late autumn and occasionally confirm that Speckled Woods breed in and around the garden. However, I have only seen the caterpillar on a few occasions, and on one occasion I saw a female egg-laying in the hedgerow margins of the garden. Others may have more luck and so here is a summary of its life cycle. In north Hampshire, there are two broods a year with first generation adults flying mainly from late March to early May, the second brood on the wing in July and August. There is, however, considerable overlap in flight times. This is a species of dappled shade, specifically spots where shafts of sunlight break through here and there. Males are renowned for being, to our eyes at least, territorial, typically basking in key vantage points and repelling any intruders by aerial combat. Eggs are laid beneath grass leaves, and because of the overlap in adult emergence and egg-laying, caterpillars can be observed from spring until late autumn. A wide range of grass species are eaten by the caterpillars although False-brome and Cock's-foot are favourites around here. Some individuals overwinter as caterpillars while others pupate; the chrysalis is suspended from a stem in deep cover. Adults are fond of aphid 'honeydew' that collects on tree foliage. If you want to help the species in the garden, leave plenty of undisturbed grass in sheltered spots such as hedgerows and along fence lines.

A Speckled Wood egg, fixed to the underside of a leaf of False-brome.

A Speckled Wood caterpillar aligned with its foodplant, False-brome.

A Speckled Wood chrysalis, just prior to emergence of the adult butterfly.

A Comma egg laid on a leaf of Common Nettle.

A newly emerged Comma caterpillar.

A Speckled Wood adult resting with its wings closed.

A full-grown Comma caterpillar.

Comma ▶

The Comma is a conspicuous and distinctive butterfly found in many rural gardens, and suburban spots too. There are two broods each year. Those adults that emerge in late summer hibernate during the winter months and appear on the wing again in March and April. They give rise to a second generation which is on the wing in June and July. Eggs are laid on the leaves of caterpillar foodplants, which in my garden are typically Common Nettle and Hop, although I did once find a caterpillar feeding on Hazel. The caterpillars are striking, with a bold white band along the back that is said to make them look like a bird dropping. The chrysalis is suspended from a twig or stem, usually in a shady spot. With wings closed, the jagged outline of the wings and markings and coloration of the underwing are a good match for a dead leaf. Hardly surprising therefore that this deception is used when hibernating, adults choosing not necessarily leaf litter as such, but sheltered spots where fallen leaves accumulate – at the base of a tangled, dense hedge, perhaps, or the base of a tree. Adopt a tidy-minded approach to these areas in the garden and you will be doing the Comma a disservice.

A Comma adult, newly emerged from its chrysalis.

A resting adult Comma with its wings closed.

A Comma adult basking with its wings spread.

Brimstone ▼ ▶

Despite being seen on the wing, off and on, from midsummer to late autumn, and again from late winter to late spring, there is just one brood of this distinctive butterfly each year. The life cycle depends on the presence of one or other of its caterpillar foodplants: Buckthorn or Alder Buckthorn. In May and June, eggs are laid on leaf buds or tender shoots, sometimes in small but scattered groups. In June and July, the caterpillars feed on the leaves and often align themselves with the midrib, making them a challenge to spot; as a clue, look for nibbled leaf margins and a caterpillar will almost certainly be close to hand. The chrysalis is elegantly suspended and harnessed beneath a leaf and can be found in June and July. Having emerged and fed, adults soon disappear into dense cover. For the most part they remain torpid, then hibernate for the next six months or so, except for the occasional foray on a sunny winter's day. If you want to encourage Brimstones in your garden, grow one of the caterpillar foodplants and ensure there is plenty of dense cover (a mass of Ivy for example) for winter hibernation. In spring, butterflies use a wide range of flowers as sources of nectar, including cultivated *Geranium* species; in the summer months Betony and garden Pelargoniums are favourites in my garden.

A group of Brimstone eggs laid on Buckthorn.

A half-grown Brimstone caterpillar.

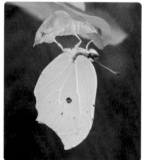

A Brimstone adult, newly emerged from its chrysalis.

A Brimstone adult feeding on a cultivated *Geranium*.

● BRIMSTONE FOODPLANTS

Brimstones lay their eggs on Buckthorn and Alder Buckthorn, both of which grow to become dense shrubs, ideal components in a hedgerow or when planted in isolation. The plants can be grown from seed (by collecting berries) or purchased online as small shrubs or bare root stems, and planted in winter. Brimstone butterflies hibernate as adults, and so pruning these shrubs in winter will not affect the life cycle of the butterfly. Buckthorn favours calcareous soils; its greenish-yellow flowers appear in clusters and its berries ripen black in autumn. The leaves are oval and finely toothed. Alder Buckthorn is the counterpart of Buckthorn that grows on neutral to acid soils, particularly on damp ground; it has pale green flowers and berries that ripen black. The oval leaves turn yellow in autumn.

Buckthorn leaf and fruit.

Alder Buckthorn leaf and fruit.

NETTLE SPECIALISTS

Common Nettle is the familiar 'stinging nettle' and needs little introduction. Its flowers are borne in catkins and its leaves are oval, pointed-tipped and toothed. Common Nettle thrives on nitrogen-enriched and disturbed soils and needs little encouragement in the garden. Tolerate it growing in forgotten corners of the garden and hedges, because its leaves are caterpillar food for many of our most iconic garden butterflies. Two of the three hibernate as adults while the other migrates south, which means that tidying up nettle patches in winter will not unduly affect the life cycles of these particular butterflies. However, bear in mind that a range of other insects, including the caterpillars of several moth species, depend on Common Nettle. The moral of the story is to avoid being too tidy in your garden.

Peacock ▼

The Peacock is one of the most familiar garden butterflies in lowland Britain and a regular and welcome feature in my garden. Although adults can be seen on the wing in many months, there is just one brood a year. Eggs are laid in May, in clusters on the undersides of nettle leaves, and the spiky black caterpillars live gregariously until it is time to pupate, typically sometime in mid-June. The chrysalis is suspended from a stem or twig and adults emerge in August. They remain active well into autumn, when they seek out hibernation spots in dense cover or occasionally in sheds or indoors. They are occasionally active in winter, if disturbed, or on unseasonably warm days, but otherwise they remain torpid until the following spring.

An adult Peacock hibernating indoors.

A group of Peacock caterpillars on Common Nettle.

Common Nettle.

A Peacock chrysalis suspended from a Common Nettle leaf stalk.

An adult Peacock basking with its wings fully spread to capture the warmth of the sun.

Small Tortoiseshell ▼

In the southern part of Britain where I live the Small Tortoiseshell has two broods a year. Adults that hatch in early autumn hibernate during the winter months in dense, sheltered undergrowth, tree hollows and occasionally in sheds and outbuildings, appearing again in spring. Eggs are laid in clusters in May or June on nettle leaves and the caterpillars feed in groups until it is time to pupate. The chrysalis is suspended from a stem or leaf petiole and the next generation of butterflies emerge in July and repeat the life-cycle process with fresh adults emerging in autumn.

Small Tortoiseshell caterpillars feeding on the leaves of Common Nettle.

A Small Tortoiseshell chrysalis suspended from a twig.

A newly emerged Small Tortoiseshell adult.

An adult Small Tortoiseshell feeding on Bramble.

Red Admiral ▼

Although this familiar butterfly may be an occasional resident, its true status is reckoned to be that of a seasonal visitor, one whose life cycle and life strategy illustrate the folly of thinking in terms of national boundaries when it comes to nature. With parallels to

A Red Admiral larval 'tent'.

The life cycle of the Red Admiral depends on Common Nettle and relies on concealment. Eggs are laid on nettle leaves and upon hatching each caterpillar constructs a 'tent' of leaves to protect itself. Metamorphosis occurs inside this silk-glued chamber, the chrysalis seen here temporarily exposed to view by teasing the leaves apart. A few weeks later, the adult emerges. Cut Common Nettle down in its prime and you stand a good chance of killing off the life cycle of the Red Admiral along with other nettle-feeding species. Leave it, and it has a habit of swamping other less vigorous species of plant. There's another conservation dilemma for you to ponder.

the Painted Lady, it is a long-distance north-south migrant traveller. Adult Red Admirals spend the winter months in southern Europe, particularly around the Mediterranean, where new generations of butterfly are produced, feeding on the flush of nettle species that appear at that time of year. As temperatures warm in spring, adults migrate northwards and appear in Britain in varying numbers, and over a staggered period mainly from April to June. New, home-grown generations of adult butterflies emerge over a staggered period and as temperatures cool in autumn they begin to migrate south again, leaving our shores and ending up where the story began near the Mediterranean. Hibernation is not part of the life strategy of the species; if you see a Red Admiral in the UK in the dead of winter, except in the most southerly of locations, the chances are it is a straggler destined to die, or an unseasonably early arrival from the south.

BUTTERFLIES ASSOCIATED WITH WAYSIDE PLANTS

A range of often-overlooked wayside plants have a role to play in the life histories of many native insects. When it comes to butterflies, one in particular stands out: Garlic Mustard, a roadside biennial that often grows in forgotten areas of gardens, and can be encouraged by scattering seeds. Its flowers have four white petals and its leaves are heart-shaped, toothed and smell of garlic when crushed. The caterpillars of two of our most attractive garden butterflies – Orange-tip and Green-veined White – feed on its leaves and pupate attached to its stems. Here they spend the winter months. Ask yourself whether or not you would squash or trample underfoot an adult Orange-tip butterfly. Assuming the answer is no, then apply the same principle to other stages in its life cycle. By destroying vegetation on which caterpillars are feeding, or to which chrysalises are attached in winter, and the effect is the same as killing an adult. And extend the same level of respect to all wayside plants because almost certainly there will be some invertebrate or other whose life depends on them.

Garlic Mustard.

Garlic Mustard leaf.

An adult Orange-tip on Garlic Mustard.

Orange-tip ▼

There is just one brood of this attractive butterfly each year. In spring, eggs are laid, often on flower buds or tender leaf stalks of Garlic Mustard as well as Cuckooflower; although tiny, they are bright orange and relatively easy to spot once you have your eye in. Look for them from late April to the middle of June, when adults are on the wing. The caterpillars, which feed throughout June and into early July, have splendid counter-shading that allows them to blend in convincingly with the stalks and elongated pods of their foodplant. The chrysalis is fixed and tethered to the stalk of the foodplant or something nearby, and remains in that state from early summer until the following spring. Cut down and destroy the stalks of the foodplant, even in the dead of winter, and you kill the life cycle of this lovely butterfly.

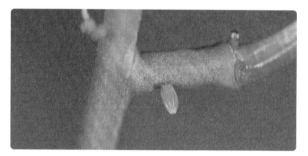

An Orange-tip egg attached to Garlic Mustard.

Orange-tip caterpillars seem to have a special fondness for the seedpods of their larval foodplant, Garlic Mustard. Counter-shading affords them excellent camouflage when they align themselves.

An Orange-tip chrysalis, attached by a silk harness to a withered Garlic Mustard stem – just the sort of thing I might have removed in my time as a tidy-minded conventional gardener.

Green-veined White ▼

Wings that are marked by darkened, greenish veins make this the most elegant and distinctive of the 'white' butterflies you are likely to come across in the garden. There are two broods each year, one that emerges and flies as an adult in spring, the other in midsummer, and its life cycle depends on cabbage family members, notably Garlic Mustard. The egg is laid singly on the underside of a leaf, and the newly emerged caterpillar eats its egg shell before feasting on the leaves. The chrysalis is attached by a harness to the stem of the plant, making it vulnerable to tidy-minded garden maintenance. See p. 138 for images of the life cycle.

A Green-veined White chrysalis, just prior to adult emergence.

CABBAGE SPECIALISTS

The natural history and success of our two 'cabbage' white species are inextricably linked to human history and can be traced back to our Neolithic forebears. They were the first to cultivate Wild Cabbage, which still grows in its original form on Dorset cliffs, and their experimentation gave rise eventually to modern-day staples ranging from Cauliflower and Savoy Cabbage to Broccoli and Brussels Sprouts. In its native location, Wild Cabbage leaves are ravaged by the caterpillars of Large Whites in particular, leaving tattered remains by early summer. Little wonder then that when presented with an almost limitless supply of food, 'cabbage' white butterflies have spread wherever brassicas are planted and grown.

In my garden, I don't actively encourage Small Whites and Large Whites but I do tolerate them and view them as integral parts of the environment. I turn a forgiving eye to their horticultural shortcomings, and if I grow brassicas, I do so inside a fruit cage which prevents egg-laying. Both are part of the cycle of life in the garden: some adults end up being eaten by predators ranging from spiders to Spotted Flycatchers, and a range of parasitic wasp species are entirely dependent on the eggs, caterpillars or chrysalises for their own life cycles to be completed.

Small White ▽ ▷

At a casual glance, this smaller cousin of the Large White could be confused with a Green-veined White, although on close inspection its inconspicuous wing venation allows certain identification. As with its larger cousin, there are two broods a year, beginning with

adults that emerge in April and May, having hatched from chrysalises that overwintered. Eggs are laid singly on brassica leaves and the caterpillars feed throughout June until fully grown. The chrysalis is supported by a silk harness and attached to a vertical surface such as a fence. Adults emerge in July and the life cycle continues with the second generation of the year pupating in late August or September, and remaining in that state until the following spring.

An adult Small White.

Large White ▽ ▷

Although the Large White is resident in Britain throughout the year, its status is complicated by influxes of butterflies from mainland Europe, in varying numbers and throughout the warmer months. In a good year, there are two broods a year, beginning with adults that emerge in April and May, having hatched from chrysalises that overwintered here. The life cycle commences with eggs being laid in clusters on the underside of brassica leaves, and the caterpillars that hatch live in groups until fully

A Small White egg, laid on the underside of a leaf of the foodplant.

A Small White caterpillar on the underside of a cabbage leaf.

A cluster of Large White eggs, laid on the underside of a cabbage leaf.

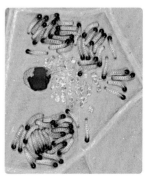

Newly emerged Large White caterpillars, and the remains of their egg shells.

grown. At this point they wander off and pupate, often attached to a vertical surface such as a fence, with the next generation of adults emerging in late July. Influxes of migrant Large Whites mean that life-cycle stages often overlap.

A full-grown Large White caterpillar.

A Large White chrysalis, harnessed by silk to a fence.

A Large White adult feeding on Betony.

SUMMER VISITORS

In my childhood, the following butterflies were the stuff of myth and legend and, decades later, they bring back memories of school summer holidays of my youth when I went in search of them. Although I still occasionally travel to hotspots to be sure of seeing them, that happens less frequently as the years go by. An encounter with one of these iconic insects is always a delight, but nowadays I find the nearer to home the sighting the greater the thrill I get. And there is nothing more rewarding than a close encounter in my garden.

Purple Emperor p. 153.

White Admiral p. 153.

Silver-washed Fritillary p. 154.

Painted Lady p. 154.

Clouded Yellow p. 155.

Purple Emperor ▼

It is not beyond the realms of possibility that Purple Emperors might one day breed in my garden, but currently the species' status is that of an annual visitor. Pamber Forest, the nearest stronghold, lies around 500 metres away, and wandering, presumably end-of-season females turn up in my garden, perhaps in search of suitable egg-laying sites. Eggs are laid on Goat Willow, and in my limited experience plants that have reached the proportions of a modest tree or large shrub are favoured; egg-laying has been observed on two such Goat Willows 200 metres or so from my garden, well outside the boundary of the butterfly's forest stronghold. Young caterpillars overwinter on buds and feed up the following spring when leaves have emerged; their shape and markings make them a good match for the foliage where they live. The leaf-like chrysalis is suspended from a petiole or twig and adults emerge, and are on the wing, in July.

An adult male Purple Emperor.

A Purple Emperor caterpillar.   A Purple Emperor chrysalis.

White Admiral ▼

Like the Purple Emperor, this species is an occasional but annual visitor to my garden, usually worn end-of-season specimens. It is unlikely to breed in my garden but does so in nearby woodland and woodland remnants. The caterpillar foodplant is Honeysuckle, but eggs are only laid on straggly plants growing in shade; the species' fate is said to have been improved by the decline in commercial coppicing of Hazel and the resulting denser canopy cover of some woodlands. Eggs are laid in July and August and the spiky caterpillar overwinters until the following spring. The extraordinary chrysalis can be found in June, suspended from a stem or twig, and adults emerge in July.

A White Admiral caterpillar.

A White Admiral chrysalis.

A newly emerged White Admiral adult resting on its chrysalis case.

A White Admiral adult, feeding on Bramble nectar.

Silver-washed Fritillary ▼

In some respects, the life-cycle requirements of this species are the exact opposite of those required by the White Admiral, often seen as the woodland consort of this beautiful butterfly. Eggs are laid on tree bark, and the tiny caterpillars spend the winter lodged in bark crevices. Come the following spring and their dependence on open woodland becomes obvious: they feed on the leaves of violets, which flourish best in full sun, and indeed larger caterpillars seem fond of basking in the open. The chrysalis is suspended from a twig, usually in deep cover, and the adult emerges and is on the wing in July and August. Silver-washed Fritillaries visit my garden towards the end of their flight period and the best thing I can do to support them is to encourage patches of Bramble, because they are partial to the flowers' nectar.

A Silver-washed Fritillary egg, laid on the bark of a Silver Birch.

A young Silver-washed Fritillary caterpillar, feeding on Common Dog-violet.

A full-grown Silver-washed Fritillary caterpillar.

A Silver-washed Fritillary chrysalis, suspended from a twig.

A Silver-washed Fritillary adult feeding on Marsh Thistle.

Painted Lady ▼

In terms of European butterflies, this is the ultimate nomad and also the supreme migrant. Working backwards, most of the Painted Ladies that appear in Britain will have their origins in North Africa or the Middle East where the winter months are spent. Transient populations develop here and there in response to winter rains and the appearance of arid-country caterpillar foodplants, notably species of thistles and their allies. As generations complete and foodplants diminish, the butterflies move on and the cycle continues. With rising seasonal temperatures, arid conditions return and subsequent generations migrate northwards into mainland Europe, some eventually crossing the English Channel. In autumn, reverse migration occurs southwards and, because of the succession of generations each year, those Painted Ladies that arrive in North Africa in early winter will be only distantly related to those that departed northwards a year previously.

An adult, feeding on Marsh Thistle.

Thistle species are the foodplants for the Painted Lady, and the caterpillar lives hidden from view inside a succession of 'tents' made from leaves bound together by silk. If you allow plants of Spear, Creeping or Marsh Thistle to grow to stately proportions there is every chance that this lovely butterfly will lay its eggs on them and you will host its caterpillars in your garden, whether you realise it or not. The chrysalis is usually suspended from a stem of the foodplant.

Clouded Yellow ▶

The Clouded Yellow is another great migrant, one that like the Painted Lady spends the winter months in southern Europe and North Africa. Like its peripatetic cousin, it also wanders and breeds in response to winter downpours and the appearance of caterpillar foodplants, notably species of clovers and related plants. As spring arrives, a succession of generations moves northwards and Clouded Yellows reach our shores (occasionally reaching my garden in small numbers) sometimes as early as May but more typically in July or August. Having a rather catholic clover diet, the species is one of the few butterflies that can make use of areas of intensively farmed grassland that have been seeded with clovers. At the end of summer, migration occurs southwards through Europe with only the occasional straggler remaining, most likely eventually succumbing to the cold.

The adult Clouded Yellow butterfly always rests and feeds with its wings closed. Only in flight are the richly colourful upperwings of the Clouded Yellow revealed.

Moths

Although there are a few day-flying moths to be found in my garden, the majority are nocturnal and require special techniques to discover their presence. An array of different methods can be deployed, and these include making use of the attraction to light by many, and a fondness for sugary substances in a few. Moths are fascinating in their own right, and most people who have never experimented with lepidopterists' tricks of the trade are amazed at just how many species live quite literally on their doorstep. There is, however, a greater

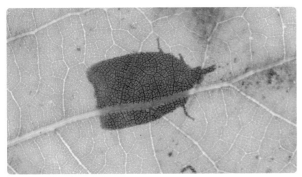

Moths are amazingly good at hiding, often in plain sight, during the daytime. However, this Green Oak Tortrix has been caught out, silhouetted and backlit by the sun as it rests on an oak leaf.

significance to observing and finding moths: using them as indicators of the biodiversity health of your garden, with hopefully increasing numbers and variety, will allow you to measure how well your garden is responding to its new management regime. Keeping and submitting records is an integral part of charting the evolution of your garden and your development as a natural historian.

IDENTIFICATION

Almost all larger moth species (macro moths) can be identified as living specimens, without the need to kill them. The process can seem a little daunting at first, but you will soon get the hang of it. You need to be aware of the variability in colour and appearance within a given species, plus regional variations and flight times, which can be crucially informative. There are several online county-based moth resources, many of which have 'flying tonight' features that allow you to see the most likely candidates in your area.

A few groups of closely related moths (for example, many of the 'minor' species) can only be reliably identified by dissecting their genitalia, and I have decided that I would rather forego the knowledge of their precise identification: from a personal perspective, satisfying my curiosity does not outweigh the moth's right to life. I apply the same principle to those micro moths that need to be killed to be recognised; they remain unidentified. This obviously curtails the list of moth species that occur in my garden, but for me that is a price worth paying.

WHAT IS IN A NAME?

From a beginner's point of view, one of the attractions when studying moths is that all the larger species have English names. These are not standard, descriptive monikers, or ones with recent origins, created to 'engage' a modern audience, for fear a strictly scientific approach would put them off the subject. Instead, many have an elegance that resonates with their history: their origins lie with Victorian entomologists and their predecessors such as Moses Harris whose interest in the subject dates back to the eighteenth century. Granted, some are a touch prosaic: Bright-line Brown-eye, Large Emerald and Clouded Drab, for example. However, many are more imaginative and in language terms as colourful as the moths themselves are attractive: Merveille du Jour, True Lover's Knot, Bird's Wing, Gothic, Maiden's Blush, Silurian and Hebrew Character to name but a few.

Mother Shipton

Setaceous Hebrew Character

Blood-vein

Clifden Nonpareil

LIFE CYCLES

As with butterflies, moth life cycles involve four stages. Firstly, adults mate and females lay eggs. Next, the eggs hatch into caterpillars that increase in size through a series of moults, each stage being referred to as an instar. Then the full-grown caterpillar pupates; although the chrysalis can wriggle, it cannot move around and

so location and protection are key, with pupation often taking place in an underground chamber or in a protective cocoon. Lastly, after a period of dormancy metamorphosis occurs within the chrysalis and the adult emerges.

Poplar Hawkmoth life-cycle:

An adult moth.

An egg, laid on a willow leaf.

A newly emerged caterpillar eating its egg shell.

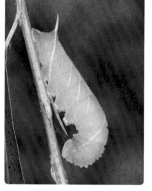

A full-grown caterpillar.

A chrysalis.

VARIATIONS ON A LIFE-CYCLE THEME

Each moth species has a subtly unique life cycle, tailored to suit its environmental needs and appropriate in terms of timing with regards to its caterpillar foodplants. In addition, a wide range of variations on the theme occur, and many unusual examples can be found in garden species.

As the name suggests, the Winter Moth is active in the winter months. Males seek out the wingless females, and mate on the stem of a foodplant shrub. You can use an LED torch to spot them in the garden – to find mating pairs, look for males that are facing head-down.

Female Vapourer moths are wingless and lay large batches of eggs in late summer.

Male Vapourers have fully functioning wings and sometimes fly in the daytime.

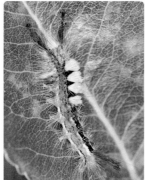

A Vapourer caterpillar is an attractive insect, covered in protective hairs.

An adult Puss Moth.

The chrysalis of a Vapourer is protected in a tough, silk cocoon.

A Puss Moth caterpillar is almost comically plump. It has a disproportionately large head and two whip-like projections at the tail.

Designed to blend in with the tree bark to which it is fixed, this hardened Puss Moth cocoon contains and protects the chrysalis.

LARVAL FOODPLANTS OF GARDEN MOTHS

Look closely enough around you and you will find that almost every native plant in your garden has a role to play in the web of life that allows healthy biodiversity to flourish. You could spend a lifetime studying and investigating the relationships and still only really scratch the surface, such is the complexity of the subject.

It is naïve to think that any one person can fully appreciate the intricacies of the relationships between the plants and animals. In many ways it is better just to embrace this inter-dependency and err on the side of caution when making judgements regarding garden management. However, to provide a flavour of the diversity, and as an indication of the range of relationships in my garden, here are a few trees, shrubs and herbaceous plants that grow in my plot along with a selection of the moth caterpillars that depend on them for food. Species where there is a very specific relationship with a single foodplant, or a small range, are highlighted in **bold**. Some rather unexpected diets are indicated as well at the end of the list.

In case anyone should suppose that this is new information, details of life cycles and larval foodplants of moths have been studied for at least a couple of centuries, and were familiar to Victorian entomologists. As an example, in the Rev. J. G. Wood's 1886 *Field Naturalist's Handbook* information about life-cycle-stage monthly occurrence and larval foodplants is listed for almost every moth species in the UK. See the References section for more information.

Pedunculate Oak: Green Oak Tortrix, Brindled Beauty, Winter Moth, Oak Beauty, November Moth, Maiden's Blush, Mottled Umber, Blossom Underwing, Grey Shoulder-knot, Red-green Carpet, **Blotched Emerald**, Great Prominent, Buff-tip, Vapourer, Pale Tussock, Lunar Marbled Brown, Yellow-tail, Black Arches, Hebrew Character, Common Quaker, Twin-spotted Quaker, Nut-tree Tussock, Scarce Silver-lines, **Merveille du Jour (above)**, Green Silver-lines, **Svensson's Copper Underwing**, Chestnut, Dun-bar, Angle Shades.

Aspen: Poplar Grey, **Chocolate-tip (above)**, Herald, Oak Beauty, Pale Prominent, Poplar Hawkmoth, Puss Moth, Twin-spotted Quaker.

Beech: **Lobster Moth (above)**, Nut-tree Tussock, Green Silver-lines.

Alder: Brindled Beauty, **Alder Moth (above)**, Lime Hawk-moth, Large Emerald, Canary-shouldered Thorn, Iron Prominent, Miller, Coronet.

Hazel: Winter Moth, Oak Beauty, Peppered Moth, November Moth, Large Emerald, **Buff-tip (above),** Vapourer, Pale Tussock, Yellow-tail, Lobster Moth, Ingrailed Clay, Dot Moth, Common Quaker, Clouded Drab, Bright-line Brown-eye, Nut-tree Tussock, Green Silver-lines, Dun-bar, Angle Shades.

Common Hawthorn: V-Pug, Brimstone Moth, Green Pug, Swallow-tailed Moth, Brindled Beauty, Winter Moth, Oak Beauty, Peppered Moth, November Moth, Common Marbled Carpet, Mottled Umber, Willow Beauty, Vapourer, Lappet, Pale Tussock, **Figure of Eight (above),** Yellow-tail, Ingrailed Clay, Common Quaker, Clouded Drab, Hebrew Character, **Green-brindled Crescent,** Grey Dagger, Knot Grass, Chestnut, **Beaded Chestnut,** Old Lady, Dun-bar.

Ash: Winter Moth, November Moth, Lilac Beauty, Privet Hawk-moth, Twin-spotted Quaker, **Centre-barred Sallow (above), Coronet.**

Rowan: Grey Dagger, **Brimstone Moth (above).**

Guelder-rose: Privet Hawkmoth **(above).**

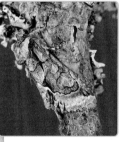

Blackthorn: Brimstone Moth, Green Pug, Winter Moth, Oak Beauty, Peppered Moth, November Moth, Mottled Umber, Red-green Carpet, Vapourer, Lappet, Pale Tussock, Figure of Eight, Yellow-tail, Ingrailed Clay, Powdered Quaker, **Green-brindled Crescent (above),** Grey Dagger, Chestnut, Dun-bar.

Wild Cherry: Green Pug, Winter Moth, **Red-green Carpet (above)**.

Small-leaved Elm: Lime Hawkmoth, November Moth, Mottled Umber, Vapourer, Pale Tussock, Common Quaker, **Clouded Drab (above)**, Grey Dagger, Chestnut.

Apple: Green Pug, Winter Moth, **Eyed Hawkmoth (above)**, November Moth, Mottled Umber, Red-green Carpet, Figure of Eight, Grey Dagger.

Sallows and willows: *Acleris emargana*, Peacock Moth, Brindled Beauty, Winter Moth, Oak Beauty, Poplar Hawkmoth, Eyed Hawkmoth, Scorched Wing, Chocolate-tip, Pebble Prominent, Pale Prominent, Swallow Prominent, **Sallow Kitten (above)**, **Puss Moth**, Vapourer, Canary-shouldered Thorn, Yellow-tail, Hebrew Character, Herald, Dot Moth, Green Arches, Powdered Quaker, Common Quaker, Twin-spotted Quaker, **Red-line Quaker**, Silvery Arches, Broad-bordered Yellow Underwing, Hebrew Character, Miller, Alder Moth, Pink-barred Sallow, Dun-bar, **Red Underwing**.

Dog-rose: V-Pug, Mottled Umber, Red-green Carpet, **Shoulder-stripe (above)**, Figure of Eight.

Silver Birch: *Acleris emargana*, Peacock Moth, Brindled Beauty, Winter Moth, Lime Hawkmoth, November Moth, Large Emerald, Willow Beauty, Scorched Wing, Canary-shouldered Thorn, Iron Prominent, Lesser Swallow Prominent, Buff-tip, Vapourer, Pale Tussock, Yellow-tail, Lobster Moth, Hebrew Character, Autumnal Rustic, Common Quaker, Clouded Drab, Silvery Arches, Broad-bordered Yellow Underwing, Scarce Silver-lines, Miller, **Green Silver-lines (above)**, Grey Dagger, Dun-bar, Angle Shades.

Alder Buckthorn: Willow Beauty (above).

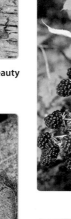

Field Maple: *Acleris forsskaleana*, Oak Beauty, November Moth, Twin-spotted Quaker, Sycamore, **Dun-bar (above)**.

Sycamore: *Acleris forsskaleana*, Mottled Umber, Broad-bordered Yellow Underwing, **Sycamore (above)**.

Elder: Dot Moth, **Swallow-tailed Moth (above)**.

Bramble: V-Pug, **Peach Blossom**, **Buff Arches (above)**, Common Marbled Carpet, Dot Moth, Green Arches, Knot Grass, Angle Shades.

Ivy: Swallow-tailed Moth, Willow Beauty, **Old Lady (above)**.

Hop: Buff Ermine, **Twin-spotted Quaker (above)**, Bright-line Brown-eye, Knot Grass, Angle Shades.

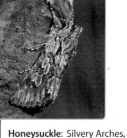

Honeysuckle: Silvery Arches, Twin-spotted Quaker, Lilac Beauty, Buff Ermine, **Early Grey (above)**.

Common Nettle: Small Magpie, Ghost Moth (roots), Setaceous Hebrew Character, Hebrew Character, White Ermine, **Spectacle (above)**, Dot Moth, Buff Ermine, Burnished Brass, **Snout**, Angle Shades.

Cleavers: Silver-ground Carpet (above).

Foxglove: Lesser Yellow Underwing, **Foxglove Pug (above)**.

Hedge Bedstraw: Silver-ground Carpet, **Barred Straw (above)**, Autumnal Rustic.

Common Ragwort: Large Ranunculus, **Cinnabar (above)**.

Primrose: Silver-ground Carpet, Barred Straw, Ingrailed Clay, **Green Arches (above)**.

Rosebay and Great Willowherb: Setaceous Hebrew Character, **Elephant Hawkmoth (above)**, Large Ranunculus.

Some moth caterpillars are not very specific and feed on a wide range of herbaceous plants (including bindweeds, knotgrasses, clovers, oraches, sorrels, docks, chickweeds, stitchworts, plantains, cultivated brassicas, Wild Carrot, Hogweed, White Dead-nettle, Common Fleabane, dandelions, burdocks, thistles): Common Plume, Riband Wave, Blood-vein, Blossom Underwing, Setaceous Hebrew Character, Hebrew Character, Pearly Underwing, Ruby Tiger, White Ermine, Silver Y, Dot Moth, Green Arches, Gothic, Large Yellow Underwing, Burnished Brass, Bright-line Brown-eye, Heart and Dart, Turnip Moth, Black Rustic, Large Ranunculus (above) (especially dandelions), Lesser Yellow Underwing (especially Broad-leaved Dock), Heart and Club, Shuttle-shaped Dart (especially Broad-leaved Dock), Satellite (early stages), Knot Grass, Rustic, Rosy Rustic (roots), Ear Moth (inside stems and roots), Old Lady, Bird's Wing, Angle Shades, Treble Lines.

Bluebell: Autumnal Rustic (above).

Grasses (notably Tufted Hairgrass, Annual Meadow-grass, Common Couch, Cock's-foot, Yorkshire-fog): Drinker (Cock's-foot), **Ghost Moth (above)** (roots), Square-spot Rustic, Large Yellow Underwing, Common Wainscot, Smoky Wainscot (especially Cock's-foot), Shoulder-striped Wainscot (especially Cock's-foot), Lunar Underwing, Ear Moth (inside stems and roots), Marbled Minor (inside stems and roots), Rosy Minor (inside stems and roots), Common Rustic, Clouded-bordered Brindle (especially Cock's-foot), Dark Arches.

Carnivorous (other insects): Dun-bar, **Satellite (above)** (late stages).

Internal deciduous wood: Leopard Moth, most clearwing species including **Yellow-legged Clearwing (above)** (oaks). See illustration on p. 168.

Lichens on tree branches: Common Footman, **Rosy Footman (above)**, Beautiful Hook-tip, Marbled Beauty.

Bracket fungi on decaying logs: **Waved Black (above).**

To give you an idea of the sheer range and diversity of UK moths, these pages show a selection of moths observed in my garden. They represent just a quarter of the total number of species recorded in my garden over the last 20 years.

V-Pug

Yellow-legged Clearwing

Acleris emargana

Small Magpie

Common Plume

male

female

Mottled Umber

Green Pug

Peacock Moth

Leopard Moth

Poplar Hawkmoth

Riband Wave

Common Marbled Carpet

Brimstone Moth

Swallow-tailed Moth

Foxglove Pug

Green Carpet

male

female

Winter Moth

Canary-shouldered Thorn

Waved Umber

November Moth

Brindled Beauty

Buff Arches

Eyed Hawkmoth

Grey Shoulder-knot

Peach Blossom

Silver-ground Carpet

Oak Beauty

Ghost Moth

Shoulder-striped Wainscot

Barred Straw

Lime Hawkmoth

Poplar Grey

Blotched Emerald

Common Wainscot

Large Emerald

Buff-tip

Common Quaker

Clouded Drab

Maiden's Blush

Lilac Beauty

Blood-vein

Scorched Wing

Green Arches

Privet Hawkmoth

Figure of Eight

Lunar Marbled Brown

Drinker

Broom Moth

Pale Prominent

Pebble Prominent

Lappet

Powdered Quaker

Lesser Swallow Prominent

Puss Moth

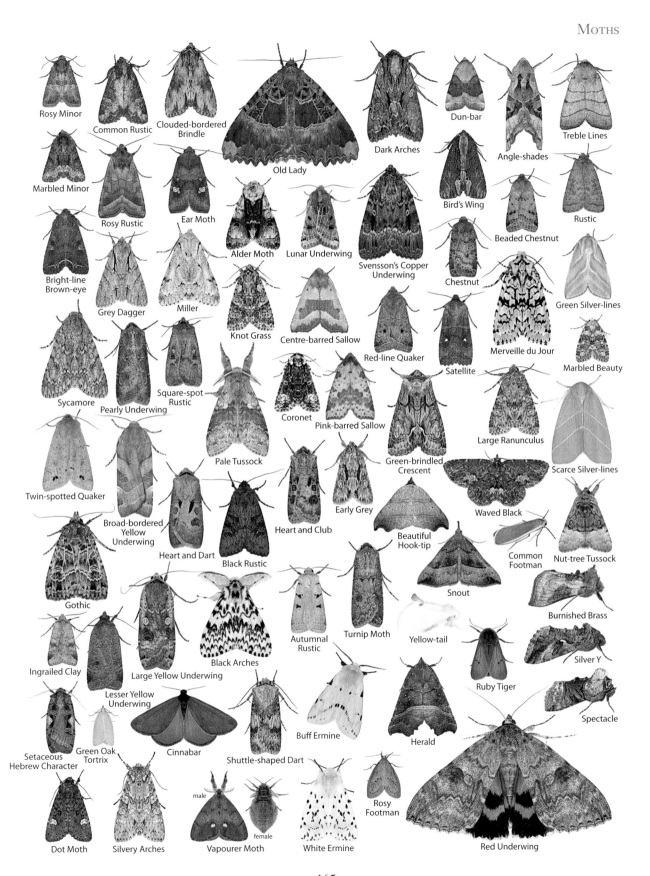

Rosy Minor

Common Rustic

Clouded-bordered Brindle

Old Lady

Dark Arches

Dun-bar

Angle-shades

Treble Lines

Marbled Minor

Rosy Rustic

Ear Moth

Bird's Wing

Rustic

Bright-line Brown-eye

Grey Dagger

Miller

Alder Moth

Lunar Underwing

Svensson's Copper Underwing

Beaded Chestnut

Chestnut

Green Silver-lines

Knot Grass

Centre-barred Sallow

Red-line Quaker

Satellite

Merveille du Jour

Marbled Beauty

Sycamore

Pearly Underwing

Square-spot Rustic

Coronet

Pink-barred Sallow

Green-brindled Crescent

Large Ranunculus

Scarce Silver-lines

Pale Tussock

Twin-spotted Quaker

Early Grey

Waved Black

Broad-bordered Yellow Underwing

Heart and Dart

Black Rustic

Heart and Club

Beautiful Hook-tip

Common Footman

Nut-tree Tussock

Gothic

Snout

Burnished Brass

Ingrailed Clay

Large Yellow Underwing

Black Arches

Autumnal Rustic

Turnip Moth

Yellow-tail

Ruby Tiger

Silver Y

Spectacle

Lesser Yellow Underwing

Setaceous Hebrew Character

Green Oak Tortrix

Cinnabar

Shuttle-shaped Dart

Buff Ermine

Herald

Dot Moth

Silvery Arches

male

female

Vapourer Moth

White Ermine

Rosy Footman

Red Underwing

DRAWN TO THE LIGHT

If you doubt the lure of illumination for night-flying moths then leave an outdoor light on after dark in the summer months to see for yourself. Taken a stage further, you can improve your catch by suspending a light over a white sheet outdoors, or you can buy or make a light trap where the moths are collected alive in a box beneath the light. The best light source is a bulb that emits ultraviolet light, to which moths are particularly receptive. Captured moths are seemingly unharmed by the experience and can be released after they have been studied and identified. Most captured moths tend to be males, reflecting the generalisation that males spend more time actively searching for females than vice versa.

On warm, humid nights exceptional catches can be made using a trap that employs a mercury vapour lamp.

BY THE LIGHT OF THE SILVERY MOON

One theory has it that moths use the Moon for navigation, or at least orientation. By maintaining a constant angle to this fixed reference point in the sky they can fly a straight course: because the Moon is so far away, the angle hardly changes even if the moth flies a considerable distance. On overcast nights man-made light sources appear brighter than the Moon to a moth's eyes, and if they use artificial light for orientation then they are in trouble: because the light source is so much closer to the moth than the Moon, the angle to the light changes dramatically over even a short flying distance. In an attempt to keep a constant angle, instead of flying in a straight line, the moth flies in a decreasing spiral, ever closer to the bulb.

Our Victorian entomologist forebears were well aware that moths are lured to light. In an era of gas lamps, an interesting observation on the subject was made by the Rev. J. G. Wood in his 1886 *Field Naturalist's Handbook*. In a section entitled General Hints he tells us that: 'For many moths artificial light has a wonderful attraction. Even in the crowded streets of London we may see moths fluttering round the lighted lamps.' After suggesting that athletic readers might try climbing lamps to remove trapped moths, he offers the following, slightly alarming advice for the collection and killing of specimens: 'It is a good plan to take the lamplighter into your service, and to pay him a certain sum for the moths which he can catch at the lamps. He may be safely entrusted with a cyanide bottle provided that you renew the poison yourself every two or three days. Do not try to make him understand the difference between common and valuable moths, but let him bring you all that he can catch. Never make a distinction in his presence and, above all, never throw away the worthless specimens until he is out of the way.'

Three Svensson's Copper Underwings and a Straw Underwing feasting on a sickly sweet 'sugaring' mixture.

SUGAR RUSH

Another tried and tested method for attracting certain species of moth is to lure them with food. The classic mixture involves dissolving sugar and treacle in warmed red wine or brown ale. If the mixture is reduced slowly over heat, it becomes thick and treacly and, when cooled, can be painted onto tree trunks and posts. Some moths find the mixture irresistible. 'Sugaring', as the technique is called, is more of an art than a science and catches are extremely variable; warm, muggy nights produce the best results.

PHEROMONES

A few years ago a neighbour gave me a couple of lengths of Grey Willow that he had cut in his garden because he had noticed at their heart were some sizeable boreholes. I stuck the cut ends in a bucket of water and promptly forgot about them until spring. On checking one day in May I noticed to my amazement that a Lunar Hornet Clearwing had emerged and was sitting there drying its wings.

Clearwings are the most atypical and enigmatic of moths. Although day-flying, they are incredibly hard to spot, being shy and seemingly wary of people. As the group's name suggests their wings are largely devoid of scales in most species. All have markings and behaviour that gives them more than a passing resemblance to various species of wasp, an evolutionary ploy, the mimicry serving as a deterrent to potential predators.

Many species of insects, especially nocturnal ones, use chemicals called pheromones, emitted by females to

A mating pair of Lunar Hornet Clearwings.

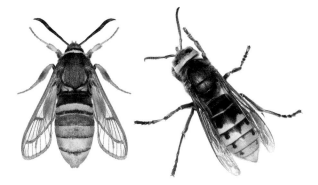

Few examples of mimicry are more impressive than the Lunar Hornet Clearwing (left) which does a convincing impression of a Hornet (right). The harmless moth cashes in on the Hornet's well-deserved fearsome reputation: not only does it look similar to a Hornet, but when disturbed it buzzes and flexes its body in an entirely believable way.

A Red-tipped Clearwing.

A furtive Red-tipped Clearwing lured close enough to photograph using pheromone lures.

It is no wonder that clearwing caterpillars are seldom encountered, since many live inside the stems or trunks of trees and shrubs. This Red-tipped Clearwing caterpillar was discovered inside a willow stem while pollarding. The stem was 'repaired', the caterpillar reared in captivity, and the emergent adult subsequently released.

attract males. That this behaviour also has relevance to diurnal insects was demonstrated by my Lunar Hornet Clearwing, which was a female: I turned my back and before I knew it a male had arrived out of nowhere and the pair had proceeded to mate. All UK clearwing species use pheromones as a means of attracting mates and this has led to the development of artificial lures that entomologists can use to attract males.

Lures provide the naturalist with a rare opportunity to observe what are otherwise extremely secretive insects. However, the formulation of these artificial pheromones was not undertaken with clearwing enthusiasts in mind and there is a darker side to the story. They were created to attract, catch and kill species that affect crops. Their origins notwithstanding, by using a range of lures, five clearwing species have been recorded in my garden in addition to the Lunar Hornet Clearwing.

THE CATERPILLAR CHALLENGE

Over the last 15 years I have recorded more than 400 species of adult moths in my garden, so clearly there's no shortage of adult lepidoptera. However, I really struggle to find their caterpillars, and over the years I have come across perhaps fifty species in my garden or close to home. But certainly not with any regularity or anything remotely approaching the numbers needed to feed a hungry brood of insectivorous birds. Given

the successful fledging of species such as Blackcap and Blue Tit in the garden, caterpillars are clearly present. So where are they hiding and why can't I find them?

Of course, failing eyesight may be part of my problem. However, my observational shortcomings notwithstanding, despite the relative abundance of moths in my garden, I have a suspicion that numbers are not what they once were, if Victorian entomologists are anything to go by. In *The Field Naturalist's Handbook*, the Rev. Wood writes that 'When I was at college, I had an average of eight or nine hundred larvae to feed and could not have done so had I not impressed a scout to run out during his few intervals of work, and procure food. Beside him a regular agent used to bring food daily, and I had one or two volunteer assistants as well.' Returning to the present, typically I might have just eight or nine (not eight or nine hundred) larvae on the go at any one time, and not for want of searching. But then again, that might be because it's just me, one person, working in the absence of scouts, servants or assistants.

Caterpillars have evolved all manner of ways to avoid being detected and eaten. Some are unpleasant to eat. Others employ defence strategies to deter predators – a coating of irritating hairs, for example. Many more prefer to avoid being seen in the first place and rely on camouflage, deception and entomological guerrilla tactics.

BEATING TRAYS

A tried and tested method of obtaining moth caterpillars, one much favoured by our Edwardian and Victorian forebears, was to hold an upturned umbrella (or specially made beating tray, or sheet on the ground) beneath a branch and whack it with a stick. While the method demonstrably works – insects and other invertebrates are indeed dislodged – it is by its very nature rather destructive. If you chance upon really productive foliage, hundreds of creatures will rain down and it is nigh on impossible to return all of them to their former home. In addition, many more will miss the tray, umbrella or sheet and fall into the surrounding vegetation. A few may be able to find their way back to the canopy but most will perish. If you do try this approach, do so with caution and try not to be overenthusiastic.

CLOSE INSPECTION

A more satisfying way of finding caterpillars is to patiently search. Many moth caterpillars are much more active after dark than they are in the daytime. Some remain inactive, hidden beneath leaves or clinging to stems, during the hours of daylight. Others undertake a daily migration, hiding low down on the foodplant (or even disappearing underground) in the day and climbing up the stems at night to feed.

Searching for caterpillars at night was accepted practice among Victorian entomologists and in *The Field Naturalist's Handbook*, the Rev. Wood advises the reader: 'After dark is perhaps the best time for discovering and capturing larvae, the light of a lantern bringing out their bodies in bold contrast to the leaves on which they are feeding.' Nowadays, LED torches are best, partly because they are so bright but also because the wavelengths of light that they emit seem to pick out invertebrates particularly well. Of course, none of this explains how insectivorous birds, which are active in the daytime, are so much more successful at finding caterpillars than I am. But then again, their lives depend on this ability.

During its time as a caterpillar (from April to June) this Red Underwing undertook a daily migration. During the daytime, it hid away in bark crevices on the trunk of the Crack Willow where it lived. After dark, it climbed several metres upwards and along stems to feed on the leaves, retracing its route as dawn approached.

Here we see the caterpillar of an Angle Shades moth feeding after dark, in this case eating the leaves of a cultivated, pot-grown pelargonium. During the hours of daylight, the caterpillar disappears from view, hiding among shrivelled, fallen leaves at the base of the plant; the only signs of its presence are nibbled leaves and a scattering of droppings.

Here is a selection of colourful, weird and wonderful moth caterpillars from my garden, alongside the adults that they turn into.

Caterpillars of the Cinnabar moth take on the chemical signature of their foodplant – ragwort species – and become toxic or unpleasant to predators. They make sure there is no mistaking who and what they are, and advertise themselves with striking orange and black stripes that are as unmistakable as they are diagnostic.

The Peppered Moth caterpillar looks like a twig, an ideal camouflage among the foliage of the various trees and shrubs on which it feeds. The adult moth flies from May to August.

The Mullein moth's caterpillar is whitish with numerous bold black spots and yellow patches; it feeds on mulleins, particularly Great Mullein. The adult moth, whose markings resemble flaking wood, flies in April and May.

The Early Thorn caterpillar is extremely twig-like and feeds on a range of native deciduous trees and shrubs. The species is double-brooded and adult moths fly in April and May, then again in August and September.

Caterpillars of the December Moth, which are finely speckled grey and yellow and resemble twigs in texture and colour, hide in plain sight. As the name suggests, adults fly in midwinter.

The Scalloped Hook-tip caterpillar feeds on birches and resembles a bit of shrivelled leaf; it often hides beneath a leaf during the daytime. The adult moth flies in May and June.

The Lappet moth's caterpillar is a contender for the largest British moth caterpillar – some individuals exceed 12cm in length. It feeds on Hawthorn and Blackthorn and rests lengthways to a stem, its hair-fringed lappets eliminating any tell-tale shadows. The adult moth flies in June and July and looks just like a fallen leaf.

The Buff-tip caterpillar is yellow-and-black and hairy, and feeds on birches and other trees. Working on the principle of safety in numbers, caterpillars congregate in groups for much of their lives. Adult moths fly in May and June.

The Lilac Beauty caterpillar feeds on Honeysuckle and Privet, and its projections and posture combine to create the appearance of dried leaf debris. The adult moth flies in June and July.

The Maple Prominent caterpillar has an angular outline, and when hiding beneath a leaf its coloration and shading match its surroundings; it feeds on Field Maple. Adult moths fly in May and June.

The Lobster Moth caterpillar is surely one of our strangest in appearance. It is ant-like in its first instar but fancifully crustacean-like when full grown. I do not know precisely what the full-grown caterpillar is attempting to mimic but it must be a success because it is incredibly difficult to find. It feeds on Beech, oaks and Hazel. The adult moth flies in May and June.

The Great Prominent caterpillar is green with diagonal stripes on each segment, which echo the veins of a leaf; it feeds on oaks. Adult moths fly in April and May.

The Knot Grass caterpillar is covered in irritating hairs and is brown with bold white dorsal spots, and a lateral white line adorned with red spots; its feeds on herbaceous plants. The species is double-brooded and adult moths fly in May and June, then again in August.

The Sycamore caterpillar is covered in irritating yellow hairs, and has orange tufts and black-ringed white dorsal spots; it feeds on Field Maple and Sycamore. Adult moths fly in June and July.

The Miller caterpillar is completely covered in long, silky hairs which serve to cloak its body and irritate anything that might attempt to eat it; it feeds on birches and other shrubs. Adult moths fly in May and June.

The Elephant Hawkmoth caterpillar comes in brown or green, and has black-and-white false 'eyespots'; when the caterpillar is agitated, the head-end can be contracted and swollen, enhancing the 'eyes' and perhaps scaring-off would-be predators. It feeds on willowherbs, particularly Rosebay Willowherb. Adult moths fly from May to June.

Guerrilla tactics: caterpillars have evolved a number of defence strategies and some use silken threads to abseil away from the threat.

REARING CATERPILLARS

Spend enough time in your garden or nearby countryside and sooner or later you will come across a few caterpillars. It can be a rewarding experience to rear them through to adulthood, and informative too if you are uncertain of the species. However, if you are not absolutely certain of a caterpillar's identity then it is probably best to only captive-rear individuals that you catch in the act of eating. Some moth caterpillars will only feed on the leaves of one species of plant and would sooner starve to death than eat the wrong thing.

Another approach is to rear moths from eggs. These can occasionally be found in the wild but a moth trap can provide a shortcut. Although most moths you catch are likely to be males, once in a while you will find a female. Distinguishing the sex of a moth is not easy in all species. If you have them side-by-side then females tend to be larger and plumper-bodied than males. However, that opportunity presents itself only occasionally. More reliably, in some larger moth species you can tell them apart by looking at the antennae: females have linear

antennae while those of the male are divided and feathery, the greater surface area this creates presumably aiding the detection of female pheromones.

It follows that if you find a moth that has feathery antennae it will be a male. If you do find a female, however, she will almost certainly have already mated and be capable of laying fertile eggs. Keep her for a few hours at dusk in a container with leaves of the caterpillar foodplant and there is a good chance she will lay some eggs. She can then be released to continue her life in the wild while you rear on the eggs. They normally take around 10–12 days to hatch depending on the species, and can be gently moved to fresh foodplant leaves near the predicted time of hatching using a wet paintbrush to soften the natural 'glue' that makes them adhere to the laying site.

Pale Oak Beauty female (above) and male (below), showing the difference between the appearance of the antennae typical of some moth species: linear in females, feathery in males.

The simplest approach is to keep your 'pet' caterpillar in a box that is sufficiently sealed to prevent escape but not airtight; air holes or a net covering are ideal.

Here are some dos and don'ts:

- Provide just sufficient fresh leaves to satisfy the feeding requirements of the caterpillar. Too much and there is a danger the vegetation will go mouldy.
- Change the food regularly (daily or every other day) and be sure to remove the old leaves and any droppings. Otherwise, the contents may go mouldy with a danger this will kill the caterpillar.

- Avoid handling or unduly disturbing your caterpillar – caterpillars are often sensitive and easily damaged, especially around the time they moult, which occurs several times.
- Don't overcrowd your container – keep just one or two caterpillars together.
- Keep the container dry and cool.
- Most moths will want to pupate at ground level or underground. When you judge that they are fully grown introduce some dry grass, leaves and mosses (checked for potential predators) and a layer of fine, dry soil.

If you decide you want to unearth your chrysalis or cocoon then delay this for at least two weeks from the time the caterpillar disappeared from view. Metamorphosis, the process whereby the caterpillar transforms into a chrysalis, is not speedy and it takes time for the chrysalis case and cocoon to harden. If the species in question lies dormant in winter and hatches in spring, be sure to replicate appropriate conditions: keep them cold, or in ambient outdoor temperatures, to avoid otherwise premature emergence in the dead of winter.

USING MOTHS TO INFORM BIODIVERSITY GARDEN MANAGEMENT

Identifying and recording adult moths in the garden is an interesting exercise in its own right and it is always useful to keep records to jog the memory in future years. Location and date are obviously important elements in the recording process and some people go to the length of noting, in addition, factors like prevailing weather and temperature.

Keeping records does, however, have a more significant role to play in the biodiversity garden, one that elevates it beyond the level of entomological trainspotting. Recording both species and numbers allows you to monitor the progress of your garden's growing suitability for wildlife, using moths as indicators.

If you want to maximise the garden's potential for wildlife, it is important to not only record species but link them to their caterpillars' foodplant requirements. This can inform, for example, how and when you manage operations like pruning shrubs and cutting grass, and what species you tolerate or encourage in any remaining ornamental or cultivated plots. Take, for

GARDEN TIGER

One of the few delights Basingstoke had to offer me as a child came at the start of the school summer holidays when I would wander the streets first thing in the morning in search of Garden Tiger moths. These I would find at the base of almost every lamppost I checked, the insects having been lured to the lights overnight. By the time I reached my teens, the moths had gone and it is at least 15 years since I last recorded the species in my garden.

As the name suggests, this moth was formerly a frequent sight in gardens across much of lowland Britain,

its hairy 'woolly bear' caterpillars having an eclectic diet that includes almost anything and everything a conventional gardener might consider a 'weed'. Nowadays, the Garden Tiger is a comparative rarity in the context of suburban and even rural gardens.

Predictably, the reasons underlying the species' decline have a human dimension. One theory has been linked to climate change: Garden Tiger moths overwinter as small caterpillars, in cocoons constructed at ground level in matted vegetation. So the theory goes, climate-change-driven increasingly mild wet Januarys followed by colder Februarys do not favour the overwintering stages.

However, I have a nagging feeling that the causes of the Garden Tiger's demise may lie closer to home. I am biased, but in this case I suspect I am right in reaching the following conclusion. That local extinction of the Garden Tiger is the result of an increasing prevalence of a tidy-minded, glyphosate-driven conventional gardening 'weed' control, and an obsession with hard landscaping, at least in the part of southern England where I live.

example a moth called the Blackneck whose caterpillars feed almost exclusively on Tufted Vetch. If I were to remove this plant from my herbaceous beds, I would deny food for the species' caterpillars, and if I dug the beds I would most likely kill its chrysalises.

New arrivals: Accidentally introduced to the UK from Asia on imported Box trees a couple of decades ago, the Box-tree Moth made its first appearance in my garden in 2022. It was a freshly emerged adult, indicating that the species had already bred there, the caterpillars feeding on the handful of Box trees that are a legacy from my days as a failed conventional gardener.

The fate of the Blackneck is inextricably linked to the presence or absence of its caterpillars' foodplant, Tufted Vetch.

Bees, wasps and allied insects

These fascinating insects are members of a large and complex group many of which defy accurate identification in the field. This is hardly surprising given their variety: depending on your source of reference there are between 6,500- 7,000 species in the UK, the vast majority being parasitic Hymenoptera. A common factor among those adults that are winged is that their membranous forewings and hindwings are linked together by means of tiny hooks, so they function and appear like a single wing. A conventional way of understanding the divisions within the group is to separate them into sawflies (Symphyta) and the rest – a group called Apocrita, itself split into (to generalise) bees and wasps capable of stinging, and parasitic wasps. Sawflies lack the 'waisted' appearance seen in other Hymenoptera where the abdomen meets the thorax.

Among insects, Hymenoptera have arguably the most varied and intriguing array of life histories and natural histories, perhaps matched only in complexity by beetles. Some live sophisticated and hierarchical social lives. Others are highly evolved parasites of other insects, with habits that are distinctly anti-social if you happen to be a potential host species. An interesting feature of the group's biology is that fertilised eggs become female

as adults while unfertilised eggs develop into males. This has shaped the social structure for many species.

Dig deeper into the literature on the subject of Hymenoptera and you will discover a complex web of intrigue and deception. It seems that for almost any species you care to mention another Hymenoptera species will have evolved to parasitise it, and there are parasites that parasitise the parasites. Rather than 'parasite' these Hymenoptera are probably better described as 'parasitoid', but that's a subject dealt with later in the section. Then there are kleptoparasites whose larvae feed on the provisions the host provided for its own offspring. And slave-making species who take over entire colonies and turn the workers to their own ends. For students of human nature and human history, there are so many parallels to be drawn between us and the world of Hymenoptera.

For the novice entomologist, the task of identifying Hymenoptera species without catching and killing them will seem daunting. However, don't let this put you off taking an interest in the group as a whole, specifically their behaviour and lifestyles generally. The more interest you take, the more you will realise just what an important role they play in the biodiversity garden, and

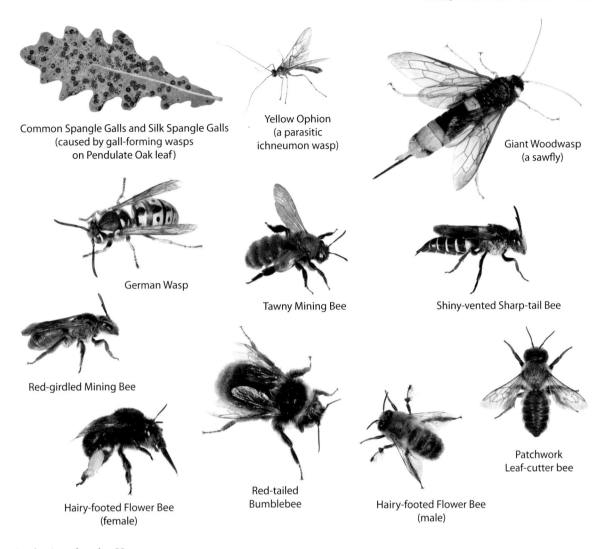

Common Spangle Galls and Silk Spangle Galls
(caused by gall-forming wasps
on Pendulate Oak leaf)

Yellow Ophion
(a parasitic
ichneumon wasp)

Giant Woodwasp
(a sawfly)

German Wasp

Tawny Mining Bee

Shiny-vented Sharp-tail Bee

Red-girdled Mining Bee

Patchwork
Leaf-cutter bee

Hairy-footed Flower Bee
(female)

Red-tailed
Bumblebee

Hairy-footed Flower Bee
(male)

A selection of garden Hymenoptera.

in the wider environment. Their functions range from pollination of flowers to predatory checks and balances on other invertebrates. Remove them and the web of life will cease to function in harmony; promote and celebrate them, and your life as well as the environment around you will be enriched. The following section covers the main groups of Hymenoptera, but restricts itself to those insects regularly encountered in my garden.

SAWFLIES

The bane of the lives of unenlightened conventional gardeners, sawflies are a varied group, some of which resemble flies, others looking rather like wasps or bees; there are 500 or so species in the UK. Despite the rather intimidating appearance of some of them, they are all harmless to humans and lack the ability to sting. The name 'sawfly' derives from the serrated margin to a female's ovipositor, which in some species is used to penetrate plant tissue and lay eggs.

Sawfly larvae are superficially like the caterpillars of moths and butterflies, but a close inspection will help you tell the difference. Both groups of insects have three pairs of true legs, just behind the head, plus sucker-like prolegs further down the length of the body: sawfly larvae have six or more pairs of prolegs while those of lepidoptera have five or fewer. Sawfly larvae also have a single pair of simple eyes, which in many of them resemble small black dots on the side of the head; moth caterpillars typically have two rows of half a dozen indistinct simple eyes. In some species of sawflies, the larvae are inclined to adopt a distinctive posture, with their tail-ends curled back above the body. They are often discovered in clusters and can defoliate entire plants in a matter of a few days. In terms of defence, if provoked some exude a fluid that is presumably unpalatable, and many are inclined to drop to the ground at the slightest disturbance. In addition to sawflies whose larvae feed externally on plant tissue, there are some species that live internally, inside stems and trunks. Regardless of how they live their larval lives, sawflies pupate, typically inside a hardened silk cocoon.

A typical sawfly.

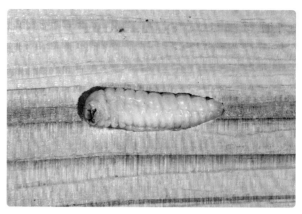

The larva of a wood-boring species of *Sirex*, living inside a pine log and inadvertently revealed when the wood was split.

A Green Sawfly.

The larva of the Figwort Sawfly is chalky-white and distinctive. Adults, which are on the wing in from May to August, are convincingly wasp-like and feed on other insects.

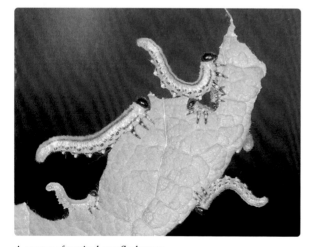

A group of typical sawfly larvae.

GALL-FORMING WASPS

A gall is an unusual and atypical growth form in a plant, one that has been induced by another organism. Many different types of insects, and indeed other forms of life, induce galls, and that includes a few species of sawflies. However, from the point of view of the casual naturalist and biodiversity gardener, those produced by so-called gall wasps (family Cynipidae) are among the most obvious and intriguing.

The detailed study of gall wasps and the galls they induce is a vast and complex subject and the domain of enthusiasts and experts. However, as with insects in general, the challenge of identification should not be a deterrent to interest or the pursuit of knowledge, particularly with regard to the extraordinary life cycles of some.

Look closely enough and almost any plant you care to mention will have a gall of some sort, not all of them caused by gall wasps, of course. Interestingly, many of these gall-inducers form the basis of a cascade of parasitic relationships. Although entomologically inaccurate, the principle of the proverbial saying 'Big fleas have little fleas upon their backs to bite 'em, and little fleas have lesser fleas, and so ad infinitum' holds true. In nature, it seems no species gets an easy ride through life. Here are a few examples to whet the appetites of curious minds.

Bedeguar Galls (or Robin's Pincushions)

If your plot of land harbours bushes of
-rose and related species, you may come across Bedeguar Galls, which are sometimes known as Robin's Pincushions. These are bright red, moss-like galls that adorn these plants, and for which a tiny wasp called *Diplolepis rosae* is responsible. By gall wasp standards the life cycle is uncomplicated. Males have been largely dispensed with and larvae will hatch from unfertilised

eggs. Adult females are on the wing in spring and early summer and lay their eggs inside leaf buds of the host shrub. The presence of a collection of larvae induces the formation of the distinctive galls and a new generation of adults emerges the following spring.

Oak Apples

If you have a mature Pedunculate or Sessile Oak in your garden or nearby, keep your eyes open for Oak Apples, which are formed from buds and appear on twigs in spring. These multi-chambered structures are induced

by the larvae of the sexual generation of a wasp called *Biorhiza pallida*, and each gall usually has single-sex occupancy. Winged adult wasps emerge in summer, and after mating, females lay eggs on surface tree roots of oaks. The larvae of the resulting asexual generation induce root galls, which differ in appearance to Oak Apples. From these galls a generation of wingless female wasps emerge in winter, and climb up the tree all the way from the roots to lay eggs in the buds. The larvae that emerge are the generation that induces the next cycle of Oak Apple formation.

Marble Gall

These distinctive galls are the work of a wasp called *Andricus kollari*, whose larvae live inside the spherical, marble-sized galls. The life cycle is more complex than first appears and involves both an alternation of sexual and asexual generations and different host species. Marble Galls can be found on the twigs of both Pedunculate and Sessile Oaks, and each contains a larva that is destined to become a winged asexual adult female. Look closely at mature, brown galls in late autumn and you will see tiny holes from which she will have emerged. These females lay eggs in the buds of non-native Turkey Oaks, and these develop in small galls and emerge in spring as a sexual generation comprising both males and females. Mated females proceed to lay eggs on the buds of Pedunculate and Sessile Oaks, Marble Galls appear and the cycle of life continues.

Knopper Galls

A relatively recent addition to the UK scene, these strange, distorted and knobbly galls form on the acorns of Pedunculate Oaks, and larvae of the tiny wasp *Andricus quercuscalicis* are responsible for their formation. Adults that emerge produce a second generation that develops in the catkins of Turkey Oak.

Cherry Galls

Aptly named Cherry Galls form on the undersides of oak leaves and are induced by the larvae of the tiny wasp *Cynips quercusfolii*. The galls remain attached to the leaf even after it falls in autumn and an asexual adult female wasp emerges in the winter. She goes on to lay eggs in oak buds, leading to the formation of smaller galls from which a sexual generation emerges and mates. Fertilised females lay eggs in young leaves and this leads to the formation of a new generation of Cherry Galls.

Cynips quercusfolii newly emerged from a Cherry Gall.

Common Spangle Galls and Currant Galls

Look beneath the leaves of oaks in autumn and sooner or later you will come across clusters of odd-looking flattened buttons. These are galls that form in response to the presence of the larvae of the asexual generation of a gall wasp. The commonest example, adorned with tufts of hairs, is the Common Spangle Gall and it is caused

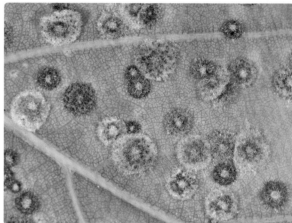

by a tiny wasp with a disproportionate mouthful of a name: *Neuroterus quercusbaccarum*. The galls eventually fall to the ground, the larvae mature during winter and the asexual generation of adults emerge in spring. These lay their eggs in oak catkins or leaves and result in the production of juicy-looking, aptly named Currant Galls. From these, the sexual generation of adults emerge and lay their eggs in the outer layer of oak leaves. The next batch of spangle galls is produced and the cycle continues. Appearing in similar spots, Silk Button Spangle Galls are aptly named and are induced by the larvae of a wasp called *Neuroterus numismalis*.

PARASITIC WASPS

The activities of members of this group are more accurately described as 'parasitoid' than 'parasitic'; the latter lifestyle involves exploiting the resources of a host but not killing it; whereas death is the inevitable outcome for a host 'parasitised' by one of these wasps. This distinction notwithstanding, 'parasitic' is the word with which the group is associated, and it best conveys their lifestyle in general terms. This is an extremely broad-church group that includes braconid and ichneumon wasps, some sizeable enough to be intimidating, others tiny enough to parasitise aphids, both adults and eggs. The fact that the group is rather neglected belies its significance in terms of representation in the UK fauna and some estimates put the species count at roughly a quarter of the entire UK insect fauna.

The problem with parasitic Hymenoptera is that many are almost impossible to identify to species level, even by experts, and among some genera there might be dozens of species that look superficially almost identical. *The Biodiversity Gardener* can do little more than to

An Eyed Hawkmoth caterpillar, eaten alive by the parasitoid wasp *Microplitis ocellatae* whose grubs and cocoons adorn its body.

AN UNINVITED GUEST

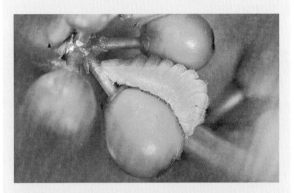

I raised this Holly Blue larva in captivity but what emerged from the resulting chrysalis was not a butterfly but the ichneumon wasp *Listrodromus nycthemerus*. Under normal circumstances I would not attempt to identify members of this challenging group of insects, but this parasitoid is well-studied and host-specific. The life cycle is straightforward if a little macabre: the adult wasp injects an egg into the plump body of a Holly Blue larva which is slowly but surely eaten alive. The larva continues to grow, but the charade ends following pupation because what emerges is not a butterfly but an adult ichneumon. A thorough account of the association between wasp and butterfly is given in Jeremy Thomas's book *The Butterflies of Britain and Ireland*, and an article by Richard Revels in the August 2006 edition of *British Wildlife* deals with the cyclical nature of the relationship. As populations of Holly Blue increase year on year, numbers of parasitoids follow in their wake a couple of years behind. When parasitoid numbers reach a level where most Holly Blue larvae are parasitised, the butterfly population crashes, followed inevitably by the population of wasps. The butterflies soon recover, the parasitoids follow suit, lagging behind by a year or two, and the cycle repeats itself.

The ichneumon wasp Listrodromus nycthemerus, *newly emerged from a Holly Blue chrysalis.*

restate the complexity and variety found in the UK and emphasise the significance of the group's members in terms of ecological checks and balances. By so doing, the aim is to foster a respect and fascination for the group.

A female parasitic wasp *Lissonota* spp. using her long ovipositor to penetrate the bark of Silver Birch in order to parasitise an insect inside, most likely a beetle larva.

CUCKOO WASPS

A number of superficially very similar members of the family Chrysidae are sometimes known as ruby-tailed wasps; the genera *Chrysis* and *Hedychrum* are examples. Collectively they are referred to as cuckoo wasps on account of their habits and lifestyle: they parasitise other Hymenoptera, notably mason bees and other solitary bees. Ruby-tailed wasps are restless creatures, constantly on the lookout, antennae twitching, for host nests. Once a nest has been discovered, the female wasp lays her eggs beside the host's eggs, and upon hatching the larvae eat those of the bee. If discovered in the act of egg-laying by the adult occupant of the nest, the ruby-tailed wasp does not give up without a fight. She

A typical ruby-tailed wasp.

curls into a defensive ball and the hard cuticle protects her from attack. As an observer, do not be fooled by its small size and beautiful appearance because this masks a painful sting, another means of defence against being attacked by the host.

SOLITARY WASPS

I am not fortunate enough have a garden that hosts solitary wasp species other than as occasional visitors. Unlike their more familiar social counterparts, which we will come to, these include species that immobilise living invertebrates ranging from caterpillars to spiders. They bury their quarry underground in excavated chambers or specially constructed paper nests, their fate to act as living larders and be consumed alive by the larvae of the solitary wasps.

SOCIAL WASPS

The wasps encountered most frequently in my garden are social wasps. As most people will be aware, these are capable of delivering a painful sting, and they are adorned with colours and markings that serve to warn the unwary of their abilities. They construct architecturally

The nest of a Hornet or wasp is an incredible feat of construction, extremely robust and yet made from the insect equivalent of papier-mâché. The coordinated efforts of the colony's workers is little short of miraculous.

Some species such as the Norwegian Wasp nest in trees, sheltered from sun and rain by the foliage.

BEES

The term 'bee' is a rather general and unscientific way of describing members of the family Apidae, insects that live varied lives according to species. The Honey Bee and bumblebees are social insects, but others live mostly solitary existences. Bees feed primarily on nectar and pollen, depending on the life-cycle stage. Females have a defensive sting and most have pollen baskets. Bees have evolved alongside flowering plants with mutually beneficial relationships being the driving force. Cross-pollination occurs when the bees move from flower to flower, and they are rewarded with sugar-rich nectar and sometimes pollen. Bees have tongues of varying length according to the species, each suited to a range of varyingly specific plants. Some bumblebees bypass the plant/insect relationship by chewing directly into the nectary of the flower.

BUMBLEBEES

Among members of the bee tribe, bumblebees are the most easily recognised. However, this easy recognition masks the fact that there are more than 20 species in the UK, each adapted to subtle and not-so-subtle differences in natural history. There are, for example, long-tongued and short-tongued species, each suited to feeding on (and hence pollinating) an entirely different range of plants; and some species that are habitat-specific.

Broadly speaking, bumblebee life histories are similar across the species range. Queen bumblebees overwinter, often in a subterranean chamber, and sometimes in holes in banks (notably the Red-tailed Bumblebee) that are used winter after winter. They emerge on warm days

impressive nests from what is, in essence, paper paste – chewed wood mixed with saliva. A summer nest is likely to contain several thousand sterile female workers whose job it is to help rear more workers, along with smaller numbers of queens and males. Only young queens survive the winter and do so by hibernating in a sheltered crevice, sometimes indoors or in sheds, emerging in spring to start the cycle again.

Social wasps are fond of fruit and other sweet substances, but the larvae are also fed on the chewed-up remains of insects. Hornets, the largest of our social wasps, are voracious predators and include in their diet other wasps and bees; in my garden the appearance of a Hornet colony usually spells the beginning of the end for colonies of other species nearby. Identification of most wasp species can be achieved by looking at the markings on the face. Some wasp species nest underground while others, including Hornets, frequently site their nests in roof spaces or sheds, along with more natural choices such as tree holes.

An Early Bumblebee foraging for nectar and pollen.

in early spring to begin the process of nest-building. A queen's first task is to restore her depleted reserves by drinking nectar, and then she can begin to build her nest. Early flowers visited in my garden include sallow catkins, and the flowers of hellebores and lungwort. Nests are typically located underground, sometimes in an abandoned vole nest. The queen makes a mound of wax and pollen on which eggs are laid, and then fashions wax pots filled with nectar. The eggs are incubated by the queen, kept warm by heat generated by her body. The developing larvae are fed on pollen and nectar that she collects and, following a brief period of pupation, the first adults to appear are female workers that help carry on where the queen started. They help to enlarge the colony, doing most of the fetching and carrying while she lays more eggs. Males appear on the scene in summer and mated future queens prepare for the coming months by fattening up before searching for a sheltered hibernation site to spend the winter. Other members of that season's colony gradually die off as temperatures drop and nectar sources disappear.

Alongside bumblebees are a sister group known as cuckoo bumblebees, which, as their name suggests, do not have the best of intentions where their hosts are concerned. Almost every bumblebee species seems to be targeted, and the process begins when a female cuckoo bumblebee enters a bumblebee hive and kills the queen. By what means who knows, but she then employs her host bumblebee workers to do her bidding and rear her offspring. I do not doubt their existence, of course, but I must admit I find it hard to be sure I have seen a cuckoo bumblebee in the field; a shiny dorsal surface to the abdomen, along with subtly smoky rather than clear wings, are identification pointers.

Over the last century, and specifically in the space of my lifetime, bumblebee numbers have declined alarmingly, in some instances catastrophically. Two species have become extinct in the UK and many are extinct or close to extinction at the local level. The underlying causes of their decline are changes in agricultural land use, specifically loss of flower-rich habitat and undisturbed soil, and more recently the use of agrochemicals. Their plight is no different from that of other less iconic groups of invertebrate wildlife, but being perceived as 'cuddly' has meant them becoming the 'poster children' for invertebrate diversity loss; their presence or absence being a symbolic indication of the health or sickness of the land. For any landowner with an open mind and a pricked environmental conscience, bumblebees, like other forms of invertebrate life, have an integrated role to play in the ecology of the countryside, in their case pollination.

The danger with icons is that, in the case of bumblebees, it can lead people to think of the group as a unified whole, with a simplistic notion that by benefitting any bumblebee you are benefitting all. That is not the case. Some are highly flower species– and habitat-specific, and no amount of planting in the garden is going to bring a heathland or upland species, for example, back from the brink of extinction. For a full and through guide to bumblebees, Dave Goulson's book *Gardening for Bumblebees: A Practical Guide to Creating a Paradise for Pollinators* is a must read. See the References section for details.

A Common Carder Bee.

A mating pair of White-tailed Bumblebees, a behaviour that is seldom observed.

HONEY BEES

I am rather partial to honey and until recently I had not thought an awful lot about the environmental consequences of beekeeping. That was, until I came across a bit of environmental propaganda associated with a planned Solar Park. In an attempt to demonstrate a positive outcome for wildlife (biodiversity net gain) the green-hyped proposal was to scatter a few seeds of mainly annual plants to create the illusion of a healthy meadow, the claim being that it then benefitted native pollinators. Needless to say, the precise species that would benefit were not specified. How could they be? But generic 'bumblebees' were cited. Anyway, as a further sweetener, literally and metaphorically, they also proposed introducing to the mix battalions of beehives. That set me thinking: how would the meagre benefits for native insects not be affected by competition from what is in essence a domesticated species being introduced on an industrial scale and accessing the same sources of nectar?

The consensus seems to be that the Western Honey Bee, to give it its full title, is extinct in the UK as a wild species; swarms that you may come across now and then are dispersing refugees that originate from man-made hives. Nowadays, the status of the Honey Bee in the UK is that of a domesticated animal, one whose role has more to do with agricultural economics than nature, and whose products – honey and wax – are valued in financial terms.

The conclusion I have come to with regard to my modest plot of meadow is that I will not contemplate introducing a hive of honey bees into the mix. I want to encourage interactions between native flowers and the struggling native insect species that visit and depend on them. The supply of nectar provided by any given native flower is not limitless. The addition of 30,000–40,000 honey bees – that's said to be the size of a typical hive in summer – to the mix, all wanting to feed on largely the same flowers, would for me provide an unacceptable level of competition for beleaguered native insects such as bumblebees.

OTHER GARDEN BEES

It would take a lifetime to get to grips fully with the UK's bee fauna and this is necessarily a rather superficial, unscientific and selective roundup of potential garden candidates. Nevertheless, as with all groups of wildlife, a lack of knowledge should not discourage an informed enthusiasm for the subject. In terms of appearance and life histories there is a lot to be enthusiastic about.

Apart from bumblebees, the remaining bee species I come across in my garden are solitary. Restricted by limited prime real estate nesting habitat, a few may appear to be colonial but, in reality, these are congested colonies of individuals not linked by any collective purpose. Amongst their number are homeless or nomad bees *Nomada* spp. that are kleptoparasites of solitary mining bees of the genus *Andrena*.

Then there are so-called blood-bees *Sphecodes* spp. that are kleptoparasites of other bees such as species of furrow bee *Lasioglossum* spp.: they invade the nests of their host, lay their eggs on the food store, and often kill and eat the host's own eggs or larvae into the bargain.

Once in a while, I spot a mason bee in my garden, typically a species called the Red Mason Bee. The construction of my cottage does not suit its requirements

The Tawny Mining Bee is an enthusiastic visitor to the flowers of currants in spring and nests in the garden. The entrances to their burrows appear like miniature volcanoes of soil here and there in the lawn. Their liking for open areas is a good reason for keeping some areas of grass mown regularly

because, as its name suggests, it has a liking for soft mortar between the brickwork of old walls and houses. The bee excavates a chamber in which to build its nest cells and, in the manner of a true professional, seals the entrance by rendering over them when she has finished. This species is an important beneficiary of artificial

● BEE HOMES, HOTELS AND HIGH-RISE

As an antidote to loss of nesting habitat, and in compensation for any tidy-minded neighbours you might have, try providing those solitary bees that nest in natural tubes with artificial nest sites. At its simplest, just cut lengths of bamboo into 15cm sections, tie them in bundles and place them strategically and horizontally in secure locations off the ground, preferably in a spot that receives plenty of sun. If you are feeling ambitious, you can always create your own high-rise 'hotel', stocking each 'room for let' with different offerings, such as drilled logs as well as hollow canes; this will soon become an extremely popular insect Airbnb. You will be amazed at how quickly the tubes and crevices are colonised and you are likely to get a wide range of species using your hotel. However, as a word of warning for those who are keen to identify their guests: where you think you might have half a dozen species, there are likely to be double that number or more. There are plenty of look-alikes to provide confusion, and certain identification of living bees in the field is not always possible.

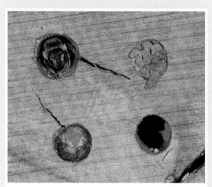

These 8–9mm-diameter holes (roughly 10cm long), drilled in a log to create a durable 'bee home', were soon occupied in early summer by Patchwork Leaf-cutter Bees. Having created a series of cells inside each tube, made from cut leaves and each containing an egg and provisioned with pollen and nectar, the filled tubes were eventually sealed with mud.

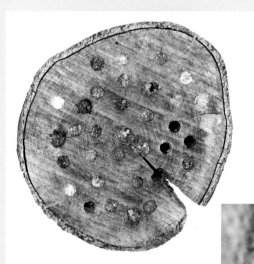

Logs drilled with 3mm-diameter holes will be favoured by a range of small solitary bee species. I have tentatively identified the ones using this log as including a species of yellow-faced bee and the other a member of the genus Heriades, perhaps H. truncorum. The tubes were also occupied by other as-yet unidentified solitary bees, along with attendant parasitoid wasps.

'bee homes' – stacked hollow tubes. In areas where the underlying soil is calcareous, a related species called *Osmia bicolor* shows there are no limits to the ingenuity of nature when an opportunity presents itself. The female bee makes her nest in an empty snail shell, seals it, orientates it so the entrance faces the ground, then camouflages it with vegetation.

If you have a keen eye, you may have come across leaves on rosebushes with perfectly semi-circular holes cut from them. These are the work of leaf-cutter bees. Females, which cut the holes with their sharp mandibles, make good use of these leaf fragments, folding and chewing them to create incubation pots for their offspring. The leaf-cutter female visits flowers, collecting pollen and nectar to stock her rose-leaf pots as food for her young. In nature a series of these incubation pots are often placed in excavated holes or in an abandoned timber beetle tunnel or borehole; they may be attracted to man-made 'bee houses' made of hollow bamboo canes. Leaf-cutters are parasitised by sharp-tail bees (see image on p. 175) that lay their eggs beside that of the host, their larvae eating first the host egg or larva inside, then its provisions.

A female Patchwork Leaf-cutter Bee returning to her nest tube with a neatly cut portion of rose leaf.

ANTS

If you are a naturalist and want to depress yourself then do a Google search for 'ants' and see how many listings portray these amazing insects as 'pests'. On a more positive note, you will also find sites where you can buy ants to keep as pets, so it is not all bad. From the perspective of a biodiversity gardener, I see them as essential ingredients in a healthy environment. Until I began biodiversity gardening, and meadow restoration in particular, I failed to appreciate just what a significant role ants play in the environment. Alongside earthworms I now see them, not me, as the real gardeners of my plot.

As far as I aware there are three species of ant that occur in good numbers in my garden, the proviso being that there is an array of superficially similar species to potentially confuse matters. Among their number is a species of black ant *Lasius* spp., which to my non-specialist eye looks like Common Black Ant. I come across colonies beneath paving slabs and most of the time these comprise egg-producing queens and sterile wingless female workers. These are the ants that 'garden' aphid aggregations, milking them for honeydew, guarding them against predators and setting chemical trails for others of their kind to follow to and from their colony. In the summer months winged males and females appear, their

In nature, small solitary bee species use dead, snapped and hollow stems of Bramble as nest sites. Remove or destroy these and you will not most likely kill a generation of these insects and remove potential nest sites for others in the area and for future generations.

A colony of ants and pupae exposed accidentally while moving a paving slab.

Winged queen ants emerging for their maiden flight.

emergence seemingly triggered by hot, humid weather in the wake of a heavy rainfall. Both sexes take flight and after mating the males die while females shed their wings and become queens of a new colony. In addition, my garden hosts a species of red ant *Myrmica* spp. that I take to be the Common Red Ant, and conspicuous

mounds are created by the Yellow Meadow Ant. The diet of the latter species includes root-associated aphids and other insects, and they function as part of the natural checks and balances of a healthy environment. Landowners beware: you disturb and disrupt your soil and kill its ant colonies at your peril.

Beetles

'If He exists, the Creator has an inordinate fondness for beetles'. That is the reply attributed to J. B. S. Haldane (1892–1964), mathematician, evolutionary biologist and all-round scientific polymath, when asked about the relationship between God and the natural world. By tongue-in-cheek inference, this possibly apocryphal quote can also be seen as a defence of Darwin's theories regarding natural selection. I too have an inordinate

fondness for beetles and although I am keen to study them, the more I learn about them, the more I realise how little I know. For any natural historian with a modicum of experience and self-awareness they are a humbling group.

Beetles belong to the order Coleoptera, and in terms of number of species they hold the world record at more than 400,000; even here in the UK more than

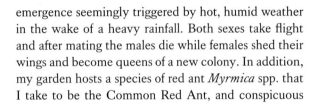

A Red-headed Cardinal Beetle taking flight: the hardened elytra (modified forewings) are spread allowing the membranous hindwings to unfurl.

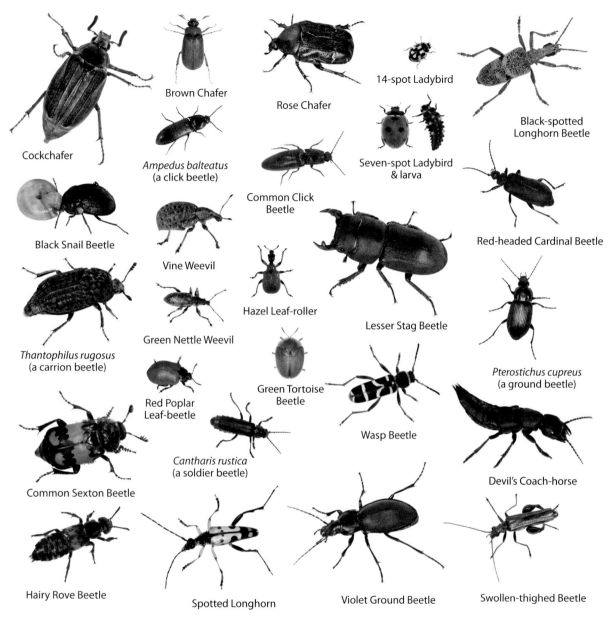

A selection of beetles from my garden.

4,000 species have been recorded. Beetles vary in size considerably, from insects hardly bigger than a flea to the bulky Stag Beetle at the other end of the scales. They are variable in terms of shape as well. However, a constant among those species whose adults have wings is that the forewings form median-aligned hardened cases (known as elytra) that conceal and protect the more delicate membranous hindwings at rest. To fly, the elytra are opened and spread and the hindwings unfold.

Beetle life cycles involve adults, which mate and lay eggs from which larvae emerge and grow. A pupal stage allows metamorphosis into the next generation of adult beetles, which have biting mouthparts, the precise structure of which, depending on species, allows them to tackle almost any and every source of organic matter. At various stages in their life cycles, there are representatives that are active predators; ones that bore into wood or eat stored grain; species that feed on pollen, leaves or other plant material; and a few that eat dead and rotting animals. In addition to terrestrial species, a few beetles have evolved to become aquatic, although when it comes to dispersal not necessarily severing their ties with the terrestrial world entirely; they are discussed on p. 238.

Given the size of the group and the scope of the book, *The Biodiversity Gardener* can only scratch the surface on the subject of beetles, and provide a taste of what might lurk on your doorstep. The following account will hopefully inspire any budding coleopterist, and provide an indication that you do not necessarily have to travel far from home to satisfy your curiosity – the exact opposite, in fact. If you are an absolute beginner in the field of beetles, it is probably no exaggeration to say that if you spend an hour or so a day searching there is a reasonable chance you could add a new species to your garden list every day from early spring to late autumn, such is the diversity of beetles. The following is an account of some of the regularly encountered terrestrial groups I have come across in the garden, with an emphasis placed on iconic and eye-catching species. Aquatic beetle species are discussed on p. 238. Given the size of the group to which beetles belong, I make no apology for this account being selective, personal and only superficially scientific; its role is to inspire.

GROUND BEETLES (FAMILY CARABIDAE)

These are active and voracious predators that are primarily ground-dwelling and mainly nocturnal. They are always keen to explore crevices and gaps beneath stones and

A Violet Ground-beetle.

fallen logs or under flaky bark, and these are the sorts of places to look for them. In some species the elytra are fused, presumably an adaptation that further protects their bodies as they scurry around in sometimes unstable environments. Of the many ground beetle species in my garden, the largest and most impressive species is the Violet Ground Beetle, which is black and shiny with a violet sheen to the margins of its elytra. Although I see the species only occasionally in my garden, I suspect that is for want of searching. As to what it eats, I imagine its diet extends to almost any invertebrate it comes across that cannot flee or fight back.

ROVE BEETLES (FAMILY STAPHYLINIDAE)

A typical rove beetle.

These beetles vary in size from tiny insects just a few millimetres long to species several centimetres in length. Despite the size range, generally they are all recognisable as 'staphys', as they are affectionately known, and have slender, elongate bodies and short elytra. As their names suggests, they are constantly on the move, and for their size they scurry along at great speed, freezing now and again as if to take stock of their surroundings before continuing their frantic activities. The diet of rove beetles is presumed to include scavenged organic material, given the predilection of many species for animal dung and corpses. There is a possibility, of course, that they visit these seemingly unappealing locations in search of prey – other insects, both adults and their larvae. One look at the intimidating jaws of a Devil's Coach-horse (see illustration on p. 187), the largest UK rove beetle, and these suspicions will be confirmed. The species is a regular in my garden and, like many of its kind, if cornered or provoked it curls its abdomen in the manner of a scorpion and emits a foul, off-putting smell.

BURYING BEETLES (FAMILY SILPHIDAE)

These are the undertakers of the beetle world, and most people are completely unaware of their presence in or around the garden. Evolution has taken them in a rather macabre direction: their life cycles are dependent on corpses. Depending on the species, they bury either small creatures whole or portions of larger ones underground, excavating the soil beneath and slowly but surely interring their prize, thereby transporting it into the underworld. Eggs are laid close to this subterranean carrion and it serves as food for the resulting larvae; the larvae of other carrion-feeding

Several species of burying beetle occur in my garden, identified by their subtly different orange-red markings.

insects are likely to feature in their diet as well. Despite burying beetles' virtues as insect pallbearers, there is no odour of sanctity about them – quite the opposite, in fact. The deeply unpleasant aroma they emit is matched by their sense of smell and ability to detect the wafting scent of decay from a considerable distance.

Assuming that you are not of a squeamish disposition, you can try an experiment to discover their presence near you. If you come across a dead mouse or roadkill

A Sexton Beetle investigating a dead shrew.

Rabbit, enclose it in a large-mesh chicken wire cocoon and peg it out in a quiet corner of your garden. Every few days, lift the corpse and inspect beneath, and the chances are you will find burying beetles have arrived along with a whole array of other beetle and insect species, all keen to make use of this organic bonanza. If you question the vital role that burying beetles play in the cycle of death and life, imagine the world in their absence, one littered with slowly decaying corpses on show all around. The Black Snail Beetle, a relative of the classic burying beetles, has more active and predatory instincts, and I come across it now again when I turn over logs or stones. It is a specialist snail feeder with a head and mouthparts adapted to the task (see illustration on p. 187).

STAG BEETLES (FAMILY LUCANIDAE)

This is an iconic group of beetles, and although the namesake is absent from my garden the two other UK members of the group do occur. The Lesser Stag

A Lesser Stag Beetle.

A Lesser Stag Beetle larva.

Beetle is a about half the size of its larger cousin and its small 'antlers' notwithstanding, it is nevertheless an impressive beast. Its larvae live inside dead and decaying wood, and in my garden that usually means fallen logs and branches that I have stacked around the margins. Burn this material and the chances are you will kill this wonderful insect. Despite its diminutive size, the Rhinoceros Beetle (see photograph on p. 108) is also impressive and it too is associated with dead and decaying wood, its larvae feeding on this material. In my garden, the most sizeable colony lives in a standing dead skeleton of a cherry tree, whose limbs are slowly but surely falling. Had I been inclined to fell and burn the tree I would have killed the entire colony of Rhinoceros Beetles.

SCARAB BEETLES
(FAMILY SCARABEIDAE)

These are a group that includes tropical Goliath and Hercules beetles. As their names suggest these are the largest insects on the planet. UK representatives are smaller but still include some fascinating insects, such as dung beetles. Among their number I see Dor Beetles lumbering across tracks nearby although I have not seen the species in the garden as yet. I do, however, come across dung-loving members of the genus *Aphodius*, notably *A. rufus*. Also included in the family are the chafers, the most conspicuous being the Cockchafer. Its larvae feed on plant roots and are despised by unenlightened conventional gardeners but beloved of any predator that discovers them.

In line with their alternative name of Maybug, the first two weeks of that month usually sees good numbers of Cockchafers on the wing in the garden. As an indication of abundance, on 9 May 2022 I recorded 67 in my moth trap. Conventional gardeners would probably call that an infestation. For me it is a sign that invertebrate populations in my garden are in a healthy state.

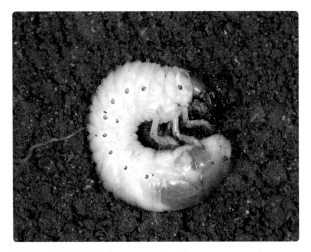

A juicy Cockchafer larva unearthed from a compost heap.

A Summer Chafer.

CLICK BEETLES (FAMILY ELATERIDAE)

These are a distinctive group whose members are overall rather cylindrical and by insect standards armour-plated. If an individual falls on its back it will try to correct this by catapulting itself into the air. On the principle of 'If at first you don't succeed, try, try again,' it continues its endeavours until it lands on its feet. The means by which this gymnastic feat is achieved involves arching the body, flexing a thoracic joint and applying tension to a peg-like projection that normally rests against the body. Eventually the tension is too much, the peg slips, the body snaps back into alignment and the energy is enough to project the insect skyward. The process is accompanied by an audible 'click' from which the group's common name derives. The most regularly encountered species in the garden is the Common Click Beetle, and its larvae, sometimes called wireworms, live underground, eat roots and shoots, and are reviled by conventional gardeners. *Ampedus balteatus* is its more colourful cousin and one that I encounter only occasionally in the garden.

SOLDIER BEETLES (FAMILY CANTHARIDAE)

These are said to have acquired their common name because their colours are reminiscent of military uniforms; dress uniforms, I assume, rather than combat gear. They have rather elongated bodies and relatively long antennae and the most regular species in my garden, the Common Red Soldier

Cantharis rustica, a typical soldier beetle.

Beetle, seems to spend most of its time visiting flowers, notably umbellifers such as Hogweed. Although its diet includes pollen and nectar, it is also a predator of other flower-visiting insects. A sister species, *Cantharis rustica*, has similar habits, and the larvae of both are active predators of invertebrates, roaming among leaf litter and soil debris, and hunting under loose bark.

A Common Click Beetle taking flight.

FURNITURE BEETLES (FAMILY ANOBIIDAE)

There are signs of the past activities of the Furniture Beetle or Woodworm in the cottage, but that comes as no surprise given its age. It is the larvae, not the adult, that tunnel into wood, their attentions focussed on softer options, so sapwood rather than heartwood of oaks, but all parts of Beech and elm. A large colony can soon turn dry wood to friable dust. In the context of a house, their actions can be seen as destructive. In nature, however, they perform a vital role: consuming and digesting dead timber and recycling the nutrients therein. Thankfully, I have not recorded its cousin, the notorious Death-watch Beetle, in the house or garden, as yet. If I did that would give me a bit of a dilemma – prioritise the conservation of a 400-year-old timber-framed building or the conservation of a native insect. I am not sure what the outcome would be.

An adult Furniture Beetle.

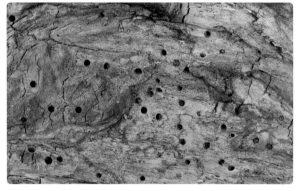

In nature, Furniture Beetle larvae construct tunnels inside dry, dead wood and play a vital role in the recycling of nutrients back to the soil.

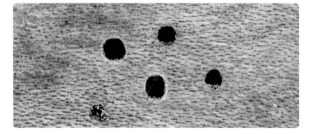

Woodworm attacks on furniture and indoor woodwork are less welcome.

CARDINAL BEETLES (FAMILY PYROCHROIDAE)

These beetles are aptly named, with the adults having mainly bright-red bodies, and two species (the Black-headed Cardinal Beetle and Red-headed Cardinal Beetle) are regularly encountered. They are active in bright sunshine, wandering over foliage, visiting flowers and sometimes taking flight. The larvae are associated with dead timber, residing beneath fallen branches and under bark. In the absence of this microhabitat, you will not have cardinal beetles breeding in your garden. See photographs on pp. 186 and 187.

LADYBIRDS (FAMILY COCCINELLIDAE)

These beetles need little introduction, their domed bodies adorned with colourful markings making their kind distinctive and instantly recognisable. Of the 45 or so species in the UK you might come across half a dozen or more in the garden, all of which will be predatory both as adults and larvae. They appear to be a group that has evolved to exploit aphids as a source of food, and it goes without saying that any biodiversity gardener should celebrate the latter to encourage the former. The most familiar species in my garden used to be Seven-spot Ladybird, Two-spot Ladybird and Eyed Ladybird. For a while, their status was overshadowed by a newcomer, the Harlequin Ladybird, with worrying fears it might displace others thanks to its extremely predatory habits. Although it is too soon to be sure, its numbers in my garden seem to be in decline, and it has possibly reached an equilibrium with its cousins. Regardless of species, all ladybirds overwinter in a state of dormancy,

A Seven-spot Ladybird.

typically in natural crevices and amongst plant debris. Burn fallen leaves or cut vegetation and the likelihood is you will be incinerating ladybirds. Assuming you are the sort of person who would not stamp on a ladybird, why would you burn one?

LONGHORN BEETLES (FAMILY CERAMBYCIDAE)

These are easily recognised by the long antennae that give the group its common name. Adults of some species feed on pollen while their larvae bore into the timber of trees and shrubs or inhabit the stems of larger herbaceous plants. While they may not be welcomed by commercial foresters, they are part of the web of life of any healthy woodland. The Wasp Beetle, with its distinctive black and yellow markings, is an occasional visitor but its cousin the Spotted Longhorn – its markings more yellow than black – is regular on flowers of many kinds in the garden. Once in a while I also come across the slightly furry-looking Black-spotted Longhorn Beetle feeding on Common Hawthorn flowers; its larvae live under the bark of fallen, decaying branches.

A Black-spotted Longhorn Beetle taking to the wing.

A Wasp Beetle, exploring the flowers of a cultivated spurge.

FALSE BLISTER BEETLES (FAMILY OEDEMERIDAE)

The Swollen-thighed Beetle is the member of this group most frequently encountered in my garden. It has narrowing, flared elytra that barely conceal the hindwings. Males possess distinctively swollen femora (the 'thighs') on their hind legs, the purpose of which is unclear. Like most of its relatives, it has a metallic sheen. Its larvae have been discovered – not by me – inside the stems of thistles, so that's another reason for treating meadow plants with more respect than as just a crop to be harvested.

LEAF BEETLES (FAMILY CHRYSOMELIDAE)

As a group these beetles have rather squat, rounded bodies with a metallic-looking sheen, and many species are colourful. Adults and their plump, grub-like larvae have vegetarian diets and many have a fondness for nibbling a patchwork of holes in leaves, sometimes eventually defoliating sprays of foliage. As its name suggests the Mint Leaf Beetle occurs on species of mint in the garden while the Green Dock Beetle is found on its namesake plant in damp spots.

A hungry Viburnum Leaf Beetle on Guelder-rose in my hedgerow.

A mating pair of Green Dock Beetles, on the leaf of Broad-leaved Dock.

The female Hazel Leaf-roller lives up to its name, rolling a Hazel leaf which protects the larva as it feeds and grows.

WEEVILS (FAMILY CURCULIONIDAE)

These are an intriguing group some of which remind me vaguely of cartoon characters. In many cases their bodies are compact and cylindrical or round, but the defining character is found at the front of the head: a snout-like beak or rostrum with mouthparts located at the tip and antennae located along its length. Weevil elytra are often hairy and occasionally fused in species that are flightless. They are vegetarians, their larvae living inside plant tissue including fruits, nuts and stems, concealed by leaves, or among roots, as is the case with the Vine Weevil.

The Acorn Weevil is associated with oaks, the female boring into a young acorn with her rostrum before inserting an egg. The larva eats the acorn and eventually bores its way out.

The Birch Leaf-roller lives its larval life inside the rolled outer half of a birch leaf, eventually pupating inside the shrivelled remains.

The Vine Weevil, whose larvae feed on plant roots, is common in my garden and is found mostly after dark with the aid of a torch.

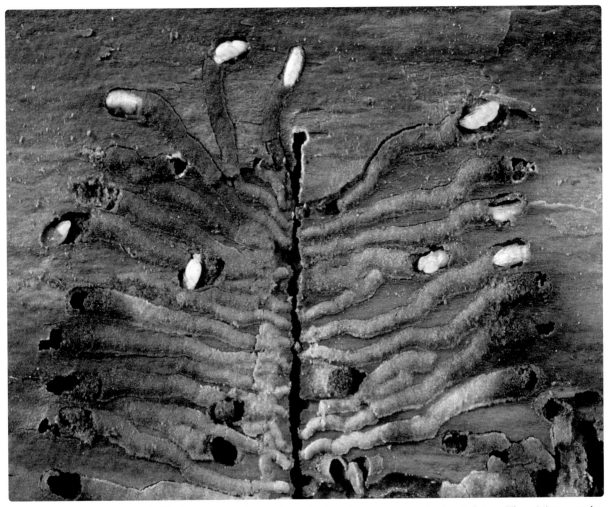

Galleries excavated by the grub-like larvae of a typical bark beetle, found beneath the bark of an Ash tree. These juicy morsels provide a tasty meal for birds such as Nuthatches and woodpeckers, which have bills capable of targeting this source of food.

BARK BEETLES (FAMILY SCOLYTIDAE)

These beetles spend virtually their entire lives beneath the bark of trees, eventually leading to peeling bark and in some cases tree death. In the case of the Large Elm Bark Beetle, its impact on the countryside has been profound as it unwittingly spreads the fungus *Ophiostoma novo-ulmi*, the causal agent of Dutch Elm Disease. Unknown in Europe before the start of the twentieth century, the fungus is said to have been introduced from Asia, mostly likely through the transportation of infected timber. In this part of north Hampshire, magnificent stately elms still graced hedgerows here and there when I was growing up. Sadly, they are now a thing of the past.

MY BEETLE WISH LIST

Over the years I have a recorded a respectable selection of beetles in my garden. However, within walking distance of the cottage there are a handful of other iconic species that I would love to discover nearer to home. Some are more likely to occur than others but nevertheless I live in hope.

Stag Beetle

A mile or so up the road, in gardens where the soil is sandy and free-draining, Stag Beetles are locally common. I fear the soil in my garden is too clay-rich to suit their needs, and the nearest I have come to seeing one close

A mating pair of Stag Beetles, plus an interloping rival male, photographed a mile or so from my cottage.

to home was a wandering male that a neighbour brought to me from their garden; for all its bulk, the species is a surprisingly capable flyer. If you live in Greater London or the Thames Valley there's a good chance you will be in the prime UK catchment area for the species. The fact that these locations are built-on is not necessarily an issue: these days, the main hotspot sites I know around here are in suburban gardens. That's probably less to do with an affinity for gardens and more because there's no alternative, but nevertheless the species hangs on and, in some instances, thrives. This just highlights the need to value the remaining natural resources of urban and suburban sites. Stag Beetles suffer when people become obsessed with perceived tidiness in the natural world. Their larvae feed in subterranean dead and decaying wood and can take anywhere up to five years to reach maturity. The clearance of dead wood and in particular the removal of subterranean decomposing roots – worse still, stump-grinding – is a sure-fire way of killing off populations of this magnificent insect. Give the beetles time to do their job and they will consume stumps and decaying roots for you, for free.

Dung beetles

The Dor Beetle provides another example of the vital role beetles play in the cycle of life and the recycling of

nutrients. They dig subterranean tunnels and provision them with dung and organic matter on which their larvae feed and develop. Imagine a world without them and the excremental consequences. In actual fact, that's precisely the world I see in my neighbourhood on land that is subjected to intensive cattle numbers. Dor Beetles, and dung beetles generally, are conspicuous by their absence. Rightly or wrongly, my assumption is, like dung-feeding invertebrates across the board, the beetles have been wiped out by ivermectins. These anti-parasitic chemicals are administered to livestock but are just as effective at killing virtually all other invertebrates. They linger and pollute the animals' dung and when spread on the land destroy a natural ecosystem. By comparison, in Pamber Forest – nominally a nature reserve – Dor Beetles are still a common sight trundling across paths. Sadly, it is tragic and disappointing to see how many get squashed under foot by visitors, either by intent or because unobservant walkers simply fail to notice the life that is right in front of them.

Glow-worm

Although many people are aware of the existence of Glow-worms, most will never have seen one, nor are they likely to the way things are going. In my youth I could have named a dozen or more spots within cycling distance of my home where you could encounter the species. Almost all are gone now, their habitats rendered worthless to them and most other native biodiversity by changes in agricultural land use, or destroyed utterly by housing and other forms of development.

Female Glow-worms, the sex that emits light, are distinctly un-beetle-like and rather similar in appearance to the species' larval stage. The role of their nocturnal 'glow', which can be turned off if disturbed, is to attract males; these are capable fliers and slightly more beetle-like in appearance than their partners. Glow-worm larvae are active predators of snails and slugs, whose internal organs they liquefy by injecting an enzyme cocktail before sucking the contents dry.

In terms of land use and abuse, the Glow-worm is a fine example of how traditional methods allowed the species to survive in the past and how modern practices are killing them. Aspects of Glow-worm natural history determine whether and where they survive in twenty-first century Britain. Firstly, there is diet: spray a field with molluscicides and you kill off larval food so the insects simply starve; spray with insecticides and the fatal consequences are as inevitable as they are obvious. Then there is the species' reproductive strategy. The subtle luminescence of a female Glow-worm cannot possibly compete with the glare of artificial light; add street and house illumination to the mix and you ruin the chances of potential mates finding a female. Seasonality is important too: glowing female Glow-worms peak in terms of numbers in July. Cut meadow vegetation too early and you destroy the three-dimensional world on which they depend – their ability to display themselves aloft like entomological beacons and attract potential mates. You also stand a good chance of macerating them in the process. In addition, there is evidence of seasonal movement between lush, damp vegetation for part of the year and drier grassland at other times. Connectivity between the two may be a factor affecting the species' survival.

Then there is the total destruction that comes with development. Although Glow-worms are nationally scarce and declining, and teetering on the verge of extinction in the borough of Basingstoke, the species lacks statutory protection. Consequently, they have no formal status when it comes to planning decisions. One of the most tragic nails in the local Glow-worm coffin came with planning application 17/02846/OUT, which was approved by Basingstoke and Deane Borough Council a few years ago. This application for housing was adjacent to a road named Swing Swang Lane.

Despite the delightfully bucolic image the byway's name conjures up, the land in question, which was owned at the time of the application by Hampshire County Council, is hemmed in on all sides by previous modern development. It represented one of the last remnants of unimproved land in the area and hosted a diverse suite of animals and plants that any self-respecting naturalist would consider notable. This included a count of 850 glowing female Glow-worms and a rare plant called Wall Bedstraw. Armed with this knowledge, anyone with an environmental conscience would have elevated the land's status to that of a sacrosanct nature reserve.

However, for those who wanted to profit from its development it was just a building plot. Despite pleading and informed argument on the part of Glow-worm supporters, an acknowledgement of the wildlife importance of the site by the county council, and a plan to mitigate the worst environmental impacts of the proposal, the planning department allowed development of the land in line with the wishes of the developers. It

A Glow-worm.

seems a forlorn hope to think that any Glow-worms will have survived. By now, their ethereal glow will have been replaced by the glare of outdoor house lighting. That is the legacy that the local council have bequeathed to future generations of Basingstoke naturalists.

Closer to home, for the moment two Glow-worm sites linger within a mile or so of my garden and it would be a dream come true if they ever graced my meadow. A forlorn hope no doubt, but a hope nevertheless and one with which biodiversity gardeners elsewhere may have more success. But as an obvious cautionary note: wage war on snails in your garden and you will never have Glow-worms.

Golden-bloomed Grey Longhorn

The length of this elegant longhorn's scientific name – *Agapanthia villosoviridescens* – is a match for the size of its impressive antennae. It lives in the pockets of old hay meadows nearby that have not been destroyed and turned to arable, or 'improved' agriculturally. Who knows, it is not beyond the realms of possibility

A Golden-bloomed Grey Longhorn.

that it might take up residence in my garden meadow someday. In sunny weather, adults delight in sitting around on stems and flower sprays. By contrast, their larvae live inside the stems of stout meadow plants such as Hogweed and thistles, eventually working their way down to the roots. So that's another good reason for not regarding these plants as 'weeds' and treating even their stems with respect as microhabitats for an array of invertebrates.

True bugs and allies

True bugs are an extremely variable group both in terms of size and shape. They range from minute aphids, perhaps a millimetre in length, to sizeable shieldbugs the size of a fingernail. Some species resemble flies while others are superficially more like beetles. What they all have in common are piercing mouthparts that are used like a hypodermic syringe to suck the juices from plants or animals. Many true bugs have wings, but some are wingless. Most are terrestrial, but a select band have evolved an aquatic lifestyle and live in ponds and ditches; these are dealt with elsewhere on p. 237.

The classification of true bugs is a complex subject, well beyond the scope of *The Biodiversity Gardener*, whose aim is to provide inspiration and not act as a field guide. Nevertheless, an introductory framework will help the reader. As a broad distinction, entomologists divide true bugs into two main groups: Heteroptera and Homoptera. To give the prospective biodiversity gardener a flavour of the range of true bugs they might come across, the following is a selection of some of the more striking examples encountered in my garden on a regular basis.

A Red-and-black Froghopper.

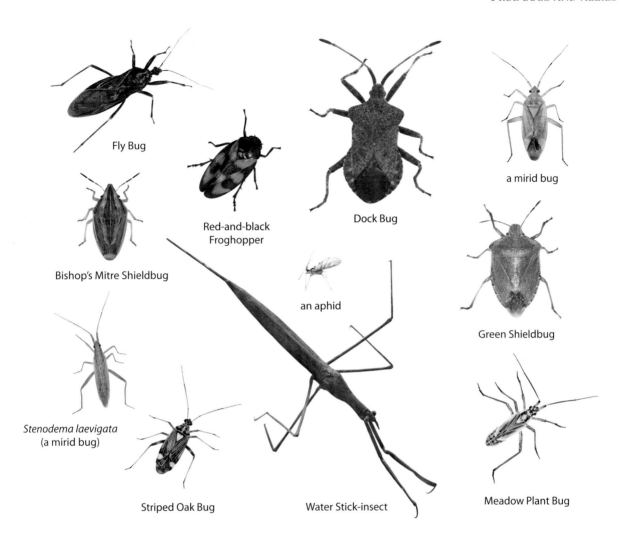

Fly Bug

Red-and-black Froghopper

Dock Bug

a mirid bug

Bishop's Mitre Shieldbug

an aphid

Green Shieldbug

Stenodema laevigata (a mirid bug)

Striped Oak Bug

Water Stick-insect

Meadow Plant Bug

BEETLES BITE, BUGS SUCK

I mean no disrespect to the excellent conservation charity **Buglife**, but now and then I find myself frustrated by the use and misuse of the word 'bug'. That must be something to do with my age. When I was growing up, a bug was a member of the order Hemiptera, a beetle was a coleopteran and the order Diptera represented flies. Nowadays there is a trend to refer to anything that walks on six legs, or indeed on occasion any invertebrate, as a bug, or worse still a *minibeast*. And to add to the confusion, in medical parlance the term 'bug' can mean a germ, microbe or bacterium. Back to the insect world, I appreciate the desire to interest non-specialists in the subject and that 'InvertebrateLife' does not have a catchy

ring to it. However, for anyone who attempts to bring clarity and precision of meaning through the use of words it can be a source of frustration. Dumbing-down generalisations are all very well if you know the subject well enough to infer what is meant, but there is a danger in using the word bug as an umbrella term. For the novice, it provides no structure to future understanding and is confusing rather than enlightening. It can be mildly infuriating to be shown a beetle or fly and asked, 'What kind of bug is that?' Or to be shown a real bug and then have to explain why it is a true bug and not just any old 'bug'. My frustration notwithstanding, I suspect this rather puerile muddying of the entomological waters is here to stay but I will always abide by the mantra 'beetles bite, bugs suck'.

HETEROPTERA

Where wings are present, heteropteran bugs have membranous hind wings but front wings that are divided into two sections: membranous at the tip but tough and hardened at the base. At rest the forewings are folded flat over the body and overlap one another; a triangular backward pointing projection of the thorax – the scutellum – is often conspicuous. By comparison, beetle forewings (the elytra) abut one another at rest. Heteroptera members include those species generically referred to as shieldbugs, together with assassin bugs, damsel bugs, capsid or mirid bugs; water bugs, which are also heteropterans, are discussed on p. 237. The larvae that hatch from eggs recall miniature versions of an adult, increasingly so through their moults and instars, although they lack wings and their markings may differ.

Shieldbugs

As you might guess, the Hawthorn Shieldbug feeds on fruits and leaves of its namesake shrub. It has an extended life, and I come across the species now and then in hedgerows in spring and summer, and while raking leaf litter – a site for hibernation – in autumn and winter. Its cousin the Birch Shieldbug is an additional garden species, but special mention must go to another birch-loving species, the Parent Bug. I have invertebrate enthusiast and expert Keith Lugg to thank for opening my eyes to its presence in my garden and now that I know where and how to look, I find it most years I search. Although well-marked, the adult

WHAT'S IN A NAME?

The moniker 'shieldbug' is both useful and potentially confusing, and the group is perhaps best thought of as shieldbugs, allies and look-alikes. The term is generic and embraces a number of true bug families, some of which do not have the word 'shieldbug' in their common names, or indeed common names at all in some instances. To confuse matters further, some families treated nominally as shieldbugs include representatives that are unlike the conventional image of the group. The families Acanthosomatidae and Pentatomidae are perhaps the archetypal shieldbugs, many shield-shaped in body outline with an obvious scutellum that is triangular and itself shield-like.

itself is rather unremarkable and would probably not arouse undue interest were it not for the parental care it extends to its offspring. Search carefully beneath birch leaves in May and June, or view them backlit, and with luck you will find a female Parent Bug standing guard over her eggs; her vigil continues as the nymphs grow, the intention being to protect them from the attentions of parasitic wasps. My entomological awakening was a contributory factor in abandoning the practice of 'beating' for insects – hitting foliage with a stick over a white sheet to catch whatever falls. In the case of a 'sitting' Parent Bug that would to all intents destroy an entire generation. Now I prefer the meticulous search approach rather than employing brute force.

A Birch Shieldbug, a match for the colourful autumn colours of its name-sake tree.

A female Parent Bug standing guard over her recently hatched offspring to protect them from predators and parasitic wasps.

What appears to be a Parent Bug crèche, presumably involving the offspring of more than one parent.

Other shieldbugs and allies I come across on the doorstep include the Forest Bug which, despite the name, is associated with shrubs as well as trees; its varied diet ranges from fruits to other insects. Searches of similar habitats also reveal the occasional Sloe Bug and the Green Shieldbug, while closer to ground level the fiddle-shaped Dock Bug is at home feeding on the sap of its namesake plants.

Other heteropteran bugs

With wings etched with tracery, lacebugs are an occasional find on thistles in the garden, the intricate fine detail only really appreciated by using a hand lens. By contrast, the rather intimidating Fly Bug is an uncommon discovery around the house. It is an assassin by nature and alternative name: both adult and weird debris-coated larva are voracious predators of other insects. The fact that they have a liking for silverfish, bedbugs and flies probably says something about my housekeeping skills.

The innocent-sounding name given to damsel bugs belies their predatory habits, and an example found in the garden is the Common Damsel Bug; its long piercing mouthparts are a sign that no small insect is safe in its presence. Capsid bugs are a varied group, most of which feed on plant sap and fruits, with many having striking markings

A typical capsid bug.

on their wings. The Common Green Capsid is rather partial to soft fruits, which does not endear it to conventional gardeners.

HOMOPTERA

Where wings are present, homopterans have membranous hind wings and, in contrast to heteropterans, front wings that are uniform and not divided into two sections; these can be membranous or toughened depending on species. Another difference lies in the orientation of the wings at rest: in heteropterans they are usually folded flat over the body, whereas in homopterans they are typically held angled in the manner of a ridge tent or

roof. Larger homopteran representatives include froghoppers, leafhoppers and planthoppers. Aphids, whiteflies, along with scale insects and psyllids are treated here as specialised homopteran groups.

Hoppers

Many larger homopteran species have the word 'hopper' in their name, an indication of their habits and abilities in response to disturbance. The Horned Treehopper is found on a variety of plants in the garden, including shrubs, while the Common Froghopper is more associated with grassy margins and herbaceous plants; it is better known in its larval or nymphal stage from the familiar frothy 'cuckoo spit' in which it lives and grows. By contrast, adults are the familiar life-cycle stage of the Red-and-black Froghopper, whose larvae live underground. The most impressive homopteran I have come across in my garden is the Eared Leafhopper. It has a diagnostic pair of 'ear flaps' projecting from the thorax and is extremely well camouflaged when resting on lichen-covered twigs and branches of trees and shrubs. Equally well camouflaged is its squat larva, which on occasions I have found on the ground beneath oak trees, dislodged by heavy rainfall and strong winds.

An Eared Leafhopper resting on a lichen-covered twig.

Aphids

Aphids have been discussed already on p. 120 but given their variety (600 or so species in the UK) and seasonal abundance, they merit another mention. The basic aphid plan involves a plump, pear-shaped body and slender antennae. Depending on species and stage in the life cycle, individuals may be wingless or winged; in the latter case both pairs of wings are membranous. Horn-like projections at the rear end are associated with the production of defensive waxy secretions. Aphids are sap suckers and, on the basis that what goes in must come out, they excrete a concentrated and hence sticky liquid called 'honeydew'; this sugary substance is attractive to other insects. As a generalisation, aphids have complex life cycles and, during the summer months, amazingly prodigious rates of reproduction. Having dispensed with the need to mate at this time of year, they give birth almost non-stop, producing several active young a day, each of these capable of producing more offspring within a few days of their own birth. The majority are wingless, but winged forms come and go when the need arises to move to new host plants. Males appear in autumn and, after mating, females lay eggs which in most species are the overwintering stage in the life-cycle. Throughout the year, aphids are hugely important as food, in themselves and via honeydew, for creatures ranging from other invertebrates to Hazel Dormice and Goldcrests.

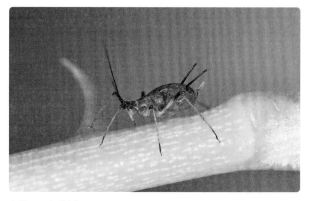

A Rose Aphid.

APHID ALLIES

Insects allied to aphids, at least in the minds of many gardeners, include the Cabbage Whitefly and species of scale insect such as the Cottony Cushion Scale. Both feed on plant sap, and elsewhere in the world scale insects have commercial significance in the production of dyes such as carmine (from the cochineal scale insect, *Dactylopius coccus,* on Agave). Manna – the biblical substance – may have been a sugary exudate of the scale insect *Trabutina mannipura*, on Tamarisk.

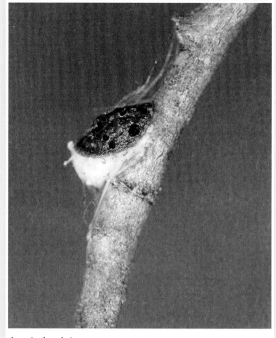

A typical scale insect.

Woolly Aphids.

True flies

There are adult representatives of most of the major insect groups that possess the power of flight, so it is no surprise that the word 'fly' is included in some of their common names. Consequently, it is helpful for the beginner to make the distinction between these groups and true flies, which are members of the order Diptera. As the name implies, these insects employ just two wings for flight; their hind wings are reduced to small club-shaped projections the function of which is to act as gyroscopic flight stabilisers.

The fact that true flies have half the complement of wings of other insects is not necessarily a drawback: some are awkward in flight, of course, but many species are fast, can stop or accelerate in the blink of an eye, and

hover motionless with the precision of a drone. As with human technology, the ability to fly would be worthless were it not for an ability to perceive the world around you and adjust your trajectory according to changing circumstances. So it is with most true flies, which have a full array of sensory organs on the head but with particular emphasis on the eyes; these hemispherical compound structures dominate the heads of many dipteran groups.

True flies are extremely numerous both in terms of abundance and numbers of species, with more than 5,000 of the latter recorded in the UK alone. Adult true flies feed on liquids and have sucking mouthparts; some simply mop up fluids, while in many instances there are

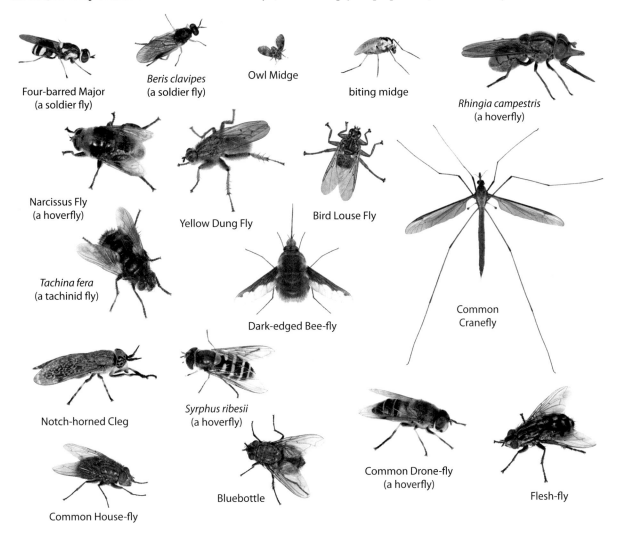

Four-barred Major
(a soldier fly)

Beris clavipes
(a soldier fly)

Owl Midge

biting midge

Rhingia campestris
(a hoverfly)

Narcissus Fly
(a hoverfly)

Yellow Dung Fly

Bird Louse Fly

Tachina fera
(a tachinid fly)

Dark-edged Bee-fly

Common
Cranefly

Notch-horned Cleg

Syrphus ribesii
(a hoverfly)

Common Drone-fly
(a hoverfly)

Flesh-fly

Common House-fly

Bluebottle

modifications for piercing the skin of animals. Across the species range, the diet is eclectic and so long as there is a fluid element, almost any and every source of organic nutrition is exploited, ranging from flower nectar to blood and dank fluids associated with dung and rotting corpses.

There are exceptions, of course, but the larvae of many dipteran species are the archetypal maggots. Lacking an obvious head and barely able to wriggle, they are seemingly undifferentiated externally and lack the architecture and complexity you find in, for example, a dragonfly larva. Don't let this apparent simplicity fool you. They play their part in the life cycle admirably and are able to exploit almost every food source imaginable, including the unspeakable; in addition to conventional feeding, filter-feeding and parasitism are among the strategies of some. In many instances, the speed at which the larvae of some true fly species grow and develop is also remarkable, taking days rather than weeks or months to mature and pupate.

Given the range of true fly species in the UK it is little wonder that almost every time I spend an hour or so in the garden in spring and summer, I see a true fly species I have never seen before, and that is just the larger and more obvious individuals. Goodness knows how many small, unobtrusive or nocturnal dipterans I am overlooking. Consequently, the following is at best a superficial account of those I come across regularly, partly in celebration of their diversity, partly as an inspiration for other people to look around for them and make their own discoveries.

An adult crane-fly *Tipula paludosa*.

CRANE-FLIES (FAMILY TIPULIDAE)

This family includes species of familiar, gangly so-called daddy-long-legs, which have slender bodies, paddle-shaped wings and extraordinarily long legs. The largest of its kind, *Tipula maxima*, is an impressive insect with dark patterning on the wings and is an occasional visitor in my garden. More frequent are its smaller cousins *T. oleracea*, a mainly spring species, and *T. paludosa* which predominates in the autumn. Their larvae – known as leatherjackets – are subterranean and feed on organic matter including plant roots. In the past, they were abundant in the soils of grassland and meadows, and were a staple part of the diet of flocks of Starlings and Rooks. In areas where intensive farming methods employ the use of chemicals, leatherjackets and flocks of feeding birds are a thing of the past. A few crane-fly species are more specialised and have larvae that live in rotting wood.

On mild winter days, midges take advantage of the apricity.

A crane-fly larva, or 'leatherjacket'.

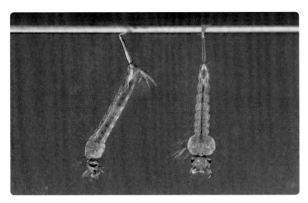

Mosquito larvae.

MOSQUITOES (FAMILY CULICIDAE)

Not to be confused with gnats and midges, this is a successful and widespread group of insects, females of which are specialist blood-suckers. By contrast, male mosquitoes feed on nectar and can be distinguished by their feathery antennae, used to locate females by detecting the high-pitched whine emitted by their wingbeats. Their larvae and pupae are aquatic, doing best in standing water free of predators; water butts and forgotten buckets of water make ideal breeding grounds.

SOLDIER-FLIES (FAMILY STRATIOMYIDAE)

Presumably the markings of some soldier-fly species reminded early entomologists of military uniforms, because the flies' habits hardly merit martial associations. Species I have encountered tend to just sit around basking on leaves or flowers. Their larvae live in a range of damp, decomposing matter from compost heaps to dung, depending on species. A soldier-fly with the delightful name of Orange Legionnaire is a garden regular.

The Banded General is a wasp-like soldier-fly.

SNIPE-FLIES (FAMILY RHAGIONIDAE)

These are alert insects that are constantly on the lookout for smaller insect prey; when a suitable victim is spotted the snipe-fly darts out and grabs the prey in mid-air. *Rhagio scolopaceus* is a garden regular. Snipe-fly larvae are subterranean.

HORSE-FLIES (FAMILY TABANIDAE)

These flies need little introduction. They are tough, fast-flying insects that specialise in puncturing animal skin and lapping up the blood, or at least females do; males by contrast feed on nectar. The females are very alert and persistent when a potential meal is spotted; the relatively huge, often beautifully patterned compound eyes are a great asset in this regard. Several horse-fly species call my garden home, including cleg-flies *Haematopota* spp., which are particularly troublesome when I am trying to concentrate on outdoor close-up photography on a warm summer's day. Horse-fly larvae are unobtrusive creatures, often partly subterranean or found living amongst damp material on the ground.

A Notch-horned Cleg and victim.

ROBBER-FLIES (FAMILY ASILIDAE)

Living up to their name, these are active predators of smaller flying insects, which they catch on the wing with the aid of their bristly legs. For much of the time they remain alert but inactive, perched on a branch or stem, watching for prey. Their larvae live in the soil and are thought to eat a range of organic matter including live prey.

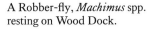

A Robber-fly, *Machimus* spp. resting on Wood Dock.

A resting Common Red-legged Robber-fly.

BEE-FLIES (FAMILY BOMBYLIIDAE)

These flies are aptly named since they resemble and behave like miniature bumblebees. They use their long proboscis to sup nectar and, in my garden, cultivated lungworts and other early flowerers are visited by the Dark-edged Bee-fly. The bee-fly's cute, innocuous appearance belies its habits: it is a parasitoid of solitary bees. Watch bee-flies for any length of time and you may spot an individual jerking its abdomen while it hovers. The chances are this will be a female flicking eggs into the burrow of a solitary bee. The bee-fly larva hatches but waits until the solitary bee larva is full grown before eating it alive.

A Dark-edged Bee-fly.

HOVER-FLIES (FAMILY SYRPHIDAE)

The group's common name reflects their aerial prowess, most being able to hover motionless for prolonged periods only to accelerate and dart away at lightning speed at the slightest sign of danger. They are a familiar and welcome sight in the garden, and the group includes some colourful, well-marked and impressively large species. Many hover-fly species are convincing mimics of wasps, bees and bumblebees, and it is little wonder that it is adults that attract most of the attention and interest. However, as is the case with that other eye-catching group, butterflies, if you want to truly benefit hover-flies in a meaningful way in the garden you need to understand and take into consideration their life cycles. Adults may be appealing to the human eye, but the life strategies of the larvae – the ugly ducklings of the insect world – are what will fascinate anyone with an enquiring mind. True, many are rather non-specific, grub-like and live in detritus scavenging on decaying organic matter. But included in their number are larvae that live in water, some with elaborate breathing tubes, specialists that feed on sap and other plant tissues, active predators of aphids, and those that live commensal lives in the nests of social insects. See p. 203 for images of adults.

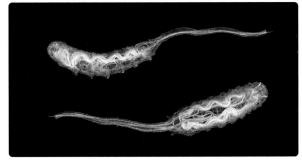

So-called Rat-tailed Maggots, the larvae of the Common Drone-fly.

A hoverfly larva eating an aphid.

TACHINID FLIES (FAMILY TACHINIDAE)

To my eyes at least, these flies have a slightly menacing air about them, although my attitude towards them may be coloured by their habits. From time to time, if I find an interesting caterpillar in the garden, I rear it in captivity. On several occasions this has led to disappointment when it transpires that what looks like a healthy caterpillar has been eaten from within by a tachinid fly larva, and what emerges is a fly and not a moth. Adults of most tachinid species have extremely bristly bodies. See p. 203 for images of adults.

HOUSE-FLIES AND RELATIVES (FAMILIES SARCOPHAGIDAE, CALLIPHORIDAE AND MUSCIDAE)

These insects often occur in the vicinity of dwellings, but if you think that where your house is concerned a 'fly' is just a fly, think again. An array of different species contributes to the mix and, depending on species, several occasionally or routinely venture indoors. These include the Flesh-fly, that gives birth to minute larvae (not eggs) that feed primarily on animal carrion; the Bluebottle that is attracted to picnics and food left out on work surfaces; the Greenbottle, one of several similar species whose larvae feed on carrion; the House-fly, whose larvae are associated with dung and organic debris generally; and the Lesser House-fly, males of which endlessly circle ceiling light fittings indoors and whose larvae eat dung and other organic waste. See p. 203 for images of adults.

LOUSE FLIES (FAMILY HIPPOBOSCIDAE)

Members of this unusual group of flies are blood-sucking parasites typically either of mammals or birds, depending on species. The one that I encounter now and then is the Bird Louse Fly, which occasionally drops on me in the garden, presumably having been dislodged from an avian host. Like others of its kind it is extremely flattened, an adaptation that allows it to scuttle under and between feathers. When it lands on a human it moves with surprising speed, often sideways in a crab-like manner; and unless caught (which is extremely difficult) it soon disappears up a sleeve or into your hair. At this point, I will be surprised if you haven't started scratching. Female hippoboscid flies don't lay eggs, but rather they produce a single, near-fully-formed pupa that only needs to harden.

A Bird Louse Fly, poised and ready to disappear between the feathers of a Great Spotted Woodpecker.

GALL-FORMING FLIES (FAMILY TEPHRITIDAE)

In addition to more conventional lifestyles, a few fly species have more unusual natural histories. So-called picture-winged flies lay eggs, the resulting larvae of which cause galls in plants; most are host plant–specific. An example is the Thistle Gall Fly, which lays its eggs in the stems of Creeping Thistle in my garden, and whose larvae cause fig- or pear-shaped swellings.

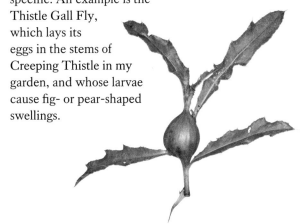

Galls on Creeping Thistle, caused by larvae of the Thistle Gall Fly, continue to be evident throughout the winter on dead stems. Remove and destroy thistle stems and you not only kill the life cycle of this interesting little fly – the larvae pupate inside the galls – but you deny birds a source of natural winter food: many galls end up being dismantled by sharp beaks and their larvae or pupae eaten. However, just because a Thistle Gall escapes the attentions of birds does not mean the fly has it all its own way. Collect a few dry galls in winter, store them in a container, and see what emerges. A fair proportion of the larvae will have been parasitised and what emerges in spring will be a parasitic wasp and not a Thistle Gall Fly.

A Thistle Gall Fly.

On a smaller scale, the Holly Leaf Gall Fly has leaf-mining larvae that live between the upper and lower cuticles of Holly leaves and cause colourful blotches.

Orthoptera

I admit to having a particular fondness for Orthoptera, having lived and worked, for a brief period, almost within walking distance of downland that is home to the iconic Wart-biter bush-cricket. Who could fail to be captivated by so impressive a beast. However, I was also intrigued by the species because there were almost as many occasions when I failed to find one as times when I was successful. This was despite the fact that an adult is the size of a small frog, its habitat is relatively short grassland, and I knew for certain they were present. The eventual realisation that they did a disappearing trick by diving head-first into clumps of Tor-grass was a lesson to me that you need to understand the lifestyle and habits of your subject to study it properly.

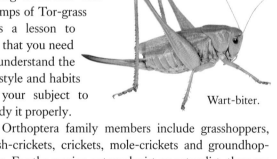

Wart-biter.

Orthoptera family members include grasshoppers, bush-crickets, crickets, mole-crickets and groundhoppers. For the novice entomologist or naturalist, they are a manageable group both in terms of species numbers and ease of identification in the field; they are also good indicators of habitat quality and management. There are 30 or so regularly encountered species in mainland Britain, with a few island-specific as well as new-arrival additions to add to the mix. Of these, nine are present in my garden, and I can see a further three within walking distance of my cottage. Expand the radius and all bar

two UK species can be found within a 50-mile travelling distance from home. Add a further 20 miles and the last regularly encountered species, Scaly Cricket, can be added to the tally.

Turning closer to home, my garden meadow's grasshoppers and grassland bush-cricket species were discussed on p. 84. In Orthoptera terms that leaves bush-cricket species associated with trees and scrub and groundhoppers. Of the three additional bush-cricket species in the garden, two are flightless. The Speckled Bush-cricket is a rotund, very long-legged species, the females of which have a sickle-shaped ovipositor. I usually spot tiny nymphs in spring sunning themselves on the foliage of herbaceous plants, with adults often moving to shrubs higher off the ground by summer. The song of the male Dark Bush-cricket sounds to my ears like a match being struck, and I come across adults hopping along in almost any vegetated part of the garden. Oak Bush-crickets differ from their above garden cousins in being primarily tree dwellers and able to fly. This latter ability, and an attraction to light, means that they sometimes venture indoors on warm summer nights when upstairs windows are open. I was more surprised to discover Common Groundhopper in the garden, partly because elsewhere I only usually come across it by chance on bare ground on nature reserves; it is most obvious when sitting on the white walls of the cottage.

Although the identification of grasshoppers and bush-crickets is relatively straightforward, assessing their numbers can be more of a challenge. In part this

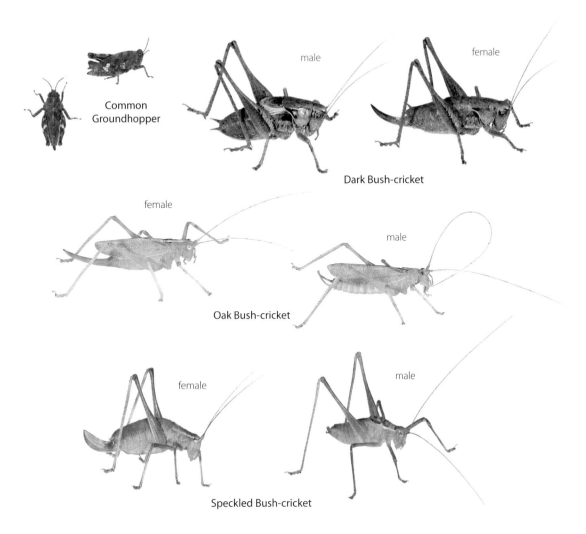

Common Groundhopper

male

female

Dark Bush-cricket

female

Oak Bush-cricket

male

female

Speckled Bush-cricket

male

Bush-cricket and groundhopper species regularly found in my garden.

is due to the animals' ability to blend in with their environment, the result being that many individuals are overlooked and population counts are usually underestimates. Thankfully, modern technology has come to the rescue. Male orthopterans sing to attract mates and although soft and inaudibly high-pitched to some ears, bat detectors can be adjusted to pick up the sounds they emit. This can be a more accurate way of assessing species present in the garden and their numbers. For more information about bat detectors, see p. 274.

A female Oak Bush-cricket on the underside of an oak leaf, fastidiously cleaning her antennae.

Terrestrial insect also-rans

In addition to the showy and iconic insects previously described, there are a number of other less eye-catching groups, some of which have only a small number of UK representatives. In many cases they live unobtrusive lives and a concerted effort may be required to discover their presence in the biodiversity garden.

EARWIGS (ORDER DERMAPTERA)

These distinctive insects can be recognised by their shiny, elongate bodies and distinctive pincers at the tail end; these are curved in males but straight in females. The Common Earwig is the species I routinely encounter, usually by chance if I turn over a stone or log, or dislodge a piece of bark. The species is mostly nocturnal and its diet comprises mainly dead and decaying organic matter, and as such their role in natural recycling is important. Female Common Earwigs show attentive parental care, guarding their 'nests' of eggs and growing young against predators.

Lesne's Earwig is a smaller, paler version of the Common Earwig and a recent addition to my garden insect 'list'. Or maybe I overlooked it in the past.

COCKROACHES (ORDER DICTYOPTERA)

Despite leaning towards the casual end of the spectrum of house pride, I do not have any of the introduced species of cockroaches living alongside me indoors. However, once in a while and usually by pure chance, I do spot the Dusky Cockroach in the garden. It is one of the three native species in the UK. If you have an aversion to this group, try to overcome your prejudice and recognise the role of native species as a natural equivalent of street cleaners, eating and recycling nature's leftovers. The fact that introduced species are seen as a plague of urban commercial kitchens, food outlets and food waste is a testament both to profligate human excess and to the resourcefulness of insects.

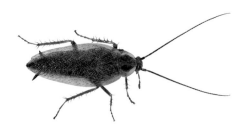

The Dusky Cockroach occurs now and then in my garden, and is considered to be a notable species by the Hampshire Biodiversity Information Centre.

PSOCIDS (ORDER PSOCOPTERA)

These are an unobtrusive group of tiny insects that have booklice among their number. Most species live outdoors on trees and shrubs and are relatively numerous if you have the patience to look closely enough. They resemble outsized aphids, having four membranous wings. However, their mouthparts are biting not sucking, and their diet includes all manner of small organic matter, from algae and fungal moulds on tree bark to pollen. Many species have a slightly hunchbacked look about them due to the shape of the thorax.

A psocid on oak.

LACEWINGS (ORDER NEUROPTERA)

Lacewings and are fairly easy to recognise as adults, having membranous, paddle-shaped wings that are held like a ridge tent over the body at rest. They have beady eyes, long antennae and a predatory diet with a particular fondness for aphids. Lacewing larvae are also the stuff of nightmares if you are an aphid, their incurved

An adult lacewing.

'fangs' piercing and sucking the life blood from their victims, leaving just papery aphid skins as a sign of their activities. Some species of lacewings attach their eggs to hardened strands, suspended like entomological fruits out of harm's way. I come across lacewings that are green in my garden. In the past I might have called these *Chrysoperla carnea* but I gather their classification is more complex and so now I tend to be vague rather than specific. I assume it is this species, or one of its

relatives, that comes indoors and overwinters in cool corners, losing its green coloration in favour of a rather sickly-looking flesh brown.

A lacewing larva.

SNAKEFLIES (ORDER RAPHIDIOPTERA)

These curious insects have the look of creatures designed by a committee rather than nature, as if some bright young spark had said 'Let's give it a longer neck'. The flexibility this extension permits presumably is an advantage in some way when it comes to feeding, their diet comprising aphids and other small insects. Their larvae are also predatory but live tucked away under bark and in crevices.

A typical snakefly, *Phaeostigma notata*.

SCORPIONFLIES (ORDER MECOPTERA)

Despite their rather intimidating appearance, these insects are harmless and get their common name from the shape of the male's abdomen, the tip of which is swollen and upturned. Both sexes have a long, rigid beak-like structure armed with jaws at the tip. They scavenge the remains of dead insects and occasionally take their lives into their own hands and raid spiders' webs.

A useful resource for anyone interested in these insects is the **Lacewings and Allies Recording Scheme**, which covers the following orders: Neuroptera, Megaloptera, Raphidioptera and Mecoptera of the British Isles. The scheme can be accessed via their website at www.lacewings.myspecies.info

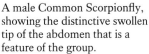

A male Common Scorpionfly, showing the distinctive swollen tip of the abdomen that is a feature of the group.

A Giant Lacewing resting on a leaf. Despite its size, this insect is easily overlooked.

INSECT ALSO-RANS WISH LIST

Although I have never seen one in my garden, the Giant Lacewing lives a few hundred yards away on a tree-lined ancient byway. It appears to have a fondness for tree-fringed streams and seasonally flowing ditches if my encounters with it are anything to go by. It is the impressive adults that I come across, now and then, resting by day on foliage overhanging the water. The larvae are said to live in moss and leaf litter in the same location. Given the presence of a seasonal stream at the bottom of my garden, I live in hope that when planted trees and shrubs have reached a size where they cast shade over the water, the species may grace my garden.

Spiders and allies

I can recognise perhaps a couple of dozen or so spider species in my garden, but know that many more from the group's 600 or so UK representatives call the plot home. The reluctance to take my studies further is not down to a lack of interest but more a reflection of other priorities and the number of hours in a day. Consequently, my approach to the spider world is to simply celebrate their diversity and abundance in my garden and be profoundly grateful for their existence. A lack of detailed knowledge could be a hindrance to managing a biodiversity garden in their best interests, and consequently I err on the side of caution and try to take into consideration the habitat and predatory requirements of the various families rather than individual species. A useful resource is the **Spider and Harvestman Recording Scheme** www.srs. britishspiders.org

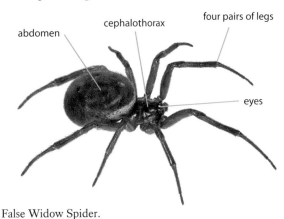

abdomen — cephalothorax — four pairs of legs — eyes

False Widow Spider.

Although mistakes are occasionally made, most people have a pretty good idea of how to recognise a spider. At the basic level, they are arthropod invertebrates, members of the class Arachnida, and have jointed legs and a hardened outer skin called an *exoskeleton*. In this regard, they are not unlike their cousins the insects. Where they differ is in having four pairs of legs not three, and a body divided into two parts not three (a fused head and thorax – the cephalothorax – and an abdomen). All spiders produce silk, as do many insects. However, spiders have perfected its use and the webs created by many species are incredible architectural structures, and beautiful to boot.

Silk is produced by glands in a spider's abdomen. In chemical terms it is a protein, one that is extruded in

Web construction reaches its apogee among members of the orb-web family Araneidae. Their webs are among the most perfect and architectural of all their kind, and as a testament to their determination a new one is often created on a daily basis.

liquid form but hardens as it is stretched and acquires incredible tensile strength. The silk that spiders produce underpins almost every aspect of their lives. It is a lifeline when they jump or move around generally; it provides protection for their eggs; many species spin webs to catch their prey; and it allows them to spread far and wide when tiny individuals of certain species are carried aloft on silk strands.

All spiders are predators. Most UK species catch and kill other invertebrates, and insects feature prominently in the diet of many. Spiders have paired fangs that are plunged into their victim like hypodermic needles, injecting a paralysing venom; in many species the

Spider webs are most striking on damp mornings, the silk strands often adorned with beads of dew.

As a testament to the tensile strength of silk, this filamentous strand easily supports the weight of a female Marbled Orb-weaver.

A Garden Spider at the centre of its orb web; these marvels of construction are constantly being repaired and are sometimes constructed from scratch each day.

venom also partially digests the prey's internal organs and the resulting soup is then sucked up by the spider through its fangs. The techniques and behaviour that spiders employ to catch their prey are varied: there are active hunters that use keen eyesight and sensitivity to vibrations to locate and catch their prey; others employ camouflage and lie in wait to launch an ambush attack; many spin elaborate silken webs to entrap their victims.

Spider reproduction is, from the male's point of view, a necessarily cautious affair because there is a fine line between being a mate and becoming a meal. Consequently, there is a fair degree of ritual involved the precise nature of which varies from species to species. It includes Morse-code tapping on safely distant strands of silk to alert the female to a male's presence and intentions. Often the gift of a dead insect is presented to preoccupy the female's predatory instincts during mating. After that, the male's role is finished and again, depending on the species, he may die of natural causes soon after or make the ultimate sacrifice and give his

life to fatten his mate. Female spiders lay eggs that are usually protected by silk in some way – a tent, a silken egg-sac or a chamber; some nomadic species carry the egg-sac with them, along with newly-hatched young.

When it comes to spiders, I hope I know enough to know how little I know. What follows, therefore, is an unscientific and highly personal account of spider groups in my garden and some of their interesting representatives.

ORB-WEB SPIDERS (FAMILY ARANEIDAE)

The aptly-named Garden Spider is the archetypal member of this spider family in my garden. Having served their reproductive function, male Garden Spiders seemingly vanish, either eaten by their mate or returning to an unobtrusive lifestyle and dying off. The species is best known by its plump-bodied females which mature in late summer and autumn; they have abdomens marked with white dots that align to form a

A female Four-spotted Orb-weaver suspended on a silken strand.

cross, and construct impressive webs that are vaguely circular or elliptical depending on the points of anchor. A number of Garden Spider relatives also live in my garden, including the Four-spotted Orb-weaver, females of which have abdomens that when swollen with developing eggs in autumn turn bright red or orange just prior to giving birth.

CRAB SPIDERS (FAMILY THOMISIDAE)

Members of this group are so-called because they look vaguely crab-like and sometimes shuffle sideways in the manner of their crustacean namesakes. By nature, they are ambush predators, using camouflage to avoid detection and lying in wait for their prey to approach close enough for a pounce attack. Species of *Xysticus* (I take mine to be *X. cristatus*) have abdomen markings that when seen in isolation are bold and striking. However, when lurking in ambush they show a remarkable ability to blend in with the surroundings and have an uncanny knack for aligning their body to make sure the markings complement their location, particularly in relation to contour shadows.

Xysticus spp.

I come across *Xysticus* crab spiders among low grassy vegetation, and occasionally lurking on grass stems just beneath the flower heads. However, the prize for master of disguise among my garden's crab spiders goes to *Misumena vatia*, plump-bodied females of which are hard to spot, their colours and posture usually a perfect match for the flowers on which they wait in ambush. To add to the deception some females adjust the colour of their abdomen to perfect their camouflage, in the manner of a chameleon but at a slower pace.

A female Marbled Orb-weaver hiding in plain sight on a dead flower head.

Misumena vatia is an extremely good match for the flower heads on which it sits. The way I often find the spider is when I notice a fly or butterfly that has remained motionless for an unnatural length of time; a closer inspection usually reveals it to be resting in the fangs of a spider.

Diaea dorsata is a small but colourful variation on the crab spider theme that is adapted to live in foliage, in particular among the leaves of oaks.

Diaea dorsata.

I occasionally find it on my clothes if I have brushed by some branches. It is well camouflaged and contracts its legs into a ball if disturbed, making it a challenge to spot just by chance.

NURSERY WEB SPIDER (FAMILY PISAURIDAE)

In early summer I come across the occasional Nursery Web Spider sunning itself on a leaf, legs spanning the foliage on which it sits. Later in the season, a male may sometimes be seen gingerly approaching the larger female with a wedding gift of an insect, an understandable precaution to avoid becoming a meal himself. Having mated, the female constructs a tent-like nest in which an egg cocoon is laid and young are raised.

A Nursery Web Spider.

COMB-FOOTED SPIDER (FAMILY THERIDIIDAE)

This long-legged, rather gangly-looking spider is a regular in my garden. Individuals are found here and there in meadow vegetation and in low shrubs, and for all their small size they are fearless attackers of insects that are trapped by their half-heartedly untidy webs; their prey is often much larger than the spider itself. The female Comb-footed Spider lays an egg sac inside a leaf that she rolls for the protection of the eggs and tiny spiderlings that hatch.

A Comb-footed Spider.

WOODLOUSE SPIDER (FAMILY DYSDERIDAE)

This spider is the stuff of nightmares for its namesake crustacean because the name reflects its dietary predilections. Take one look at its fangs and you will be left in no doubt that it is weaponised for the task of piercing the armour plating of woodlice. Just be thankful it is only around an inch long, and not a foot in length, because otherwise coming across one would be terrifying. Despite its fearsome attributes, the

A female Woodlouse Spider guarding her eggs, which were accidentally exposed while moving logs.

Woodlouse Spider is rather reclusive, at least during the daytime. It is most frequently encountered under stones or beneath stored logs in sheds and greenhouses; any damp shady recess where woodlice might hide in daylight will serve as a potential refuge.

WOLF SPIDERS (FAMILY LYCOSIDAE)

As a group wolf spiders live rather nomadic lives, roaming across fallen leaves and open areas in search of prey, which they locate using their keen eyesight. As a consequence of using vision as their main sensory cue, they seem mainly diurnal, and are particularly active on sunny days. Once spotted, their victim is pounced upon and quickly dispatched. Wolf spiders are represented by an array of species in the UK, some of which are highly habitat-specific. Overall, they are a bit tricky to separate, but as a group adult females share a common character: for a while the female carries around her egg sac beneath the tail end of the abdomen, and clusters of spiderlings cling to her body for a short while once they hatch. A member of the genus *Pardosa* is the one I encounter in my garden. Its association with leaf litter, both as an adult in summer and as spiderlings at other times, is another good reason for never burning this natural resource.

A Wolf Spider female carrying her egg sac.

FUNNEL WEAVER SPIDERS (FAMILY AGELENIDAE)

These spiders spin an untidy sheet web, at the centre of which is a tunnel into which the owner retreats when danger threatens. The function of the web is to aid feeding: if the spider senses vibrations on the silk it rushes out to catch its prey. Webs and tunnels are usually located in crevices in walls, banks or tree bark. The apogee of the approach is seen in the Labyrinth Spider, which lives in tangled vegetation and creates a labyrinth of silken tunnels leading away from its tunnel entrance. From a personal point of view, the

A sheet web and tunnel entrance.

only drawback of having Labyrinth Spiders in my meadow is that they number grasshoppers among their favourite dishes, and I happen to have a fondness for my grasshopper population.

House Spiders are the larger and more impressive cousins of the Labyrinth Spider. As their name suggests, they make our homes theirs and create untidy, tunnel-entranced webs in forgotten corners in cool houses, outbuildings and sheds. The House Spider is the archetypal representative, less common than of old in part because a newcomer, the Daddy-long-legs Spider, is able to subdue and kill its much larger counterpart.

Keen eyesight and fearsome-looking fangs are among the armoury of this Common House Spider.

A Daddy-long-legs Spider and spiderlings.

DADDY-LONG-LEGS SPIDER (FAMILY PHOLCIDAE)

House-cleaning is one of my least-favourite chores, and so I pity the life of maids in domestic service in past eras. In Victorian times, advice to housekeepers and owners to measure the thoroughness and integrity of their servants is said to have included placing a penny beneath a carpet and monitoring the outcome. After cleaning work had finished, if the penny was still there the servant had failed in their duties, and if it was missing they were a thief. The only satisfactory outcome was for the servant to return the coin to their mistress. Today, the twenty-first-century housekeeper can abandon the need for deception in favour of technology to judge the attention to detail of anyone tasked with

house-cleaning. An LED torch is the answer, and shone under chairs and into ceiling corners it is the perfect tool for highlighting the silken mess created by Daddy-long-legs Spiders. If I were to be judged on my housekeeping skills in this manner, I would be deemed an abject failure. The Daddy-long-legs Spider is not itself housetrained when it comes to tidiness, and in terms of design and execution its web skills are virtually non-existent. However, what it lacks in terms of the quality of its silk it makes up with quantity. If disturbed, this alien and relative newcomer spider has a tendency to vibrate like mad. It is an effective predator of other household invertebrates, including native spider species as large as a House Spider.

HAMMOCK WEB SPIDERS (FAMILY LINYPHIIDAE)

The horizontal hammock webs made by these tiny spiders are easiest to spot when backlit by the low angle of the sun. Members of this group are a challenge to identify to species level. One of their number, the so-called Money Spider, is a great adventurer: carried aloft by silken strands, it is borne by the wind far and wide, sometimes alighting on your clothing.

Neriene montana

Drops of dew adorning the fine strands of a hammock web.

● SPIDER ALLIES

The arthropod class Arachnida includes a range of other invertebrate spider relatives that share some or all of the characters of their more familiar cousins, most notably their four pairs of legs. Their representatives include ticks, mites, false scorpions and harvestmen, and I encounter representatives of each in my garden.

Once in a while, I will notice I have picked up a tick in the garden, presumably one dislodged from a passing deer. If you worry about the transmission of Lyme disease, monitor any skin discoloration or rash that develops after being bitten and seek medical advice.

Burying beetles such as this Black Sexton Beetle are often burdened with mites Poecilochirus carabi, which scurry around on the beetle's head and thorax. The mites breed in carrion and are important recyclers; the beetles serve merely as a means of transport from one carcase to another, and this harmless relationship is known as phoresy. I defy anyone to study this photograph for any length of time and not feel the urge to scratch.

Red spider mites are a familiar sight in the garden, wandering across the ground or on foliage. There are a number of mite species that are red and although Tetranychus urticae is often referred to as the Red Spider Mite, the group is probably best treated in general terms. Some are sap suckers and not welcomed by conventional gardeners, but the myriad others that live in leaf litter and soil are significant and vital members of the recycling community.

Although you would never know it from external appearance, the distinctive nail galls that form on the surface of the leaves of lime trees Tilia spp. are caused by a mite called Eriophyes tiliae.

False scorpions (sometimes called pseudoscorpions) are easily overlooked but nevertheless widespread and common in leaf litter and compost heaps. Their scorpion-like pincers are not there for show and help these tiny predators catch and subdue smaller invertebrate prey.

Harvestmen are arachnids with small, rather flattened-rounded bodies and disproportionately long legs; they bear a passing resemblance to a Daddy-long-legs Spider but live outside, don't make webs and are generally much more active. I come across them on walls, in leaf litter and in meadow vegetation. Some species are predators, others scavenge or have a varied omnivorous diet.

JUMPING SPIDERS (FAMILY SALTICIDAE)

As their name suggests, these spiders are capable jumpers, and their leaping abilities are put to good use when pouncing on unsuspecting prey such as flies. Their athletic prowess is matched by their vision and proportionately huge eyes dominate the front of the head. The most familiar species in the garden and on the walls of my cottage is the Zebra Spider, so-called because of its striking markings. Although they appear to make fearless leaps into the unknown, if you look closely you will see that jumping spiders have an insurance policy in the form of silk strands that anchor them to the point from which they leapt.

A Zebra Spider and prey.

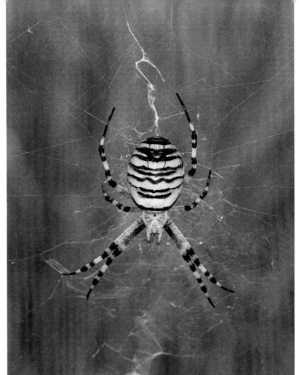

A Wasp Spider.

SPIDER WISH LIST

I saw my first Wasp Spider in the Mediterranean decades ago. This southern species made its first appearance in the UK in the 1920s and nowadays I occasionally come across this unmistakable spider near to home, the closest location being perhaps five miles from the cottage. I have seen Wasp Spiders on far-flung locations such as the Isles of Scilly and so have every confidence in the ability of the species' spiderlings to disperse and colonise new ground. I hope to welcome them to my garden in due course.

Invertebrates of the underworld

As members of a healthy environment, and integral to the ecology of any thriving biodiversity garden, the invertebrates of soil, compost, leaf litter and decaying wood are unsung and often-overlooked heroes. Many of the failings of modern farming, from the polluting use of chemicals to water run-off and flooding, can be blamed on ignorance of these creatures, the roles they perform and the world they inhabit. This is not a mistake a biodiversity gardener should make: in a stable environment their functions range from the recycling of organic matter to the maintenance of soil structure and its aeration. They are also fascinating in their own right.

No one location will be quite like another in terms of its underworld invertebrates. The geological make-up of the soil is important, not only in terms of its chemistry but in its ability to retain or drain water, and the types of plants that it supports as a consequence. Hence, whether the soil is acidic and free-draining, or neutral and water-retentive, will influence, for example, the tree species that thrive, the chemistry of the leaf litter and fallen timber and, ultimately, the organic component of the soil. This in turn will have a bearing on the soil's invertebrate inhabitants.

Soil is so much more than just a growing medium. It is a habitat in its own right and home to the myriad invertebrates that live nowhere else. Were it not for these creatures, organic matter falling on the land – be that leaves, timber, herbaceous plant material, or animal corpses and dung – would just lie where it fell for all eternity. It is these species that break down larger objects at the macro level, incorporate their remains and other fallen organic matter below ground, and recycle the nutrients.

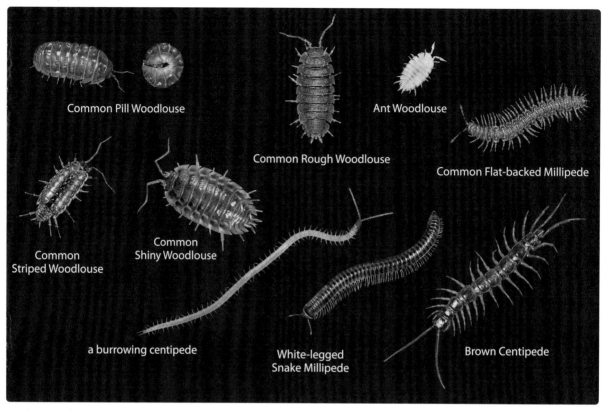

Common Pill Woodlouse

Ant Woodlouse

Common Rough Woodlouse

Common Flat-backed Millipede

Common Striped Woodlouse

Common Shiny Woodlouse

a burrowing centipede

White-legged Snake Millipede

Brown Centipede

A selection of soil and compost arthropods from my garden.

A range of organisms live only within dead wood, with some residing under the bark of fallen logs and a few requiring standing dead timber. And the stage in the decay process also has a bearing on the fauna: some creatures act as the advance guard while others tackle the wood when decay has rendered it softer and more friable. Fallen logs and indeed larger stones create a microclimate of their own beneath them, and the resulting near-constant humidity is vital for creatures that are prone to desiccation.

Healthy soil, compost, leaf litter and decaying wood offer a range of feeding opportunities for an array of different invertebrates. Some consume decaying organic matter, be it animal or plant in origin; others eat plant material or the hyphal threads of the fungal agents of decay; and there are carnivores that eat other invertebrates. Looking at the bigger picture, these creatures represent the natural recyclers and predatory checks and balances that maintain a stable underworld environment. The biodiversity gardener tinkers with this balance at his or her peril.

Many of the invertebrates that spend their lives or part of their life cycle in soil, leaf litter, or in association with decaying timber, have been mentioned before. These include, for example, certain types of beetles and true flies whose larvae have evolved to live in this habitat, many spiders and allied arthropods (false scorpions and mites), plus earwigs and ants. To be added to the tally of underworld invertebrates are springtails and bristletails, creatures so small they are often overlooked but whose numbers can be astronomical. Leaving them on one side, here are a selection of other, larger invertebrates not discussed so far, whose importance in the cycle of life cannot be overstated.

EARTHWORMS

The significance of earthworms in the web of life was recognised and explained by Charles Darwin in his 1881 book *The Formation of Vegetable Mould Through the Action of Worms, with Observations on their Habits* (see the References section for details). There are 30 or so species

An earthworm dragging dead leaf material back into its burrow.

Earthworms are segmented worms and members of the phylum Annelida. They are not to be confused with unsegmented so-called roundworms of the phylum Nematoda, which are important, if tiny, members of the leaf litter and surface soil communities. Most nematodes feed on living plant material (roots for example), decomposing matter or fungal hyphae. They do not have things all their own way, however, since there are fungi that catch them in a hyphal noose and digest them from within.

of what might loosely be described as earthworms in Britain. Their diversity is reflected in their particular ecological niche and feeding requirements. The classic species live in soil, in grassland and woodland, eating dead and decaying plant material, creating humus in the process and mixing and aerating the soil as part of their job description; they live in burrows, and the 'spoil' of shallow burrowers is deposited on the surface as familiar worm casts. Some species are more tolerant of nitrogen-rich mediums and are compost specialists while others live under the bark of decaying fallen timber. Earthworms also have relatives that live in freshwater. For more information, visit **The Earthworm Society of Britain** website at www.earthwormsoc.org.uk

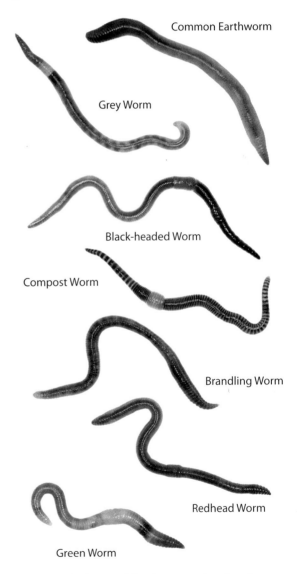

Here is a small selection of the 30 or so species of earthworms that are found in the UK. Each one is adapted to subtly different soil strata, conditions and habitats and all have a vital role to play in ensuring a healthy soil environment.

Mistle Thrushes have an uncanny ability to spot any worm ill-advised enough to be active near the soil surface in daylight.

COMPOST HEAPS AND WORMERIES

I have met people who are determined not to have a compost heap in the garden for fear of being overrun by rats. I can only speak from personal experience but have no evidence that those in my garden encourage these unwelcome rodents, despite the fact that they occur in the general area. Perhaps part of the reason is that all my organic kitchen and vegetable waste goes into a sealed wormery, something that these days I would not be without. If you are interested in using one, just type the word 'wormery' into an online search engine and you will discover plenty of alternatives for sale. Before you know it, everything from banana skins to carrot peelings is turned into rich compost that periodically I use to enrich my remaining vegetable plot. The agents of decomposition include earthworms of course, but also armies of woodlice and slugs.

MILLIPEDES

Millipedes are myriapod arthropods that are placed in a class called Diplopoda. A typical millipede has a long, segmented body with two pairs of legs per segment. Many millipede species are cylindrical but a few are distinctly flattened, an adaptation to a life spent in the spaces behind the bark of decaying timber or the interstices beneath the log itself. Millipedes are prone to desiccation and are usually most active after dark or on damp days; even on these occasions they seldom break the cover of leaf litter. Their diet comprises mainly decomposing leaves and damp and decaying wood in the advanced stages of decomposition. A few have more eclectic diets ranging from living plants to fruits, and some take an interest in decomposing animals.

More than 60 species have been recorded in Britain, many of which are either rare or so habitat-specific that you are unlikely to come across them by chance. However, a few species are common and widespread, and among the most striking is the White-legged Snake Millipede. Other species, associated with rotting wood, leaf litter, and

A Pill Millipede.

compost, include the Blunt-tailed Snake Millipede; flat-backed millipedes such as *Polydesmus angustus*; and the Pill Millipede, which can roll itself into a ball if threatened. For more information about millipedes, the **British Myriapod and Isopod Group** www.bmig.org.uk provides a range of useful resources.

CENTIPEDES

Sometimes lumped together in the same breath as millipedes, centipedes are their opposites and counterparts in terms of lifestyle and natural history. These myriapod arthropods are members of the class Chilopoda and are active and voracious predators, something that can be surmised by a head that is armed with fang-like poison claws. When discovered, a typical response is to scuttle away at speed, the progress of their segmented bodies aided by the single pair of legs per segment. Long and slender species live mainly subterranean lives but others are active above ground, generally remaining hidden beneath bark or under stones and logs in the daytime, emerging after dark to hunt.

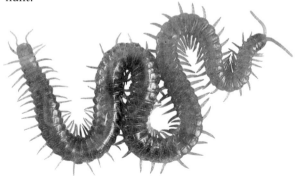

A Western Yellow Centipede.

More than 50 species of centipede are found in Britain, and many require close examination and an expert eye to ensure correct identification. Some are scarce and habitat-specific but there are several common species and group representatives to be found on the doorstep. The most frequently encountered garden species are members of the genus *Lithobius*, *L. forficatus* probably being the most ubiquitous of the lot, and sometimes referred to by the common name Brown Centipede. Other species live and hunt underground, mainly in surface layers but also in compost, and these include the Western Yellow Centipede and species of *Geophilus*. For more information about centipedes, the

British Myriapod and Isopod Group www.bmig.org.uk provides a range of useful resources.

If you come across small, pale centipede look-alikes in a soil sample they may be creatures called pseudocentipedes or symphylans. Unlike their relatives, these members of the class Symphyla are not predators but consume subterranean plant material, both decomposing and living.

CRUSTACEANS

These arthropods are placed in the subphylum Crustacea and are extensively represented by species that live in freshwater and the marine environment. There are, however, terrestrial crustaceans and those that most people are familiar with are woodlice. These distinctive creatures are members of a subdivision order called Isopoda, and are recognised by their rather flattened body shape, the dorsal surface of each segment protected by hardened plating. Adult woodlice have seven pairs of legs plus a number of superficially leg-like appendages; most species have conspicuous antennae and rudimentary compound eyes. The group's eclectic diet includes decaying plant material such as wood, organic matter generally, fungal hyphae and occasionally living plants. Woodlice lay eggs from which tiny juveniles emerge; adulthood is reached after a series of moults, and empty, pale woodlice 'skins' are sometimes found under logs, bearing testament to this process.

Of the 50 or so species of woodlice recorded in Britain there are a number of regularly encountered species. These include the Common Shiny Woodlouse, the Common Rough Woodlouse and the Common Pygmy Woodlouse. Species with a distinctly southern bias to their distribution include the Common Striped Woodlouse, and the Common Pill Woodlouse (popularly referred to as a 'pillbug'). The blind, white and subterranean Ant Woodlouse has been discussed on p. 87. For more information about woodlice the **British Myriapod and Isopod Group** www.bmig.org.uk provides a range of useful resources.

SLUGS AND SNAILS

Slugs and snails belong to the phylum Mollusca, the obvious difference between the two being that, for the most part, the former have unprotected bodies while the latter have shells into which they can retreat wholly or partly. Because of the calcium component in shells, as a general rule snails are more numerous and varied on neutral to calcareous soils than acid ones. Both slugs and snails are sensitive and vulnerable to desiccation and are most active after dark or diurnally during spells of extremely wet weather. Otherwise, they retreat underground or beneath logs and stones to avoid drying out. Elsewhere in hotter, seasonally drier parts of the world, snails ride out the arid summer months in a state of torpor known as aestivation. For the time being at least, however, the effects of a Mediterranean-type climate are not felt in the UK, and mollusc activity and behaviour is dictated by our fickle and generally temperate weather patterns.

In terms of diet, some species of slugs and snails feed on living plant material, much to the annoyance of gardeners. Many species also feed on decaying organic matter, including rotting wood, fungal hyphae, and composting vegetable matter, and play a key role in the recycling of organic matter and nutrients to the soil. A few are predators and there are species of slugs that feed on other slugs. Molluscs are hermaphrodites,

NEW ZEALAND LANDHOPPER

The crustacean order Amphipoda is a mainly aquatic group, but keen-eyed naturalists may occasionally come across a terrestrial representative in the garden – the introduced New Zealand Landhopper. It spends the hours of daylight in retreat and is sometimes discovered when moving flowerpots and the like. The jury is out on the environmental impacts that New Zealand Landhoppers have on native wildlife, but based on past experience with other alien invaders their spread and success is not likely to be without adverse consequences. That we cannot imagine what they might be serves to illustrate the paucity of our knowledge rather than the reality.

A New Zealand Landhopper.

Garden Snail

Garden Snail

Copse Snail

Kentish Snail

White-lipped Snail

White-lipped Snail

Brown-lipped Snail

Smooth Glass Snail

Leopard Slug

Strawberry Snail

Arion ater complex

Netted Slug

Dusky Slug

Irish Yellow Slug

A selection of slugs and snails from my garden.

possessing both male and female reproductive organs. Following what are often elaborate snail's pace courtship rituals, individuals cross-fertilise one another and lay eggs in clusters in secluded, damp locations. The young that hatch resemble miniature adults and grow incrementally; that includes species with shells, the size of which enlarges to accommodate the body of its owner. In addition to their recycling role, slugs and snails are food for a wide range of other creatures, ranging from birds to Hedgehogs and predatory insects. Remove them from your environment and you not only deplete your own natural world but harm the prospects of all manner of other creatures that depend on their existence, thereby running the risk of derailing the web of life.

Snail identification

In theory, snail identification should be a relatively straightforward affair, because within a given species or genus the shell shape is reasonably constant. However,

bear in mind that as a snail grows so does its shell, so size is not always helpful. Furthermore, there may be subtle differences between the shell shapes of mature and juvenile animals, to the extent that the shells of young animals in some species may be hairy while in adults they are smooth. On the whole, superficially similar group members are best left unidentified or confirmed by those with experience, expertise and an appreciation of variability: those who know which characters are essential for the identification of a given species.

Living up to its name, the snail species I encounter most frequently is the Garden Snail, although smaller individuals could be mistaken for the Copse Snail. I usually come across the latter in damp vegetation, including beds of nettles. The Brown-lipped Snail and the superficially similar White-lipped Snail occur in the garden too, and a close look at the mouth of their humbug shells is needed to distinguish between the two. Spend time searching among leaf litter and under fallen logs and stones, and others to be discovered include the

Slippery Snail and the Discus Snail. You may also come across species of *Oxychilus* with their shiny flattened shells, and their number includes the Cellar Snail and the Garlic Snail, which does indeed give off an odour of Garlic if disturbed. Use a torch to search low-growing vegetation on a wet evening and you should find the Strawberry Snail and the Kentish Snail, the latter having a southerly bias to its distribution.

Slug identification

Slug identification and family recognition requires a close look at external features. These include the presence or absence, and extent if present, of a dorsal keel behind the saddle-shaped mantle; the presence or absence of fingerprint-like concentric ridges or grooves on the mantle; and the location of the breathing hole (pneumostome) on the mantle.

Members of the family Arionidae lack a keel and have no patterning on the mantle. Large *Arion* species include the Black Slug (which, confusingly is also available in red) plus a complex of superficially similar, mainly introduced species including the Large Red Slug and the Spanish Slug. Smaller members of the family include the Dusky Slug and Silver Slug, the near-ubiquitous Blue-black Garden Slug, and the Brown Soil Slug.

A Yellow Slug.

Members of the family Limacidae have a keel running along the rear half of the tail end behind the mantle, and fingerprint markings on the mantle itself. Their numbers include the Leopard Slug, the Yellow Slug and the similar Irish Yellow Slug. As its name suggests the Tree Slug climbs tree trunks, especially in wet weather, and grazes on lichens and algae. By contrast, the introduced Greenhouse Slug, and the superficially similar Balkan Three-banded Slug are more interested in cultivated plants.

Members of the family Milacidae have keels along the full length of the tail end behind the mantle, the surface of which is grooved. They include the Budapest

The shelled slugs *Testacella* spp. (members of the family Testacellidae) are so named because of their fingernail shells. Their diet comprises mainly earthworms and as a consequence they live mostly subterranean lives. They can sometimes be found above ground in wet weather, or at other times in compost heaps or under stones.

Slug and Sowerby's Slug, both of which are competent burrowers and avoid daytime desiccation in this manner; after dark they emerge to feed on plants. In contrast, members of the family Agrolimacidae have a short keel and they include the introduced and abundant Netted Slug, and the Chestnut Slug with its pale-rimmed breathing hole.

For more information about Slugs and Snails, **The Conchological Society of Great Britain and Ireland** www.conchsoc.org is the best first port of call.

Pond life

The parish of Pamber is not blessed with an abundance of bodies of standing water. Outside of its boundaries, some ten miles away, there are linear waterways in the form of the Basingstoke Canal to the south, and the Kennet and Avon Canal to the north; and on the fringes of the Thames Valley, again a dozen or so miles from

Pond creatures don't spring fully-formed from the mud or materialise from thin air, they colonise newly formed ponds by dispersing from existing bodies of water. In the context of my pond, one such source of aquatic biodiversity is the Basingstoke Canal.

my cottage, are a mosaic of flooded gravel pits. A mile or so away from my cottage is a large moated house built in the late fifteenth century. Apart from that, there is evidence to show that there were also two moated farmhouses near my cottage. The farmhouses remain but the moats have long since been filled in or reduced in size. As a consequence, in the immediate vicinity of my cottage, bodies of standing water are represented in the main by ponds. These are typically relatively small in size and lack the feeder and drainage streams that are usually associated with lakes.

In the grand scheme of things ponds are ephemeral, and in the absence of human intervention they have a limited lifespan due to natural vegetation colonisation and succession. Here in north Hampshire, they are reliant on man to extend their lives, and in many instances, people created them in the first place. It is little wonder, therefore, that pond inhabitants are adapted to the transient nature of these small bodies of water, some of which historically would have dried out now and then. An advantage for those species that specialise in living in seasonally drying ponds is that, unless intentionally stocked, they are unlikely to harbour fish, which are utterly dependent on water for their entire lives. That is one less predatory factor to influence the evolution of the life histories of pond-dwelling specialists. The downside is that an ability to wander far and wide and colonise new locations is a prerequisite for the long-term survival of a pond-adapted plant or animal.

PONDS THROUGH THE AGES

Given their scattered and isolated locations, ephemeral nature and low density, it is surprising perhaps not that ponds support *some* forms of life but that *so many* species are able to thrive there. Well, perhaps not so surprising if the evolution of the landscape of lowland southern England, indeed the temperate northern hemisphere, is considered. Imagine an environment evolving in the wake of the last Ice Age with temporary pools of glacial meltwater forming and colonisation by a progression of increasingly vigorous plants taking place. Then picture ponds subsequently being created along watercourses by fallen trees, or perhaps intentionally dammed through the action of Eurasian Beavers (present in the British landscape until hunted to extinction in the sixteenth century). And finally, a pond's inevitable surrender to successional colonization by vegetation – herbaceous plants, then scrub, then woodland. Regardless of origin, on an evolutionary or geological timescale all these natural ponds would have been 'here today, gone tomorrow' habitats. An ability to cope with this environmental transience would have been an important factor driving the evolution of pond-colonising creatures.

As the centuries progressed, and humans began to alter the British landscape, an ability to control and manage the water supply would have been an essential part of daily life. Man-made ponds would have played an important part in this management process and, in wildlife terms, these were replacements for those created by natural forces. Fast forward to the time of the 1838 Tithe Awards and Maps for Pamber and there is written and visual evidence for the existence of ponds associated with farmsteads. Like their natural predecessors, even these would have been fickle environments for freshwater life. They would have been subject to climatic vagaries, potentially drying up in summer, or subject to the whims and management skills of their human custodians. The naturally selected

Common Frogs bred in my pond in its first season, and newly metamorphosed froglets emerged in June and July.

colonising abilities of successful pond inhabitants are as essential today as they were in the Victorian era or millennia ago.

The life of a pond may seem temporary and ephemeral when viewed through the prism of a human lifespan. However, in terms of the cycle of life and lifespan of pond inhabitants, a year or two is an eternity, and provides time to occupy a pond with enough success that subsequent generations can disperse and colonise new habitats. The pond I created in my garden is a perfect example, and a testament to the colonising ability of pond dwellers. In its first year it was colonised, seemingly out of nowhere, by five species of amphibians – every one that could reasonably be expected, including the Great Crested Newt – and at least seven species of dragonflies and damselflies.

CONTEMPORARY PONDS

Today, garden ponds assume a new significance in environmental terms if we want to maintain the legacy of standing water freshwater life that has been passed down to us through the ages. In the past, a pond would have taken days if not weeks to create, and years to become so overgrown that its value to what we conventionally think of as pond species came to an end. Today, a pond's creation, decline and fall has changed pace, and a waterbody can be created or destroyed in a matter of hours. This is not idle conjecture. I can think of two instances, over the last three years and within a mile of where I live, where precisely the latter has happened. The ponds' fate was to be infilled with builders' rubble, and their previous existence obliterated by a blanket of soil. Therefore, if you have any concerns for native aquatic life, this reinforces the significance of creating ponds, large or small, of your own; and it underlines the urgent need to secure their future for as long as possible. Do not worry if over time they lose their conventional aesthetic appeal and become overgrown. That is not the end of the world, and such new habitats will become the new world for a different suite of freshwater-associated creatures, albeit ones with which you may not yet be acquainted.

With the above in mind, my pond began life not as a garden feature but as a complement to the suite of local habitats that I was trying to foster on my doorstep. It has succeeded far better than I could have hoped in adding variety and complexity to the diversity of wildlife that

There is a more serious side to pond-dipping or pond-watching. By monitoring and recording the species you encounter, and their relative abundance, you will gain an understanding of the success or otherwise of your endeavours. You will also be able to gauge the quality and variety of standing water life in the area. As an example, if amphibians colonise quickly, you can be certain that there is a breeding pond nearby with a healthy metapopulation living their terrestrial lives in the general area. If your amphibian tally includes Great Crested Newt then your conservation antennae really should be twitching.

I suggest that, like me, you do not introduce anything, apart perhaps from a few aquatic plants at the start of the project, just to kick-start the process and aid aeration. Monitoring and recording the appearance of new arrivals to your pond will be part of the fun. Following the progress of colonisation will give you an understanding of the ability of pond invertebrates to come and go, and will inform your appreciation of the ecological significance of these small bodies of water in the twenty-first century. If they are maintained over time, garden ponds really do have the potential to become reservoirs of aquatic life from which pioneers will move to other sites as time goes on. That is exactly the process that allowed settlement of my pond and its transformation from a relatively lifeless pool of water at the start to the bustling, complex haven for freshwater life that it is today.

POND DOS AND DON'TS

Historically, the role of man-made ponds in my part of the world would have been purely functional. There were a few larger bodies of water that acted as stew ponds, stocked with fish for the table; an example can be found at Pamber Priory (Sherborne Priory) whose origins date back to the twelfth century (see p. 30). However, the likelihood is that, from a human perspective, in previous eras most ponds were seen merely as bodies of water, mainly for the benefit of domestic livestock. The fact that they nurtured the wildlife legacy we see today was not intentional but merely an unintended consequence of their existence.

POND PLANTS

It is hard to be sure, but based on observations of ponds near me that are not in people's gardens, and receive minimal human intervention, truly aquatic plant life

There are few more rewarding sights for any pond creator than that of an emerging adult dragonfly. For early risers among you, the larva of this Brown Hawker left the water at around 3.00 a.m., had finally settled on its emergence spot by 5.00 a.m. and had emerged and begun drying its wings an hour later.

has established itself in my plot. As well as providing a sense of satisfaction that comes from creating something worthwhile, it also brings back happy childhood memories; anyone with an interest in natural history will surely recall the delights of pond-dipping. On an occasional basis and with a respectful appreciation of the disturbance it causes, I rekindle those memories. However, these days my pond exploration is undertaken less frequently with a net than in the past, and with more emphasis on pond watching than pond-dipping. By creating your own pond, you too will generate a new ecological dimension to the array of wildlife your plot of land supports. As it has for me, it may also reawaken a latent passion for freshwater life; for those memories to translate into action, all that is needed is a net, a shallow tray and a keen and enquiring mind.

Common Duckweed.

it comes to plant introductions. The same applies to water-lilies and allies (*Nymphaea* spp., *Nuphar* spp. and *Nymphoides* spp.) which in terms of stature can quickly become dominant in small ponds; the fact that some may be native in the wider sense does not mean they are environmentally appropriate for a particular pond, or are favourable regarding the ecological niches to which its native pond invertebrates have evolved and are adapted. On the plus side, submerged aquatic plants produce oxygen via photosynthesis, and provide a three-dimensional structure to the aquatic environment. They help turn what would otherwise be little more than a drinking pool into a thriving and healthy freshwater environment. However, to maintain a pond as a pond the plants need cautious management.

When it comes to plants that grow around wetland margins, perhaps the best advice is to think in terms of proportion and scale: the size and spreading capacity of the plant you are contemplating introducing versus the size of your pond. Look at ponds and wetlands in your area to gauge the colonising potential of any contenders when they are left to their own devices. With a small pond, I would urge extreme caution with regards to any of the larger sedge species that like to grow with their feet in water, Greater Pond-sedge being among them. Before you know it they will have taken over, and in the context of a small pond that will be the beginning of the end unless you constantly address the progress of colonisation.

is relatively limited and comprises species of water-starwort and Common Duckweed and not much more. Many people's perception of pond vegetation is based on marginal colonisers that subsequently span the divide between land and water. These are valuable in their own right, of course, but, if left unchecked, they lead inexorably to a pond becoming wholly vegetated and well on its way to being a damp, terrestrial habitat. Yellow Iris and Floating Sweet-grass, in my experience, are among the many architects and accelerators of this process.

Common Water-starwort.

When it comes to the perceived value of a pond, conventional gardening advice appears to equate something that is colourful and pleasing to the human eye with an aquatic environment that is beneficial to wildlife. The two are not necessarily mutually exclusive, of course, but given that I wanted my pond to be true to its local heritage, I find beauty in what occurs naturally, and fulfilment from an appreciation of the largely unseen web of life that it supports.

Plants that are sometimes suggested as aquatic introductions for ponds tend to be those that I associate more with lakes, canals and sluggish river backwaters than small homestead ponds in my area. These include Opposite-leaved Pondweed and species of hornwort. When introduced to small bodies of water they usually thrive, so be careful what you wish for when

If you have the patience, then wait for natural colonisation to occur. However, if you want to kick-

Introduce White Water-lily to your pond and you may come to regret it after a few years, by which time the plant will have increased in size dramatically.

Chief among the botanical offenders is Public Enemy Number One New Zealand Pigmyweed *Crassula helmsii*, which will smother a small pond in a season, out-compete most native species, and render any project worthless.

start the process, then I hope by now you will have got the message that you need to exercise extreme caution with what you introduce. The source of any introduction is also important. The greatest risk comes from the introduction by accident or design of non-native species that subsequently run amok and displace native ones.

Overall, perhaps the best pond-related advice is to never accept gifts from strangers, or even from friends come to that. If you buy plants, use reputable suppliers, and even then I would still urge caution and quarantine as measures to be taken prior to the introduction of any plants. Inherent in this approach is the need to be able to identify offenders. If your aim is to create and nurture a pond that benefits the greatest variety of native wildlife and species most suited to and dependent on small ponds, then do not introduce fish. Even if your pond is the size of a lake my advice would still be to let nature take its course and not introduce fish.

PRACTICAL POND-DIPPING AND FRESHWATER SAMPLING

Looking back at my past actions, I suspect that my approach to pond-dipping was, to put it kindly, overenthusiastic, and will have caused untold damage to the freshwater habitats I sampled so eagerly. In terms of havoc, repeatedly and vigorously sweeping a net through a pond is akin to trampling through or flailing a flower-rich meadow (or in conventional gardening terms, an herbaceous border). Nowadays I am more circumspect and sample the pond using a net only occasionally, and I hope the concern for my aquatic catch reflects the obligation I feel towards their welfare. That being said, I do still engage in pond-dipping

● WELCOME AND UNWELCOME VISITORS

As an avid birdwatcher, I have mixed feelings when it comes to birdlife visiting my pond. I welcome the Blackbirds, Song Thrushes and Robins that come to drink and bathe. And I am thrilled when I spot a Grey Wagtail bobbing around the margins, or by the very occasional sighting of a Kingfisher perched on an overhanging oak branch. However, there are other birds that are less welcome and a few that I would probably discourage. Again, as with plants, it is a question of scale and proportion on one hand, and the ecological role I want the pond to play. Mine is a small pond, one where native invertebrates and amphibians are the creatures I want to benefit most.

I get occasional visits from Mallards and prospecting Mandarin Ducks, but I certainly do not want to encourage their permanent residence, something I could easily do if, for example, I fed them. Before long I would have no aquatic vegetation left, the pond's marginal vegetation would be 'puddled' and grazed beyond

recognition, and the water would be polluted through nutrient enrichment from their faeces. I like both species in the right context, but for all these reasons I feel they are not compatible with my small pond. I also dread the day when a Moorhen turns up. Again, I have nothing against the species, but their eclectic diet has a predatory dimension, one that I saw with my own eyes a few years ago on a nearby pond. In the company of a couple of friends, I spent an hour or so watching the pool in the hope of spotting Water Voles, which had been reported in the area. While we sat there, a Moorhen worked its way around the margins, picking off tadpole after tadpole with alarming success. Finally, it scored big-time and pulled an adult female Great Crested Newt from the depths, which it dragged to dry land, disabled by repeated pecks and then swallowed whole. In my small pond, a resident Moorhen would not be good news for its amphibians, or its invertebrate population.

now and then. For me it brings back fond memories of simpler, less troubled times. It may do the same for others of a similar disposition; or for novice naturalists it could be the perfect introduction to the complexity of life that lives beneath the water's surface, and be a way to engage the next generation. So, to that end, the following are some thoughts and suggestions for the way forward.

The standard pond-dipping tool of the trade is a net, typically a long-handled, stout-framed item with a mesh size that allows silt and small particles to pass through whilst retaining larger objects such as leaves, pondweeds and of course, aquatic creatures. Rather than simply swishing the net through the water, my favoured method, which minimises destruction and disturbance, is to slowly ease the net into the water down and below the aquatic vegetation and then to lift it to the surface with a smooth but swift action.

The contents of the net are then ready for inspection and the best option is a shallow white tray already filled with water from the pond. It is important that the net contents are placed in water for two reasons: firstly, because aquatic creatures will ultimately die if deprived of their natural medium; and secondly, most creatures will only start moving around, and hence become more visible, when submerged. Environmental etiquette demands that creatures lingering in the net and those in the tray should be returned to the pond, rinsed off in the water.

The time of year has a bearing on what you might find in your pond sample and, indeed, whether you should be sampling in the first place. For example, if you have amphibians in your pond and care about their survival, pond-dipping is best avoided from the point that courtship begins until a time when tadpoles have metamorphosed into tiny adults. Locations vary and timing differs but, in my pond, I limit my investigation to observation rather than exploration from late February to early June. Arguably, any budding pond naturalist is born with the best equipment for understanding pond life without the need to purchase anything. Furthermore, they can easily train themselves and hone their skills to make best use of this kit. Your eyes are the best assets you will ever have, and patience and observational skills can be learnt, honed, and enhanced, to make the best use of this kit.

Many pond creatures are surprisingly sensitive to movement, especially when a moving object such as a human observer breaks the skyline. Having stationed yourself strategically on the bank, if you have the patience to sit still for a couple of minutes, aquatic life will return to normal. Amphibians will emerge from cover and move about, and insect larvae and adults will begin to scuttle around. Look for tell-tale signs of movement as your first clue. Many pond creatures are much more active after dark than in daylight, and certainly more visible and easily picked out using a bright LED torch.

The lingering scientist in me still occasionally wants to quantify what I observe, either out of nostalgic curiosity or in an attempt to monitor progress. An example might be assessing the number of male amphibians lingering around the pond margin at the start of the breeding season. However, sounding a note of caution, even the most sophisticated non-parametric statistical methods cannot account for some variables in nature. My amphibian studies demonstrated this when I attempted systematic amphibian monitoring one spring: I would cautiously work my way round the pond margin once an hour, marking on a sketch map everything I saw. In that particular season (in 2021), a typical count just before sunset was 32 Palmate Newts, 41 Smooth Newts, 5 Great Crested Newts, 5 pairs of Common Frogs in amplexus and 15 Common Toads. Similar numbers would be recorded just after sunset. However, as dusk turned to total darkness subsequent counts revealed that almost everything had vanished.

Both Palmate and Smooth Newts (the former shown here) are avid consumers of the eggs and developing embryos in frogspawn.

That happened on successive nights and it puzzled me greatly – until I set a camera trap. It turned out that between counts, when I retired to the cottage for an after-dark cup of tea, a pair of Mallards would alight on the pond in what seemed to me to be total darkness. With prenuptial vigour they would chase each other round and round, the male sometimes nearly drowning the female, disturbing everything aquatic in the process before flying off to who knows where. Had I not uncovered these wildfowl shenanigans I would have been tempted to think I had discovered some amazing new facet to amphibian behaviour. More dangerously, had I elected to monitor the pond late in the evening rather than at dusk I would have concluded it was devoid of amphibian life.

Pond life evolves and changes over time, and as a water body matures new species appear and flourish while others fade and disappear. That pattern of change has been noticeable among the amphibians in my pond. Although it has become much harder to observe due to the increasingly vegetated submerged world, the relative abundances of Common Frogs, Common Toads and the three newt species have changed over time. Common Frogs appear to have taken a particular hammering as newt fortunes and populations have risen – the latter are avid consumers of embryos and developing tadpoles in the spawn to the point where only a few froglets reach the metamorphic stage nowadays, whereas in the pond's first couple of years of life hundreds would emerge.

Dragonflies, those consummate colonisers, also come and go in terms of species. Initially Common Darter and Broad-bodied Chaser were dominant but for now at least Southern Hawker and Emperor Dragonfly are in the ascendent and rule the Odonata roost. Colonisation by dragonflies provides more information than just a pond's health: their speed of arrival at a pond and the succession of species says as much about the health and abundance of other ponds in the vicinity. Dragonflies also provide opportunities for monitoring colonisation and population levels without necessarily sampling water. More about that later in this section.

Recommended resource: **The Freshwater Habitats Trust** is a valuable online resource for all things relating to garden ponds and the wider aquatic environment. Visit www.freshwaterhabitats.org.uk

THE VARIETY OF LIFE

Entire books have been written on the subject of pond life and the identification of aquatic creatures. It is not the role of *The Biodiversity Gardener* to replicate such an ambitious target. Instead, the following is the most basic of introductions to the wealth of life you might encounter if you create a wildlife pond in your garden, or already have one, with a nod to the species you might also come across in ditches and slow-flowing streams.

Some invertebrates are aquatic throughout their lives, while others are terrestrial and airborne as adults with other stages in their life cycles (that might include eggs, larvae or pupae) being aquatic. The requirements of all life-cycle stages need to be considered when managing your biodiversity garden, with terrestrial as well as aquatic habitat and feeding requirements respected in terms of management and planting.

UNSUNG HEROES

The most important ingredients for a thriving, wildlife-rich pond are the plants and animals you cannot see either because they are so small or insignificant that they are overlooked, or because you lack the eyes to see them. These unsung heroes, some of which are microscopic and super-abundant, underpin the cycle of life in freshwater. Tiny creatures, ranging from protozoa and rotifers to microscopic crustaceans such as ostracods, help recycle nutrients from organic

Two examples of microscopic life in my pond: left, a water flea (a free-swimming crustacean); right, an ostracod (a bivalve crustacean). Both are smaller than pinheads.

detritus at the bottom of the pond, and in turn serve as food for larger creatures. In the water column, planktonic algae contribute to oxygenation of the water and live alongside, and are sometimes eaten by, free-living crustaceans such as water fleas and copepods. With echoes of a coral reef in miniature, tiny *Hydra* (see illustration on p. 125) use stinging tentacles to catch prey in the manner of their marine relatives the sea anemones, and there are even freshwater sponges that live in ponds. More sizeable overlooked creatures lurk in the murky depths if you take the time to look, and these include three phyla of worms: nematodes, annelid worms (earthworm relatives and leeches), and platyhelminth flatworms. Operating checks and balances on one another, this community of unsung heroes ensures a healthy body of water in which larger, more familiar creatures can prosper.

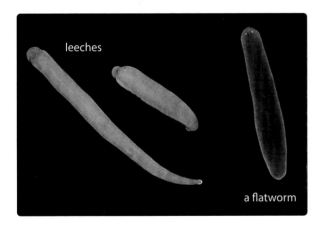
leeches
a flatworm

WORMS

The term 'worm' is a generic and non-specific one that embraces several animal phyla, of which two have larger representatives in my pond. Annelid worms (phylum Annelida) – best known as terrestrial earthworms – have a few representatives that live in the soggy margins, but their most familiar representatives are leeches. These have segmented bodies, suckers at either end and a diet, depending on species, that can be predatory or blood-sucking. So-called flatworms belong to the phylum Platyhelminthes, a group that includes some notorious internal parasites – flukes and tapeworms – of animals, including humans. The pond representatives of the group are entirely harmless to us, however, and glide around feeding on diatoms and other small pond organisms.

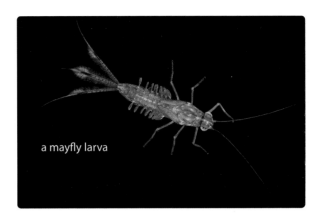
a mayfly larva

MAYFLIES (ORDER EPHEMEROPTERA)

Most of the members of this insect group are associated with flowing water but a few favour still conditions, including ponds. The Pond Olive is one such species and it quickly colonised my pond. As the group's scientific name suggests, adults are relatively short-lived, although the Pond Olive may survive for ten days or more, roughly the adult lifespan of some of our butterfly species. Adult mayflies do not feed and have two pairs of wings that are folded over the body at rest while their body adopts an elegant curved posture. There are two whip-like projections at the tail end (some species have three). Mayfly larvae or nymphs have six legs, gills projecting from the sides of the abdomen and three projections known as cerci at the tail end. Mayfly larvae feed on algae, diatoms and detritus generally, and those of the Pond Olive roam around, many becoming food for predatory pond inhabitants. Mayfly larvae undergo a partial metamorphosis and go through a 'subimago' stage before moulting to become fully adult.

CADDISFLIES (ORDER TRICHOPTERA)

Caddisflies are another group of insects that, throughout their life cycle, span the divide between aquatic and terrestrial lives. Represented by 200 or so UK species, adults bear a passing resemblance to micro moths and live terrestrial lives. By and large they are shy and retiring creatures and scuttle away if disturbed, or fly off using their two pairs of wings. They have long, slender antennae, small beady eyes and rather spindly legs. Adult caddisflies are mostly nocturnal and spend the hours of daylight hiding under leaves and foliage, or among moss and emergent vegetation. The group is best known for its larval stage and in particular their

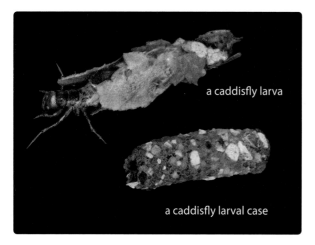

a caddisfly larva

a caddisfly larval case

Caddisfly species such as *Potamophylax cingulatus* (seen here), *Limnephilus sparsus* and the Grousewing, which I catch occasionally in my garden moth trap, are perhaps individuals that have strayed from the stream, or they might be overlooked pond dwellers.

case-building skills, these being constructed from debris particles bound together by silk. Each caddis family, and in some cases individual species, is unique or nearly so in terms of the material and method of construction. Caddisfly larvae have a head and thorax hardened with chitin but the rest of the body is soft and vulnerable, their delicate gills protected by the case in which they live.

Most caddisfly species are associated with flowing water or lakes, but a number have larvae that live quite happily in ponds and ditches. Although there are excellent keys and guides to caddisfly identification, I find the process trickier than it might first appear. For absolute certainty they need to be killed and adult features such as wing venation and genitalia scrutinised under the microscope; a similar approach is needed with larvae where, for example, gill structure is a useful feature. Since I am not prepared to kill these engaging creatures to satisfy my curiosity, I content myself with the recognition of a few easy-to-identify species, and identification to family level of the rest. The trade-off and the resulting conservation consequence is that caddisflies in my pond and stream are under-recorded, and this approach potentially undermines the power of datasets to protect wildlife.

Caddisfly species in my pond with which I am reasonably confident regarding identification include *Limnephilus lunatus* and the Mottled Sedge. For the latter to survive in a body of water, overhanging vegetation is crucial – see p. 112. Caddisfly larvae are sensitive to disturbance and if alarmed, for example when the contents of a net is emptied into a tray, they retreat into their cases and remain seemingly lifeless

for several minutes. Patience is the friend of the pond watcher and as another tip, like many other pond invertebrates, caddis larvae are much more active after dark, their movements easily spotted with the aid of a bright torch.

STONEFLIES (ORDER PLECOPTERA)

Of the 30 or so UK members of this insect group, most are associated with streams and, with a clue in the name, their larvae have a body shape designed so they can flatten themselves to the surfaces of rocks and boulders and cling on without being washed away. A few species are associated with slow-flowing streams and ditches. I sometimes see adult *Nemoura cinerea* on the bank of the stream at the bottom of my garden and occasionally in the vicinity of the pond. Adult stoneflies prefer to scuttle away rather than fly, and that behaviour combined with their rather insignificant appearance

a stonefly larva

An adult stonefly *Nemoura cinerea*.

An adult alderfly *Sialis lutaria*.

means they are easily overlooked. They have a slender body, two pairs of wings that are typically wrapped around the body at rest, two long slender antennae and two superficially antenna-like projections at the tail end. Larval stoneflies bear a passing resemblance to wingless versions of their adult counterparts and their diet varies, according to species, from predator to detritivore.

an alderfly larva

ALDERFLIES (ORDER MEGALOPTERA)

Three species of this insect group are found in our region. However, they are similar enough to require examination of their genitalia for certain identification, and most people, including me, are happy to ascribe the name *Sialis lutaria* to observations in the field as the most likely contender. Alderflies have two pairs of similar smoky-coloured wings with conspicuous dark veins. These are held over the body at rest in the manner of a ridge tent, giving the insect a passing resemblance to a large, dark lacewing. Alderflies are rather sluggish insects that wander over vegetation, occasionally flying a few feet if the fancy takes them. Their diet comprises mainly pollen and they are associated with streams, lakes and larger ponds where their larvae are free-

living among debris at the bottom. In appearance the larvae have elongated, tapering and clearly segmented bodies, and powerful jaws to match their predatory diet. There have three pairs of legs, plus paired feathery gill projections on the abdominal segments and a single projection at the tail end.

DRAGONFLIES AND DAMSELFLIES (ORDER ODONATA)

This distinctive insect group is divided into members whose adults have dissimilar front and hind wings (dragonflies, suborder Anisoptera) and ones with similar wings (damselflies, suborder Isoptera). The life cycles of both groups are broadly similar. Adults lay eggs, usually in water but sometimes beside it, from which larvae hatch. These are always aquatic and undergo a series of moults that permit growth in body size. Some species will emerge as adults from eggs laid the previous summer. Influenced by geographical

Compound eyes dominate the head of dragonflies such as this Brown Hawker.

location and water temperature, others take two years (sometimes longer) to reach the point where they will metamorphose into adults.

Dragonfly adults have large and mobile heads and proportionately huge compound eyes that befit their predatory lifestyle and the fact that they hunt in flight. The two pairs of mainly clear, strikingly veined wings are held flat in one plane at rest. Dragonflies are superb fliers, capable of sustained hovering and rapid acceleration and manoeuvrability. The abdomen is long, segmented and often colourful. Eggs are laid randomly in water, inside water plant stems or in waterside vegetation, depending on the species. Their larvae are active predators that use an extensible mask and fangs to capture prey – the insect equivalent of a chameleon's tongue. Among dragonflies, there are three main larval body forms: elongate, seen in members of the genus *Aeshna* for example; squat but active larvae such as species of *Sympetrum*; and ambush predators that are squat and hairy, and live in pond debris, examples of which include members of the genus *Libellula*. All dragonfly larvae breathe by means of so-called rectal gills, oxygenated water being pumped in and out of their rear ends; in streamlined species rapid expulsion of water via this route serves as a means of jet propulsion to escape danger. Depending on the species, dragonfly larvae emerge from the water in spring or early summer and metamorphose into adults.

An Azure Damselfly.

As befits their name, damselflies are dainty and slow-flying by comparison with their larger cousins. Nevertheless, they are active predators, but ones that target smaller invertebrates, usually spotting prey on vegetation rather than catching it on the wing. Adult damselflies have large, near-spherical compound eyes and almost identical transparent (in most species) forewings and hindwings, with venation and markings that aid classification and identification. Damselflies hold their wings above the body at rest. Their larvae are slender and predatory, and use an extensible mask and fangs to capture prey. They breathe using three paddle-shaped gills at the tail end, the shape and markings being useful in identification.

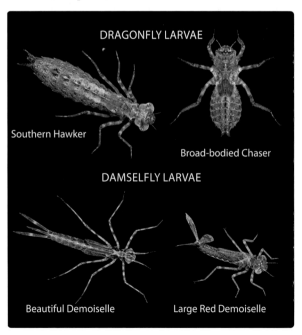

DRAGONFLY LARVAE

Southern Hawker

Broad-bodied Chaser

DAMSELFLY LARVAE

Beautiful Demoiselle

Large Red Demoiselle

Dragonfly exuviae, such as this Southern Hawker, tend to be robust and can be removed from vegetation intact. Stored carefully, they will last for years.

Damselfly exuviae, such as this Large Red Damselfly, are rather delicate and are best collected and stored while still attached to the vegetation on which they emerged.

For a few weeks after emergence, adult dragonflies and damselflies have a tendency to disperse from water, and they often feed over terrestrial habitats. When fully mature they return to water, and the prospect of mating and egg-laying becomes a priority. Some species demonstrate a degree of territoriality, and although there is always a lot of coming and going, this is the time you might want to monitor and count identified individuals to allow comparisons year-on-year. A more accurate indication of the previous year's population is provided by the larvae, not by any intrusive means but by employing fieldcraft. When larvae emerge and metamorphose into adults they leave behind their larval skin, something that naturalists call an *exuvia* (plural 'exuviae'). This tough, chitinised husk, although brittle, can be extracted, accurately identified, and numbers of exuviae counted for future comparisons. It is a good idea to build up a reference collection, and field observation will allow you to appreciate the sort of marginal and emergent vegetation dragonflies and damselflies need to complete their life cycles.

TRUE FLIES (ORDER DIPTERA)

Adults of this group of insects have one pair of functioning wings, the hind pair being reduced to club-shaped structures that aid aerial stability. The presence of the group in the biodiversity garden has already been discussed on p. 203 but it is worth mentioning them again in the context of freshwater, because the larvae of some are associated either with water itself or with inundated soggy ground; the larvae of soldier-flies are adapted to the latter habitat. Some water-associated true fly larvae are found in temporary bodies of water, and mosquitoes are quick to colonise puddles and buckets of water (see illustration on p. 205). By doing so, they avoid many of the predators associated with more permanent bodies of water. Others have evolved to live in more extreme conditions: the Common Drone-fly, as elegant as any other hoverfly as an adult,

has larvae that colonise stagnant water so revolting that little else could cope, breathing air through a long periscopic siphon (see illustration on p. 206). Look closely and almost any body of water in the garden, big or small, temporary or permanent, will harbour the larvae of some true fly species.

WATER BUGS (ORDER HEMIPTERA)

Many species of aquatic true bugs are capable of flight, which is how they colonise new water bodies so quickly. Like their terrestrial insect cousins, water bugs have proboscis-like mouthparts designed to pierce and suck. Many representatives are predators, and this group includes those that employ ambush and stealth tactics. Their numbers include the Water Scorpion and the Water Stick-insect (illustrated on p. 199). Other species are much more active, including species of lesser water boatman, which swim the right way up using paddle-shaped front legs to propel themselves; they feed on plant material. Their larger cousin the Common Backswimmer (or Water Boatman) swims upside down

a typical aquatic true fly larva

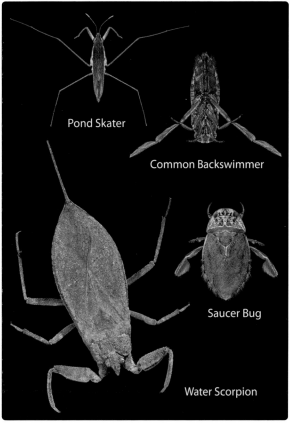

Pond Skater

Common Backswimmer

Saucer Bug

Water Scorpion

and is surface-buoyant. Specially evolved eyes allow it to see above and below the surface film at the same time. It uses its back legs for swimming, and its predatory diet extends to prey the size of small tadpoles. Pond Skaters also live at the surface, but in their case, they skate on top of the surface film, propelled by their middle legs. They are both predators and scavengers, their invertebrate diet including creatures that have fallen into the water and become trapped by the same surface film that underpins a Pond Skater's way of life.

WATER BEETLES (ORDER COLEOPTERA)

As members of a vast and varied group of insects, several families of beetles are adapted to a life in freshwater and are referred to collectively as water beetles. Their larvae are tied to the aquatic environment, but most water beetles leave the water on a regular basis, typically after dark, and are capable of flight; this explains why they can colonise newly created ponds so rapidly. The adults are usually recognisable as such, having hardened front wings called elytra that cover the body

A female Great Diving Beetle.

and create a smooth, streamlined outline. Regardless of diet, all water beetles have biting mouthparts and many are predators. Quick to colonise my pond in its infancy were whirligig beetles, familiar to any observant naturalist and known for swimming in endless circles on the pond surface, often in what look like swarms. Both adult and larval whirligigs are predators.

Some water beetle species crawl and amble among pond vegetation, but so-called diving beetles have refined the art of speed-swimming and have particularly streamlined bodies. An air supply trapped beneath their elytra gives them buoyancy, and means that they have to grasp on to something to remain submerged; the air supply is replenished by sticking the abdomen through the surface film. The hind pair of legs is used for swimming and is often fringed by hairs to increase the surface area. Diving beetle larvae are typically elongate and, like the adults, they are predators. The larvae of members of the genus *Dytiscus*, which includes the Great Diving Beetle, are particularly fearsome.

AQUATIC MOTHS (ORDER LEPIDOPTERA)

Many species of moths are associated with larval food-plants that grow around the margins of water or in damp ground. However, the larvae of a few members of this insect group are truly aquatic, and a couple have colonised my pond. In a manner reminiscent of caddis larvae, those of the Brown China-mark construct a rudimentary case from pieces of leaf and feed on the underside of water-lilies and other plants with surface-floating leaves. Tiny, but abundant in my pond, the Water Veneer is another example of a moth whose larvae are aquatic and make a loose case of leaf fragments to protect themselves.

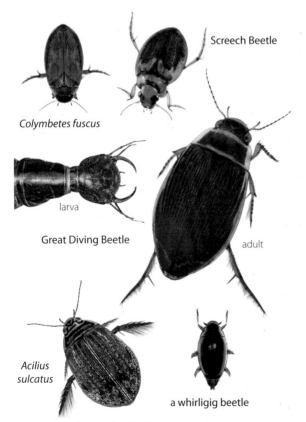

Colymbetes fuscus

Screech Beetle

larva

Great Diving Beetle

adult

Acilius sulcatus

a whirligig beetle

A selection of water beetles from my garden pond.

A fully winged female Water Veneer, the life-cycle stage and form that disperses and colonises new aquatic habitats. Most females of the species possess only rudimentary wings, cannot fly and live submerged aquatic lives.

FRESHWATER CRUSTACEANS (SUBPHYLUM CRUSTACEA)

Crustaceans are arthropods, and as a group they are far better represented in aquatic environments than on land; a few examples now call my pond home. Like others of their kind, they have an outer exoskeleton that is moulted as they grow; multiple pairs of legs and leg-like appendages; and some are competent swimmers.

Among the range of pond crustaceans there are numerous small but important scavengers and filter feeders, which in turn serve as food for others. They are important components in the cycle of life in a healthy pond. They include water fleas such as *Daphnia* spp. (see illustration on p. 232) that have transparent bivalve shells from which the head and limbs extend; they swim jerkily through the action of the second pair of bristly antennae. Adding to the planktonic pond mix are tiny copepods, recognised by their pear-shaped body, paired antennae and projecting tail filaments. Like water fleas they swim with a jerky action, females carrying with them paired egg sacs. Most copepods are free-living but

some species are parasitic, attaching themselves to, for example, the skin or gills of fish. What they lack in size ostracods make up for with numbers. You will need to look closely to see them, however, since they are smaller than pinheads (see illustration on p. 232). Seen through a hand lens or microscope, they are like miniature bivalve molluscs. They are constantly on the move, scurrying around by the action of their projecting antennae.

Not all my pond crustaceans are creatures in miniature. The Water Hog-louse, which is related to woodlice and bears a passing resemblance to its terrestrial cousins, is one example. It seems to spend most of its time in the debris at the bottom of the pond and moves at a fairly slow pace. The Freshwater Shrimp is another of my pond residents, and it is also present in the stream at the bottom of the garden. It can be recognised by its laterally flattened arched body, and the array of legs and appendages that are used to scurry along the bottom and walk and climb among pondweeds; when alarmed it can swim in a jerky and brief manner, using its tail and tail appendages. Freshwater Shrimps have a varied diet and are themselves food for many other creatures. Males carry eggs in a brood pouch.

FRESHWATER MOLLUSCS (PHYLUM MOLLUSCA)

Terrestrial molluscs in my garden have been discussed on p. 223, but a few aquatic species have taken up residence in my pond. Among the more surprising of the arrivals was that of a tiny bivalve called the European Fingernail Clam. I did not knowingly introduce the species and I have no idea how it arrived, but nowadays it is verging on the abundant. Like other bivalves, my tiny clams can clamp their shells shut to protect the soft body and are surprisingly agile, moving by means of an extensible foot. They filter-feed and supply themselves with oxygen from water that flows into and out of siphons extended between the open shells. Larger species of bivalves, not those associated with ponds, have larvae that are parasitic on fish.

The remaining molluscs in my pond are, for the most part, easily recognised as snails, having obvious spired shells (for example species of *Lymnaea* and *Physa*) or coiled shells (for example species of *Planorbis*). A few freshwater snails have a plate called an 'operculum' that can be used to seal the mouth of their shells, but none of my pond species have that feature. Typical

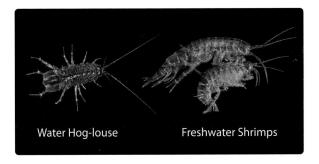

Water Hog-louse   Freshwater Shrimps

Great Pond Snail

European
Fingernail Clam

Wandering Snail

Pfeiffer's Amber Snail

Great Ramshorn
and egg mass

Margined Ramshorn

A selection of freshwater molluscs from my garden pond.

pond snails are called 'pulmonates' and as the name hints, they have an internal chamber that acts as a rudimentary lung, air being replenished periodically at the surface. My pulmonate snails are grazing herbivores that feed on algae and diatoms as well as plant material. In larger ponds elsewhere, but not currently my own, I have come across the Lake Limpet. Like its seashore counterparts it has a grazing diet that includes algae and diatoms; it can be found attached to larger plant stems and stones.

POND LIFE WISH LIST

The pond in my garden is relatively new and currently does not harbour Water Spiders, as far as I know. As its name suggests, this species lives underwater. It uses its silk-weaving skills to make a bell-shaped web, woven between plant stems. This it stocks with air that is transported from the water surface trapped by hairs on its body. I have come across the species in some pretty isolated spots – a pond on the top of windswept Lundy Island, for example – and I live in hope that my small body of water may one day be colonised by this fascinating creature.

A Water Spider.

Amphibians and reptiles

All our native amphibians and reptiles face threats in one form or another and few are thriving. Particularly at risk is the Common Toad and according to the report 'Amphibian and reptile declines – UK perspective' on the conservation charity Froglife's website, the species has declined by 68 percent over the past 30 years. The threats are almost all as a result of human activity. The solution to the problem also lies with us, and everyone can do their bit to help.

GARDEN HAVENS

The importance of gardens for wildlife, including amphibians and reptiles, lies in their sheer size. According to the Office for National Statistics' *UK natural capital: ecosystem accounts for urban areas* profile, an estimated 29 percent (520,000 hectares) of urban areas in Great Britain comprise residential gardens; see the Reference section for a link to their website. So, on the basis of size alone, these potential sanctuaries

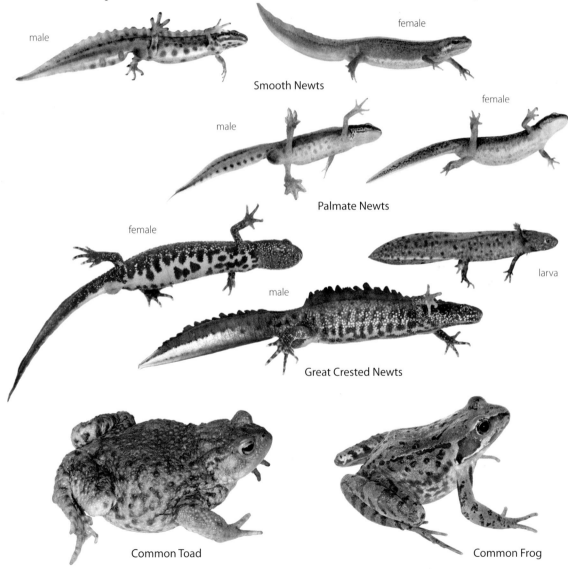

male

female

Smooth Newts

male

female

Palmate Newts

female

larva

male

Great Crested Newts

Common Toad

Common Frog

Of the seven native species of amphibians in the UK, these are the most likely garden candidates.

clearly have a role to play in conservation if managed appropriately. Then there is the notion of connectivity. In isolation, an individual garden may have little impact on the fate of wildlife in Britain. But collectively they can, in terms of size and connectivity, particularly if an integrated approach is adopted and endorsed by community spirit.

LIFESTYLES AND LIFE CYCLES

Reptiles are terrestrial creatures, although the Grass Snake has a definite affinity for water. From a garden-management perspective, UK amphibians are best regarded as terrestrial animals too, but ones that have to return to water to breed, for a brief period in spring. All our reptile and amphibian species hibernate to a greater or lesser extent, depending on prevailing weather. Outside the breeding season, amphibians tend to wander on dry land, with newly metamorphosed young animals being particularly inclined to disperse far and wide. In general, amphibians return each spring to the pond where they were spawned.

Of the six native species of reptile found in the UK, the most likely garden candidates are Grass Snake (left and above) and Slow-worm (right).

Amphibians lay their eggs in water, and the developing tadpole is protected by a bubble of jelly. In the case of the Common Frog, eggs are laid en masse, as frogspawn. After a couple of weeks, tadpoles emerge and become free-living, growing and developing front legs, and then hind legs. Their diet switches from being a largely vegetarian grazer to a more carnivorous animal; eventually the tail is resorbed and a young froglet is the result.

Reptiles also produce eggs. In the case of the Slow-worm they hatch internally and after the yolk supply has been depleted, tiny young are born. Grass Snakes, on the other hand, lay a clutch of eggs in a grass mound or compost heap, using the heat generated by decomposition to promote development. Depending on temperature, incubation can last between two and three weeks, during which time the female often guards the clutch.

When it comes to diet, all adult amphibians and reptiles in the UK are carnivorous. Invertebrates, including slugs as well as more active creatures, feature in

Grass Snakes are generally unobtrusive and wary creatures that will see you coming before you see them. However, because they shed their skins periodically, evidence of their presence is easy to spot.

A few years ago, a neighbour gave me a clutch of 20 or so Grass Snake eggs that he had retrieved from a pile of wood chippings he was about to burn. As an aside, this illustrates the folly and environmentally unfriendly nature of bonfires in general. Anyway, I installed the eggs on a damp bed of compost in a gently heated aquarium and hoped for the best. Unbeknownst to me, the heater packed up, and when I discovered this mishap I assumed that was the end for the eggs. Thereafter I only looked at the tank once in a while, and on day 41 of incubation I decided to give the eggs a 'decent burial' in one of my compost heaps. However, to my great surprise and delight, lo and behold I found a young Grass Snake lurking in the bottom of the tank, so I hastily restored the set-up. All 20 eggs hatched in the end, the last emerging on day 50. I guess the moral of the story is to have patience when it comes to nature and never give up.

A Grass Snake hunting in my meadow.

An Adder.

A Common Lizard.

the diet of Common Frogs, Common Toads and newts, while surface and subterranean invertebrates, including ants, are eaten by Slow-worms. The Grass Snake is a more active predator and its favourite prey will be the amphibians in your pond. Larger individuals will tackle nestling birds and small mammals.

REPTILE WISH LIST

As far as I am aware, Adders do not occur in my garden today, and the nearest I have come to seeing a Common Lizard is one squashed on the adjacent road. However, good populations occur within walking distance of my cottage, in gardens that back onto heathland and

woodland in the parish. Given the history of land use surrounding my cottage in earlier centuries, I see no reason to rule out their having occurred here in the past. Adders need to be respected, not feared. They will only strike as a last resort, after extreme provocation. The best advice to give to any gardener fortunate enough to have Adders in residence is to not confront them. Once they know they have been spotted, they will quickly disappear into the undergrowth. Common Lizards love to bask in the sun, so if you have them in your garden, provide them with sheltered, south-facing clearings where they can warm themselves. One of the worst things you can do for Common Lizards is to own a cat.

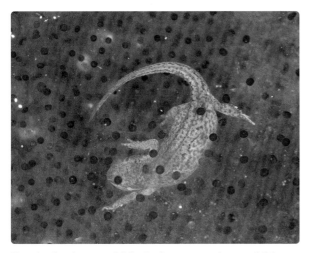

Even in the absence of fish, don't expect native amphibians to live in peace and harmony: this Smooth Newt is gorging itself on frogspawn embryos.

NEWT EGGS

Unlike frogs and toads, our three species of newts attach their eggs singly to the leaves of aquatic plants. In many instances, the leaf will be wrapped around the egg and glued in place as a means of protection, and this is another reason why it is important to stock your pond with aquatic plant species with relatively small leaves – water-starworts, for example. Great Crested Newts seem particularly partial to the surface-floating leaves of Floating Sweet-grass. If you keep your pond 'clean and tidy' and free of aquatic plants, newts will be denied the opportunity to breed. Remove aquatic plants in the spring, and you will kill embryo newts.

A Palmate Newt egg.

GARDEN PONDS

If you create a pond from scratch do not be tempted to introduce fish – they will eat small amphibians as well as freshwater invertebrates, including the larvae of damselflies and dragonflies. If you inherit an existing fish-stocked pond (these are unlikely to be species that are appropriate for a pond) and want to encourage native wildlife while keeping your fish, consider 'zoning' off a fish-free area using chicken wire. You can then move frogspawn to this 'safe zone' each spring and improve the chances of tadpoles not being eaten.

COMPOST HEAPS

Being open to the elements, compost heaps provide easy access for amphibians and reptiles both as daytime refuges and as sites for winter hibernation. In addition, sun-drenched heaps also act as sites for Grass Snakes to lay their eggs. As any seasoned gardener will tell you, a thriving compost heap generates a lot of heat, and the reptiles take advantage of these natural incubators. Indeed, Grass Snakes actively seek out warm compost heaps in the garden (and manure heaps on farms) and females seem to know exactly where in the mound to lay their eggs.

Female Grass Snakes lay their eggs in leaf mounds and compost heaps.

SAFE REFUGE

In the wild, amphibians and reptiles seek daytime and winter refuge beneath fallen logs and compacted tangles of branches. In the garden you can replicate these havens using broken clay flowerpots, old roof tiles and log piles. Nature reserves often deploy 'reptile mats', which benefit the cold-blooded creatures by providing warmth as the mats catch the sun; they also allow numbers to be surveyed. Try this in the garden – old dustbin lids make good homemade 'reptile mats', as do offcuts of butyl liner used to make your pond.

CONNECTIVITY

This buzzword is used by conservationists and planners alike, and it has some genuine merit beyond its use as jargon. Gardens have the potential to play a real role not only as havens for wildlife but as corridors connecting widely separated biodiversity hotspots. However, look at your garden from the perspective of a small amphibian. How could you move from 'a' to 'b' if an insurmountable obstacle such as a fence was placed in your way? We all value our privacy, but if you have a fence try to make sure there are significant gaps at ground level. The same principle is applied on a larger scale for Hedgehogs, of course.

MOWING THE GRASS

Come the summer months and young amphibians will begin leaving your pond and dispersing in the garden. Newly metamorphosed frogs and toads are barely the size of a fingernail and easily overlooked as they lurk in the grass. Be extra vigilant when mowing from June to September. Progress slowly and keep an eye open for movement in front of the mower to avoid shredding the tiny amphibians inadvertently. They are prone to desiccation and least likely to be active in sunshine in the middle of the day – that's a good time to mow the lawn. Avoid mornings and evenings, overcast days and occasions when the grass is damp.

The broken remains of a clay flowerpot can provide a safe and secure hibernation spot for newts during the winter months.

GARDEN ORGANICALLY

In their terrestrial lives, amphibians eat invertebrates as do Slow-worms, and their diet will range from slugs to insects depending on predilection and time of year. If you attempt to control or eliminate invertebrates you will obviously harm your garden's natural biodiversity and directly affect amphibian and reptile food supply. Think about the consequences of your actions in the garden, and never poison your garden with pesticides.

BEYOND THE GARDEN

There are a number of things you can do to help amphibians and reptiles beyond the boundaries of your garden. Your local toad patrol will always be glad of a helping hand, rescuing migrating animals as they attempt to cross roads. Consider giving up some of your time to become a 'Toad Patroller' – visit the Froglife website for more information. In addition, there are a number of county and national organisations whose role it is to help the conservation of amphibians and reptiles, including the **Amphibian and Reptile Conservation Trust**.

Toad patrols around the country require volunteers to rescue migrating amphibians from being squashed and killed by cars as they cross roads.

Birds

A 2020 report entitled *The State of the UK's Birds* informed us there were 19 million fewer pairs of native breeding birds in 2017 than in 1966 (see References section for details). Examining the decline in more detail, comparing numbers in 2019 with those in 1970, particularly hard-hit were farmland indicator species (a 45 percent decline) and woodland indicator species (a 27 percent decline). More recently *Birds of Conservation Concern 5 (BOCC 5)*, published in December 2021 (see References section for details), reported that today more than one in four bird species in the UK are in serious trouble. The report uses an evidence-based tiered, 'traffic light' system that places all of the UK's birds into one of three categories in increasing order of conservation concern – Green, Amber and Red. The UK Red List for birds now stands at 70 species, a net increase of three from the last update in 2015.

The House Martin moves from Amber to Red in the Birds of Conservation Concern 5 report because its population declined by 57 percent between 1969 and 2018.

During the first Covid lockdown in 2020, there was a brief period of compliance which meant the ambient noise of Pamber's countryside – whining chainsaws, the visceral rumble of diggers and the angry, staccato roar of silencer-free all-terrain vehicles – was replaced by the sounds of nature. One of the delights was the arrival of a Cuckoo in mid-April, which took up residence in my garden and called day and night for nearly six weeks. As is the way with the species, it changed its tune in June. By the time it flew away in July the sound of the Cuckoo had been replaced by the contemporary noise of the countryside.

This depressing downward trend has been reflected at the local level in the parish of Pamber. Two decades ago, in the first few years of living in my cottage, I recorded 19 of the currently Red-Listed species either in the garden or within a 500-metre radius. These were: Grey Partridge, Lapwing, Woodcock, Turtle Dove, Cuckoo, Lesser Spotted Woodpecker, Marsh Tit, Skylark, Starling, Fieldfare, Song Thrush, Redwing, Mistle Thrush, Spotted Flycatcher, House Sparrow, Tree Sparrow, Grey Wagtail, Yellowhammer and Corn Bunting. Some were occasional and unpredictable non-breeding visitors, of course, but, based on observations over the last five years, the following are now extinct in the immediate vicinity as breeding species: Grey Partridge, Turtle Dove, Tree Sparrow, Yellowhammer and Corn Bunting. All are farmland birds and their decline is attributable here, as elsewhere in the UK, to modern-day, industrialised farming practices; the two remaining farmland species that still cling on – Lapwing and Skylark – have a patchy distribution and declining numbers in the parish that reflect, and are a consequence of, agricultural land use.

One or two pairs of Song Thrushes usually attempt to breed in my garden, using the dense cover of hedges and patches of scrub to conceal their mud-lined nests. Their presence is easiest to detect by listening for the song of territorial males.

FEED THE BIRDS?

Given the decline in bird populations across the board, it is perhaps a surprise that I no longer provide artificial food in my garden and began weaning myself off bird-feeding at the start of my biodiversity gardening adventure. I realise there are arguments in favour of 'blanket' feeding, the obvious one being that natural food is so depleted in the countryside around me by farming that I would be helping beleaguered birds by feeding them. However, I decided I didn't want to create a dependency, concentrate birds in one spot, foster unnaturally elevated populations of certain species, or contribute to the environmental cost and carbon footprint associated with growing, processing and distributing artificial bird food. What I wanted to achieve was an ecological balance, with the garden itself providing enough natural food to satisfy the requirements of species appropriate to the location and habitat, and at population levels that were sustainable and not enhanced. As for growing food to feed birds, the consequences are profound enough if the food is grown in the UK; if it comes from overseas, you can add the carbon cost of global transportation to the mix.

In early summer, parent and juvenile Green Woodpeckers visit the garden and benefit from the insects living in standing dead wood, and the bonanza provided by the meadow's anthills.

Two or three pairs of Blackcaps either breed in the garden or have territories that include its margins. They benefit from scrub cover for nesting, and naturally occurring garden invertebrates serve as a source of food in spring and early summer.

I cannot help feeling that this 'growing land' would be of greater benefit to birds in particular and biodiversity generally if it were returned to a natural environment.

An article in *Birdwatch* magazine by Jack Shutt and Alexander Lees entitled 'Why do we feed our garden birds?' provides a compelling overview of the subject. A *British Birds* journal article by Richard Broughton, Shutt and Lees entitled 'Rethinking bird feeding – are we putting extra pressure on some struggling woodland birds?' is an in-depth study on the same subject. See the References section for more details.

Underpinning my approach is the primary aim, which has been to create a garden for wildlife across the biodiversity spectrum, not just birds. I try to ensure that the small plot provides enough natural food for species appropriate to the habitat. So, I leave thistle heads to reach maturity as a source of seeds for Goldfinches; standing dead wood remains until it falls as a habitat for wood-boring invertebrates which in turn feed Nuthatches and Great Spotted Woodpeckers; I encourage invertebrate-rich shrubs and trees and avoid the sort of over-pruning that would result in a loss of winter food for insectivorous birds.

NEST BOXES

I have a few open-fronted nest boxes in the garden but I have removed all bar four of those that are hole-fronted, for reasons that I will explain. During the years when I fed birds in the garden, the main beneficiaries were not species under threat but in the main Blue Tits and Great Tits. These are birds that are confident around people and whose populations, on consideration, I am sure I was boosting. In the back of my mind, I recalled a conversation with a bird-ringer friend who had undertaken colour-ringing mark-recapture on birds in his garden. It turned out that while there might be perhaps five or six Blue Tits on or in the vicinity of his feeders at any one time, the true number of birds that used them in a day regularly exceeded 200. Blue and Great Tits were also the species that occupied all of my hole-fronted nest boxes.

I have nothing against Blue Tits and Great Tits and I might encourage them if I lived elsewhere. But in my particular location, I had a nagging feeling their elevated populations were adversely affecting more vulnerable and less pugnacious species, specifically during the breeding season. Being hole-nesters, suitable nesting spots are a limiting factor for Blue and Great Tits, which is why hole-fronted boxes are so readily used by both. My fear was that by supporting and potentially elevating populations of these two belligerent species during the winter months, and boosting their breeding

By not underpinning Great Tit and Blue Tit populations in my garden, it is my hope that nearby breeding Marsh Tits suffer less competition for nest holes than would otherwise be the case.

success in my garden with boxes, I was creating a ripple effect of enhanced populations in the surrounding remnants of woodland. I wanted to avoid the possibility that, by dint of sheer numbers, they would outcompete other hole-nesters for natural sites in the vicinity. Marsh Tit, which is now Red Listed and regular in and around the garden, was the species I had in mind specifically. Plus, potentially also that declining national rarity Lesser Spotted Woodpecker, which persists in the neighbourhood and which I see now and then in my garden. If I was fortunate enough to live in an area where Redstarts and Pied Flycatchers bred, I would be concerned about the impact that elevated populations of Blue and Great Tits would have on the ability of these seasonal visitors to find unoccupied natural nest holes by the time they arrived in spring.

By not providing artificial food that benefits Blue Tits and Great Tits, the aim has been to allow their numbers to reach the natural carrying capacity of my garden. I have left a couple of hole-fronted nest boxes on the side of the cottage to cater for the needs of those few birds that are resident, and to discourage them from seeking nearby natural sites and outcompeting Marsh Tits. For the latter species, I have moved two hole-fronted nest boxes to the wooded end of the garden and keep them rammed full of wood shavings throughout winter and early spring; Marsh Tits (also a hole-nesting species) like to feel they have excavated their nest site, so I read, so the hope is this compromise solution benefits them. It is hard to be sure I have got the balance right, and it is not advice for others to necessarily follow. However, it is based on considering the impacts on the environment around me if I continued with 'wholesale' feeding. It has meant sacrificing the pleasure gained from feeding birds and losing the instant gratification that came from feeling I was doing something good.

KNOCK-ON EFFECTS

Further suggestive evidence for the ripple effect when it comes to competition for nest-hole sites can be found from a seemingly unlikely source in the vicinity of my cottage. In a nearby area of semi-natural ancient woodland, a Hazel Dormouse recovery project has been underway for the past five years, the site having been provisioned with 20 dormouse boxes. To provide context, after emerging from hibernation Hazel Dormice will use boxes during spring and summer for

With entrance holes located on the back, dormouse nest box construction and placement is designed to discourage use by birds.

diurnal snoozing and breeding, but will not or cannot use them if they are already occupied by nesting birds, specifically tits. In addition, they seem to have a dislike of boxes that show signs of previous occupancy in the form of abandoned bird's nests.

Despite the best endeavours of the team, for the first three years there was near 100 percent occupancy of the boxes by either Blue Tits or Great Tits by late March, rendering them unusable by Hazel Dormice when they emerged from hibernation later in spring. Late breeding attempts (which invariably failed) by the birds often continued into summer and Hazel Dormouse occupancy of the boxes was zero. Although artificial food is not provided for birds in the woodland itself, feeding does occur in neighbouring gardens. The hard-to-prove contention was that, as a consequence, the populations of Blue Tits and Great Tits were elevated to levels that would not be supported in nature. Consequently, the overflow population had nowhere else to breed except in the woodland, and this elevated bird population, arguably caused by human intervention, was hindering the recovery of the beleaguered Hazel Dormice. The project had to go to extreme lengths to combat this problem. Traditional hole-fronted, bird-friendly boxes were installed right beside the dormouse boxes. There was near 100 percent occupancy of the new boxes and the birds'

instinctive territoriality ensured the neighbouring dormouse boxes remain bird-free.

Another consideration was the impact that populations of Blue and Great Tits, elevated beyond the natural carrying capacity of the garden by artificial feeding and nest boxes, might have on the garden's invertebrates during spring and summer. Caterpillars (primarily those of moths) are an important source of food for the growing chicks of both Great and Blue Tits. The latter species is well-studied and according to the British Trust for Ornithology each chick can eat 100 caterpillars a day. Consequently, to feed an average brood of ten chicks, adults need to find as many as 1,000 caterpillars a day. On average it takes 18–21 days from hatching to fledging or leaving the nest box. The result is that potentially up to 20,000 caterpillars might be killed and eaten to raise a single Blue Tit brood. At one time I had 12 boxes in the garden, all occupied each spring with either Blue Tits or Great Tits, with the majority reaching the point of fledging. Assuming the caterpillar consumption of Blue and Great Tits to be similar, that's potentially 240,000 caterpillars being killed and eaten during the breeding season alone. When balancing the needs of Blue and Great Tits to feed against the stability of the invertebrate populations in the garden and the web of life that depends on them, I came down on the side of the invertebrates.

I have reduced the number of Blue and Great Tit nestboxes in my garden to two. In theory, that means potentially 200,000 fewer caterpillars are consumed by these two species during the breeding season than in the past when nestbox numbers were higher. Mortality in life-cycle stages notwithstanding, 200,000 caterpillars translate into an awful lot of adult moths, which serve as food for hungry bats.

THE UNINTENDED CONSEQUENCES OF CONCENTRATING BIRDS

If the pandemic has done anything, it must surely have reminded us in the UK that the chances of contracting or spreading contagious diseases are greatly increased by close proximity to members of the same species. In the case of coronaviruses, breathing the same air is the key to spreading Covid-19 as well as the common cold. Elsewhere in the world, accessing the same water and food, combined with poor hygiene, are means by which many pathogens and parasites spread through a human population.

Garden feeding stations are implicated in the Greenfinch's demise, and so hygiene and cleanliness are the watchwords if you do decide to feed the birds in your garden.

No surprise then that there are consequences for birds if we encourage them to concentrate in unnaturally close proximity and in elevated numbers. A case in point is the Greenfinch. Once a familiar garden bird, the species has been moved directly from the Green to the Red List in the *BOCC 5* report after a population crash of 62 percent since 1993 due to the disease trichomonosis. This is caused by the parasitic protozoan *Trichomonas gallinae*, an infection that is spread primarily by the consumption of contaminated food and drinking water, or by birds feeding one another with regurgitated contaminated food during the breeding season.

Another case in point are gruesome afflictions seen in Chaffinches, the external manifestations being frilly-looking canker growths, warty swellings and bloody lesions on birds' feet and legs. Causal agents are a virus called the *Fringilla coelebs* Papillomavirus and a skin mite of the genus *Knemidocoptes*. The afflictions may not in themselves cause the death of an individual, but they most certainly reduce the odds against its survival. If a bird cannot perch or walk properly, or loses its feet through infection, this will hinder its ability to feed and roost, and the best outcome is probably a speedy death in the talons of a Sparrowhawk.

The fact that similar diseases affect caged birds is suggestive. The implication is that, in the wild, encouraging birds to repeatedly use the same perch or hop on the same ground is the likely way by which the afflictions are spread in a population. Although I have no empirical evidence to demonstrate a link between artificially feeding Chaffinches and the spread of leg and feet infections, I can offer some anecdotal indicators. On a visit to the New Forest in Hampshire in January 2022, I came across a couple of flocks of Chaffinches, both 50 or more strong, feeding in the leaf litter off the beaten track; none of them appeared to have any signs of infection. Next stop was a car park feeding station; this attracts Chaffinches and other species that routinely sit, one after the other, on the same perches, or feed on the same patch of ground. Of the 30 or more Chaffinches observed, all had some signs of infection. More background information can be found by visiting the British Trust for Ornithology website and from the *Frontiers in Veterinary Science* article listed in the References section.

Experience taught me that another consequence of feeding birds in a relatively rural garden was that

Chaffinch infected with *Fringilla coelebs* Papillomavirus and skin mites.

Grey Squirrels and Brown Rats were unintended beneficiaries. This placed me in the unenviable position of having to decide whether or not to kill or control these unwelcome visitors. In the case of Brown Rats, my reluctance to encourage them will need little explanation. But in the case of Grey Squirrels the damage caused by these alien mammals perhaps needs some qualification, and two examples spring to mind.

That Grey Squirrels, an alien species in the context of the UK, damage Hazel nut crops in the autumn is all too obvious in my garden; witness the shattered remains of nuts beneath the bushes. Hazel nuts are important in the autumn diet of the Hazel Dormouse (there's a clue in the name), and Grey Squirrel damage affects their chances of fattening up for hibernation. Evidence exists for the presence of Hazel Dormice as close as 200 metres to my garden, and therefore I felt that anything that benefitted squirrels was likely to harm the prospects for Hazel Dormice, thanks to the ripple effect of spreading populations.

The second example relates to the impact of Grey Squirrels on nesting birds. The last two attempts by Spotted Flycatchers to nest in my garden ended in failure; in one instance I saw the predatory culprit – a Grey Squirrel – but not in time to prevent destruction; on the second occasion strong circumstantial evidence suggested the same villain. Consequently, rather than face the ongoing choice of whether or not to control squirrels and rats, I now opt for the easier option of not encouraging them.

My approach to benefitting birds is personalised to this particular garden and it would certainly be different if I lived somewhere else – in an urban or suburban environment, for example. There, in all likelihood, I would do everything that I could to help populations of species now associated with human settlements. Starling, Swift and species with 'house' in their name – House Martin and House Sparrow – would be top of the list.

SPARROW CLUBS

The House Sparrow is an interesting case in point, a species that flies over my garden but seldom settles, despite the presence of modest flocks as close as 300 metres away. House Sparrows are commensal birds, and although welcome by and large in the UK today, that has not always been the case. In times past, along with anything else that competed for food or affected standards of living, the humble sparrow would have been seen as the enemy. In historical context, the term 'sparrow' may well have been a catch-all that included not only House Sparrows but also Tree Sparrows, and possibly assorted grain-feeding finches and buntings too. Sparrows eat grain and happily dismantle thatch to build their untidy nests, and these would have been among the crimes that put them in the spotlight. The latter habit presumably explains why the thatched portion of my cottage has been covered in wire mesh for as long as I have known it.

At one time the killing of sparrows was institutionalised by the establishment of 'Sparrow Clubs', whose aim was not to celebrate the birds but to strive towards maximising their destruction. There are said to have been Sparrow Clubs in every parish in Britain including Pamber, their members being dedicated to the destruction of adult birds as well as their eggs and chicks. Prizes were awarded for those who killed the most.

To understand the genesis of Sparrow Clubs, or at least incentivised sparrow-killing, we probably need to go back to the Poor Laws. The legislation, whose origins stretch back as far as the sixteenth century, was designed to provide relief to the poor. It required Overseers of Poor for every parish to levy Poor Rates (a tax by any other name) on parish householders who were not paupers, the amount collected being determined by the value of the property that they owned or occupied. On the debit side of the accounts, some of the payments were made to the poor in return

Pages from the Pamber Overseers of Poor 1795–1814 (Hampshire Record Office reference 15M70/PO1) for 1801 provide a snapshot of our ancestors' relationship with sparrows. Accounted for by the presentation of heads, the going rate was 1d for three sparrows killed, which according to the National Archives currency converter equates to 18 pence, or roughly 6 pence per sparrow, in today's money. More than 1,000 sparrows were killed and paid for in 1801, along with Hedgehogs, the going rate for which was 2d per animal, or 36 pence today. I am grateful to Stephanie Albery for alerting me to the existence of this document.

for killing birds (named as 'sparrows', and presumably mostly House Sparrows), the tally being measured by the number of heads handed over for inspection.

Another interesting reference to rural sparrows can be found a 1907 book entitled *The Country Month by Month* (see References for more information). On page 180, the authors Jean Owen and George Boulger provide the following personal account: 'William Howitt has told how, in his boyhood in Derbyshire, he used to get away on summer evenings with the village boys, who, with a ladder, visited the eaves of every cottage, and even of the church, for sparrows' nests. The eggs, nestlings, and even old birds, which they sometimes caught in the nests, were sold by them, according to an old parish custom, to the overseer of the poor. They received a penny for every three eggs, and for every two young birds, and the same for the head of an old bird; for a harmless hedgehog they got fourpence, and a shilling for a weasel, because these were supposed to work great havoc on the farms. The lads found it a paying joke to watch this parish officer, after selling him a lot of sparrows and their eggs; for he was at times, presumably under pressure of parochial duties, wont to throw the birds' heads into the street. These they would pick up and sell over again. Some lads, too, trading on the ignorance of the overseer, would put amongst them, and get payment for, the heads of hedge-sparrows, buntings and larks, for which the parish allowed nothing.' Regardless of era, it seems that boys will be boys.

At this point, it is worth introducing Eleanor Ormerod (1828–1901), an indomitable Victorian English lady who was an enlightened aesthete, highly regarded for her prowess in the field of agricultural entomology and her particular interest in what she regarded as 'pests'. Revered in farming circles for her rather personalised understanding of what today we would call ecology (the inter-connectivity of life) and her 'innovative' ways of controlling insect pests, she was reviled by others. And she had an uncompromising attitude towards House Sparrows, which she appears to have regarded as 'avian rats'. There is a slightly perverse, simplistic logic to Eleanor's thinking regarding House Sparrows: they eat grain (amongst other things) and therefore they must be causing deprivation in rural communities.

For a detailed account of Eleanor Ormerod, a good read is *Bugs and the Victorians* by John F. M. Clark, particularly the chapter entitled 'A Female

Nowadays, House Sparrows live largely commensal lives alongside people, benefitting from scraps of food discarded or provided intentionally.

Entomologist' (see References). In summary, Eleanor's campaign against the House Sparrow followed a typical course for the time: in the first instance a letter to *The Times* in which she called for their extermination. Inevitably there followed a crusading pamphlet and thereafter she campaigned for the revival of the 'Sparrow Clubs', which by that time had fallen out of fashion as the human population became more urbanised.

In the context of sparrows, this is Eleanor Ormerod's legacy, but unwittingly she did stir up a storm of protest from 'nature lovers' and those concerned with animal welfare. So perhaps she should be remembered as well for unintentionally creating a groundswell of feeling that contributed to the genesis of what today we call conservation. That includes the birth of the RSPB – initially the Society for the Protection of Birds – founded in 1889 by another redoubtable Victorian lady, Emily Williamson (1855–1936).

By the end of the century that followed Eleanor Ormerod's death in 1901 her wish was coming true with regards to House Sparrows. Populations crashed, and today in the UK the species is a cause for conservation concern and Red Listed. Since the mid-1970s, urban sparrow numbers have declined by 60 percent, with populations in the countryside following a similar trend. And in London, numbers of cheeky cockney sparrows fell by 60 percent between 1994 and 2004. The jury is out regarding the causes, but most people reading this can guess the candidates: lack of winter stubble; sanitised, industrial farming methods; a catastrophic decline in insect numbers in part due to the increased 'efficiency' of modern pesticides (seasonally, invertebrates comprise

Who knows whether Sparrow Club members' efforts were restricted to House Sparrows, but it would be no surprise if Tree Sparrows (seen here) were also in the firing line.

up to 75 percent of a House Sparrow's diet); a tidy-minded approach to gardening; the list goes on.

Contempt for sparrows is not a uniquely British phenomenon, and China provides another shockingly vivid example. In 1958, the founding father of the People's Republic, Mao Zedong (a.k.a. Mao Tse-tung), launched the so called Four Pests Campaign against rats, mosquitoes, flies and sparrows, as part of an effort to improve the lot of the Chinese people. With military-style efficiency birds were shot, eggs and young were destroyed, and communities collaborated to create noise and disturbance to keep the birds in the air until they died of exhaustion or dehydration. Tree Sparrows and House Sparrows were no doubt vilified in the same manner and it is easy to imagine that no distinction was made between them and a host of other passerine species in the heat of the moment.

The Great Sparrow Campaign was so successful that China virtually eliminated 'sparrows' (and presumably other passerine farmland birds as well) within two years.

In the absence of an understanding of House Sparrow diet and ecology it is easy to imagine how, in the past, a flock might have been viewed as akin to a plague of locusts as it descended on a crop. Sizeable House Sparrow flocks are a thing of the past in the UK, but these Spanish Sparrows in southern Europe give a flavour of the scene.

However, there were unintended consequences, and far from seeing greater crop yields, harvests crashed. The architects of the Campaign had failed to consider the insectivorous component of the birds' diet and without predatory control, the insects wreaked havoc on the crops. This led ultimately to what has been called the Great Chinese Famine that claimed the lives of an estimated 20 million people.

EGGS AND NESTS

I have never collected birds' eggs nor felt an urge to do so. However, I was brought up in an era where it was an acceptable, if not accepted, practice amongst children raised in rural or even suburban locations. Most grew out of the hobby, of course, but a dangerous few continued and joined the small band of fanatical

RED KITES

The sight of a Red Kite soaring over my garden is now a regular feature and always an uplifting one. However, unlike others I know I am not tempted to feed them. They do perfectly well without supplementary feeding, and besides, I have an inherent distaste for the commercial production of frozen mice and day-old male chicks, the latter by-products of industrial egg production. In keeping with the Shakespearean image of the species as one associated with waste, carrion and corpses, around here Red Kites appear to thrive on roadkill and discarded remnants around lay-by burger vans. The cynic in me sees the return of the Red Kite to north Hampshire as not so much a conservation success story as a testament to a species' ability to benefit from human impact on the environment and the excesses of twenty-first-century life.

If burger vans and roadkill must send
That which we discard back, our monuments
Shall be the maws of kites.
(With apologies to Shakespeare: Macbeth, 3.4.84–86)

collectors whose modern-day status, quite rightly, is that of pariahs. A consequence of the shift towards outright condemnation of egg collecting was that, for decades it seems, birds' breeding biology became almost a taboo subject. Thanks to this avian cancel culture, there was a period when you could read a book about British birds and be forgiven for not realising that wild birds actually laid eggs or made nests.

The subject has, to a degree, been rehabilitated in recent years, partly in recognition that sections of society now lack even a basic understanding of the range of environmental and habitat requirements of nesting birds, let alone an ability to identify nests or eggs. I am not of course advocating that garden owners should actively search for eggs or nests – the exact opposite, in fact. But an understanding of where birds nest can help with conservation management when, for example, you make a chance discovery of a nest in a hedge, discover the remains of an egg that a parent bird has removed from a nest, or come across a failed clutch when repairing an old nest box in winter. Underpinning this is the need to be able to identify what you come across. For more information about nesting birds and the law see p. 322.

IN PRAISE OF JAYS

Jays are intelligent birds. Like several other members of the crow family, they put their powers of observation to good use in spring when the eggs and nestlings of other birds feature in their diet. This has contributed to the species having a bad image in some sectors of society. That Jays eat eggs and chicks is not in dispute. However, these are only components among a much more varied diet. There is another side to the life story of the Jay, one that should be placed on the credit rather than the debit side of the accounts. In autumn, they collect acorns and bury them here and there in open ground. This cache of food is returned to in winter and early spring and those acorns that are overlooked or forgotten are the genesis of new oak woodland.

Perhaps less well appreciated are other components in the Jay's diet, in particular invertebrates. In their 1907 book *The Country Month by Month* (see References), Owen and Boulger recount the following, with regards to Cockchafers (in particular their soil-dwelling larvae, which were perceived as a pest in those times) and

A Jay gathering acorns in autumn.

Jays. On page 180 we read: '... in reference to this troublesome cockchafer, let me tell of an observer who has recorded that having carefully watched a nest of young jays which he found, he noticed that each of the five birds while still very young devoured at least fifteen full-sized grubs in one day, with of course very many more of a smaller size. The parent birds and their family consumed about two hundred every day. As the grub continues in that state for four seasons, the observer reckoned that this single pair with their family alone, without reckoning their descendants after the first year, would destroy eighty thousand grubs of one of the most destructive creatures that we have. Think of that when at the entrance to some cover you see the murdered body of an ill-fated jay hanging from the branches of a low tree.'

LEAVE WELL ALONE

As a word of caution, if you chance upon a nest in your garden then resist the temptation to pay return visits to 'see how things are going'. Even if you don't realise it, in some way or another you will always alarm the parent birds, who will almost certainly exhibit subtly or overtly abnormal behaviour. Altered stress-related behaviour may not always be obvious to our eyes but you can guarantee that it will not go unnoticed by egg-predator specialists such as Magpies and Carrion

Crows: being able to spot even subtle signs that a bird is nesting is an ability that is hard-wired into their natural history. By paying repeat visits to a nest, you will be increasing the chances of it being discovered and the clutch of eggs or nestlings consumed.

Carrion Crows are patient observers, watching for tell-tale indications of nesting.

THE INTERESTING CASE OF THE CUCKOO

In rural settings there is an outside chance a Cuckoo may favour your garden with its presence. Although males advertise themselves with their eponymous song, females are unobtrusive for obvious reasons: they are nest parasites and want to spot the signs of breeding birds without alerting their potential hosts to their presence. Each Cuckoo female is genetically 'programmed' to be host species–specific and in the context of a garden, likely candidates include Blackbird, Robin or Dunnock. In the case of the first two, Cuckoo eggs are a reasonable mimic for those of the host species: eggs that do not resemble those of the host are sometimes recognised as such and ejected. Consequently, it is hard to explain why the eggs of Cuckoos laid in Dunnocks' nests are so dissimilar and yet successful.

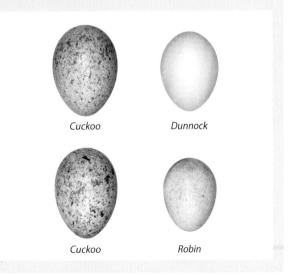

Cuckoo   *Dunnock*

Cuckoo   *Robin*

The eggs of bird species that routinely or occasionally nest in gardens. Each egg is depicted at life size.

Swift
Clutch: 2–3 eggs. Nest: shallow cup of debris, sited on level surface often in a loft space; will use a nest box.

House Sparrow
Clutch: 4–5 eggs. Nest: tangled mass of plant material, usually sited in a cavity and often in artificial locations.

Long-tailed Tit
Clutch: 6–8 eggs. Nest: beautifully constructed sphere of moss, lichens and spider silk, sited in a dense, usually spiny bush.

Chiffchaff
Clutch: 4–7 eggs. Nest: domed, woven mass of plant material, sited on the ground in dense cover or low in a bramble patch.

Great Spotted Woodpecker
Clutch: 4–6 eggs. Nest: cavity excavated in a tree.

Nuthatch
Clutch: 4–5 eggs. Nest: located in a natural tree hole, the entrance often plastered with mud.

Marsh Tit
Clutch: 7–9 eggs. Nest: dense mass of moss, animal hair and fine grass, usually sited in a natural cavity, very occasionally a nest box.

Goldcrest
Clutch: 6–8 eggs. Nest: spherical ball of woven moss, lichens and spider silk, usually attached to end of conifer branch.

Treecreeper
Clutch: 5–6 eggs. Nest: cup of fine grass and moss, sited behind peeling tree bark or in a natural crevice.

Wren
Clutch: 5–6 eggs. Nest: spherical mass of plant material, sited in a bush or cavity.

Coal Tit
Clutch: 9–10 eggs. Nest: deep cup of moss, sited in a natural cavity, very occasionally a nest box.

Chaffinch
Clutch: 4–5 eggs. Nest: woven cup of fine grasses, moss and animal hair, often sited in fork of a tree or shrub.

House Martin
Clutch: 4–5 eggs. Nest: cup of mud, sited under house eaves.

Dunnock
Clutch: 4–5 eggs. Nest: cup of twigs and moss, sited deep in a bush well off the ground.

Great Tit
Clutch: 7–9 eggs. Nest: dense mass of moss, animal hair and fine grass, sited in a cavity or nest box.

Greenfinch
4–5 Clutch: eggs. Nest: lined cup of woven stems, moss and animal hair, usually sited in the fork of a tree.

Swallow
Clutch: 4–5 eggs. Nest: cemented cup of plant debris and mud, usually sited on a ledge in a barn or similar artificial structures.

Robin
Clutch: 4–5 eggs. Nest: bulky mass of leaves with a woven cup, sited in a range of locations including inside sheds and outbuildings.

Blue Tit
Clutch: 8–10 eggs. Nest: dense mass of moss, animal hair and fine grass, sited in a cavity or nest box.

Bullfinch
Clutch: 4–5 eggs. Nest: neat cup of woven grasses and stems, hidden deep in the cover of a bush or shrub.

Spotted Flycatcher
Clutch: 4–5 eggs. Nest: woven shallow cup of plant material, on a ledge on side of house.

Pied Wagtail
Clutch: 4–5 eggs. Nest: cup of plant material, sited in a cavity.

Blackcap
Clutch: 4–5 eggs. Nest: delicate cup of fine grasses, sited low in a dense shrub or bramble patch.

Goldfinch
Clutch: 4–6 eggs. Nest: neat woven cup of fine grass, moss, animal hair and spider silk, sited on an outer branch of a tree.

Jay
Clutch: 4–5 eggs.
Nest: platform of
twigs on which
sits a cup of
grass, often sited
in a tree fork.

Magpie
Clutch: 5–6 eggs.
Nest: impressive-
ly large mass of
twigs, spherical
in shape and
lined with mud,
usually located in
a dense tree.

Tawny Owl Clutch: 2–3 eggs. Nest: sited
in a tree cavity; will use a nest box.

Sparrowhawk
Clutch: 4–6 eggs.
Nest: twiggy
structure, often an
embellished former
Woodpigeon or
Carrion Crow nest,
located in a tree
canopy or close to
the trunk.

Starling
Clutch: 4–7 eggs.
Nest: untidy mass
of plant debris,
sited in a natural
cavity but also in
house roofs.

Blackbird
Clutch: 3–4 eggs.
Nest: cup of
twigs, lined with
mud and grass,
sited in a range
of locations
including
inside sheds and
outbuildings.

Feral Pigeon Clutch: 2 eggs. Nest: shallow
cup of debris, usually sited in a cavity.

Carrion Crow
Clutch: 3–4 eggs.
Nest: bulky mass
of twigs, usually
sited high in
a tree.

Jackdaw
Clutch: 4–5 eggs.
Nest: untidy
mass of twigs,
sited in a cavity
and sometimes
in a chimney or
other artificial
structures.

Mistle Thrush
Clutch: 4 eggs.
Nest: cup of
twigs, cemented
inside with mud
and lined with
fine grasses, sited
in a tree.

Woodpigeon Clutch: 2 eggs. Nest: flimsy
platform of twigs, sited in a tree or shrub.

Collared Dove
Clutch: 2 eggs.
Nest: flimsy
platform of twigs,
sited in a tree
or shrub.

Song Thrush
Clutch: 3–5 eggs.
Nest: cup of
twigs, smoothly
lined with mud,
sited in a tree
or on a ledge.

Pheasant Clutch: 6–12 eggs. Nest: concealed,
unlined depression in cover on the ground.

Mammals

Mammalian visitors to, and residents of, my garden are only occasionally easy to spot; generally, they are rather unobtrusive and secretive, and many are nocturnal. However, there are ways of improving the chances of observation or at least of registering their presence: many species leave signs that can be detected and read by the discerning eye.

UNGULATES

Although stray ponies, and even on one occasion a cow, have found their way into my garden, deer are the largest mammals to visit on a regular basis. Unsurprisingly, I see signs of their presence much more frequently than I see the animals themselves. Roe Deer are the most regularly encountered species and although the garden is far too small to support them, it lies within the home ranges of one or more of these animals. They come and go, as do the intermittent sightings, as animals are killed on roads, die of natural causes or abandon habitats due to change of land use or repeated dog disturbance.

Observations often relate to early morning encounters. In summer, these tend to be 'courting couples', for want of a better expression, or rival male bucks. Roe Deer are the only members of their kind in the UK to employ delayed implantation as part of their breeding biology: although mating occurs in July or August, fertilised eggs remain in the doe's uterus for several months before foetal development begins. As a consequence, a nine-month pregnancy is followed by sightings of mothers and fawns in spring.

Muntjac are also present and are heard more often than they are seen, their dog-like barks often continuing for hours on end. They have an annoying habit of nibbling young shoots of planted saplings, so I make sure I protect anything I particularly value by the creation of miniature 'dead hedges' of branches. On occasions in the past, I have had Fallow Deer in the garden. Sizeable herds live within 1km to the north and south and disturbance occasionally causes them to scatter; in April 2022, I watched from my garden more than 50 Fallow Deer feeding in a field to the south of me.

A Roe Deer (left) and Muntjac (right) passing through my garden.

A Hedgehog mother and young.

INSECTIVORES

Moles, Hedgehogs and shrews belong to a group of mammals previously referred to as insectivores. This generic name does not do justice to the dietary range of these mammals, which, depending on species, includes almost any and every type of invertebrate they encounter. In addition, a few have more ambitious predatory tendencies and tackle vertebrate forms of life. Moles are evident in my garden thanks to the eruption of molehills here and there in the lawn and meadow. I welcome them for the contribution they make to aeration of the soil and, given their diet of earthworms, you should take their presence as a sign of healthy, invertebrate-rich soil. Molehill soil provides a great medium for growing native plants from seed and for potting on seedlings.

Hedgehog: friend or foe?

The Hedgehog's adorable media persona belies its distinctly predatory habits, which extend from invertebrates to small birds and other mammals if the opportunity arises. When it comes to loving or loathing them, context and location are all-important,

as is history: the Pamber Overseers of Poor 1795–1814 (Hampshire Record Office reference 15M70/PO1) records that killing Hedgehogs was rewarded financially, the going rate being 2d per animal. That's 36 pence in today's money according to the National Archives currency converter.

In the present day, on mainland Britain, where they are native, their presence is broadly speaking welcomed, and indeed they are often actively encouraged in urban and suburban gardens. However, matters are different elsewhere. Take for example the Outer Hebrides, one of Europe's most important breeding locations for ground-nesting waders including Lapwing, Dunlin, Ringed Plover, Redshank and Snipe. Somebody had the bright idea of introducing half a dozen or so Hedgehogs to South Uist in 1974, so the story goes, with the intention of controlling garden slugs. The animals soon multiplied, spread and turned their attentions to the eggs and chicks of the birds. At their zenith, they were responsible for more than half of all nest failures annually, resulting in a catastrophic decline in wader breeding success. The consequence is that Hedgehogs on the Outer Hebrides are the target of eradication and removal projects, with the hope that their elimination will reverse the precipitous decline of breeding birds. For more information, an article on the NatureScot website is a good starting point (see References for details).

A more extreme and tragic example can be found 'down under'. It sounds barmy nowadays, but in the 1870s Hedgehogs were introduced, along with all manner of other European species, to New Zealand to make human settlers feel more at home. The spiny, four-legged pioneers took to their new surroundings with a vengeance and there are now more individuals in New Zealand than in the UK: the country's Department of Conservation (DOC) puts numbers at between two and four per hectare. Bear in mind that New Zealand's endemic fauna evolved over millions of years in the complete absence of terrestrial mammals, and they have no defence against the menagerie of predators – domestic cats, rat species, Stoats, Possums, Hedgehogs and the like – which human settlers brought with them.

The result has been an ecological catastrophe, and as an indication of this 42 percent of New Zealand's endemic bird species have been driven to extinction since the arrival of humans, dating back to the first Polynesian settlers. Hedgehogs contribute to the on-going decline in native wildlife generally, eating their way through everything from ground-nesting birds' eggs to endemic species of weta (like giant bush-crickets). In contrast to their image in the UK, DOC describes Hedgehogs as pests and offers advice on how to discourage Hedgehogs in the garden along with methods for catching and killing them. New Zealand's long-term aim is for the islands to be rid of all non-native mammalian predators.

Scattered around the garden are bits of tree bark and remains of clay roof tiles, placed there in the main as refuges for amphibians and reptiles. However, once in a while shrews of both terrestrial species nest beneath them. If you do discover such a nest, such as this Pygmy Shrew's, then resist the temptation to keep lifting the cover. You run the risk of causing the parents to desert their offspring.

A Pygmy Shrew.

Shrews

I neither encourage nor discourage Hedgehogs and they are only very occasional visitors to my garden. I take more interest in, and have more concern for the garden's shrew population. Both Common and Pygmy Shrews must have reasonable populations in the garden

A Common Shrew.

A Water Shrew.

spring morning in 2005 I counted 23 individuals from various window vantage points in the cottage. Nowadays, numbers in the area have plummeted and I might see one a week at most, and that is invariably a brief encounter. Anecdotal evidence suggests the most likely cause of recent declines is viral Rabbit Haemorrhagic Disease. Brown Hares still occur sparingly in the neighbourhood but I have not seen the species closer than 500 metres to the garden for more than 10 years. Factors affecting the species' decline are familiar: destruction and degradation of open farmland due to changes in farming methods; and occasional illegal hare coursing with dogs.

judging by the times I encounter them by chance. As a testament to its inquisitiveness and climbing skills, the latter species is an occasional visitor indoors, including on a couple of occasions a bedroom upstairs.

Shrews are short-lived animals, and it is not unusual to come across an unmarked corpse of an individual that, on the face of it, has seemingly died of old age. It was just such an encounter that alerted me to the presence of Water Shrews in the stream at the bottom of my garden. I came across a freshly dead individual one spring on a path, and later that year saw the occasional individual alive and well in the drying bed of the stream itself.

Lagomorphs

For a period of a few years after I moved to the cottage, Rabbits were frequent visitors to the garden: early one

Young Rabbits tend to be more approachable and bolder than their adult counterparts.

Mustelids

Weasels and Stoats, which were such a feature of my childhood growing up in north Hampshire, are in essence now extinct at the local level. As with most declines in wildlife, their disappearance is likely to have something to do with modern farming methods. Targeted poisoning and trapping, and the cumulative effects of rodenticide poisoning, may have contributed to their downfall. However, there may be a more prosaic reason for their decline: they have simply been starved out of existence. Year-round use of the land, regular ploughing and monoculture crops are hardly conducive to the build-up of small mammal populations. And for a variety of reasons Rabbits, a favourite food for female Stoats in particular, are a rare sight nowadays.

Adult Rabbits are typically wary and alert.

Farming neighbours occasionally tell me that the countryside is overrun with Badgers and that they are the cause of almost everything that ails British wildlife: from the demise of Hedgehogs, ground-nesting birds, and woodland flora to the spread of Bovine Tuberculosis (BTb). I have long since abandoned trying to address this blinkered mindset and unpick the flawed logic that underpins the species' role in the blame game. Suffice to say that impartial science reveals the Badger to be, not a monster, but merely an omnivorous member of the countryside with an undeserved reputation. The reasons why it became a BTb scapegoat, and has since acquired such a pariah status among many in the farming community, date back to the 1970s. The motivation seems more sociological than pseudoscientific, with a whiff of political expediency and populism lurking in the background. To help unpick the story, an interesting read is an open access book (downloadable) entitled *Vermin, Victims and Disease* by Angela Cassidy, specifically the chapter called 'How the Badger Became Tuberculous' (see References for details).

I see occasional signs of Badgers in the garden and see one in my car headlights nearby now and then. However, if I knew of a sett (the name for a Badger's underground home) in the vicinity, the last thing I would do is tell anyone about it. I know of one nearby that, I subsequently discovered, was dug out by men and dogs; who knows whether the operation was undertaken with or without the tacit consent of the landowner. To put all the above in context, and to highlight the inherent contradiction in their status, Badgers are supposedly safeguarded under the Protection of Badgers Act 1992, which means it is an offence to wilfully kill, injure or capture a Badger, or attempt to do so.

Two other mustelids occur in the general area. Otters are making something of a comeback along the course of the River Loddon, into which the stream at the bottom of my garden eventually feeds. The closest I have come to seeing one nearby was a roadkill corpse, that of a large male. Signs that Otters are in the area are also evident in human responses to their presence: the species' return is not welcomed by all. A few miles north of my cottage lie a series of flooded gravel pits, some of which have suffered the fate of becoming 'carp lakes'. These are leased by syndicate clubs, stocked with prize fish and polluted with wheelbarrow loads of 'boilies' (nutrient-rich ground bait, whose ingredients can include dried blood, fish meal, powdered milk,

maize flour, that sort of thing) in order to catch said fish. You can spot these lakes from a distance because their banks are usually populated by isolated and lonely sentinels, almost always men, contemplating their next catch. On a post-lockdown stroll in 2021 I passed by one such lake, expecting to be able to view the water but only to discover it had been completely surrounded by maximum-security fencing. On chatting to one of the 'locals' I discovered this was to prevent Otters from gaining access and 'stealing' their prize fish. The larger specimens grow to monstrous proportions and are caught repeatedly by syndicate members; some even have names. They would cost a small fortune to replace if eaten by an Otter.

Until about five years ago I received regular calls from neighbours telling me about roadkill Polecats on highways nearby; and occasionally someone would be kind enough to even leave one on my doorstep. There is ample scope for confusion with well-marked escapee Ferrets and Polecat/Ferret crosses. However, looking at the markings closely and measuring the biometrics of skulls, seemed to point towards these animals being genuine Polecats, which are said to be making something of a comeback, having been driven to near extinction.

Rodents

Of all the mammal groups in my garden, rodents are the ones that I encounter most regularly and that have the most significant populations. Wood Mouse and Yellow-necked Mouse are the commonest and both make regular incursions indoors, especially in autumn and winter, and particularly during prolonged periods

A Wood Mouse.

The part of north Hampshire where I live is something of a hotspot for Hazel Dormouse, thanks to the heritage of woodland cover; specifically, the history of hazel coppicing, and the network of hedgerows and tree lines. The epicentre used to be nearby Bramley Frith, a woodland that was truly ancient in terms of its lineage, one that dated back to the Domesday Book, and among its trees it boasted a

A Yellow-necked Mouse.

few that were more than 500 years old. I use the past tense because it was purchased, gutted and degraded by the Central Electricity Generating Board to build a substation (see p. 91) at its heart, the process of environmental attrition continuing under its subsequent owner National Grid (see p. 331).

Closer to home, there are Hazel Dormice in Pamber Forest, the boundary of which lies around 500 metres from my garden. There is a recovery project underway in a nearby woodland, and a summer nest was discovered in 2020 around 200 metres from my cottage in Hazels

of cold weather or heavy rain. I live-trap both species regularly and liberate them at a distance I judge to be far enough away from my house for them not to make a quick return.

When I first moved to the cottage Harvest Mice were regularly noted. Occasionally a living animal was observed but more typically I would discover one of their tennis-ball-sized nests constructed in rank vegetation. At the time, the likelihood was that these occasional visitors to my garden, and temporary residents, came from nearby hay meadows. Now that these grassland habitats have been destroyed the species appears to be all but extinct near me; the last time I saw a Harvest Mouse in my garden was four years ago, and that was the first I had seen for three years. Natural grassland that is left to its own devices – precisely the sort of habitat that would fail to meet Natural England's prescription for 'favourable status' – is exactly what Harvest Mice seem to like, at least in my experience.

A Wood Mouse.

A Yellow-necked Mouse.

A Harvest Mouse.

A Field Vole.

that line the ancient byway adjacent to the garden. As far as I know Hazel Dormouse does not occur actually in my garden. However, who knows what might happen in the future once the Hazels planted to augment existing shrubs are mature enough to fruit, and once the restored hedgerows provide connectivity. It is important to keep that word – connectivity – in mind when considering Hazel Dormice: apart from time spent nesting (in a hole at ground level, amongst tree roots) they are arboreal, shun the ground and will not willingly cross it.

Field Voles and Bank Voles seem to occur in good numbers in my garden and the latter species is also an occasional visitor into the house, appearing in live traps set for mice. As their name suggests, the Field Voles live in my tiny meadow, while the Bank Voles appear to favour hedge lines and areas of maturing scrub with dense leaf litter and plant debris. I occasionally come across winter caches of Common Hawthorn seeds, stored by the latter species beneath fallen tree bark or in a dilapidated nest box.

I first realised there were Water Voles in the stream at the bottom of my garden when I came across a neighbour's cat in the act of killing and eating one (see p. 277). The population persisted for a few years but I have not noticed any tell-tale signs of late. If you think you might have Water Voles where you live, look for flattened, water-level platforms of vegetation where voles like to nibble their food, and look for small piles of greenish droppings. Your sense of hearing can also help you locate Water Voles: listen for the distinctive 'plop' as a vole, startled by your approach, quickly submerges. As to why Water Voles no longer appear to live in my

stream, the jury's out. I have no evidence for American Mink (often cited as instrumental in the species' demise) being present although that cannot be ruled out. More likely I suspect the cause is unsympathetic waterway management upstream and downstream, and insidious pollution by run-off of agrochemicals degrading the overall environmental quality of the waterway.

The last two rodents that I encounter regularly in the garden are Brown Rat and Grey Squirrel, and unsurprisingly they are less welcome. Although I don't adopt a seek-and-destroy approach, I do actively avoid anything that would encourage them, and that includes the collateral benefits to them associated with feeding birds. More on that subject on p. 249. I don't regard Brown Rats as inherently evil and, away from the scope of my garden, they have many admirable qualities: intelligence, resourcefulness and a wariness of humans

A Brown Rat.

among them. These are just the qualities that allow them to thrive in modern Britain, and to take advantage of the seemingly unlimited food generated by the wasteful nature of human society, and the way we exploit the land. I am less forgiving of Grey Squirrels. In the absence of any meaningful natural predatory control, these alien invaders are not welcome in my garden.

Rodent nests

At some point in their lives most small mammals construct insulating or cushioning nests for themselves or their offspring. With many species these are sited either underground or hidden from view and hard to discover; they are not necessarily well-constructed enough for it to be immediately obvious what they are. However, those made by the Harvest Mouse and Hazel Dormouse are extremely well-built and remain intact long after being abandoned by the animal that made them.

The nest of a Hazel Dormouse is about the size of a Seville Orange. Summer nests, which are located well off the ground, often in tangles of Honeysuckle (or in a nest box), comprise mainly a woven ball of stripped Honeysuckle bark with a central chamber.

The Harvest Mouse is our smallest rodent and its summer nest is about the size of a tennis ball. It is an intricately and tightly woven ball of intertwining grass fibres sited among the swaying stems of meadow plants. If you discover one in your biodiversity garden or meadow then it is a sure sign that you are on the right track when it comes to promoting native wildlife.

Hazel Dormouse winter nests include proportionately more leaves and grasses in the Honeysuckle-bark-mix than summer nests and are located underground, or at ground level among a tangle of roots.

A Harvest Mouse nest.

A Hazel Dormouse nest.

The nest of a Field Vole is usually located underground and accessed via a tunnel. In this instance, the tunnel and nest, which comprised a tangle of dry grass stems, was discovered beneath a reptile mat near the garden's meadow.

Nibbled nuts

In good years, mature Hazel shrubs in your garden or on land you own will produce an abundance of nuts. Several species of insects have evolved to make use of this bonanza, and rodents too are extremely partial. Wildlife enthusiasts are usually keen to discover signs that Hazel Dormice are present in their area. Most nibbled examples turn out to be false alarms but sooner or later, if the species really is present, you will find a nibbled nut with the definitive signs of Hazel Dormice in action.

Hazel Dormouse To access the nut, a Hazel Dormouse first creates a hole, then uses its incisor teeth to chisel around the hole in a circular fashion to enlarge it. The result is an inner edge that is extremely smooth, the angle of the cut edge relative to the surface of nut being 90 degrees or more. The overall effect of the end result is rather like a miniature clog.

Wood Mouse The typical approach of a Wood Mouse is to gnaw an initial hole then enlarge this with its nose outside and lower incisor teeth inside. These leave radial teeth marks on the cut slope of the hole with the animal's upper incisors leaving scratch marks on the outside of the nut.

Yellow-necked Mouse A Yellow-necked Mouse opens a Hazel nut in a similar way to a Wood Mouse: nose outside and lower incisor teeth inside the hole, radial teeth marks on the cut slope and scratch marks on the outside of the nut.

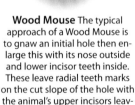

Bank Vole Having created an initial hole in the nut, a Bank Vole will enlarge the opening with its nose inside the shell. The lower incisor teeth leave a series of tooth marks on the slope of the cut and outside of the shell is barely scratched or marked.

Grey Squirrel Experienced Grey Squirrels can sometimes crack a Hazel nut neatly in half but most either shatter their shell in attempts to open it or leave a jagged cut margin.

The Hazel nuts that survive the nibbling attentions of rodents may go on to produce the next generation of shrubs, and indeed Hazel nuts are surprisingly easy to germinate: either bury them in the ground where you want them to grow, or grow them in a pot and plant them out once they reach a height of half a metre or so.

CARNIVORES

Domesticated carnivores (dogs and cats) notwithstanding, the Fox is the natural apex mammalian predator in my part of north Hampshire. It is an occasional visitor to my garden, detected mainly by droppings – strategically placed to mark territorial ownership – and the pungent smell associated with scent-marking. In my part of the world Foxes tend to keep a low profile, and who can blame them: aside from the few enlightened residents who manage land for wildlife in the general sense, overall attitudes towards them are on the intolerant side of indifference.

Like almost every British mammal going, provide a hungry Fox with a concentrated source of food and it will try to exploit it. Hence their interactions with alien Pheasants should come as no surprise, nor should the consequences for a resident near me who kept chickens housed in flimsy, congested outdoor cages where security was lacking. The outcome was as inevitable as it was tragic – a Fox got in and killed many of the birds and the owner's solution was to find somebody to shoot the Fox. This he succeeded in doing with little trouble. There is seemingly no shortage of people – invariably men of a particular temperament – willing to undertake this sort of task and for whom killing things for pleasure is seen as a legitimate and validated country pursuit. I suspect there are few people in the parish that would bat an eyelid at this or be in the least bit surprised.

With Biblical resonance, the attitudes of many around me still adhere to Medieval principles towards animals, that they exist for one of three reasons: as food, as beasts of burden, or for sport and pleasure. In the twenty-first century you might have hoped that humanity had evolved just a little bit. However, from local experience I fear it will be a while before a majority accepts that wildlife needs no more reason to exist than do humans; their 'role', if one needs to be ascribed, is as part of a balanced and sustainable global environment.

SKULLS AND OWL PELLETS

Owl pellets are easy to handle and odour-free, and can be teased apart after soaking in water. They provide valuable insights into the populations of small mammals in the vicinity. Here, we see undigested Bank Voles bones (from more than one animal) gently removed from the regurgitated pellet of a Tawny Owl.

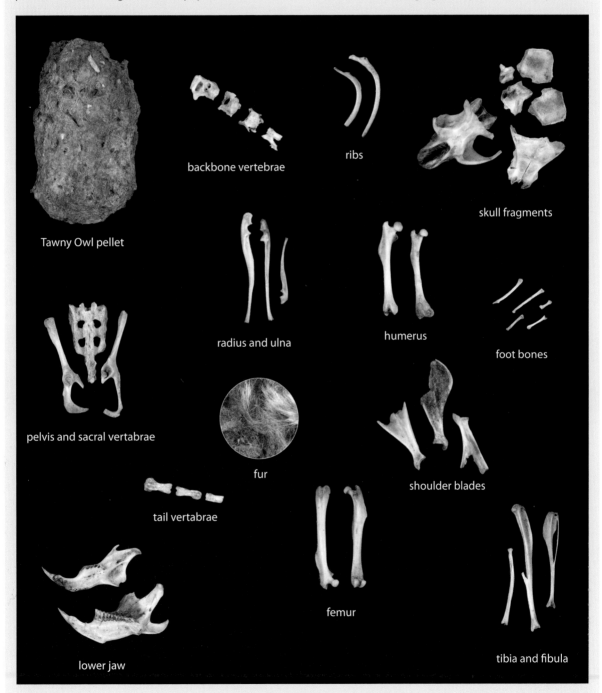

Tawny Owl pellet

backbone vertebrae

ribs

skull fragments

radius and ulna

humerus

foot bones

pelvis and sacral vertabrae

fur

shoulder blades

tail vertabrae

lower jaw

femur

tibia and fibula

A communal winter roost of Brown Long-eared Bats in a loft space.

BATS

Bats are a fascinating group of mammals but attract relatively little attention, apart from experts and dedicated enthusiasts. They have a number of intriguing characters, among these being that they are the only group of mammals capable of sustained and active flight, and furthermore they can fly and orientate in complete darkness. As a consequence, although some species occasionally emerge from their daytime roosts to hunt for food at dusk, bats are essentially nocturnal animals. They use a complex echolocation system to navigate and locate prey at night, and judging by their success their ability to move around in complete darkness matches the efficiency in daylight of vision in birds.

Bat biology

Operating in darkness, bats use echolocation to understand the world around them; specifically it is the mean by which they navigate and locate food. The system is akin to sonar: a bat emits short bursts of high frequency sound that bounce off objects; the sound 'echoes' are picked up by the animal's ears and provide a three-dimensional picture of the neighbourhood. Bat echolocation is so sophisticated that they can determine the direction and speed of movement of something as small as a midge. Without this ability, bats would not be able to feed.

British bats feed on nocturnal insects such as moths and beetles, food that is only abundant from spring to autumn. As a consequence, bats would have difficulty finding enough food during the cold winter months, and so they hibernate. The months of November to

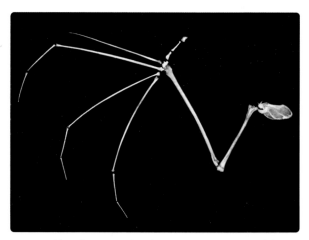

Bats are the only mammals to have mastered the art of flying and do so using membranes stretched over extended finger bones; in birds, the wings are supported by limb bones.

March are spent in a state of torpor, one where their body temperature drops considerably. Hibernation sites are typically used communally and although cool, keep a reasonably constant temperature and humidity.

Bat detractors

I have lost track of the number of times I have heard house owners and landowners utter, in unguarded moments before they realised where my loyalties lay, words to the effect 'Bloody things, all they do is ruin your plans and cost you money – best to get rid of them before they cause you trouble.' Judging by the number of times I have intervened with inaccurately completed planning application forms, I would say the attitude is commonplace among everyday folk. At the other end of the social spectrum, I was told about a patrician island tenant who used his privileged connections to overrule the requirement for a bat survey to be undertaken on one of the properties in his kingdom. I would have been tempted to dismiss this claim as hearsay except that the person who told me answered to a higher authority than Natural England – he was ordained – and the property in question was a church. So, yes, bats really do need all the friends they can get, and more than that they need advocates willing to stand up for them, challenge their detractors and thwart their enemies.

Bat detectors – studying and helping bats

Apart from nurturing an environment where there is enough insect food for bats to eat, there is another way you can help the group. In times past, there would

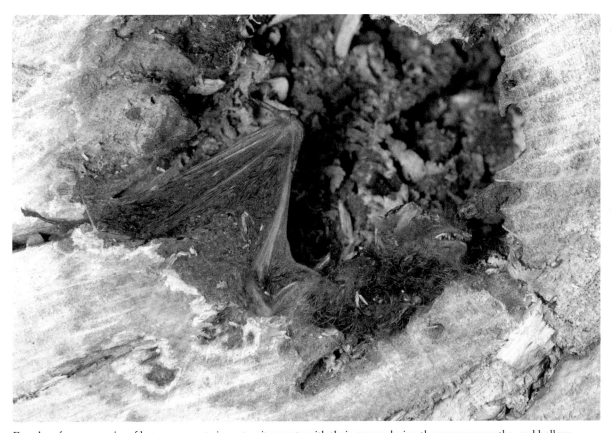

Females of many species of bats congregate in maternity roosts with their young during the summer months, and hollow trees are favoured sites. Predictably, tree surgery undertaken at this time of year can have fatal consequences, as it can in winter when bats hibernate in such sites. This Daubenton's Bat mother was chain-sawed in half, inside the nursery roost she occupied, by contractors working on behalf of Hart District Council, which is adjacent to Basingstoke. More than 50 other bats were in occupancy at the time. Hart District Council was prosecuted and fined for the offence but that was little comfort to the dead and injured bats.

have been any number of places where bats could have roosted during the daytime or hibernated in winter. Depending on the species and the season, sites in the parish of Pamber would have included natural holes and crevices in trees, the crumbling brickwork of old bridges, roof spaces and barns. In our increasingly sanitised, hermetically sealed and 'tidy' world those haunts are diminishing. You can provide substitutes in the form of bat boxes, bearing in mind that each species – there are 18 regularly recorded in the UK – is likely to have subtly different requirements and different seasonal preferences. The **Bat Conservation Trust** is a good source of information, so visit their website at www.bats.org.uk for more details.

In the past, studying bats was a daunting prospect. To the novice, the subject seemed inaccessible and shrouded in a cloak of mystery worthy of a secret society. Only those who had undergone ritual initiation and been granted a bat licence were allowed to participate. To outsiders, studying bats was a dark art, literally and metaphorically, and woe betide any amateur who transgressed. To a degree, the secrecy is understandable given that it is all too easy to accidentally destroy or ruin a bat hibernation or maternity roost site without

Locating boxes on different sides of this tree gave bats a choice in terms of shade and the temperature of their daytime roost.

New technology has brought good news to would-be bat enthusiasts and unlocks this hitherto inaccessible subject for the novice. Using a range of devices, including smartphone plug-ins, now anyone can lawfully identify bat species with as much certainty as a licenced bat worker and record numbers and feeding patterns, once you know the limitations of the device and yourself as a user.

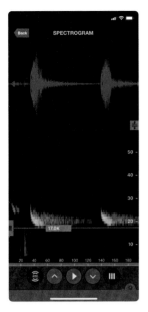

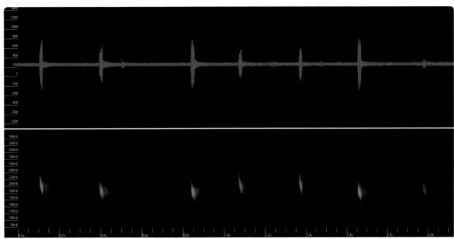

This is the spectrographic (or sonographic) representation of a recording of a feeding Noctule. Firstly, as viewed on the smartphone to which the device (in this case an Echo Touch Meter 2) was attached; and secondly, the recording's appearance when analysed using accompanying computer software.

realising it, and given the level of contempt felt for bats by many developers.

Knowing what is around you is of more than passing interest to the biodiversity gardener. The real significance comes from knowing what species are present and thereby ensuring that the environment you are nurturing is optimal for them. It also allows concerned individuals to compete on a level playing field with professional ecologists when it comes to challenging evidence provided by surveys submitted in support of planning applications. Buy one of these devices and become your own bat guardian and advocate.

Local bats

Eight species of bats have been recorded in the parish of Pamber, partly based on observations of individuals but also using analysis of their call signatures. This figure is likely to be a minimum number because some bat genera (notably species of *Myotis*) require expert eyes and ears to interpret their sonograms, and many individuals will not be identifiable to species level with any degree of accuracy. Given that proviso, species known for sure are: Common Pipistrelle; Soprano Pipistrelle; Serotine; Brown Long-eared Bat; Noctule; Natterer's Bat; Whiskered Bat or Brandt's Bat; and Western Barbastelle.

Until recently, identifying which bat species were present in my garden was a matter of conjecture and

educated guesswork. However, now that I have purchased my own state-of-the-art bat detector, confident determination has replaced tentative speculation. To illustrate this change in fortunes, here is a summary of

With a good view, well-lit or in silhouette, long-eared bat species can be identified as such in the field. A bat detector would have been needed to confirm that this individual was a Brown Long-eared Bat and not its Grey cousin.

recordings made between 21.00 hrs and 22.00 hrs on 4 June 2022, from a stationary spot in my garden, the number being the number of recordings, not necessarily the number of bats: Western Barbastelle, 3; Natterer's Bat, 2; Leisler's Bat, 2; Noctule, 20; Common Pipistrelle, 22; Soprano Pipistrelle, 23; Brown Long-eared Bat, 1. Visual observation of some of the individuals indicated that they were following a circuit, hunting over my meadow and tree-lined stream, then continuing along the ancient byway with which my garden is contiguous.

The presence of the Western Barbastelle is of greatest significance among the local bats because of its rarity and sparse national distribution. Like all bat species, it is protected by the Wildlife and Countryside Act of 1981, but the Western Barbastelle is also a UK Biodiversity Action Plan priority species.

Injured bats

Sadly, many people's only encounters with bats are with injured individuals – collisions with cars and being caught by nimble cats are among the commonest causes of injury. Fortunately, there is a network of committed bat enthusiasts across the country who care for injured bats and rehabilitate them. If you find an injured bat, visit the Bat Conservation Trust website for information or contact the RSPCA.

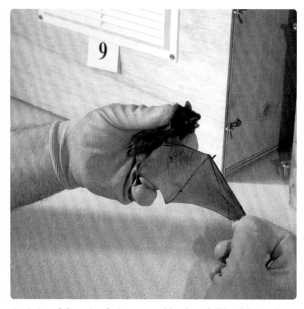

An injured Serotine being nursed back to full health in a bat hospital.

MAMMAL TRACKS AND TRAILS

In contrast to most birds, mammals are generally rather secretive and many are most active after dark. Consequently, the naturalist often has to rely on tracks and trails to indicate their presence, rather than seeing the animals themselves. Muddy paths provide ideal conditions for larger mammals to leave tell-tale 'footprints' while a decent fall of snow (a rare event these days in southern England) is a much more rewarding blank canvas. It is surprising just how much information can be gained by discovering and interpreting the clues that mammals leave.

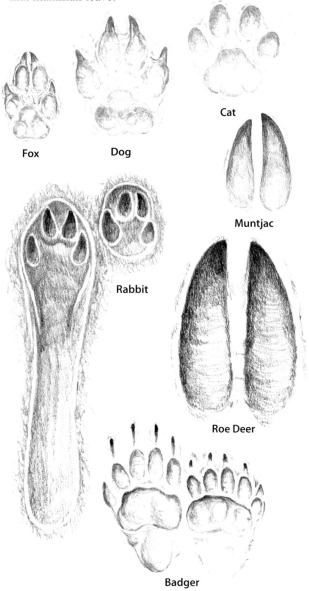

Fox

Dog

Cat

Muntjac

Rabbit

Roe Deer

Badger

Pets and domesticated animals

I like close encounters with nature as much as the next naturalist but regard the wildlife in my garden as just that – wild. While some of the animal visitors tolerate my presence, I have no desire to tame them or treat them as pets. Those that pass through or are resident in my garden are subject to the laws and vagaries of nature, albeit with a bit of a helping hand from me in terms of habitat provision. These days my engagement with animals as pets is restricted to, for example, finding an interesting caterpillar in the garden and rearing it through to adulthood.

My past interactions with other people's pets in the context of my garden have seldom endeared me to either animals or owners. The first I knew of Water Voles being present in the stream at the bottom of the garden was when I stumbled upon a neighbour's cat in the act of killing one on my lawn; despite my best endeavours I was unable to save the victim in time. On the canine front, during a particularly cold snap many years ago now I had scraped away snow to reveal leaf litter and provided windfall apples for the benefit of winter thrushes. While I was enjoying the scene an off-the-lead dog ran into the garden, snatched a Redwing and crunched the life out of it. On confronting the owner, I was told 'It's in his nature', to which I replied 'That's precisely why the creature should be under control or on a lead'. My language was more colourful than that when I asked the owner to remove their dog from my garden, but the result was that I fenced in much of the plot (with ground level access for small creatures) to reduce the chances of repeat incursions. From that point onwards, my attitude towards other people's pets in my garden hardened.

I have no wish to offend friends of mine who own and love their pets. And in a former life, I was part of a family that had a dog and was ruled by a cat. I appreciate that these two species provide company for their owners; and there is little doubt that for some they combat loneliness and provide a sense of purpose in their lives. In the past, I probably felt the same. Nowadays, however, I cannot see this companionship as anything but an illusion; and I cannot shake off the feeling that the relationship is more about the pet conditioning and training its owner than the other way round. Partly for these reasons, but mainly on environmental grounds, I have made the conscious decision not to own a cat or a dog in the future. For what remains of my life, I want to minimise my carbon footprint and impact on the environment generally. Owning and feeding a cat or dog would have the opposite effect and only add to the problem, making me responsible for appreciably increasing my overall carbon consumption. And I can't help feeling that if the nation's passion for pet welfare – primarily focused on just two species: cats and dogs – could be channeled into environmental concern across the wildlife spectrum, then there would be more advocates for the environment and conservation would be better resourced than it is today.

Turn back the clock a couple of centuries and domesticated cats, along with working and pet dogs, would have been fed largely on scraps. And there would have been far fewer of them. Cats in particular would have had to earn their keep by catching and eating rodents. Today, a significant proportion of pets I have come across consume the processed contents of tins and packets, not offcuts of meat destined for the table. Therein lie some of my concerns, an example of which might start with the carbon-liberating and biodiversity-destructive production of plants here and elsewhere in the world to feed to animals. Having served their purpose, these are then killed and, using energy-hungry processes, turned into food for pets. Add to that plunder of the marine environment for similar reasons. And all for the benefit, in the main, of two species kept for personal gratification. If it is not intuitively obvious that this industrial-scale sequence of events is ecologically barmy, you might want to read up on the subject. A good start would be Brenda and Robert Vale's book *Time to Eat the Dog? The Real Guide to Sustainable Living*. Further background is provided by a 2018 article in the British Veterinary Association publication *In Practice* entitled 'The impact of dogs on the environment' by authors Giles Groome, Jonty Denton and Phil Smith; and 'The environmental impacts of food consumption by dogs and cats' by Gregory Okin; and 'The ecological paw print of companion dogs and cats' by Pim Martens, Bingtao Su and Samantha Deblomme. See the References section for more information about these articles and books.

REIGNING CATS AND DOGS

As I mentioned, the decision to not own a pet is a personal one, and *The Biodiversity Gardener* is not the place to argue the case to persuade others to follow suit. However, it might be useful to explain my reasoning in a bit of detail. Firstly, there are the staggering levels of methane and nitrous oxide (measured in carbon dioxide equivalence) generated in producing processed food for the UK dog and cat population; that alone is enough to put me off. Then there is the way the food is produced and the land it takes. As an example, in their thoroughly researched book *Time to Eat the Dog? The Real Guide to Sustainable Living*, Brenda and Robert Vale calculate the amount of land it takes to feed a medium-sized dog, assuming the food is processed and comprises animal protein and vegetable matter. At a rough guess, the land required for production is around 30 percent greater than the size of my biodiversity garden. This is a plot that if I were so inclined could produce enough food to sustain a small family of humans.

If the production of pet food happens to include land that was once Brazilian rainforest and now grows soya (to feed to animals in the UK, the offcuts of which are turned into pet food), you can add habitat destruction and transportation carbon consumption to the environmental cost of owning an omnivorous or carnivorous pet. A 2021 estimate by the Pet Food Manufacturers Association cited UK pet numbers as including 12 million dogs and 12 million cats. I have come across figures that are larger, but regardless of that it still means that an awful lot of land and environmental consequences are devoted to feeding creatures whose primary purpose in life, in the context of the UK, is human indulgence.

LOOK WHAT THE CAT BROUGHT IN!

Only the most blinkered of owners would deny that cats are predators (obligate carnivores to be precise) and that they kill things. The fact that even well-fed animals retain their predatory instincts is self-evident to any owner with an open mind; and tacitly acknowledged, for example, by the existence of toy mice sold to cat owners to pander to the killing urges of their pets. A Mammal Society review entitled *Domestic Cat Predation on Wildlife* by Michael Woods, Robbie McDonald and Stephen Harris attempted to quantify

A neighbour's cat caught in the act of consuming a young Rabbit.

the scale of the problem in the UK, and shed some informed light on the subject. The report extrapolated from a sample of 986 cats, with their owners recording what prey was brought home. The authors estimated that a British population of approximately 9 million cats would have killed something like 92 (85–100) million prey items over the five-month study period (April to August 1997) including 57 (52–63) million mammals, 27 (25–29) million birds and 5 (4–6) million reptiles and amphibians. For each group, the first figure represents the mean, with the statistical extremes shown in brackets. Stating the obvious, these numbers do not take into account those prey animals killed and eaten away from the home, nor those simply killed and discarded.

In recognition of the harmful impact of domestic cats on native wildlife, there are instances where environmental mitigation accompanying planning applications for new-build houses and estates in the country has included a lasting requirement for house owners not to own cats. An example is a 68-home development at Cliffe Woods near Rochester in Kent, where the threat to Red-Listed, ground-nesting Nightingales was the underlying reason for the proposal. Quite how such policies, if adopted, would be enforced and policed long-term I am not sure.

THE COUNTRY'S GONE TO THE DOGS

Information is sketchy but the last recorded capture and killing of a Wolf in Hampshire is said to have occurred near Freemantle in 1212, with a bounty of five shillings being paid; at a guess, that's perhaps £600 in today's money. The last to be killed in England is said to have been in 1290. However, the Wolf's lineage lives on in the form of domesticated dogs, whose super-abundant populations have a far greater impact on wildlife across the board than a carrying-capacity population of their ancestors would ever have done.

The problem lies not with the existence of dogs per se but in their numbers and also the level of disturbance that they are allowed to cause. It affects those people who do not appreciate dogs running amok, of course, but the real issue regarding disturbance relates to the destruction of wildlife and natural habitats. Over the past few years, I have talked to naturalists and rangers from Northumberland and Lancashire to the Isles of Scilly and Sussex; people who are tasked with the responsibility of managing sites for wildlife and protecting nature. Without exception, the most significant problems they face are dog-related, with the animals' owners often adding to the troubles. The issues range from the wholesale destruction of nesting colonies of terns and waders on the coast, to disturbance of sensitive wildlife on lowland heaths and the physical destruction of Natterjack breeding ponds by constant dog incursions.

On local walks I seldom see anyone without at least one dog, typically off the lead, and further afield I suspect the story is repeated. I recall a visit a few years ago to a woodland nature reserve in the Chilterns, the aim being to renew an acquaintanceship with the Narrow-lipped Helleborines that once grew there. On arrival I was greeted by a signboard asking members of the public to restrict the number of dogs each person brought with them to five. Indeed, it seemed like every visitor apart from me had read the notice and brought their canine quota with them. Predictably, the woodland floor was trampled bare, ground flora was non-existent, birdlife was absent, you hardly dared kneel on the ground for fear of being smeared with faeces and, instead of summer fruits, the bushes were festooned with bags of dog excrement. Unsurprisingly, as a natural historian I felt out of place and abandoned the woodland to its two-legged and four-legged regulars.

PETS AND CONSERVATION

In an attempt to say thank you to the natural world, which has made my life so fulfilling, I am a trustee of a conservation grant awarding charity called **Birds on the Brink** (see the References section for details). As a sad indictment of the times, several of our recent grants have gone to projects that have the specific aim of excluding dogs as well as humans from vulnerable coastal breeding sites for ground-nesting species such as Ringed Plover, Oystercatcher and Little Tern, and winter roosting sites for species such as Dunlin. Except where fencing protects them, all of the species are essentially prevented from being able to nest on

A Birds on the Brink grant helped provide fencing at Hayling Island on the Hampshire coast to protect nesting birds and winter-roosting waders from disturbance.

At high tide, waders such these Dunlins, which were photographed at Hayling Island, need time to rest and recuperate. Generally, it is only private sites or fenced-off areas that provide the sanctuary from disturbance that they need.

● RECENT CANINE SEDIMENTARY – a new geological stratum in the making?

Apart from the revolting side of close encounters with dog excrement, there are issues that arise from the organic pollution it causes if left on ground. Collecting faeces in plastic bags is bad enough, bearing in mind the carbon consumption associated with manufacturing the bags and incinerating the filth or burying it in landfill sites. But leaving the bags hanging in trees and undergrowth for all eternity is surely an even greater environmental obscenity.

According to data from the Groome, Denton and Smith article 'The impact of Dogs on the Environment' (citing figures provided by Okin's 'Environmental impacts of food consumption by dogs and cats') the UK dog population produces 1,300 tonnes of faeces each day plus 6 million litres of urine. See the References section for publication details. Imagine the public's reaction if the equivalent in human excrement and urine were either deposited in the countryside or bagged and paraded while out on a morning's constitutional, ending up in landfill or incinerated with the fumes becoming part of the air we breathe.

suitable areas of the English coast by disturbance of one kind or another.

I became convinced of the need for an exclusion-zone-fencing approach when I visited Hayling Island one winter's day. On chatting to a lady dog owner whose pets were repeatedly flushing exhausted, winter-roosting Dunlins and Ringed Plovers, I was told it was the birds' fault because they 'taunted' her poor dogs, and in any case 'the birds always come back to the same spot' so they must enjoy the game. Yes, that really was the reasoning behind justifying her dogs' behaviour.

Another example of the impact of dogs on the environment comes in the form of veterinary flea and tick products: the active ingredients include the chemicals fipronil and the neonicotinoid imidacloprid. Currently banned for agricultural use in the UK and European Union because of their ability to kill invertebrates across the spectrum, and for the environmental harm they cause, they are still freely and widely available in pet products. Research by Rosemary Perkins, Martin Whitehead, Wayne Civil and Dave Goulson has demonstrated the contamination of British waterways with fipronil and its toxic breakdown products, and other pet product chemicals (see References section for details). Assuming farmers are not still using stockpiles of these chemicals, the contamination is assumed to arise when treated dogs are allowed or encouraged to enter waterways, the pesticides then leaching into aquatic environments. The danger is that levels of these hideous chemicals accumulate and kill freshwater life, thereby wrecking entire ecosystems. If you want more information on the subject, then visit the website of the charity Buglife. For my part, I am not willing to take the risk, and will not let a dog anywhere near my pond or stream.

PECKING ORDER

In a past life, and partly in an attempt to live 'The Good Life', I kept a few chickens for eggs. At the time, that seemed a rather natural and environmentally harmonious thing to do, but today my views have changed and hens, which would in essence be pets in my context, are no longer part of my plan. I guess it all boils down to the question of what you feed them on. If left to their own devices and given the freedom to roam I have no doubt the native biodiversity in my garden would suffer. They are truly omnivorous birds

and apart from plant matter, I have seen chickens catch and eat everything from caterpillars, earthworms and beetles to juvenile Slow-worms. The other option is to cage them and feed them artificially, but then you need to consider the carbon- and energy-wasteful, environmentally damaging aspects of producing the food they are given to eat if this is bought-in. Nowadays, my egg consumption is greatly reduced, and wherever possible I source them from neighbours who have no desire to foster biodiversity in their gardens but adopt a free-range policy towards poultry.

HOBBY HORSES

Prior to the invention and rise of the internal combustion engine, the role that horses played in the rural environment of Pamber was much more profound than it is today. For the majority of the population, those who worked the land, they were the people carriers of their day, transporting both individuals riding horseback and groups in carriages and carts. They were also the haulage vehicles and tractors of the time, dragging loads and invaluable on the land when it came to pulling ploughs. In a pre-mechanised era, horses used purely for equestrian pleasure were likely to have been restricted to the higher end of the social spectrum. Horse racing satisfied a competitive streak among the wealthier landed classes; it also allowed them to flirt with speed and indulge any gambling predilections they might have. And of course, there was the institutionalised pursuit of hunting on horseback with all its aristocratic leanings.

Nowadays, the functional roles that horses played in the past have been largely replaced by mechanical alternatives. And some of the equestrian pastime pleasures have been traded for technology too. For example, the desire to indulge a love of speed in the countryside has trickled down the social ladder and today finds outlets among owners of quadbikes and scrambling bikes, allowing teenage mentalities to persist into old age. Despite these changes, however, today there are still plenty of horses in the parish of Pamber. The difference is that they are, in essence, pets, or perhaps hobby horses would be a better way of describing them. They are kept for fun and recreation, not as work horses.

In terms of their impact on the environment, there are subtle differences between grazing by horses in the

past and the situation today. In the past, most animals would have been put to work for much of their lives, and on the move during any given day. Modern day horses live more sedentary lives, which is significant both in terms of grazing pressure and the dung that comes out the other end. A few native wildlife species benefit from continual, intensive grazing, for example the tiny plant Mousetail, and some species of wax-cap fungi. However, most cannot tolerate constant close-cropping. And almost nothing, except perhaps Common Nettles, will tolerate the intensive manuring that results from elevated stock levels defecating and urinating in one spot. If the horses in question have been dosed with ivermectin then that is disastrous for biodiversity. This veterinary drug, whose stated purpose is an anti-parasitic, persists in manure and is toxic to the forms of life that would normally decompose the dung and recycle the nutrients to the soil.

A member of the buttercup family, Mousetail can be found here and there around the margins of horse-grazed fields.

Plants: a botanical overview

I find it easy to fall into the trap, when talking to others about natural history, of ascribing roles to plants and animals in nature, rather like job descriptions, as a simplistic way of trying to explain, for example, why aphids exist or why Otters eat fish. This implies an overarching master plan where there is none, and it exposes the human need to discern order where we see chaos. Neither is an appropriate way of interpreting nature; a better way to look at the world is to think of species being driven by evolution to occupy every available ecological niche, their structure, physiology and behaviour tailored by natural selection to best exploit the resources that present themselves. Plants and animals simply exist. During their lifespans they compete with one another, even with members of their own kind, to maximise their own reproductive potential.

PLANT LIFE AND
THE BIODIVERSITY GARDEN

Focussing on plants, without the need for you to do anything in your garden, every available ecological

niche will be occupied by one species or another. All photosynthesise and liberate oxygen and in that sense all of them contribute to the well-being of the environment. Many will compete with each other, almost all will be food for one or many species of animals, and their roots will contribute structure to the soil and aid water retention, thereby benefiting others. It is impossible to calculate the complexity of the web of life and multitude of interactions and dependencies in my garden and frankly I don't want to. I am happy to accept the fact, understand some of the more superficial relationships and simply celebrate the complexity and the environmental benefits that result.

Conventional gardeners will acknowledge that artificial plant communities in herbaceous borders evolve and change over time. If left to their own devices, what is sometimes described in pejorative terms as 'nature taking over' follows, as if that were somehow a bad thing. This is biological power play at work in the world of plants, a process that underpins vegetative succession – the drift over time, in terms of species present, towards the climax community appropriate to that particular bit of land. In most terrestrial areas of lowland Britain that means woodland. Vegetative succession needs to be acknowledged if you want to help native biodiversity, and it highlights the need to have a clear understanding of what you want to achieve in terms of habitat creation and encouragement.

If your goal is on a grander scale than my garden, and some form of rewilding with woodland features in the mix, then your options vary. Of course, you can plant trees and, assuming the species are appropriate to the area where you live, hope that over time these isolated specimens consolidate and evolve into a woodland proper. However, you might want to consider an alternative, which is the do-nothing approach. The initial stage in the process will be grassland and over time this will be colonised by the likes of Brambles, which make ideal protective nurseries for sapling trees that have seeded themselves. Most likely your local Jay population will plant acorns for you and within 20 years you will have a truly natural woodland in the making. My guess would be that your infant woodland will harbour appreciably more biodiversity than that in a regimented planting scheme of a similar age. And it would have done more ecological good along the way, the evolving scrub having fostered species that call this stage in succession home, allowing their populations to build up and colonise elsewhere.

A shining example of what can be achieved by a hands-off approach to environmental recovery comes from New Zealand's South Island; namely the Hinewai Reserve ecological restoration project on the Banks Peninsula. Owned by the Maurice White Native Forest Trust, the aim has been to foster natural regeneration on its 1,250 hectares and as a result fabulous forests, akin to those that cloaked the land before human settlers felled them, are returning under their own steam; more than that they are positively flourishing. Interestingly, Gorse, introduced by settlers from Europe, is part of the plan at Hinewai; seen by many New Zealand farmers as an invasive plague, here it acts as a protective impenetrable nursery for seedling trees, and dies out once native forest takes over. Human intervention is now restricted to the removal of alien introduced species where they pose a threat to native plants and animals. It is an example of selfless and environmentally responsible land management the likes of which we could do with having more of in the UK.

My plot of land is miniscule by comparison with Hinewai and since there is no hope of restoring wilderness to the part of southern England where I live, I have opted for what I see as the next best thing: promotion and protection of those man-influenced habitats that historically nurtured the native biodiversity I value. One of these habitats is grassland, and being an intermediate stage in the succession of vegetation, intervention and management with clear aims and targets are what I aim for. Again, as discussed previously, successional habitats have an important role to play, since what are dismissively referred to as scrub and overgrown rank grassland are the sources of much of the biodiversity people prize today.

BOTANICAL AND HORTICULTURAL ETIQUETTE

Here is a plea to gardeners of all hues, from conventional to aspiring biodiversity advocates: consider the consequences of your actions and act with environmental responsibility. Let us start with the disposal of garden waste; the notion that anything organic from the garden can be described as 'waste' is part of the problem. I once heard a French chef say, slightly tongue in cheek, that it should be a criminal offence for anyone to throw away stale bread. He was not talking about avoiding waste but referring to stale bread as a valuable ingredient. I suspect he did not have sliced white in mind but no matter. The same principle applies to most organic output from the garden, be that cut grass, hedge trimmings or fallen branches. Carefully distributed or composted, all forms of organic matter are likely to make a valuable contribution to a biodiversity garden. Their removal will diminish the value of your plot for wildlife.

Taking responsibility for the consequences of your actions has another significant dimension, beyond that of exporting your problems so that they become somebody else's. Dumping garden material in the countryside is the botanical equivalent of littering and fly-tipping. Apart from being antisocial, it can pose a real threat to native wildlife. Many of the horticultural plants grown in conventional gardens are not native to the UK and some are invasive botanical thugs that, in the absence of natural checks and balances, can quickly take over and smother out more delicate native species. Liberate them in the countryside and some run amok, displacing and killing native plants with all the knock-on consequences for other wildlife associated with those species. Even seemingly innocuous plants such as Variegated Yellow Archangel, a widespread garden plant, pose a threat. Much more vigorous than its native subspecies cousin, when liberated into the wild it quickly spreads and overwhelms delicate native species. As with other plants listed on Schedule 9 of the 1981 Wildlife and Countryside Act, it is an offence to plant or otherwise cause it to grow in the wild, and convicted offenders face a fine of up to £5,000 and/or six months imprisonment.

LIVING WITH THE PAST

Many prospective biodiversity gardeners will be working with small plots and either starting from scratch or, like me, undergoing a managed retreat from conventional gardening. It might help give a flavour of those plants that are worth encouraging and championing, and those hangers-on from cultivation that, due to their botanical thuggery, you might want

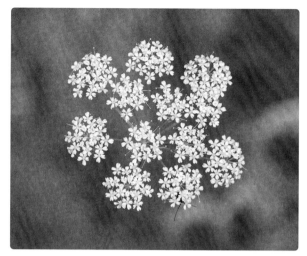

In its favour, Ground-elder is an excellent nectar source for a wide range of insects.

A drift of Snowdrops in late winter.

to discourage. From a native biodiversity perspective there are not many of the latter and none that require anything more than occasional removal.

Previous owners of my cottage planted Snowdrops and daffodils in the lawn and I see no reason to remove or discourage them despite the latter being represented by a range of non-native cultivars. Clumps of Summer Snowflake grow here and there, better known locally as Loddon Lily. Although the stream at the bottom of my garden is part of the catchment of the river after which they are named, the snowflakes are undoubtedly introduced here. Again, they look happy enough and I cannot imagine they pose an ecological threat so they are welcome to stay.

Ground-elder is a plant that thrives on disturbance and is seen by gardeners as a foe. Back in the days when I was a conventionally minded gardener, I followed received wisdom that it was Public Enemy Number One and unless I relentlessly dealt with the problem, I deemed myself a failure as a gardener. Consequently, for years I slavishly tackled Ground-elder, knowing in the back of my mind that my labours would only ever end in disappointment. The secret to overcoming the perceived threat it poses is a change in mindset; the real problem, such as it is, is solved by providing long-term soil stability.

Even back in the bad old gardening days I had a sense that the more I did to try to remove Ground-elder, the more disturbance I caused and the better it thrived. Nowadays, I no longer bother and my attitude to this particular species might serve as a blueprint for others of its kind. Put simply, I tolerate it. It grows here and there in the lawn but as the years go by its presence diminishes as meadow soil stability increases. Ground-elder does still grow in my remaining herbaceous beds and on banks but again, because I don't disturb the soil its seasonal dominance is in decline.

Although I have learned to live with Ground-elder, I do resent the rise of one of its umbellifer relatives, namely Hemlock Water-dropwort. That's not because I have an inherent dislike of the plant but because its spread into my garden, which has occurred over the last 15 years, is a direct consequence of its ascendency in local ditches and waterways due to nutrient enrichment run-off from agricultural land. That is pollution by any other name and the eutrophication it causes is a botanical reminder of a problem that most people either ignore or are unaware of.

In a former gardening life, I saw Common Nettles, which thrive on disturbed and nitrogen-enriched soils, as a problem. Nowadays, this is not a plant that I lose sleep over, quite the reverse in fact. In the part of the garden reserved as a meadow, nettles have all but disappeared and I welcome the species for its relevance to butterflies where it grows in forgotten corners and margins.

My garden soil has a strong clay component and is neutral in pH. As a result, fortunately I do not have to deal with the problem of Rhododendron, which likes acid conditions. And I am lucky not to have had Japanese Knotweed imposed on the garden by previous owners.

To reinforce warnings about pond plants, I suggest you do not buy any unless you are 100 percent confident both in your ability to identify them and of the identification skills of the person selling them. Bear in mind that just because a plant comes with a label that does not mean it is accurately identified, nor that it is free of contaminating companions. If you have any doubt regarding the suitability of the plants you have purchased for the purpose you have in mind, then at the very least quarantine them first.

The ascendency of Hemlock Water-dropwort in local ditches has taken place in my lifetime, the plant benefiting from fertiliser run-off from farmland.

There are lists available online of invasive species, but those aquatic species you must not buy or accept under any circumstances include Floating Pennywort, Nuttall's Waterweed, American Skunk-cabbage and Parrot's-feather. The impact of New Zealand Pigmyweed on native British wildlife and habitats is discussed on pp. 66, 115 and 230.

When the times comes to clear some of the vegetation from your pond do not be tempted to liberate what you remove into the wider world. Take care, in the manner described on p. 115, to safeguard as many of the pond invertebrates as you can when you remove pondweeds. Having done so, the plants that remain are probably best composted.

NECTAR THROUGH THE SEASONS

British natural history and ecology has evolved over millennia, and the resulting web of life has resulted in refined and nuanced ecological relationships and dependencies. Those between flowers and insects are examples of ones that are mutually beneficial, the plants getting pollinated and the insects getting fed. A range of adaptations characterise the relationship, having evolved to maximise the chances of pollination success: insect mouthpart structure tailored to flower shape is an example. However, time of flowering is also a factor. To minimise competition, some plants bloom at either end of the floral season and have evolved to benefit from insects that like to get an early start and are active in late winter, and those that are on the wing in autumn; with species that hibernate, these are often one and the same.

Examples of early risers are moths such as Early Grey, Common Quaker and Clouded Drab that contribute to the night shift, with post-hibernation queen bumblebees and butterflies such as Comma and Brimstone active in the day. At the end of the season, night shift moths include Large Yellow Underwing, Lunar Underwing and Setaceous Hebrew Character, while queen bumblebees and wasps are busy in the daytime fattening up before hibernation. To maximise the benefits to both insects and plants, the biodiversity garden can provide valuable sources of nectar for at least ten months of the year.

Grey Willow
(February to March)

cultivated Lungwort
(February to May)

Selfheal
(April to June)

Germander Speedwell
(April to June)

cultivated French Crane's-bill
(May to August)

Creeping Buttercup
(May to August)

Greater Bird's-foot-trefoil
(June to August)

Creeping Thistle
(June to September)

A selection of seasonal nectar sources in my garden.

Primrose
(February to May)

Blackthorn
(March to April)

Daisy
(March to October)

Cowslip
(April to May)

Common Comfrey
(May to June)

Common Hawthorn
(May to June)

Elder
(May to July)

Hogweed
(May to August)

Bramble
(May to August)

Oxeye Daisy
(May to August)

Tufted Vetch
(June to August)

Spear Thistle
(July to September)

Common Fleabane
(July to September)

cultivated Michaelmas-daisy
(September to November)

Ivy
(September to November)

Fungi

There is so much more to a fungus than just a toadstool or bracket, and the main body is invariably far more extensive but hidden from view. The significance of hyphal threads and the mycelium that they form are discussed on p. 108. Sometimes this mycelium is inadvertently discovered if you break off a piece of bark on a decaying tree stump.

Hyphae not only comprise the body of the fungus, they also fulfil a multitude of different tasks, which includes feeding: they produce enzymes to digest organic matter externally, and the resulting nutrients are then absorbed along with water from the growing medium. Sexual reproduction is a feature of fungal natural history. Hyphae from different colonies fuse, and toadstools, in their many different forms, are their fruiting bodies. These are themselves composed of tightly packed hyphae and their function is to produce and disperse spores, typically by means of gills or pores on the undersurface; these structures increase the surface area for spore production and release.

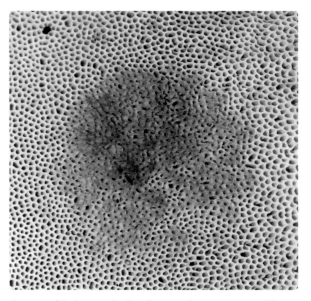

Species of *Boletus* and related genera have pores not gills on the underside of the cap. In some, these change colour when bruised, a character that can aid identification.

Fungal mycelium comprising a mass of hyphae.

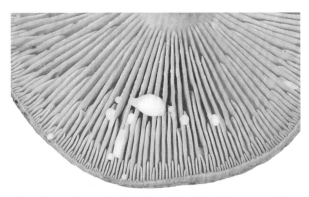

The gills on the underside of a toadstool cap increase surface area for spore production. In milkcap species, minor damage causes the release of latex-like, milky fluid.

Countless millions of spores are released by a fungal fruiting body over its lifespan, and a hint of this can be seen in this time-lapse image of spore release by Honey Fungus toadstools.

FUNGAL LIFESTYLES AND GROWING HABITATS

Most contemporary naturalists are aware that fungi play a vital role in decay and the recycling of nutrients from dead organic matter back into the environment. The extent and variety of fungi are hinted at in autumn when toadstools appear from growing media that range from dead wood and leaf litter to humus-rich soil. However, many fungal species are much more than agents of decay: they have a complex and entirely positive relationship with living plants, and trees in particular. These symbiotic, mycorrhizal partnerships, where the fungus sheaths the tree roots and its hyphae extend into the soil and penetrate the tree's root cells too, are discussed on p. 108. Many of the toadstools that adorn the woodland floor in autumn are the fruiting bodies of these partnerships.

The relationship between a few fungal species and trees is less benign and parasitism is well documented, as are instances where fungi invade an already diseased or damaged tree, hastening its end. It is a short step from this strategy to that found in the Honey Fungus, which is capable of penetrating seemingly healthy trees and ultimately causing their demise. Elsewhere in the natural world, there are fungi that parasitise insects, and in a few cases they even attack their own. There seem to be no limits to the extraordinary ways in which fungi make a living.

Members of the fungal genus *Russula* form mycorrhizal associations with the roots of a range of trees, depending on species. The Charcoal Burner, seen here, is associated mainly with oaks.

IDENTIFICATION

With the exception of a few iconic species, identifying fungi is a challenge, even when comparing individuals of the same species. This is partly because they are so variable, both as they grow and as they mature. Although the subject of fungal identification is beyond the scope of this book, the following section offers some pointers to help you hone your skills and improve your chances of correct identification when referring to a guide on the subject.

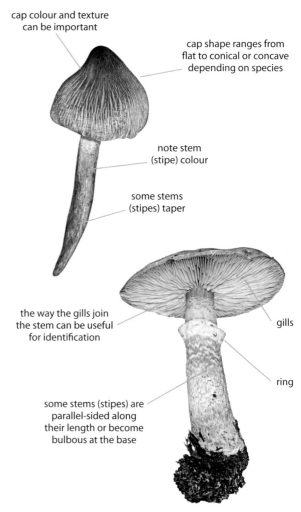

cap colour and texture can be important

cap shape ranges from flat to conical or concave depending on species

note stem (stipe) colour

some stems (stipes) taper

the way the gills join the stem can be useful for identification

gills

ring

some stems (stipes) are parallel-sided along their length or become bulbous at the base

If you can, resist the temptation to pick fungi in order to identify them. Instead, make notes and try using a small mirror to scrutinise the gills and undersurface of the cap.

- **SIZE** Most species vary considerably in terms of size. Like all living organisms, they need water and nutrients to thrive, and a shortage or abundance of either will affect the size. The sizes provided in field guides will be rough guidelines and nothing more.
- **CAP SHAPE** This feature in a toadstool can be extremely useful and indicative. For instance, a cap might be pointed, domed and rounded, or dimpled and depressed in the centre.
- **TEXTURE** A cap's surface is generally a reliable characteristic and may be, for example, smooth, fibrous, granular, hairy, wrinkled or glutinous.
- **STEM** The texture and colour of the stem can be important features in identification as can the presence or absence of an attached ring.

- **SMELL** A few toadstools have a distinct smell: some are pleasant – aniseed for example – while others have more pungent aromas.
- **MILK** A few fungi, notably species of milkcap (*Lactarius* spp.), produce what looks like 'milk' when damaged or nicked.
- **GILLS AND PORES** Using a small mirror if necessary, study the structure, arrangement and colour of the gills or pores, and their attachment to the stem.
- **HABITAT** Most fungi are habitat-specific and might be found, for example, in grassland or deciduous woodland but seldom both. Some woodland species form symbiotic relationships with specific tree species and will not grow on others; this is an invaluable aid to identification.

GARDEN FUNGI

To follow is a brief selection of species found in my garden to provide a flavour of what other biodiversity gardeners might expect.

Fungi associated with trees

Boletus cisalpinus
In the garden usually occurs in the vicinity of Pedunculate Oak or Silver Birch.

Birch Brittlegill
Grows among fallen leaves and mosses in association with Silver Birch.

Leopard Earthball
Grows among surface roots and fallen leaves in association with Pedunculate Oak.

Fungi of dead wood and decaying organic matter

Blistered Cup
The cup-shaped Blistered Cup grows on enriched ground in the vicinity of well-rotted compost heaps and leaf mulch.

Striated Earthstar
Grows in well-rotted leaf litter and organic matter, with a persistent colony in a large pot of Pelargoniums of all places.

Winter Fungus
As its name suggests, the Winter Fungus appears in clusters during the winter months on dead tree stumps and logs.

Verdigris Agaric
Appears now and then on leaf mulch, and in the decaying carpet of grass and moss in the meadow.

Redlead Roundhead
This striking fungus grows on wood chips and twiggy debris, but only after it has decayed and compacted.

Candlesnuff Fungi
The distinctive spore-producing bodies of a fungus that grows in well-rotted wood, both branches and stumps.

Collared Earthstar
The Collared Earthstar grows in well-rotted leaf litter and organic matter, often in association with a buried, decaying log.

Jelly Ear
The unmistakable Jelly Ear grows most frequently on the standing dead branches of Elder.

Grassland fungi

Pleated Inkcap
A delicate species found in short grass. Discovered in the morning after overnight rain and seldom lasts more than a day.

Slimy Waxcap
This rather unassuming toadstool grows in short grass, usually in short grass around the margins of the meadow in the garden.

Spangle Waxcap
Like many other species of waxcap, it favours unimproved grassland, and has associations with grassland mosses.

Meadow Waxcap
As waxcaps go, this is a relatively large and striking species that appears in the meadow in early autumn, sometimes in small groups.

Golden Waxcap
The bright yellow fruit bodies of this waxcap appear in short, unimproved grassland, and is reckoned to be associated with meadow mosses.

Cedarwood Waxcap
Named for its smell, not its associations, the Cedarwood Waxcap grows in the lawn and is associated with the mosses that thrive there.

Meadow Coral
This distinctive fungus is reckoned to be a good sign of unimproved grassland. It grows here and there in the meadow, sometimes amongst and overshadowed by grasses.

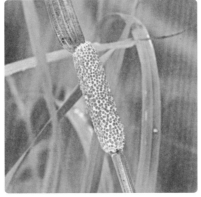

Choke
A distinctive fungal fruiting body. Lives within the grass, favouring Cock's-foot, and forms a symbiotic relationship, improving the efficiency of the plant's photosynthesis.

Ergot
The spore-producing body of Ergot, which contains psychoactive alkaloid chemicals, is shaped like a miniature blackened banana and grows from the ears of various grasses.

Parasites, predators and gall inducers

Entomophthora muscae
This fly is infected with spores from the dispersal stage in the life-cycle of a fungus called *Entomophthora muscae*. Prior to killing the fly, the fungus alters the insect's behaviour so it climbs to an exposed spot on a shrub, ensuring good spore dispersal. If the fly had been infected by a stage in the life cycle that produces resting spores it would have been induced to crawl down to the ground before dying so the spores could more easily enter the soil.

Scarlet Caterpillarclub
Appears occasionally in short grass fringing my meadow and its colourful appearance belies its rather sinister natural history. The 'club' is the fruiting body of a fungus that infects and kills the larvae of soil-dwelling moth caterpillars, notably species such as the Ghost Swift.

Isaria farinosa
Above ground, *Isaria farinosa* appears as tiny, floury forks, rather like a tiny Candlesnuff Fungus. Trace the stem into the ground and you will find it growing out of the remains of the pupa of a micro moth. Easily overlooked, they appear most frequently in mosses growing beneath Pedunculate Oaks.

Alder Tongue
Altogether otherworldly, Alder Tongue appears in early autumn and is a gall caused by a fungus that infects the cones of Alder. The galls resemble fiery tongues that burst from otherwise healthy looking cones.

FUNGAL FORMS

Considering that fungal fruiting bodies have all evolved to serve the same dual functions – the production and dispersal of spores – their appearance is extraordinarily varied. Bearing in mind that there are several thousand species of larger fungi in Britain alone, the following examples are just a snapshot of their many, varied forms.

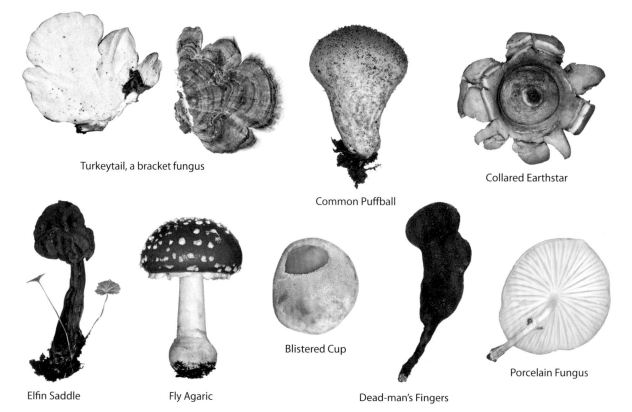

Turkeytail, a bracket fungus

Common Puffball

Collared Earthstar

Elfin Saddle

Fly Agaric

Blistered Cup

Dead-man's Fingers

Porcelain Fungus

294

SPORE PRODUCTION AND DISPERSAL

The role of a fungal fruiting body is to produce spores and to aid their dispersal. In the simplest instances, spores are produced all over the relatively smooth and unadorned surface of the toadstool. However, increasing the surface area available for spore production means that greater numbers can be produced and a variety of ingenious means of achieving this have evolved. These include the creation of gills, pores or teeth on the underside of the toadstool or bracket in question, and as a consequence countless millions of spores are liberated in the life of a single toadstool. Because spores are generally dispersed by the wind it follows that the higher their liberation takes place away from the ground, the more chance they have of being carried far and wide. This is why toadstool caps are carried aloft on a stalk and bracket fungi fruiting bodies appear on trunks or branches of trees, well off the ground.

Simple spore-producing surfaces

The fruiting bodies of some fungi such as the earthtongue *Geoglossum cookeianum* (below) are simple structures with spores being produced over the whole surface.

Pored toadstools

Members of the genus *Boletus* (and many bracket fungi too) have tubes on the undersides of their caps, inside of which the spores are produced; they are released via external pores.

Gilled toadstools

Most of the common toadstools with which we are familiar have radiating gills on the underside of cap. Classic examples are found in the genus *Agaricus* (seen below) and the group includes several edible species such as the Cultivated Mushroom. Released spores fall from the gills and are carried by the wind; if a cut cap is placed on a sheet of white paper, a detailed spore print is produced.

A growing mushroom.

The underside of the cap showing the gills.

A spore print.

Toothed fungi

A few unusual fungi increase the surface area available for spore production by producing teeth, either on the underside of the cap in the case of hedgehog fungi (genus *Hydnum*), or all over their external surface in the case of species like the Bearded Tooth (seen below).

Cup fungi

In the case of cup fungi, spores are usually produced on the inner surface and are washed out by raindrops. With the Common Bird's-nest (seen below) and related fungi, however, the spores are borne in egg-like packets and it is these that are flung out of the cup and dispersed by falling rain.

Puffballs and earthstars

These unusual organisms belong to a group called the 'stomach fungi' and their spores are produced inside a rounded sac that opens via a terminal pore. If raindrops hit the sac, the internal pressure is enough to puff out a plume of spores (see p. 292). Some species are anchored to the ground but in the case of the Collared Earthstar (seen below), stability is improved by the sac's outer casing spreading and forming radiating arms.

● LICHENS

Pinning down a strict definition for lichens has always been difficult. To the novice, they may look like primitive, non-flowering plants. But in reality, they are strange organisms created by mutually beneficial relationships between fungi (which are not plants, after all) and tiny photosynthetic partners that live inside the fungal body. The appearance of any given lichen species is determined by the species of fungus involved and the partner; a partner can be either an alga or a cyanobacterium (a bacterium capable of photosynthesising), and some fungi play host to either form of partner.

In the context of a garden, lichen communities are found mainly on tree bark, as here in the case of a species called the Common Orange Lichen, or on shaded bricks and roof tiles.

A Stinkhorn, often first detected by smell.

Animal agents

Fungi enthusiasts are often appalled by the havoc wreaked by slugs on toadstools, especially if the season happens to be a dry one when other sources of water are in short supply. It is certainly true that slugs ruin the appearance of otherwise pristine toadstools but do they do any real damage? Probably not, unless the toadstool in question fails to mature as a consequence: undigested spores are inadvertently transported by the slugs themselves and often taken underground. Indeed, research suggests that in some fungal species, slugs are among the most important agents of spore dispersal. There are parallels with the Stinkhorn, and related species, whose spores are produced in stinking slime that attracts feeding flies, which in turn spread the spores when they fly off.

A Dusky Slug feasting on a toadstool.

● ALIEN INVADERS

Like all things in the natural world, Britain's fungal complement is constantly changing. Sadly of course there are plenty of losses, mostly associated with habitat destruction and degradation. But there have also been some gains in recent years, notably species introduced inadvertently by man. The Redlead Roundhead (p. 292) and the Red Cage Fungus (above) are spreading thanks to the increased use of woodchip mulch, which they find much to their liking; the former is now locally abundant in some flowerbeds. But perhaps the weirdest of all is the Starfish Fungus (below), which hails from the Southern Hemisphere, and now grows in a few spots in southern England; it emits an unspeakable smell that attracts flies, which disperse its spores.

A lightweight net used for catching insects.

Monitoring and Recording Wildlife – Making the Most of Your Garden, Both for Biodiversity and for You

Approaches to the study of some groups of animals have been covered elsewhere in the book, and these include: butterflies on p. 139; moths on p. 155; beetles on p. 186; dragonflies on p. 235; pondlife on p. 226. To follow is some more general advice about equipment, along with techniques for observation and study applicable to more than one group. As a top tip: never explore your garden without a pocket full of pots. I try to use as little plastic as possible. However, in my clumsy hands, I reluctantly accept that screw-top plastic pots are better than glass ones, which sooner rather than later I manage to smash, or cardboard ones that I crumple.

Nets

Nets come in all shapes and sizes that are designed to capture a range of different creatures. Fine-mesh, large-mouthed nets are good for a range of subjects but their deployment is inadvisable anywhere near brambles or roses, or other snags: before you know it the fabric of the net will be in tatters. At the other end of the spectrum are heavy-duty sweep nets.

The trouble with sweep nets is that they have a tendency to encourage a rather indiscriminate and overenthusiastic approach. This has the potential to result in damage not only to delicate invertebrates but also to the environment in which they live. To put things in perspective, transport yourself back to your conventional gardening days and imagine the impact vigorous sweep-netting would have had on a precious herbaceous border. You should treat, for example, your meadow, or indeed any meadow, with the same respect you would somebody's prize Dahlias.

Pond-dipping

Exploration of freshwater and the study of pondlife has been discussed on p. 112 but it is such a fascinating subject that it deserves a further mention. One of the main tools of the trade are long-handled pond nets, robust enough to allow the user to sweep through vegetation and debris. Bear in mind that the very act of pond-dipping is a disruptive, not to say destructive, process from the point of view of the complex and relatively stable world of pond creatures. So, act with circumspection. Rather than employing frantic action, try gently immersing the net to the depths, causing as little disturbance as you can to the vegetation as you go, and then sweep up towards the surface. It is useful to have a range of smaller nets for more delicate work.

Try pond-dipping at night. You will be amazed how much more activity there is after dark, and with the aid of a bright LED torch in the hands of an assistant you can target specific creatures more effectively than in the hours of daylight. Such torches are also invaluable for examining your catch in a tray, in part because they are so bright, but also because the 'cold' wavelengths of light they emit seem to pick out invertebrate bodies particularly well.

When it comes to examining your catch, the first and best piece of advice is to keep each sample size small. Resist the urge to collect a net full, because unless you have a huge examination tray, sifting through the collected material in a thorough and systematic manner becomes an impossible task. In addition, some delicate creatures will be killed if they are smothered and compressed by a mound of vegetation. Your sample should always go into a tray, or wide bucket containing clean freshwater from the pond or water body from which you are sampling: some creatures cannot survive for long out of water. Leave the sample undisturbed for a few minutes, then look for signs of movement as invertebrates begin to feel confident enough to begin scurrying around.

Pond-dipping top tip – When examining and providing a temporary home for pond creatures, never use tap water. There is a good chance that it will contain levels of chlorine – used to treat and sterilise the water – that will kill your precious catch. And in some cases, drinking water that comes from the tap also contains microplastics. It is best to use the water from the water body that you sampled, or rainwater.

It is useful to have three or four smaller water-filled trays to hand into which prize specimens can be transferred. Spoons and paintbrushes are the ideal tools of the trade for this process and it is a good idea to separate what might otherwise become warring factions. To aid observation and appreciation of your catch, both black trays and white ones are useful, depending on which background contrasts most effectively with the bodies of pond creatures in question.

Binoculars

Once the badge of honour of hard-core birdwatchers, modern binoculars now serve the interests of a wide spectrum of naturalists. Their impressive capabilities and modern technology come at a price, needless to say. There is no pair of binoculars that could be described as the best for wildlife-watching, only a range of alternatives each favoured by some but not by others. For me, the main considerations are weight, optical quality, durability and an ability to close-focus. The binoculars that I currently use, and have no wish to be parted from, have the optical parameters 8x32, the former number relating to magnification, the latter the diameter of the objective lens and an indication of how bright the image is. A minimum focus distance of around 2 metres allows me not only to examine in detail the feather patterns of a bird, but also to scrutinise features needed, for example, in the identification of dragonflies.

Part of the toolkit of the generation of naturalists I grew up with was a decent magnifying glass; anyone with any sense tended to carry two or three with them, because they had an uncanny ability to get lost even when strung on a cord around the neck of their user. These days, although they have the uses, magnifying glasses or hand lenses have been to some extent replaced by smartphone cameras and digital cameras as a means of examining something in close-up. You can also try reversing your binoculars and peering through the objective lens with the eyepiece moved as close to the subject as is necessary.

Photography

Photography has a role to play in both in celebrating the beauty of nature and in recording your findings for posterity. Given the amazing advances in digital technology, it is also a useful tool for identification either in the field, reviewing and enlarging images on the back of the camera, or in the subsequent examination when images are scrutinised on a computer screen back home.

Photography can be an invaluable aid to identification, but one that comes with a warning: be aware of its limitations. For example, shadows can take on the appearance of genuine physical features. An apparent absence of a crucial feature may simply mean it is not captured by the depth of field of the image, or you have not photographed your specimen from an angle where it

You do not necessarily need a sophisticated camera set-up to capture good quality images which provide a useful record of your local wildlife.

is visible. Pretty images and ones where the deportment of your subject enhances the composition may not necessarily be the best photographs for identification purposes.

These days there is little to choose between different camera manufacturers, other than perhaps build quality, weight and price. Unless you are operating at the professional end of the spectrum, in which case probably you will not be reading this, almost every camera make, model and system will produce adequate if not excellent results if used properly. Do not be drawn into the addictive world of camera envy where buying new equipment is subtly portrayed as the way to solve all your problems. Dig a little deeper and it is usually opportunity that is the missing ingredient for dissatisfied photographers, not underperforming equipment. Most failures are the result of, for want of a better expression, operator error rather than system failure.

Get to know the inner workings of your photographic system, find a system that works for you and stick with it is the best advice that I can give.

LENS CHOICE

Canny manufacturers of camera equipment come up with never-ending ways of parting avid photographers from their money and the constantly evolving range of lenses is a good example of this business model. From a naturalist's perspective, and with plants and invertebrates in mind, there are two types of lenses that will be most useful for capturing the beauty of nature and taking images that also aid identification. A wide-angle zoom – perhaps covering the range 17–35mm – will allow you to capture scenes and habitats, and place individual plants and animals or groups in the context of their environment. A macro lens is the invaluable lens of choice for close-up work. Ideally it should be one that at its closest focus has a magnification ratio of 1:1 – at minimum focus that means the size of the subject as it appears on the camera sensor is the same as the size of the subject in life. This sort of magnification allows me magnificent enlargement and scrutiny of details so minute that I cannot see them in the field with my aged

Bird photography is the domain of hardened enthusiasts with deep pockets, and is not appropriate for the average biodiversity gardener. You will need a lens with a focal length of at least 500mm and ideally 600mm to capture a good quality image of wary subjects like this Barn Owl. In terms of cost, for a decent model multiply the focal length by 20 and you will come close to the pound equivalent. Add to that a whole set of accessories – heavy duty tripods and the like – and you arrive at an outlay equivalent to the cost of a modest new car.

Fortunately, some garden birds become accustomed to their human companions, and species such as this Robin can occasionally be photographed with modest telephoto lenses.

eyes, even with the aid of a hand lens. A macro lens with a focal length of around 100mm is ideal because of the working distance from the subject it allows: wary species are easier to capture without having to approach too closely and cause disturbance, and the potential for you to cast a shadow on your subject is reduced.

CAMERA FUNCTIONS

Many cameras have a range of automatic shooting modes, designed to make the life of a casual user simpler. However, rather than rely on a generic approach based on somebody else's idea of what you want, I would suggest avoiding these shortcuts. Far better to understand your camera system and subject, and appreciate and control those variables that influence whether the resulting image is sharp and pleasing, or a blurred disappointment.

Most camera and lens systems have an autofocus function, which can be an invaluable advantage in the field, especially if your subject is on the move: the camera's ability to focus will be quicker than your reactions. However, the camera cannot read your mind – at least not yet – and it will only focus as programmed. Therefore, if you set it up to use a range of focal points you have no guarantee that it will choose to focus on the part of the subject you want to be sharp; or indeed not necessarily on the subject itself if, for example, something more prominent and closer to the camera presents itself. An alternative is to choose a single, precise focal point for the autofocus system to use. Stating the obvious, perhaps, make sure that you orient the camera so that the focus spot aligns with exactly the part of the subject you want in focus, or move the focus point in-camera appropriately. In reality, however, nature photographers often do not have the luxury of time on their side.

When you focus on a specific part of a subject, manually or using autofocus, more than just the precise spot you have focussed on will be sharp in the resulting image. This is called the depth of field and the degree to which things other than the focal point are sharp is influenced by the aperture of the lens, itself indicated by the 'f' number in use. This is something over which you have control: the larger the f number, the greater the depth of field. For macro work you might want to use an aperture of f16 as a starting point. Or if you intentionally want to throw foreground and background out of focus, f4 might be the aperture of choice. Another thing to bear in mind is that as a rule of thumb, at any given focal point a third of the depth of field will reside in front of the focal plane, two thirds behind.

Shutter speed is an important consideration, especially when both you and your subject are moving. You can, to a degree, overcome the problem of you and your equipment moving by either using a tripod or inbuilt image stabilisation. However, bear in mind that this gyroscopic addition to your camera may compensate for any wobble on your part but it has no effect on the movement of the subject. A butterfly on a swaying flower is always going to need a shutter speed of perhaps 1/500 second or more to 'freeze' movement and minimise blur if that is your intention.

An alternative or additional approach to reduce movement in your subject is to use something to shield the wind, and a wide-mouthed net is a great improvised option – especially if deployed by a willing assistant, or even a reluctant one. The beauty of a net is that it 'diffuses' rather than diverts the power of the wind, thereby reducing annoying eddies.

LIGHTING

Generally speaking, natural light produces the most consistently pleasing photographic results when the subject is the natural world. However, images taken in daylight also have the potential to produce disappointing results until you appreciate the shortcomings of this source of light. When direct sunlight is the source of light, the most satisfying results are usually those taken when the sun is relatively low in the sky, and with the light behind you. In practice that means before the sun has climbed beyond, say, 25 degrees above the horizon and after it has sunk below it.

Most naturalists know from experience that many species of animals are only active or easy to observe in the middle of the day, and consequently often in less-than-ideal photographic light. In this regard, dull, overcast days can be better than glaring sun. However, there will be plenty of occasions where you want to photograph in harsh light when the main consequences are harsh shadows and extreme contrast. There are a couple of ways these issues can be addressed. A low-tech method is to use a reflective surface to soften the shadows – foil-covered boards on which shop-bought cakes are sold are ideal. A more sophisticated and infinitely more expensive approach is to use flash, and specially designed macro flash systems are in the armoury of many serious close-up photographers.

If well-used, flash is a great addition to the palette of any natural history photographer. But it needs to be used with a degree of sympathy to avoid unnatural and garish results. The use of flash has been likened to the use of make-up: for a natural look, you know you have applied too much when it is obvious make-up is being used. As a further word of warning, with some cameras the flash will only synchronise, and therefore have the intended effect, up to prescribed shutter speeds. If, for example, that speed was 1/250 of a second that might be too slow to freeze movement of your subject if that was your intention, and the result is likely to be double imaging.

From the outset it can be a useful exercise to decide on your photographic aims and aspirations. For example, you might want to capture images as a way of celebrating the beauty of nature, or alternatively your intention might be to use them solely for identification. That is not to say you cannot achieve both, but it is sometimes helpful to separate the two. This leads on to the subject of processing because it is always worth bearing in mind that the files you download from your camera to your computer are just the starting point. The art of processing is beyond the scope of this book, but suffice to say the end result produced for the purpose of printing in a book will be different from that required for

I sited a trail camera beside the stream at the bottom of my garden in early summer and left it there for a few weeks as the watercourse began to dry up. These are a selection of the birds and mammals that passed through its fixed-point field of view.

use on the web or social media. Before you undertake any processing, the key message is to save your original photographs as an untouched archive. And remember to back them up.

TRAIL CAMERAS

When I began taking photographs back in the 1980s, I would never have dreamt that technology would advance in the way it has. Among the more remarkable achievements is the development of 'trail cameras'. These self-contained, all-weather digital cameras can be left outside for weeks on end and, triggered by movement, will capture anything that moves within sensor range, day or night. The names assigned to some models often hint at an association with hunting and covert operations. Despite these sinister undertones, from a wildlife perspective they are ideal tools for getting to know what is going on behind your back.

Foes become friends

Nowadays, I feel sorry for anyone who sees Moles, earthworms or ants as enemies in the garden. For those in whom this mindset lingers, I would say some further education is needed before embarking on a biodiversity gardening project, and I hope that by reading the book to this point many will have begun to see former gardening foes as biodiversity friends. It is fitting, therefore, to adapt some conventional gardening techniques as applied to perceived 'pests' and turn them in to sampling techniques. The difference being, the aim is not to kill your 'enemies' but to befriend and make peace with them, then study them and let them go, having recorded their presence and marvelled at the complexity of the natural world.

If ever there was a group with a pariah status among unenlightened gardeners, it is slugs and snails. All manner of techniques are deployed to 'control' them, with the language and imagery of battle used to promote the revolting chemical warfare waged against them. From the perspective of biodiversity gardening, these methods are a ghastly irrelevance, but some methods at the more benign end of the armoury spectrum can be turned to positive use. Take, for example, so-called 'beer traps', which are trays or jars of stale beer or other sweet and sickly concoctions, into which slugs and snails and all manner of other creatures crawl and drown. If the liquid is replaced with a beer- or diluted honey-soaked tissue or cloth then you can turn a death trap into a ready-made sampling vessel, from which molluscs and other invertebrates can escape if they need to. Since slugs and snails, and many other invertebrate groups, are mostly active after dark, scrutiny at night with a bright torch is a productive way to observe the comings and goings.

There are other conventional gardening techniques used to 'control' slugs, snails and other invertebrates, ones that are sometimes portrayed as environmentally friendly. One suggestion that I have come across is to site old roof tiles in shady nooks and crannies and lift them in the dead of winter and height of summer to discover lurking snails, respectively hibernating or aestivating. Advice about what to do with the said snails ranges from removing them and stamping on them to 'relocating' them outside of the garden. I guess that is better in some ways than chemical poisoning and the collateral harm that causes. However, I use the technique to discover what is present in my garden and celebrate it, not destroy or remove it.

A tried and tested technique among naturalists and sampling ecologists of my generation is the use of so-called pitfall traps. These are exactly what the name suggests: a jar or some other container with vertical, insurmountable sides, sunk into the ground to the rim and into which passing creatures fall. Ground-level wanderers such as beetles are particularly inclined to drop in. The trouble is that so do other creatures such as shrews, which quickly die of starvation, as do the invertebrates themselves if left for days on end. Or they drown if a rain guard has been omitted from the design. The conclusion: this is an effective technique but not one to be used unless you are willing and able to check the trap on an almost hourly basis.

An upside-down approach to pitfall traps is to site upturned flowerpots here and there in the garden, stuffed with straw and baited with, for example, a banana skin or apple core to entice invertebrates. The plan is that you tip the contents into a tray periodically and examine the catch. Some conventional gardeners

Six-belted Clearwing males attracted to a pheromone lure – an impregnated rubber bung.

use it as a way to catch, then kill, snails in particular. I use the baited pot method for study and recording. If you have a taste for the macabre you can try baiting the pot with carrion, if you discover a dead mouse for example. There is every chance you will attract one or more species of burying beetle, and more about them can be found on p. 189.

Pheromones are chemicals emitted by an animal that alter the behaviour of another member of the same species. In the context of my garden, their significance is exemplified in their use by female moths to attract males. This is clearly not something easy to witness among nocturnal species, but day-flying clearwings are a different matter. Advances in chemistry in recent decades have reached the point where artificial

pheromones are manufactured and sold to attract and kill perceived pests. Moth enthusiasts can purchase artificial pheromones to observe clearwings and certain other day-flying species, but this does not alter the fact that these chemicals exist because they were engineered to kill (see p. 167 for more information).

As a failed conventional gardener, that is the limit of my experience and advice because I never really wanted to kill 'pests' even back in the bad old days, hence I never sought out additional methods of biodiversity mass destruction. Others with more grounded experience in gardening will no doubt come up with all manner of other adaptations to tried and tested 'control' techniques that can be modified and used in study rather than destruction.

Botanical survey and study

In the context of biodiversity gardening, some find it interesting to add a scientific dimension to their studies. The use of a standardised technique allows comparisons to be made between one site and another, different locations within the same site, and to monitor changes over the years. Ecologists and botanists use a range of techniques and one of the simplest survey methods employs quadrats. A frame, typically a metre square, is placed randomly in a meadow, for example, and the numbers of each species growing within the frame are counted. Undertake the operation a dozen or so times and the counts will give you an average outcome that can be compared with sites elsewhere, or in the same location with previous and future years. Of course, that does rely on the surveyor's ability to be able to identify with certainty the species being recorded.

Quadrat surveys appeal to the analytical end of the naturalist spectrum but may not be appropriate to all, and if your plot of meadow is small then this systematic approach may not be warranted. The purely analytical side of my nature died a long time ago. So, like me, you may choose simply to marvel at your meadow's plant community and monitor changes on almost an individual plant basis.

Fieldcraft

Fieldcraft is a concept that is familiar to anyone who is keen on mammals and birds, where their favoured subjects have keen senses, designed in the main to make sure they are fully aware of the environment around them, specifically threats. The subject has its origins in hunting, shooting and fishing but the same principles apply to wildlife-watching, the difference being the watcher wants to observe not kill the subject under observation.

For a lucky few, fieldcraft is just common sense by another name. However, for others it represents a range of techniques that need to be learned. Mammals have a keen sense of smell and the direction of wind needs to be considered so that close approach is attempted from a downwind direction. Sudden movements will give away your presence if your subject has good eyesight, so stealth and an ability to remain motionless are key. Active concealment so you blend in with the background is another thing to consider; camouflaged clothing or netting and canvas hides are part of the armoury of many dedicated wildlife watchers. Fieldcraft is not an art that is useful exclusively in the domain of birds and mammals. The concept is also valuable when studying other animal groups that possess acute senses. For example, dragonflies and many butterfly species have superb eyesight and are extremely wary of any blundering attempt to creep up on them.

Patience is a said to be a virtue in the way we live our lives and so it is when it comes to observing nature. One of the most satisfying and rewarding techniques, if you can call it that, is just to sit still. Position yourself in a spot where you anticipate something interesting might happen and let nature come to you. As an example, having identified a nectar-rich flower that is popular with insects, get up close and personal, remain motionless and enjoy the results. Sudden movements are your enemy.

Keeping and submitting records

Contributing information to national wildlife databases and organisations is worthwhile in the sense that it adds to the bigger biodiversity picture: it allows trends in distribution and numbers to be discerned, assessed and quantified in a manner that the powers that be are theoretically obliged to take seriously. Personally, I wish I still lived in an era where I could mind my own business and just be a naturalist. But those days are gone, and anyone who cares about the environment now has a moral responsibility to contribute in whatever way they can to the fight to save British wildlife; data collection and submission are tools in this process, and this action is sometimes referred to as citizen science.

Government announcements in autumn 2022 mean it is worth bearing in mind the potential for future watering down or scrapping of existing legislation. With that caveat in place, the following represents my understanding and experience of some of the legislative frameworks at the time of writing.

In theory, gathered and collated information can be used to inform conservation management and, potentially, government environmental policy as well. In practice, a cynic might say all that data collection does is provide wonderfully granular detail charting the decline in British wildlife. I hope that is overly pessimistic. I agree it is debatable as to what extent government actually acts on presented statistics and data and listens to advice that is offered. But the process still needs to be undertaken, because in the absence of evidence there is absolutely no reason why anyone should consider the environment at all, and no direction for leaders to follow if they did. All concerned need to be in possession of indisputable facts. Only then can they be called to account if subsequent decisions harm wildlife and the environment.

At the individual level, it is unlikely that any one biodiversity gardener will be able to influence government thinking and policy. However, at the local level the importance of record-keeping and observation assumes greater significance and has the potential to result in tangible benefits. Reasons for ensuring your local records are kept and submitted to locally appropriate databases will become clear in the next chapter.

On a personal note, the records I have kept over the years from my garden and the ancient, tree-lined byway with which it is contiguous have contributed to the decision by Hampshire Biodiversity Information Centre to designate the byway a Site of Importance for Nature Conservation. Once implemented, this will provide the site, and its immediate surroundings, with a degree of protection from future change of land use and abuse.

RECORDING SCHEMES AND DATABASES

A wide range of organisations collect data on the natural world at the local, county, regional and national level. In theory individual and local information should filter up through the system to become part of the national database, thereafter becoming accessible and available to interested parties throughout the region. In practice, to an outsider the process can appear subject to the same frailties that affect all aspects of human endeavour: rival factions that sometimes compete rather than cooperate; envy and harboured grudges; and a peppering of system failures and human error to spice up the mix. At times it must seem like herding cats to anyone tasked with coordinating the system.

RECORD-KEEPING – AN OVERVIEW

All records make a contribution to conservation, and there are number of ways that their addition to the system can be achieved, ensuring that they are accurate and verified. Routes to submission include county recorders and recording schemes; specialist societies; and organisations that operate at the national level. For many naturalists, all they want to do is submit a record to ensure somebody else knows about it. Sometimes the route by which this can be achieved can seem daunting and perplexing in equal measure. However, do not be put off, because whichever valid route you choose, with persistence and by understanding the system, you will succeed. Individual records are always welcome, but it is worth bearing in mind that contributing to systematic national recording schemes (like the National Plant Monitoring Scheme or Breeding Bird Survey) provides most benefit to wildlife conservation.

As an aside, an overview of UK record-keeping might help make sense of the system. The Biological Records Centre (run by the UK Centre for Ecology and Hydrology) is the overall database hub for almost all biological records; it is funded in part by government, and in part by charity. The exception is birds, for which the British Trust for Ornithology is the responsible organisation.

While browsing the internet you may have come across a website called iRecord. This is a forum for sharing wildlife sightings and photographs, but it also has a more serious side: it is a portal via which individual records as well as systematic studies can be submitted for inclusion in the national database. Talking of which, the National Biodiversity Network is a repository of this information. It is also another route via which records can be submitted. It shares as well as stores its data, and its mapping schemes and atlas are particularly useful for naturalists interested in a deskbound exploration of their local natural history.

Local Environmental Records Centres (LERCs) provide another tier of biological information, and ones relevant to where you live can be found by searching online. In my area, and under the Hampshire County Council umbrella, the Hampshire Biodiversity Information Centre (HBIC) is a database of biological records for the county. It is not a comprehensive account of the status of every species in the county across all locations and is only as good as the records it receives. Typically, the records are only added to the database if they come from a verified observer, or are submitted via the route of an 'approved' county recorder for the particular wildlife group in question. In theory that means that all its records are accurate and verified.

LERCs provide information to national databases, but as a cautionary note, not all interested parties supply them with information. Some bypass that particular system and submit records directly to national databases; if verified these eventually find their way onto the National Biodiversity Network, and then become accessible to the public. Records submitted directly to national databases do not necessarily filter back to LERC databases, reinforcing the point that, when using these as sources of reference, absence of evidence is not evidence of absence.

Special mention should go to the recording and reporting of species with nominal statutory protection, for example those with schedule 1 designation under the Wildlife and Countryside Act 1981 (with amendments). When it comes to bolstering the legal protection afforded to a given area of countryside, or challenging a planning application, they are your allies: iconic species whose presence, in theory, should provide a protective umbrella for other wildlife. However, being able to use the status of these species to fight for conservation requires their presence to have been reported and accepted into the recording 'system' in the first place. Therein lies more of a challenge than you might think.

As examples of schedule 1 protected species relevant to north Hampshire, and the pitfalls associated with studying, recording and reporting them, let's take Great Crested Newt, Hazel Dormouse and bats of all species. To study and survey these species, a licence is required and, at the time of writing, the body overseeing them where I live is Natural England's licensing department. Obtaining a licence requires time – years in some cases – and in some instances considerable financial outlay for training.

Having attempted to go through the process of obtaining a licence, it can seem like an individual's attempts to help conservation are being intentionally thwarted by the powers that be. Unsurprisingly, this sector is now largely the domain of professional ecologists for whom licensing is an investment and these pieces of paper become licences to print money. For you, as a wildlife-concerned individual, the lack of

● BIRDTRACK

Among those whose passion in life is wildlife, there is a disproportionate interest in birds, and it is not surprising that this focus of attention has resulted in advances in the field of avian data collection. Thanks to modern technology you can now record and store your bird records online via a tool called BirdTrack. This allows you to submit records for the greater good, access your own records back through time, keep up to date with what others are seeing, and monitor, for example, current migration patterns and trends. BirdTrack was created through a partnership between the British Trust for Ornithology (BTO), the RSPB, BirdWatch Ireland, the Scottish Ornithologists' Club and the Welsh Ornithological Society. Through collaboration with appropriate sister organisations, BirdTrack also allows you to record sightings of mammals, amphibians, reptiles, butterflies, dragonflies and orchids.

a licence is potentially more than just an annoyance. It will mean that you are unable to undertake legitimate surveys and studies of protected species. Of equal significance, you will find it hard to submit records that become accepted and included in databases used by developers and decision-making planning authorities.

If you have the time and money, you could of course go down the ecologists' route of getting licences for Great Crested Newts, Hazel Dormice and bats. However, there are easier ways to proceed if the goal is to ensure observations and sightings translate into validated environmental records. In the case of Great Crested Newts, an option is to persuade a friendly licensed individual as to your ethical credentials and ability to identify amphibians, and you can become an Accredited Agent; via your 'supervisor' your records will be accepted. With Hazel Dormice, contact the People's Trust for Endangered Species (see References section) or the mammal group in your county wildlife trust. With the landowner's permission, you may be able to initiate a study project using dormouse boxes (see p. 251). In the case of bats, new technology (such as the device discussed on p. 272) allows anyone to record and submit audio (.wav) files to the county recorder. You need no greater expertise than an ability to use a smartphone app and a bit of computer software for your records to rank alongside those submitted by bat licence holders.

As far as wildlife is concerned, you name it and there is almost certain to be a specialist society, charity or organisation that focusses its attention on the group of plants or animals in question. In some instances, their remit will include admirable ways of encouraging and enabling the recording and verification of species. Many have impressive online resources, and the most useful are listed in the References section.

Freshwater pollution

Pollution caused by the application to the land of agricultural fertilisers is recognised as a problem at the global level and is the subject of a sobering document entitled *Soil Pollution* produced by the World Health Organisation (see the References section for details). Agricultural fertiliser pollution has many sources: synthetic agrochemicals are significant, as are those that are organic in origin, such as treated human sewage and animal waste that is produced on an industrial scale, for example from the intensive farming of chickens and cattle. In the WHO's document, the impact on the land itself is considered along with pollution of freshwater (and ultimately coastal marine environments) that results from run-off from the land.

Agricultural fertilisers are intended to promote plant growth, and so it is unsurprising that when they find their way into freshwater through run-off from the land they have the same effect. However, their unnaturally elevated levels favour some species more than others and this invariably leads to the process known as eutrophication, which was discussed earlier.

Near where I live, local waterways are no strangers to insidious pollution caused by the enrichment of water by agricultural run-off. To a practised nose it is evident in the very smell of the water, and those with a botanical eye will notice the effects too: an absence of plants that should adorn the banks and grace the aquatic environment of a healthy stream or ditch, with the proliferation of species that benefit from elevated levels of nutrients such as phosphorus and nitrogen; Hemlock Water-dropwort is a case in point where I live. Nutrient enrichment of ditches and waterways is likely to have come from run-off of synthetic fertilisers applied to the land; once in a while, animal slurry and 'treated' human sewage waste are also spread on fields. Sometimes the pollution is obvious, and on several occasions the stream at the bottom of my garden has become coated with frothy scum of unknown origin or chemical nature; despite contacting the Environment Agency's pollution hotline, I am not aware of any action having been taken.

MONITORING FRESHWATER POLLUTION

The Freshwater Habitats Trust has a website that provides a wealth of information about what constitutes good quality water and advice and links on how to monitor pollution. Their *Clean Water for Wildlife Technical Manual* is worth a read (see References for more information).

Death and destruction on Silchester Brook caused by the release of raw sewage into the waterway by Thames Water. Fish were not the only creatures to die, of course, and the stream's invertebrates were also wiped out.

Occasionally, pollution can be dramatic and catastrophic. A mile or so north of where I live, a watercourse known as Silchester Brook runs through Pamber Forest. In the summer of 2010, during a period of heavy rain it was subject to an illegal discharge from a Thames Water sewage works. The sewage killed life downstream for a length of several kilometres. The lingering smell that accompanied the sight of the dead fish was a reminder of this awful pollution. Silchester Brook is part of the network of waterways that run through Pamber Forest and eventually into the River Loddon. This network includes ones known to host one of the UK's rarest insects

the Scarce Brown Sedge, the caddisfly mentioned on p. 27. Winchester Crown Court fined Thames Water more than £60,000 for the reported incident, a sizeable amount but little more than a slap on the wrist in the context of the company's turnover.

While environmental vandalism should always be condemned, it is worth reminding ourselves of the role that we, as humans and members of society, have to play. We hardly need to be reminded of the origins of sewage, and in our own small way, and as members of a population that has grown by something like 50 percent in the last century, we all contribute to a problem that others have to resolve.

If you are interested in discovering the levels of waterway pollutants and contaminants in your general area, the Environment Agency has a network of monitoring sites across the country. Budget cuts mean that the level of monitoring is less thorough than it once was, but it is still of interest in providing, for example, an indication of whether a given waterway has got cleaner or more polluted over time. The website can be found at environment.data.gov.uk/water-quality/view/explore

The Freshwater Habitats Trust's website has links to a number of relatively cheap home-use devices and kits that can be used for sampling and monitoring. See their *Clean Water for Wildlife Technical Manual* for advice on monitoring pollution.

To satisfy your curiosity you can also have water samples analysed by professional laboratories that specialise in this service. To demonstrate that the process is possible for the layperson, I had a go myself and used South East Water Scientific Services to analyse water samples from water sources in my garden and surroundings for two pollutants that are often associated with agricultural run-off and human intervention: nitrates and phosphates. The sample sites were my well (as groundwater), my pond (which is entirely fed by rainwater), the stream that borders my garden, Silchester Brook (close to an Environment Agency sampling point, downstream of the sewage treatment works that caused the pollution incident mentioned above), and rainwater as what I naïvely thought would be a 'control' akin to distilled water.

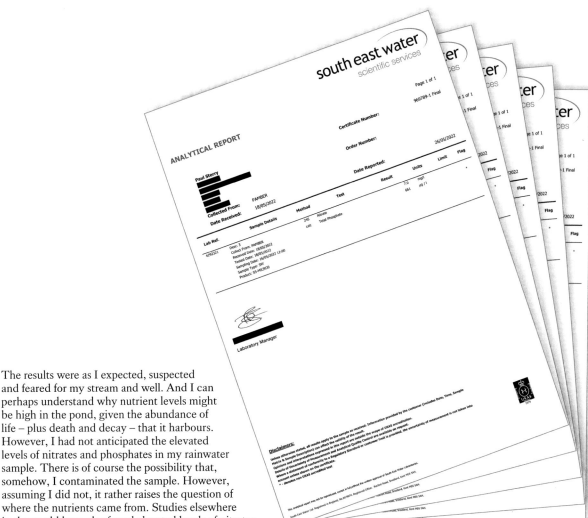

The results were as I expected, suspected and feared for my stream and well. And I can perhaps understand why nutrient levels might be high in the pond, given the abundance of life – plus death and decay – that it harbours. However, I had not anticipated the elevated levels of nitrates and phosphates in my rainwater sample. There is of course the possibility that, somehow, I contaminated the sample. However, assuming I did not, it rather raises the question of where the nutrients came from. Studies elsewhere in the world have also found elevated levels of nitrates in rainwater along with pesticides. According to the Freshwater Habitat Trust's *Clean Water for Wildlife Technical Manual*, reference levels of nitrate and phosphate are as follows: clean water: <0.5mg/l nitrate, <0.05mg/l phosphate; some evidence of pollution: 0.5–1mg/l nitrate, 0.05–0.1mg/l phosphate; high or very high levels of nutrient pollution: >1 mg/l nitrate, >0.1mg/l phosphate.

Sample date	SEW certificate reference	Water type	Total Nitrate mg/l	Phosphate ug/l	Phosphate mg/l
18-Jun-22	969787-1 Final	rainwater/control	46.8	236	0.236
20-Jun-22	969789-1 Final	pond	7.0	661	0.661
21-Jun-22	969790-1 Final	well/groundwater	5.5	226	0.226
22-Jun-22	969806-1 Final	stream	31.6	308	0.308
19-Jun-22	969788-1 Final	Silchester Brook	13.3	1191	1.191

A Call to Action

After agricultural land use, the most significant factors driving the loss of wildlife-rich habitats and biodiversity in the part of north Hampshire where I live are urbanisation and industrialisation of the land. Issues range from change of land use in the countryside – often a step in the direction of urbanisation – to the development of land for housing. The loss to wildlife through these routes is irreversible. If you care about the environment and have adopted a wildlife-friendly approach to managing your garden or land then sooner or later the aspirations of others will impact upon you. You will then be faced with two options: either stick your head in the sand and pretend it is not happening or scrutinise developments and try to influence things for the betterment of wildlife.

Experience has taught me not to become too dependent on others for support or assistance when it comes to the fight for wildlife. Sooner or later, allies will gradually lose interest, worn down by attrition or distracted by other aspects of their lives; or they might not have been allies in the first place. And, with a few exceptions, you are unlikely to get meaningful help from statutory bodies or conservation charities. Of course, it is still a good idea to talk to as many people as possible in an attempt to engage them: as you lose former allies others may replace them.

Relying on your own resources might seem daunting at first but it will become less intimidating with time. To fight your own battles, a basic understanding of the planning process and the legal structures that nominally protect the natural world is invaluable. Why is planning important? Because it provides a legal framework whereby wildlife and biodiversity can either be destroyed or partly protected.

Troubling developments

In autumn 2022, the UK government signaled its intention to dismantle key elements of environmental law, 'sweeping away red tape' and 'streamlining the planning process' in the name of growth, growth and yet more growth. Although currently it is impossible to know where events will lead, the conservation sector is right to be alarmed. Changes to the Wildlife and Countryside Act, for example, could conceivably mean that only plants and animals under imminent threat of extinction globally would be afforded protection in the UK; that would remove safeguards for most currently-protected plants and animals. Presumably, all other species – i.e. most British wildlife – would then need to be nominated for protection by assessment. But assessment by whom and based on what information? It is hard to imagine, for example, that the construction industry would not lobby for the removal of environmental red tape in the name of increased profit, sorry 'economic growth'.

Perhaps that is overthinking things and the announcements were just rhetorical bluster. However, if nothing else, when seen against a policy backdrop of economic growth at any cost, they hint at the ambitions of some in power and those who whisper in their ears; and a vision of their brave new world. In the absence of a crystal ball, who knows what environmental planning law will look like in the future, assuming it exists at all. As a result, this chapter deals with the situation as I have experienced it and attempted to deal with it. Future environmental campaigners may have to modify their approach if the legal frameworks really do change for the worse.

Is resistance futile?

The initial arbiters of development in your area, and its environmental impact, will be your Local Planning Authority (LPA). Regardless of their environmental aspirations, they operate within the guidelines of a National Planning Policy Framework; in addition, they will have created their own Local Plan to provide a development and sustainability framework to guide the way they operate. In theory, they should factor in environmental law and their own guidance when it comes to planning decisions. In practice, however, the small print often allows for subjective interpretation, with the result that something a concerned naturalist might regard as unlawful, egregious or immoral is permitted. Of the hundreds of employees on the payroll in your LPA, the number of people with natural history as their passion in life is likely to be tiny. An inclination to unwaveringly stick to bureaucratic rules will be an advantage when it comes to climbing the promotional ladder.

As a result, through a combination of legislation and predisposition, and despite apparent safeguards, experience tells me that there is an inherent presumption, hard-wired into the system, in favour of development. Increasingly in recent times, the law as it applies to the natural world has been watered down thanks to tweaks to the system, and an increasingly pro-development economic recovery narrative. Depressing that may be, but I suppose it's hardly surprising, given human nature and that, put simply, people can vote, wildlife cannot.

Land development is the default way of achieving economic growth for many in the population, and on the whole councils love it for the illusion of prosperity it brings. This inherent bias notwithstanding, by understanding the basic principles underpinning the planning process you may gain insights into the ways in which the system is exploited and manipulated by wily developers and their agents, and tactics you can use to fight back on behalf of wildlife. Once in a while you might be able to stop development or at least temporarily halt it. More often, and equally significantly, by challenging and using the system, you stand a fighting chance of influencing the way in which development takes place; and thereby achieving the least awful outcome for wildlife.

Do not expect arguments based on common sense, ethical or moral environmental factors, or stated environmental *aspirations* on the part of any given council, to be taken seriously. Sadly, those will cut no ice and you are better off using a council's own policies and guidelines, and statutory law, to remind them of their obligations and environmental best practice.

Do not expect your actions to necessarily make you popular with nearby residents, and certainly not with prospective developers. With so much money at stake, I have come across instances of attempts at intimidation, more direct physical threats and even a dirty tricks smear campaign involving unfounded allegations of sexual misconduct. The shenanigans would not look out of place in a Tom Sharpe novel and would be hilarious were they not so serious. Things have not progressed to an episode of *Midsomer Murders*, but who knows what the future might bring?

Lastly, do not expect organisations that a newcomer to the game might reasonably assume to be on the side of the environmental angels to necessarily be in your corner; nor council employees tasked with environmental responsibility come to that. At times, their actions may come across as obstructive to put it kindly. Consequently, you will need to acquire a degree of resilience because the process can be soul-destroying; as life experiences go, it probably ranks alongside booking your own prepaid funeral. However, give up and the battle is lost before it started.

Escape to what was the country

In terms of biodiversity loss in my part of the world, it is not house extensions or loft conversions that are the issue. It is the drive to build new houses – those 'much-needed' five-bedroom, three-car-garage mansions-in-miniature – that increasingly litter what was formerly open countryside. Generally speaking, these are not properties intended to meet a local need, and they are certainly not affordable to ordinary local families.

Before and after. There is an irony to the way roads on new housing estates are often named – after the very habitat or species they have destroyed. Loss of open countryside to development is not unique to contemporary Basingstoke of course, nor is nostalgic dismay regarding environmental degradation. In the 1939 novel by George Orwell (born Eric Arthur Blair, 1903–1950) *Coming Up for Air*, protagonist George Bowling revisits his boyhood home only to discover progress has taken its toll: a favourite fishing pond is filled with rubbish and houses have replaced the country estate in which it sat. Orwell grew up in Shiplake, 15 miles from where I live.

Instead, they appeal to those enriched by relocation from more affluent areas in the London orbit, in the case of north Hampshire; those perhaps who want to escape to the country while failing to appreciate that by buying open countryside new-build houses they are destroying the very thing they sought.

Given that land in the UK as elsewhere on the planet is a finite commodity, continual bit-by-bit new build in open countryside is environmental death by a thousand cuts. It is only a matter of time before the land runs out. What then, you might ask? Of course, that will not be a problem that my generation has to deal with. Like them, I will be long gone. Either interred as a woodland burial resident or cremated so that my ashes can be thrown in the faces of environmental detractors and climate-change-deniers; that would almost justify the added carbon consumption associated with cremation.

In the past and in my part of the world, open countryside was seen as sacrosanct, but no longer. In part, what is driving the building frenzy – specifically the urge to submit speculative planning applications – is that there is more money to be made from building houses than there is from farming. A local landowner – one who still actually farms much of his land – explained the economics to me in broad terms: he might make perhaps £50 per acre per annum profit on land that is farmed; this jumps to £800 per acre per annum income if the land is given over to a solar park; and depending on the terms and the size of the development, anything from hundreds of thousands of pounds to millions if planning permission for housing is obtained. Fuelling the process are government-set targets imposed on local councils for house-building.

Perhaps things will change for the better if reported alterations to the proposed Levelling Up and Regeneration

Bill become law: Bob Seely, MP for the Isle of Wight, and others appear to have succeeded in their campaign to make housing targets advisory, not mandatory; and for brownfield sites to be prioritised oven greenfield land. Until those changes become law, however, in Basingstoke that means dozens of new houses here, hundreds there –

each year, every year. The blight of new housing is not evenly distributed throughout the borough, of course, and in Orwellian fashion, all parishes and boroughs may be equal but some are more equal than others. Hence there are areas that are sacrificial in terms of housing and development while others still remain sacrosanct.

Plan of action

My experience is limited to my local planning authority, Basingstoke and Deane Borough Council (BDBC), and this may not necessarily translate in all regards to other areas. As a further caveat, planning law is not set in stone (or should that be bricks and mortar) and evolves, but seldom in a way that benefits wildlife in a meaningful way. As a result, the following overview represents just a snapshot of my limited understanding of the situation in 2022. To further complicate matters, at the time of writing, Basingstoke's planning system is temporarily out of kilter because of the council's failure to meet its 5-year Housing Land Supply targets. From where I sit, present-day house-building seems more like a free-for-all than a sustainable, planned process. I can only hope that the former planning status quo will be restored soon, or that proposed changes to the Levelling Up and Regeneration Bill, making housing targets advisory rather than mandatory, actually become law.

I am not an expert in planning law and my reluctant involvement has come about through bitter desperation. The process has been made more distasteful because of inevitable exposure to the seamy, self-interested side of human nature and the bureaucratic nightmare that outsiders face when dealing with local government. Depending on where you live, planning decisions will be made by a council planning officer who may or may not be in possession of the full facts, and may be open-minded when it comes to wildlife legislation or dismiss its significance. It's a matter of luck as to where on the spectrum any given individual sits. If there is a case to be made for factoring wildlife into any decision, you can usually make a difference by ensuring that the authorities are in possession of all the facts, and that they are reminded of the legislation and their legal obligations.

Information about environmental planning law can be found online and a few conservation organisations offer basic practical advice; an example can be found

on the Berkshire, Buckinghamshire and Oxfordshire Wildlife Trust (BBOWT) website (see the References section for details). However, on the basis that personal experience can also provide insights, here's a bullet-point summary of the planning process as I have experienced it:

- The planning process begins when an application is submitted either by the landowner or by an agent acting on their behalf.

- Most initial applications will have either the suffix FUL or OUT after the planning reference number. As it suggests, FUL means an application for full planning permission and will be detailed. OUT denotes an outline planning application, testing the water to see whether or not a proposal is likely to be approved by the planning authority. It requires fewer details about the proposal to be submitted. From a cynical perspective, it can be seen as a way for a developer to flush out the opposition and address concerns raised when the time comes for a FUL application. Therefore, if you suspect a given application will progress from outline to full, it may be tactically wise to keep some of your arguments in reserve. There is an additional form of planning application that has the suffix PIP (planning in principle). That relatively recent addition to the developers' palette will be discussed separately.

- Part of the process for a FUL application involves the submission of a form that includes in essence honesty tick boxes about the presence or absence of protected or notable species and habitats on the site and in the vicinity.

- The applicant may or may not submit some form of ecological survey voluntarily at this stage or may be required to do so by the planning department.

- Comments and objections can be submitted up to

the point where a prescribed deadline has passed; in reality the actual deadline is the point when a decision on an application is about to be made.

- A member of the planning department – a case officer – will have been assigned to the planning application that interests you, and under the supervision of somebody higher up the pecking order they will make a decision to approve or refuse the application. Case officers often tend to be junior and attempts to communicate with them can be frustrating, with non-committal responses at best. To get a more informed feel for council thinking it can be a useful exercise to talk to or meet more senior and experienced planning officers.

- If the planning application is approved, and there have been more than six objections, the application is passed to the council's Development Control Committee (DCC) for consideration. The DCC is likely to comprise a dozen or so elected borough councillors.

- If the planning application is refused then the application can be referred to the DCC by a local councillor. You may ask why any councillor would do that, but I imagine you can probably guess the reason.

- The DCC meets periodically to consider a number of applications at any given sitting. Members of the committee will have read the basic paperwork associated with the application that interests you, but there is no guarantee that they will have extended their due diligence to include having read your own submission. It does not hurt to send every member a summary of your reasons for objection individually in advance of the DCC meeting; their email addresses will be available online via the council's planning portal. You might also want to check on the voting record of councillors on the DCC panel; you can bet the 'opposition' will be doing that.

- Applicants and objectors can speak at the DCC meeting and make their case. The time available is short – typically 2–4 minutes depending on the number of speakers – so you need to be concise. DCC meetings are usually recorded and live-streamed and the experience is intimidating if you are not used to public speaking. And, of course, the 'opposition' is likely to be present, staring you in the face. It is, however, worth the effort, and in my limited experience unless the DCC has, behind the scenes, already reached a consensus, a plea from you

stands a chance of making a difference. However, when you speak, you must avoid introducing into the mix anything personal or irrelevant in planning terms. Heartfelt and evidence-based presentations are good, but vitriol will undermine your case.

- If the planning application is refused by the DCC then the applicant has the right to take the application to Appeal. That costs the applicant virtually nothing but the council's defence of their original decision costs the taxpayer dearly. If the appeal overturns an original planning decision to refuse an application, then, short of funding a Judicial Review yourself (which is hugely costly), sadly that is the end of the story.

If an appeal upholds the original planning decision to refuse then what often happens is that resilient developers, and applicants in it for the long haul, start the above process again by simply submitting a subtly revised version of the original application. Sooner or later, there's a good chance this approach will bear fruit, and there are firms of consultants whose business model it is to help clients overcome unfavourable (to the client) planning decisions. An architect friend of mine told me of one development consultant he met who boasted that if a client was willing to wait five years, he could guarantee to get any application they wanted approved. Throw enough money at a planning application, try, try, try again and eventually you will win is the mantra.

PERMISSION IN PRINCIPLE

From an environmental and biodiversity perspective, one of the worst changes to the planning process occurred with the introduction of a type of application called Permission in Principle (PIP) development. Designed to streamline the process of obtaining planning permission for housing developers, it separates the process into two stages: firstly, a PIP application is assessed as to whether, in principle, the land in question is suitable for residential development; once that has been established, the second stage relates to Technical Details Consent (TDC) and deals with the practical side of development. Once the principle of development has been established, some form of housing will be built, and it then becomes a case of arguing for the least awful outcome for wildlife.

In theory, biodiversity and the environment considerations should carry the same importance as they do in the conventional planning world, not that this amounts to a huge deal. However, in practice and in my experience, ecological factors carry even less weight and council planning departments struggle to find reasons to refuse the PIP stage of the process. There appears to be a presumption that all environmental damage, large or small, can be mitigated or compensated for. Even if an Environmental Impact Assessment were to demonstrate, at the TDC stage, that an application would be too damaging to proceed, as I understand things, any previously-approved PIP remains in place.

MODIFYING PLANNING LAW TO BENEFIT WILDLIFE

Some of the harm to wildlife caused by development in open countryside may be addressed by changes to the proposed Levelling Up and Regeneration Bill, although who knows what the law will actually say when passed, and what loopholes it will contain. However, it will not resolve all problems. If there is anyone reading this who cares about the environment and has the ability to influence the planning process at the statutory, government level, here is a plea on behalf of beleaguered wildlife, and indeed the threatened countryside.

- Scrap PIP legislation.
- Require VAT to be applicable to new-build developments.
- Prevent developers from having multiple bites of the cherry and, if first refused, deny them the ability to submit endless variations-on-a-theme planning applications for essentially the same project. It is not a reasonable way to operate the lawful planning process, it wastes countless hours of council time and taxpayers' money, and it is unfair to members of the public who, exhausted and demoralised by this war of attrition, one by one give up the fight.

- Legislate so that granted planning permissions are measured against a council's housing targets. Reduce the length of time for which permissions are valid to one year or require developers to pay rates on unbuilt houses until they are constructed and sold. Currently, they only count against housing targets when a spade goes in the ground. Consequently, there is a tendency for developers to stockpile land with granted planning permission and only develop when the financial climate suits them. With targets to meet, this helps skew the council planning system in favour of approving more and more applications in the hope of meeting government-set housing targets.

- Legislate so that, regardless of an Inspector's decision, the cost to applicants of appealing against planning refusals is not borne by councils (and hence taxpayers) unless gross negligence can be demonstrated; and that council costs associated with defending decisions at appeal are automatically paid for by the applicants if they lose.

- Require councillors tasked with making planning decisions to take a proficiency test regarding environmental matters and legislation that have a planning dimension.

Challenging planning

In order to challenge the planning process on lawful environmental grounds, sources of biological and environmental information include:

- Where I live, Hampshire Biodiversity Information Centre (HBIC) is a database of biological records for the county that falls under the umbrella of Hampshire County Council (HCC). It has its limitations: it is not comprehensive, it is only as good as the records it receives, and not everyone submits records to HBIC. This reinforces the important point that absence of evidence is not evidence of absence.

Its records are updated periodically, not on a rolling basis, so that there is a time lag between information being submitted and appearing in the database.

- National Biodiversity Network (NBN) receives biological records from across the UK and presents them in database form and as maps; these can be accessed online. There is by design an overlap with HBIC in terms of the records they include. However, some important and significant records find their way onto NBN when they are missing from HBIC.

- The Department for Environment, Food and Rural

Affairs (DEFRA) provides an online service in the form of something called the DEFRA MagicMap. Despite the unpromising-sounding name it is a sophisticated tool, capable of being interrogated at a level of detail sufficient for anyone scrutinising a planning application. It works using a range of mapping overlays that display useful things such as habitat type, boundaries of Sites of Special Scientific Interest (SSSI) and Sites of Importance for Nature Conservation (SINC), SSSI buffer zones, the boundaries of DEFRA Priority Habitats and much more.

- The Environment Agency has an online service that can be used to scrutinise river courses and associated land which is graded according to Flood Risk. In planning terms, it is not just the risk of flooding relating to the land itself that is considered, but the consequences for flooding downstream of building on land which then contributes to rapid water run-off.

- None of the above sources of information are foolproof, and this serves to emphasise the importance of local knowledge, submitting records and making certain that key information actually gets incorporated into local and national databases.

Statutory protection and legislation in the context of north Hampshire is as follows:

- Site of Special Scientific Interest (SSSI) status is a statutory land designation afforded to areas that represent what, at the time of designation, were considered to be the best examples of our natural heritage, be that plant communities, animals, geological and land formations, or a combination. They do not provide an exhaustive inventory of *every* good wildlife site and there are plenty of other undesignated sites that, to use the jargon, 'meet the criteria required for SSSI designation'. Having been through the process of attempting to get additional sites designated, I would rate the chances of new SSSIs being created as slim to zero. Where I live, they are currently administered by Natural England; elsewhere they are administered in a devolved manner by NatureScot and Natural Resources Wales.

- SSSIs are fringed by Impact Risk Zones, which can be viewed on the DEFRA MagicMap site, and which in theory should influence development. In

In theory, the Hazel Dormouse is a protected species. In practice, this status seldom provides the degree of protection that concerned naturalists would wish.

practice, I am not sure what good they do, and I have encountered instances where Natural England's Sustainable Development team have raised no concerns regarding planning applications for house-building within Impact Risk Zones. Nevertheless, they are worth bearing in mind when challenging assertions made by developers.

- SINCs are sites that are considered important for nature conservation. They lack statutory protection but the wildlife they harbour contributes to the bigger ecological picture. In the case of Hampshire, they are administered on behalf of local authorities by HBIC. Again, they do not represent a comprehensive list of every good wildlife site in an area. If you find a spot that you think merits SINC status you stand a better chance of achieving designation than with SSSI; you will of course need to back up your opinion with hard facts such as botanical and breeding bird surveys and moth-trapping records. SINC status elevates the difficulty for landowners to, for example, change agricultural use or stand a chance of successfully building housing on or near a SINC site.

- A select band of species have nominal protection under the Wildlife and Countryside Act 1981 (with amendments). In the case of planning applications in north Hampshire, protected species include Hazel Dormouse, Great Crested Newt and all species of bat. A knowledge of their presence in a given area – not just the plot of land subject to development – will seldom prevent development, but it will make life more complicated for developers and may force them to factor the environment into their plans in a meaningful way. To ensure that any aspirational promises become reality requires close independent scrutiny and comment, and it is unlikely your local council will monitor the situation beyond perhaps the initial stage of compliance, and sometimes not even then. So that is another role for local, individual guardians of the countryside.

- The UK Biodiversity Action Plan (UK BAP) is a well-intentioned strategy and framework aimed at conserving and protecting existing biological diversity, and enhancing it wherever possible. Whether it achieves those goals is anyone's guess, but local authorities are aware of its existence, and it underpins the planning concept of Biodiversity Net Gain. Again, this is a seemingly worthy goal, but deeply flawed when it comes to its use in planning applications. There are a number of UK BAP priority species such as Common Toad and Water Vole whose presence in an area again raises the stakes.

- Whether this is true of all local authorities I do not know, but BDBC decisions are informed by various Support Planning Documents, including ones that relate to biodiversity. As part of planning requirements, developers are required to factor in buffer zones for perceived important wildlife habitats such as established hedgerows, tree belts, woodlands and watercourses, with the buzzword 'connectivity' also playing a part. The planning department will not necessarily know of the existence of all habitats relevant to any given planning application and developers are unlikely to raise the issue. That's where individual local knowledge can make a difference.

- Under the Wildlife and Countryside Act, with a few exceptions, all wild birds have a degree of protection. The relevance to planning comes in timing, so that it is an offence to intentionally damage or destroy the nest of any wild bird while it is being built or used. That has a bearing on the timing of any development, but there is always a get-out for offenders with that little word 'intentionally'. It is notoriously hard to prove intent. Quite how this bird-related aspect of the Wildlife and Countryside Act applies to farmers I am not sure, specifically with regards to nesting Lapwings and ploughing, and grass-rolling and Skylarks. And how it is possible to obtain forestry felling licences to undertake work in spring and summer is a mystery to me: I have yet to come across any woodland that does not harbour nesting birds of some sort in these seasons.

Here is a Citizen's Biodiversity Advice guide to what you can do for the benefit of wildlife:

- Check the Planning Application form and specifically check the tick boxes relating to the presence and proximity of protected and notable species and habitats; make sure there have not been any oversights on the part of the applicant.

- The council may be on its toes and request ecological surveys and reports to be undertaken and submitted. If the developer in question is canny, they will have submitted one as part of the application process and ahead of being asked. These reports, and the application itself, will be scrutinised by the council's biodiversity team, but they are typically swamped by cases and do not necessarily have all the facts to hand. When I say 'team' it is worth checking with your local authority: depending on the importance placed on biodiversity in the planning process by your council, they might only have one full-time employee tasked with the role, or none at all. In this regard you can help them out.

- If you have detailed knowledge of a local area's natural history you may be in a position to comment on ecological surveys and reports submitted on behalf of the applicant. You will also have access to the same database information as the applicant and their representatives, and you may find interesting omissions that can be pointed out to the planning department.

- It is important to write letters of objection, but for your arguments to be taken seriously and weighed in planning decision-making you must stick to facts, specifically those that are valid considerations in planning law. At all costs, letters of objection should avoid including personal feelings.

- By all means encourage others to write letters of objection. But for these to be taken seriously and have planning weight, they are best written in the letter-writer's own words. Covering the same ground as your letter is fine, but carbon-copy replication or a repeating a 'blueprint' letter is best avoided.

- Timing is crucial. Do not go in all-guns-blazing straight away. Instead wait until the tenth or eleventh hour for all the supporting documents to have been submitted, then study them thoroughly before you write a response.

SCRUTINISING AND CHALLENGING ECOLOGICAL SURVEYS

I have come across a few ecological consultants whose integrity I respect and I dare say that there are others out there somewhere who retain a moral compass. However, based on documents submitted in support of planning applications in the borough of Basingstoke I do not have a high regard for the job they do. I rank them on a par with estate agents, and their roles are not dissimilar. Both are employed to act in the best interests of their clients and both aim to benefit from the relationship.

In my limited experience, reports submitted by ecological consultants have a tendency to dress up and bolster the ambitions of their clients. There is usually devilish attention to detail when it comes to proposed environmental mitigation, lengthy cut-and-paste repetition of wildlife legislation, and much is made of the illusion of biodiversity enhancement through development. By contrast, there is often scant regard for anything natural that fails to conform to the fiction that building houses benefits wildlife. To the discerning reader, the underlying subtext establishes that it is not what the document reveals that is important but what is conceals.

One thing that you, as an independent scrutineer, can do is to check the methods and detail as revealed in any ecological report, including the way that publicly

available information and data have been presented. In the case of north Hampshire, I have not come across an ecological report that uses anything other than HBIC as a source of information for its deskbound 'surveys'. Typically, this puts ecological consultants at an immediate disadvantage because they are relying on incomplete data; other sources of information and local knowledge play a role that can be used by you, the scrutineer.

A central tenet of such ecological reports, and of current planning logic, is the concept of biodiversity net gain or loss. In theory that sounds like a good approach, but in practice I cannot think of any instances near me where it has not been used as a way of legitimising habitat and wildlife destruction. Overall, the way the system is used by developers is often to downplay the existing biodiversity and wildlife value of a site prior to development, and to emphasise the supposed benefits of biodiversity net gain achieved by environmental 'mitigation' and 'compensation' associated with building.

One example might be a planning application to build a house on a meadow. A typical low-budget ecological report may at first glance look professional and intimidating but will comprise 80 percent cut-and-paste repetition of wildlife law, local planning law and guidelines, and methodology. Once you have read a dozen or more of these dismal submissions you will begin to see a pattern emerging. The rest will be made up of the actual body of the report which typically comprises a one-day, out-of-season site visit and a trawl through the databases of HBIC and DEFRA MagicMap.

Regarding a hypothetical planning application for housing to be built on a meadow, here is a cynic's view of the ecological consultant's methodology:

- Step one – Undertake a site botanical survey in the dead of winter, find nothing of note and declare the land to be low-grade grassland on the basis of its seeming botanical impoverishment.

- Step two – Propose scattering a few seeds in an attempt to create a gaudy wildflower meadow somewhere on the development plot. Mention the benefits to so-called 'pollinators' – don't worry, there is no need to be specific about the alleged beneficiaries: generic reference to 'bees' or 'hover-flies' is all that's required. Then suggest planting a few hedgerow trees and shrubs, and advocate digging a small pond. Hey presto, like a conjuring trick, you have now created the illusion of biodiversity net gain.

- Step three – Undertake a deskbound search of HBIC, focus on protected and notable species but make sure the self-prescribed search radius you employ excludes anything of note.

From a developer's point of view, the beauty of the biodiversity net gain approach is that the council is most unlikely to ever check that these aspirational promises translate into compliance, and almost certainly they will never oversee compliance long term.

In this particular hypothetical case, flaws in the plan that could be highlighted to the planning department include:

- A failure to mention that most grassland plants are herbaceous and die back in winter and that for any meaningful assessment of botanical merit a site needs to be surveyed multiple times throughout the floral season, not in the dead of winter.

- The search radius used in any deskbound 'survey' can make the difference between the presence or absence of a given species being quoted by ecologists in a support document. You can check the process and point out any shortcomings.

- Use local knowledge and access other sources of data such as NBN and you may uncover a different picture regarding biodiversity of the area. This is where an independent individual can play a key role in making sure the planning department has all the crucial information.

- Scrutinise the mitigation plans carefully. Notwithstanding the proviso that you can scatter seeds but you cannot plant a meadow, proposed seed mixes for 'meadow creation' are seldom entirely appropriate for the local area. That is something that only local knowledge can expose. As an example, a new-build 'meadow mix' near me included seeds of Wood Vetch, a rare and declining UK species that does not occur in north Hampshire and the presence of which would have caused a sensation

among local botanists. You can also check that any tree and shrub species destined for a proposed hedgerow planting truly reflect what actually grows in existing local hedgerows. Just because a species may be native to the UK does not necessarily mean it is locally appropriate.

- Ask the legitimate question of who will maintain these supposed biodiversity net gains, and what is to stop future homeowners, for example, turfing or paving-over the 'meadow', or filling in the pond? You already know the answer to that question, but it does not hurt to point out the reality of the situation.

If this hypothetical case were in Hampshire, then the ecologists' deskbound 'survey' would consist of interrogating the HBIC database. However, as with all complex systems glitches occur and not every submitted record will necessarily find its way onto the system straight away. This happened with some validated and submitted records of Hazel Dormice and Great Crested Newts in the parish of Pamber. So, independent scrutineers need to keep in mind the possibility that vital data may be missing from your county biodiversity records database.

Planning officers are generally not wet behind the ears when it comes to ecological tricks of the trade, but the danger is that an overwhelming case load may lead to environmental indifference. It can only help if you do some of the planners' work for them by dissecting ecological reports, and it will not hurt if the said ecological reports are discredited in the process. If you have a reasonable level of knowledge of your local natural history, you are almost certain to know more about the wildlife significance of the site in question and the local area throughout the seasons than any paid-for ecologist, who in all likelihood will only have visited the site once, maybe twice. Being able to repeat wildlife and planning law chapter and verse is useful but not essential. The trick is to present the facts in a way that complies with the law and local planning guidance as interpreted by planners and exposes the inadequacies of any ecological supporting documents.

Protected and notable species

In the back of the minds of some of the founding fathers of protected species legislation and UK BAP priority species guidance, there might have been the thought that by protecting symbolic plants and animals, their habitats as well as the species themselves would be safeguarded. If that was the intention then it has failed as far as I can see. I cannot speak for the whole of the UK, but in the vicinity of where I live protected species legislation seldom meaningfully benefits the species it purports to protect, and it often legitimises the destruction of natural habitats through land development or exploitation. The small print seems to actually work in favour of developers by providing ways to overcome that irksome issue of wildlife. In short, by making protected species the focus of attention, no regard needs to be paid to the rest of biodiversity, nor is it.

Take reptiles as an example. Imagine a plot of land that has dry, sandy soil and supports populations of Adders, Slow-worms and Common Lizards. Armed with this knowledge, you might imagine a developer would say, fair enough, this site is so good for wildlife I will leave it alone and shift my attentions elsewhere. Not a bit of it, and in full compliance with the law, a ghastly perimeter of plastic fencing will be erected around the site; and matting will be littered on the ground inside in the hope that a few destitute reptiles will crawl under, and those that do are collected and removed. Pity the poor reptiles that do not seek shelter, for like their fellow amphibians and other forms of wildlife their fate will be to be bulldozed into the next world. And what happens to those few, those lucky few, those band of reptilian brothers that were collected, you might ask? Often their fate is enforced relocation to a site that is deemed 'suitable', usually one that already holds their kind at carrying capacity with no room for extras.

Amphibians fare little better. Currently Great Crested Newts are protected under the Wildlife and Countryside Act in England, but who knows for how much longer. They are such an annoyance to developers and we would not want to stand in the way of building back Britain, would we? Currently, a reasonable person might assume that having this elevated status would mean that 'crestie' breeding habitats were sacrosanct. Furthermore, given that, like other amphibians, Great Crested Newts are in essence land animals obliged to return to water briefly to breed, you might assume that their terrestrial habitats would also be no-go areas. Not a bit of it, and it is just a question of money: pay a 'licensed' consultant to collect and remove as many Great Crested Newts as possible, and then feel free to fill in the pond, or build right up to its margins, and to hell with other amphibians and other wildlife. Job done. In statutory terms, that is probably called 'sustainable development'.

These days a request to destroy ancient woodland no longer seems to raise a planning eyebrow especially if you play the 'over-riding public interest' card and offer to plant a few trees as compensation. Who cares if these include inappropriate species, and who knows if anyone actually checks on compliance with any promises made. If the said woodland destruction is set to destroy Hazel Dormouse habitat, then hey, no problem. Catch a few Hazel Dormice, plant a few Hazel whips and that is the mitigation and compensation element of planning sorted. If the development happens to include a road that dissects the said woodland, then introduce a few rope bridges and connectivity is miraculously restored. Build houses right next to a Hazel Dormouse habitat, and there is no need to worry about the impact of the army of rampaging cats and dogs that new homeowners will bring with them: just plant an embryo hedge as a buffer zone and ask the cats and dogs to keep out. That will do the trick, or at least it will in terms of compliance with the law.

Development not only destroys habitat and wildlife but also isolates and separates remaining populations of species such as Adders.

Statutory nature conservation bodies

The need for statutory nature conservation became apparent once the dust of World War Two had settled and the country had lived through a decade of austerity. Aesthetics crept to the fore and for those able to appreciate the finer things in life, the nation's natural heritage was placed on a par with its art and history. The golden age for nature conservation arrived with the formation of the Nature Conservancy Council (NCC) in 1973 and particularly the era when the late Derek Ratcliffe (1929–2005) was its chief scientist. However, the rot set in in 1991. Probably as punishment for disloyalty, NCC was dismantled, the budgets of its nationally-devolved offspring slashed year-on-year, and their remit and ability to aid conservation increasingly curtailed. The body responsible for England has gone through spasmodic changes down the years, first called English Nature, and since 2006 Natural England. At the time of writing, it is this entity whose administrative remit covers the part of north Hampshire where I live. For how much longer, who knows? Only time will tell.

I have mixed feelings when it comes to Natural England. On the ground, I admire many of the National Nature Reserves for which it is responsible, and I have yet to meet a site manager or reserve warden who is not committed, knowledgeable and passionate about the land over which they have stewardship. In addition, many go far beyond the call of duty and their job is also their passion in life. And Natural England's role in grand schemes such as the restoration of lowland raised bogs – the Marches Mosses for example – is to be praised. However, when it comes to the corporate, bureaucratic face of Natural England and their reaction to the concerns of individual members of the public, I am less impressed.

To varying degrees, we all live in social bubbles and reinforce our views of the world by mixing with and talking to those who by and large share our outlook. I dare say that many in Natural England move in circles that applaud the sterling job they are doing in balancing the demands of their paymasters and influencers and achieving the 'best outcome' for nature. Given the restrictive parameters under which they operate, there may be some truth in that. However, in the circles I move in – stakeholders in the local environment – it is a rather different story. From landowners to concerned naturalists, I know few who have a kind word to say for the organisation when it comes to support sought or received regarding local conservation issues – the things that really matter to people on the ground.

My admiration for many aspects of Natural England's work notwithstanding, I am somewhere in the middle of the spectrum of attitudes towards the organisation as a corporate entity. Numbed by disappointment, I work on the assumption that it is unlikely to help the local wildlife causes that I am involved with, and I am seldom disappointed in that regard. Part of the problem with other people's attitudes and mine stems from expectation. I have to keep reminding myself that nowadays Natural England is an advisory body not a campaigning one; and it has no meaningful independence from government and is unlikely to openly confront the powers that be. It exists to apply and interpret the law as written by government. A reasonable person might argue that, surely, it is Natural England that advises the powers that be about legislation, so that any legal shortcomings are their fault. In their defence, I suppose I would have to state the obvious: that advice can be given but government can always choose to ignore it.

Nowadays, the overwhelming feeling I have when I think about Natural England is pity. Pity for the combative, fully-toothed organisation it once was; pity for those of its employees who are committed naturalists with an environmental conscience; and pity for all the wildlife that suffers as a consequence of its prescribed inability to tackle biodiversity loss in the part of the world where I live.

Why this hostility towards Natural England, you may ask? In part the problem is its government-imposed remit and underfunding. That is something that the organisation can do nothing about. Government attitude towards conservation, and hence the role Natural England must play, should perhaps be seen as reflecting the attitudes of the electorate. Where I live, I cannot think of many people who would vote to strengthen and extend the powers of Natural England and increase its funding; the majority, if asked, I suspect would want to restrict the organisation's remit further to eliminate wildlife from the planning and land-use processes completely. So, it is down to anyone who cares not just to complain but campaign, and not to Natural England but to those who ultimately exert control over them and define their powers and funding.

There's a cautionary note to be sounded to detractors of Natural England inside the conservation world, myself included perhaps: be careful what you wish for. There is a chance that your criticism may give behind-the-scenes anti-environmental lobbyists just the ammunition they need to whisper into the ears of government and do away with statutory nature conservation bodies altogether. That's far-fetched you may say. However, based on the trajectory of erosion of nature conservation to date, it would be a logical end goal for those who want to profit from the land at any environmental cost and wish to remove obstacles in their path.

For individuals on the receiving end of corporate Natural England, the organisation does not do itself any favours. An inability to help wildlife at the local level invariably comes across as *unwillingness* to help, the corporate equivalent of 'Not my job, mate'. Rather than find creative ways to help conservation at the local level, the perception is of an organisation that loves to throw obstacles in the path of any individual who wants to protect wildlife. Furthermore, do the following statements from the organisation's website convey to you a passion for natural history and conservation? Their stated aims include: 'being a values-led organisation that delivers excellent service standards to all partners, organisations and communities engaged in achieving Nature's recovery'. They also aim for 'people connected to the natural environment for their own and society's wellbeing, enjoyment and prosperity' and 'improvements in the natural capital that drives sustainable economic growth, healthy food systems and prospering communities'. What that actually means is anyone's guess but regardless, at a personal level, I certainly do not feel that I have been delivered 'excellent service standards'. Nor do the Common Toads, Great Crested Newts and Hazel Dormice I represent, but I will come to that later.

It is tempting to dismiss Natural England as a harmless irrelevance when it comes to the planning process. However, complacency in that regard is dangerous. Don't assume that their perspective regarding conservation will align with yours. Unless you present a watertight and compelling case, their comments, if they have been sought, are more likely to

be listened to than yours. A clue to the danger is hinted at on the Natural England website in its 'Who We Are' mission statement, which says: 'Our purpose is to help conserve, enhance and manage the natural environment for the benefit of present and future generations, thereby contributing to sustainable development.' So, no explicit mention of managing the environment for the benefit of *wildlife*, and the old-school naturalist in me finds it alarming that Natural England should have a sustainable development department in the first place. Local experience has taught me that, when it comes to meaningful benefits to wildlife, the words 'sustainable' and 'development' when used in conjunction are not compatible. They might be in a Kafkaesque parallel universe but not in my world.

Although biodiversity and environmental impact have successfully contributed to planning refusals locally, I can only think of a couple of instances near me where they have been the *sole* reasons for stopping development. Those meagre successes have all been the result of the action of individuals acting alone. The best advice that I can give to any prospective campaigner is: do not rely on others; and be careful what you wish for before any attempts are made to engage conservation bodies including Natural England as allies. A few local examples may help explain this advice.

UPPER CUFAUDE FARM

Not far from me there is a site called Upper Cufaude Farm, which at the time of writing remains open countryside and as rural as anywhere in this part of north Hampshire. But not for much longer. It is separated from a Basingstoke estate called Chineham (itself the size of a small town) by a railway line. To set the scene, I recall a meeting reported in the Basingstoke Gazette on 26 February 2019 at which the Basingstoke MP met the local Wildlife Trust to discuss an aspiration for a 'Wilder Chineham and Sherfield Park'. Ironically, Chineham really had been 'wild' in a past life, but that was before Basingstoke & Deane Borough Council (BDBC) gave the green light for thousands of houses to replace most of the wildlife. Upper Cufaude Farm was owned, at the time of writing, by reportedly cash-strapped Hampshire County Council, and permission has been granted by BDBC for developers to build 350 houses on the land, with all of the extras that such a development entails (Planning reference 19/00018/OUT).

Prior to its impending development, residents of 'wild' Upper Cufaude Farm included Great Crested Newt and Hazel Dormouse, both of which are nominally protected species. Given the proximity of the site to Chineham – the site being championed for 'rewilding' – you might perhaps have expected some comment from the Wildlife Trust? However, having looked at the documents associated with the planning application I cannot see anything from them. Perhaps the site will have to be 'dewilded' by having houses built all over it and then populated by a new set of residents – potential Wildlife Trust members – before it interests the organisation?

Fascinatingly, an example of Natural England's helpful advice regarding Upper Cufaude Farm was contained in a document relating to the site's population of Skylarks, a species that is Red Listed in the latest *Birds of Conservation Concern 5* document. Natural England stated 'that the proposals will result in a residual impact on skylark but that this can be offset by providing offsite compensation via means of a financial contribution to a farmland wildlife project that benefits skylark.' Yeh, that will work – there are so many 'farmland wildlife projects' in the vicinity to choose from and I am sure the local Skylarks will be happy to comply. The use of euphemistic phrases like 'residual impact' and aspirational advice about 'offsite compensation' shed light on the mindset and workings of twenty-first-century statutory nature conservation.

TOAD RAGE

In addition to managing land for wildlife rather than for profit, there are a number of practical ways in which you can help conservation in your local area. Wildlife trusts are occasionally on the lookout for volunteers although, given my fondness for the 'habitat', I would avoid helping with anything that smacked of generic 'scrub-bashing'. Another way to support wildlife is to help with so-called toad patrols: across the country there is a network of sites where volunteers rescue amphibians as they try to cross roads on migration. Visit the charity Froglife's website to find out more. As it happens, 500 metres or so up the road from Upper Cufaude Farm is a prime example, one that also illustrates how local government and statutory nature conservation work in harmony for the betterment of wildlife, or not as the case may be.

But first, let me set the scene. Once upon a time there was a rural byway called Cufaude Lane, a single-track lane along much of its length, lined by majestic elm trees and renowned in local naturalist circles for its amphibian abundance. Back in the day, it was the sort of lane where grass grew down the middle of the track and you could walk its three-mile length on a summer's evening and encounter one or two cars at most.

From the 1960s onwards, things began to change for the worse. Dutch Elm Disease accounted for the landscape's majestic trees; increasingly industrialised land-use put paid to the local Tree Sparrows; and house-building at either end of the lane went into overdrive. Nowadays, there are thousands more houses at either end of Cufaude Lane than there were fifty years ago, and hundreds of cars per hour use it as a peak time rat run. During spring migration, amphibians are obliged to cross Cufaude Lane from wintering land on the east to breeding ponds on the west. The volume of traffic means amphibian carnage on the road during spring migration, when peak movement at dusk coincides with going-home time for residents of Basingstoke to the south and village-cum-town Bramley to the north.

Back in 2015, friend and local naturalist Andrew Cleave initiated a toad patrol to help save some of the amphibians, a tally of species that includes not only Common Toads, but also Common Frogs, Smooth Newts and Great Crested Newts. Thanks to volunteer patrols, what would most likely have been 100 percent mortality given the volume of traffic has been reduced to 25 percent killed by cars. Although this is an improvement, every squashed toad feels like a bereavement for the volunteers.

Back at the start of Covid lockdown in 2020 Hampshire County Council (HCC) took the welcome decision to install a 'toad tunnel' at a strategic point on the amphibian crossing zone. This would not have happened had toad patrollers not raised the profile of Cufaude Lane's amphibians and provided empirical evidence of numbers. Well-intentioned, the construction comprised an under-the-road subway pipe and barriers to direct amphibians to the mouth of the tunnel. The unconventional nature of the design notwithstanding, the barriers were intentionally temporary, the aim being to refine their location using advice and evidence from patrollers before anything permanent was installed.

SERIES TWO

TOAD RAGE

The nightmare on Cufaude Lane continues...

Hosted by the Borough of Basingstoke, 2020 sees the welcome return of this
toad-on-the-road reality series that charts the everyday struggles of amphibians
as they attempt to cross the
specially engineered Cufaude Lane Racetrack.

WHO LIVES? WHO DIES? YOU DECIDE!

COMING SOON TO A BLOG NEAR YOU
CATCH UP with SERIES ONE on social media

Warning: contains scenes of animal cruelty that any decent human being will find offensive.

This is an example of an advert used to raise the profile of the problem and gain media attention. The moniker Toad Rage stems in part from the anger that volunteer toad patrollers feel on behalf of the dead amphibians but also from the mouthfuls of abuse hurled at them now and then by passing motorists, irritated by having to momentarily reduce speed. As an example of the increasing disconnect between the UK public and nature, while I was on patrol one night a car stopped and the driver asked me 'What are you doing?' I replied that I was collecting migrating toads to save them from being squashed by cars, to which the driver asked 'What's a toad, mate?'.

You think that sounds reasonable? Not a bit of it, and the subsequent chain of events continue to be as baffling as they are depressing. Shortly after the tunnel was installed (in 2020), so the volunteers were told by HCC ecologists, Natural England (NE) instructed work on the installation to cease, which it did, because HCC did not have an appropriate Great Crested Newt licence. At the time, the volunteers had no reason to doubt what they were being told, although they were

puzzled by HCC's failure to foresee the need for a licence. There was an additional requirement that HCC introduce openings (they were called 'strategic gaps') along the length of the barriers, which it did, so as not to 'interrupt' newt migration. There is a breeding pond roughly 500 metres from the toad tunnel and this was presumed to be the reason for the intervention.

Predictably, the inevitable consequence of introducing gaps in the barrier was that every species of amphibian found its way through the openings and onto the road only to be squashed by cars unless spotted by volunteers; this rendered the entire project pointless. Despite pestering and cajoling on the part of the toad patrollers, there followed virtual radio silence from HCC ecologists and NE for a year or more. The only change came about through the actions of a disgruntled landowner who took it upon himself to dismantle much of the barrier. From that point until the summer of 2022, a dumped pile of plastic piping served as a memorial to this taxpayer-funded project, and a metaphor for a road to amphibian hell paved with good intentions.

In August 2022, an email from Natural England's Wildlife Licensing Service finally arrived in response to the toad patrollers' pleading enquiries and an invitation to attend a site visit. Would this be the response that would save the environmental day, they wondered? Not a bit of it: having previously indicated they would attend a meeting, NE declined the invitation to discuss the situation on site. The letter itself was bewildering, making no sense to anyone on the receiving end and giving the distinct impression that wires had been crossed, or parallel universes were being inhabited. Reading it, you could be forgiven for thinking that NE was referring to a project that was about to start, rather than one that had been abandoned as a consequence of their intervention.

A flavour of the confusion that the letter created can perhaps be gleaned from the following statement: 'NE's understanding is that HCC are very aware of the GCN in locality, but based on the information they presently hold, HCC have concluded that they can confidently pursue the toad tunnel installation project without detriment or impact to the GCN population and therefore do not consider that they need a licence to undertake these works.' And that 'As a Regulator, Natural England cannot specify if a licence is required to undertake works. That is the role of the ecologist connected with the project.'

The toad patrollers were left wondering whether the initial story about NE's intervention was correct or whether they had been misled at the time. If, however, the story was correct, then why the intervention in 2020, and the responsibility washing-of-hands in 2022? I guess we will never know, and in any case, I doubt any further attempts to achieve clarity from NE would achieve that result. The letter ended with the helpful advice: 'In the absence of a licence, any activity that could constitute a wildlife crime should be reported to the Police directly for them to conduct an investigation.' That hardly filled me with confidence, for reasons I will explain in due course.

Returning to the subject of the pond which harboured the Great Crested Newts that were presumably behind Natural England's reasoning for halting work on the toad tunnel, there's a further twist in the tale. The pond has been subjected to a massive building project literally on its doorstep, and Natural England saw no reason to require a Great Crested Newt licence to be in place. Given the organisation's bureaucratic attention to detail, and the letter from NE's Wildlife Licence Service, they are probably complying with the letter of the law. In the strange world of statutory conservation logic it obviously perfect sense to them, but it is beyond me. However, is it any wonder that Natural England is not held in universally high regard by the outside world, if social media postings are anything to go by? And that's putting it mildly.

The saga of Cufaude Lane's amphibians got worse by an order of magnitude when a planning application (22/00444/PIP) was submitted to build four new homes on a field that sits at the heart of the main migration route for Common Toads and other amphibians. If you had to choose a place to build houses, and to destroy wildlife and block an amphibian migration route, you could not pick a more effective location.

Initially, the applicants and their agents neglected to advise the local council of the true environmental significance of the land. Fortunately, toad patrollers were able to point the council towards empirical data and prior evidence held in their possession. In part, the latter relates to the previous topic of the development on Upper Cufaude Farm and a document, lodged on the planning portal, submitted by consultants Aspect Ecology and entitled 'Toad Mitigation Option Study and Proposed Strategy'. It was compiled following

a meeting that took place in the Basingstoke council offices where those present included Cufaude Lane toad patrollers, the council planning officer associated with the development of the Upper Cufaude Farm site, the author of the Aspect Ecology report, and representatives of developers Croudace Homes. The aim of that meeting was to discuss ways in which the developer could address the impact on Common Toads caused by building 350 homes in open countryside. The catastrophic consequences for the rest of Upper Cufaude Farm's native biodiversity were not up for discussion at the meeting.

Read this independent report and you will discover that the field subject to planning application 22/00444/PIP is identified as significant with regard to amphibian migration on Cufaude Lane. Furthermore, Aspect Ecology suggested that a toad tunnel (in addition to the one installed by Hampshire County Council) be installed close to the spot where the entrance to planning application 22/00444/PIP was proposed.

This document adds further weight to the argument that seemingly uninteresting and ordinary fields can have genuine wildlife significance; and that location, not just botanical make-up, can elevate one particular field's importance above a neighbouring plot. It also demonstrates the folly of viewing prospective developments and proposed environmental mitigation in application-by-application isolation and not in a joined-up manner. Adopt the former approach and potentially overlapping and conflicting environmental mitigation plans mask their collective damaging impact on the environment. That provides another example of death by a thousand cuts for the environment in general, but in this instance for toads and other amphibians in particular.

The saga continued and, to the dismay of toad patrollers, a Basingstoke & Deane Borough Council planning officer recommended approval of application 22/00444/PIP (on land of prime importance for Common Toad migration). However, when the Development Control Committee examined the case on 7 December 2022, they made the unanimous decision to refuse the application, in part because of the impact it would have on Common Toads. Others in a similar situation might benefit from knowing the legislative arguments that the toad patrollers used in support of refusal, and those which the councillors referenced in their decision. The toad patrollers cited the following: UK Biodiversity Action Plan Priority Species status; National Planning Policy Statement section 9; Basingstoke & Deane's Local Plan (regarding Biodiversity, Geodiversity and Nature Conservation); the advice of Basingstoke & Deane's biodiversity team; and appeal precedents regarding the refusal of PIP applications in open countryside. In the decision letter, factors included: the adverse impacts on the conservation status of Common Toads (named as key species S41 in the letter); harm to linkages between designated sites and key habitats; and contravention of the Natural Environment and Rural Communities Act, the National Planning Policy Framework (July 2021) and Policy EM4 of the Basingstoke and Deane Local Plan 2011–2029.

Closer examination of evidence presented on behalf of the developers provides red flag insight for other campaigners; specifically, how presentation of county database information (in this case HBIC) has the potential to muddy the waters. The Preliminary Ecological Appraisal, compiled by an ecologist on behalf of the applicants, stated that 'The HBIC data search returned four records of common toad (Bufo bufo) within two kilometres of the site between 1997 and 2015'. When challenged by the DCC as to toad numbers, the planning officer repeated this statement, which is technically correct. However, what it does not reveal is that those four records represent hundreds of animals, and not four as perhaps an uninformed person might assume; there is, of course, a risk that the word 'just' creeps into such statements by inference. Fortunately, in this instance the DCC committee members knew their stuff about local Common Toad populations. However, in the absence of informed oversight, there is a danger that a false equivalence is created between accurate and unhelpful ways of presenting information, not to mention between facts and hearsay.

Cufaude Lane's amphibians can breathe a collective sigh of relief, at least for now. However, it is worth bearing in mind that if the planning conversation had been about a nationally significant population of Common Frogs, which have no statutory protection, it is unlikely that their plight would have figured in the decision-making process. This highlights the need for environmental planning advocates to concentrate on adverse impacts to key species relevant to any given location, as well as general biodiversity.

BRAMLEY FRITH

Let us return to the subject of Bramley Frith, which lies a mile or so from Cufaude Lane in one direction and a similar distance from my cottage in the other direction. This was the ancient woodland (mentioned on p. 91) that had its heart ripped out by the CEGB to accommodate an electricity substation. Fast forward to the era of National Grid, and an environmental centre was established there, which came into its own under the direction of Andrew Cleave. During his 15-year tenure, as well as educating school children and hosting university students, Andrew established Bramley Frith as a Natural England Hazel Dormouse recovery site where he trained prospective licensees (you need a Natural England licence to handle the species). He was nominated for an MBE by National Grid for services to environmental education and received the award in 1995.

The seemingly idyllic partnership between industry and conservation came to an abrupt end in 2005, if memory serves, when National Grid announced its intention to enlarge the substation by expanding into, and hence destroying, more ancient woodland. This was in response to increased demand for electricity that was forecast as a consequence of projected plans for house-building in Basingstoke. To his credit Andrew, aided by a team of supporters, fought to save the woodland and even came up with alternative plans that would have enabled expansion of the substation without eating into the remaining ancient woodland. Requests for support from almost all conservation charities were met by stony silence or outright refusal, except for The Woodland Trust, who funded a challenge in the High Court, led by renowned environmental advocate David Wolfe QC.

That particular chapter in the Bramley Frith saga gets a lengthy mention in *Silent Summer*, a book edited by Norman Maclean (see the References section for details). What does not come across is the involvement of Natural England and their role in this sorry tale as indicated by the heading under which the Woodland Trust brought the High Court case: 'The Woodland Trust v Natural England and National Grid (Interested Party) CO/4897/2007'. Natural England was the Defendant and National Grid the Interested Party – a body that was directly affected by the outcome of the challenge. Leafing through the correspondence associated with the campaign to save woodland at Bramley Frith, it was interesting to be reminded that endorsement for National Grid's approach to woodland management was provided by The Tree Council. At the time, National Grid worked in partnership with The Tree Council; they no longer do so, and according to their website at the time of writing The Tree Council now numbers Network Rail among its partners.

The High Court ruled in favour of The Woodland Trust and issued an injunction that halted National Grid's plans. However, the relief among those trying to save ancient woodland was short-lived: a successful appeal quickly followed and overturned the injunction. The Woodland Trust ended up footing the massive legal bill; the environmental centre closed; Andrew and his team lost their jobs and were barred from the site; and the woodland was duly felled. Unsurprisingly, Natural England were not flavour of the month among those trying to save Bramley Frith's ancient woodland.

NOT MY JOB, MATE

Recently, a landowner near me embarked on a dewilding project in spring. While people's attentions were elsewhere, a stream was dredged, adjacent trees and shrubs were felled, and dredged material was deposited on land beside the watercourse. As a result, the flow of the stream (which lies in Environment Agency Flood Zone 3) was altered; trees and shrubs containing occupied bird nests were destroyed; and the work strayed on to an ancient byway and public footpath that comes under the jurisdiction of Hampshire County Council.

A group of concerned citizens immediately reported the incident to a range of authorities including the following: Hampshire Police; the Environment Agency; Basingstoke & Deane Borough Council's Tree Officers and Biodiversity Team; Hampshire Highways; and Hampshire Footpaths. A request for Tree Preservation Orders (TPOs) was made for the remaining gnarled, ancient pollards; or for this short stretch to be added to the boundary of a contiguous TPO area (at the time of writing, the TPO notification process was underway for the rest of the byway).

When reporting the incident, and requesting TPO status, the environmental significance of the habitat was made clear: along with the rest of the ancient byway, this stretch was in the process of having Site of Importance to Nature Conservation status conferred upon it by HBIC; Hazel Dormouse had been recorded in a contiguous length of the byway less than 200 metres away; Water Voles had been recorded on the stream; in spring 2022, Western Barbastelle and six other bat species had been recorded in the immediate vicinity of the trees for which TPOs were requested; and the trees in question were blessed with plenty of crevices and holes in which bats might roost or use as nurseries.

No action was taken by anyone in authority at the time, nor by the time of writing, and here are a selection of responses and advice from the various bodies:

- **Hampshire Police**: no response
- **Environment Agency**: they acknowledged that they had no record of any work being approved or sanctioned by the Environment Agency. However, as far as local residents are aware no investigation was undertaken nor action taken.
- **Basingstoke & Deane Borough Council's Tree Officers**: at the time of writing, the request to confer Tree Preservation Order (TPO) status on the trees had been refused, despite the process of conferring TPO status to the rest of ancient byway being underway. The advice from Tree Officers included the following: that matters relating to the Wildlife and Countryside Act are the responsibility of the Police; hedgerows are the concern of council Biodiversity Officers and not the Tree Officers; TPOs can only be made to preserve the 'amenity value' of trees; that Tree Officers apply an 'expediency test' to determine whether the tree or trees in question form a strong enough 'amenity asset' to warrant a TPO, and whether or not it would not be expedient to do so.
- **Basingstoke & Deane Borough Council's Biodiversity Team**: that any alleged breaches of wildlife-related legislation should be reported directly to Hampshire Police.
- **Hampshire Highways**: that tree works can take place during the bird nesting season as long as the trees were checked for nests prior to the start of works and none were found that would be disturbed by the planned works. That was rather the point – clearly the trees and shrubs were not checked in advance of the planned work, otherwise nests would have been discovered.

- **Hampshire County Council's Countryside Service**: that the reported incident had been resolved to their satisfaction and that the case had now been closed.

As an aside, Government guidance on Tree Preservation Orders states: "'Amenity' is not defined in law, so authorities need to exercise judgment when deciding whether it is within their powers to make an Order' and that 'Orders should be used to protect selected trees and woodlands if their removal would have a significant negative impact on the local environment and its enjoyment by the public. Before authorities make or confirm an Order they should be able to show that protection would bring a reasonable degree of public benefit in the present or future.'

One phrase in the above stands out: 'Orders should be used to protect selected trees and woodlands if their removal would have a significant negative impact on the local environment.' That suggests to me that 'environmental impact' is indeed part of the remit of Tree Officers tasked with the 'expedient' task of deciding, in tree terms, who lives and who dies.

Perhaps Tree Officers might consider widening their vision of what constitutes the 'amenity value' of a tree? Government guidance on Tree Preservation Orders clearly indicates that the process is subjective. Given this, I would suggest that 'amenity value' should be assessed through the eyes of the beholder – in this case those who actually use the ancient byway in question and gain pleasure from its existence, and not someone sitting at a desk. For anyone interested in natural history or indeed local history, the stature and heritage of trees, and their associated wildlife, are precisely what constitutes the 'amenity value' of our native trees and woodlands. I am also curious to know what a Tree Officer's 'expediency test' might look like. I am probably wrong, but to an outsider and in the absence of an explanation it could be interpreted as meaning 'Can I be bothered with the extra paperwork?'

Regardless of the final outcome of this sorry saga, it serves as a lasting reminder of the obstacles faced when concerned citizens try to protect the natural world. Sometimes it can feel like you are not only fighting environmental detractors, but the entire system as well.

The moral of the story

I read somewhere that a noted wit was once asked why he always took an instant dislike to people, to which his reply was 'I find it saves time'. In a similar vein, when it comes to matters where biodiversity, self-interest and bureaucracy rub shoulders, I find it saves time to always assume the worst of others. That way, on the rare that occasions that I am proved wrong, I get a nice surprise.

Photographed in the dry summer of 2022, this image illustrates the mosaic of habitats – from meadows to willow-fringed watercourses – that have been nurtured and encouraged by managing Manor Farm land for wildlife. Thanks to the work of sympathetic neighbours, it also demonstrates the potential for wildlife connectivity to play a key role in restoration of the countryside, with meandering, biodiverse corridors linking the land in the foreground with distant woodlands that form part of the National Trust's Vyne Estate.

I Am Not Alone

When I began my biodiversity gardening project, it felt like I was bucking a local trend (perhaps that should be 'going against the grain') and I admit to feeling isolated at times. However, it was comforting to discover that I was not alone, and gradually I came across example after example of others who, independently of me, had embarked on similar journeys. My advice to anyone in a similar position to me is that there will be kindred spirits near you if you take the time to seek them out. Find them and you will have moral support and practical advice you can call upon, resources that are especially useful when facing challenges and your spirits are low. Here are the stories of three pioneering couples, told in their own words.

Manor Farm
by
Adam Rattray and Jenna Burlingham, Hampshire

Five years ago, my wife and I invited a friend – who was also a freshwater expert – to come and look at the one-acre lake on our land. He looked at the striped lawns leading up to the water's edge; the sharp edges; and the neatness of the recently cut hedges and shrubs. After reflection, he turned to us and said, rather pointedly: 'What you have here is a swimming pool, not a pond.' This depressing statement – which, at first, we did not understand – set us on a journey that, to date, has led to us rewilding 85 percent of the ten acres of our land.

To provide a bit of context, our land at Manor Farm is located on the outskirts of the village of Sherborne St John, north-east of Basingstoke. The settlement has an ancient heritage: the Sherborne element of the village's name means "bright water" in Anglo-Saxon and a farm of the same name is mentioned in the Domesday Book. The house has not been part of a fully operational working farm since the 1940s, when the then-owners sold much of the farmland, and the house became a private dwelling. The farmhouse itself was rebuilt in the late eighteenth/early nineteenth century in imitation of the Tudor architecture of our local 'great house', The Vyne.

Returning to the visit by that freshwater expert, what he was alluding to were the ways in which we had been looking after the lake – mostly cutting right up to its edge and taking away all debris. The result meant we had left precious few areas for those amphibious animals – from insects to amphibians – that seasonally span the divide between water and land, depending on the pond to breed and feed for parts of the year, returning to the cover of waterside vegetation at others.

What was true of the pond was also true of our fields. Historically these were ancient meadowlands that until the middle of the twentieth century most likely would have flooded in early spring, produced a crop of hay later in the season and experienced periodic grazing in winter. However, since that time the regime has been different and in recent years the fields had been grazed continuously to a playing-field surface by horses. At the end of additional 'topping sessions' in March, July and September, when the vegetation was cut, you could have played cricket on these ancient meadowlands. Worse still were the chemicals that were used – the herbicides in particular – to create a bright-green monoculture of grass.

We started to read about natural renewal, and watched YouTube videos by environmentalists such as Isabella Tree and Charlie Burrell; and visiting the Knepp Estate was a transformative and eye-opening experience. We began to realise that what we were doing, though it looked estate-agent 'pretty', was contributing to the collapse in biodiversity and wildlife across the board that was setting off alarm bells across the country.

Our Manor Farm site is crossed by three chalk streams that combine to feed a mill pond further downstream from our lake. Together with our fields, my wife and I felt this patch of Hampshire countryside offered remarkable possibilities for the renewal of nature. One thing led to another and a chance meeting with Pete West of the Hampshire and Isle of Wight Amphibian and Reptile Group led to an introduction to Paul, the author of this book. Under their guidance, we have learned to mostly let go, to let nature do what it wants rather than continually interfering with the process of natural restoration.

This does not mean we have abandoned the fields entirely. We have planted thousands of whips to restore the hedgerows that border the site, and created a series of shallow pools to add to the wetland margins. The fact that Tubular Water-dropwort and Common Spike-rush – notable plants for this area, that like to grow with their 'feet' in water – managed to cling on and survive decades of intensive agriculture gives us hope that wildlife restoration under nature's own steam is an achievable goal.

By combining forces with some of our neighbours, a 'wildlife corridor' more than 1.5km long has been created, harbouring not just meadows, scrub and hedgerows, but seven ponds and two modest-sized lakes. Large piles of dead wood have been created for the benefit of those invertebrates – insects in the main – that depend on this habitat. In particular, we had in mind the likes of Lesser Stag Beetles, whose larvae live inside dead timber. However, we will be rather pleased if this insect's larger cousin, the Stag Beetle, makes an appearance in the future. It can be found in good numbers a few miles to the north of Manor Farm, so we live in hope.

It has not been plain sailing, of course. Trying to persuade some of our neighbours as to the value of what we are doing has been challenging. And there have been plenty of walkers (on the public footpath that cuts through the property) who see the result as unsightly, and our management of the house and grounds lazy and irresponsible. It is certainly true that the place does not look as it did between about 1947 and 2017: the wildlife corridors created on either side of the approach to the house have raised eyebrows among friends and visitors, as previously these now-lush, grassy areas were striped to Wimbledon perfection as a continuation of the formal gardens.

But the reward has been worth it: there has been an explosion of insect life, and butterflies of many species stream across the fields as I write; and there is deafening bird song in spring. We now see more deer, Badgers and Hedgehogs than we did in the past. And most excitingly of all, having not seen a snake in years, Grass Snakes are now regular. Most remarkable of all, there have even been two reliable sightings of Adders in our fields.

Inspired by our efforts, our immediate neighbour has created a wildlife garden at the end of his land, widening the natural corridor that flanks the exit stream from our lake. Even more powerfully, our neighbours with the mill pond (who have undergone their own environmental journey independently) have left huge areas of their 10-acre plot to 'rewild', and planted long hedgerows. Together, we have created a large area between our two properties for nature to return, and hopefully set an example for the thousands of walkers who pass through our acres on the (shared) public footpath.

Pete West said that reptiles and amphibians – and insects and other invertebrates – would return to our land if we provided the conditions for them to do so. He has been proved right. I cannot thank our friend – the freshwater expert – enough for starting us on our rewilding journey. We would also like to thank Paul for his help and encouragement: he and others have taught us to let go and see what happens, rather than to continually interfere with the land. We are now lucky enough to be temporary guardians of a small patch of rewilded England. Every day we walk in it, and every day we are rewarded.

The Hughes Family Wilding Project
by
Karl Hughes and Nicola Hughes, Pamber, Hampshire

A few years ago, as a family we purchased a parcel of land adjacent to our house and garden. Our relationship with that plot has changed over the years, and involved an unexpected and enlightening journey. Our attachment to and empathy for it has grown in parallel with the evolving habitat recovery that is in progress. And the wildlife biodiversity that has appeared on our doorstep has enriched our lives.

THE BEGINNING

When a 12-acre piece of agricultural land immediately behind our house came up for sale we discussed whether it was something we should or would want to buy. My wife and I talked about it at length, and we also spoke to our neighbours to explore whether there was any interest in buying the land collectively. Although many of our neighbours expressed concern over what would happen to the land if we did not buy and retain control of it, only two of them voiced a genuine desire to purchase.

Initially, my pragmatic wife questioned the wisdom of spending several thousand pounds buying an empty field that previously had only been used for arable and as grazing land. However, after a lot of deliberation eventually we made the decision to purchase a third of the land, acquiring 4.5 acres that linked to the rear of our garden. The remainder of the field was bought by our two interested neighbours, and none of the purchasers really knew what they wanted to do with the land at that stage. However, what we had in common was that we all wanted to be in control of what happened to the land in the future, and we also perceived it to be a financial asset.

THE EVOLUTION

To begin with, collectively the field's new owners only really thought of the land as a 'nice to have' financial asset. We did not divide the land up into thirds and continued to grow farm crops in the field as a whole. The reality of ploughing, seeding, growing, and cutting crops meant that we, as a family, could not really enjoy the area. We were restricted to walking around the perimeter and found that the most enjoyable days were those when the crops were cut; for a brief period, every year we could actually walk through the field and enjoy sitting on the straw bales.

It dawned on us that we were not really getting any pleasure from farming the land. That realisation, together with the belief that it would add more financial value to our asset, meant we applied to change the land use from arable to equestrian and proceeded to build a stable. However, we quickly realised we did not want the additional responsibility of owning horses, nor did we want to rent out the stable and have other people accessing and using the field. A turning point came when one of our neighbours decided to partition their third of the field because they wanted to graze animals on it and needed to secure the perimeter. At this stage we thought our only options were: growing crops, which we had tried and did not like; equestrian use, which we had ruled out; or grazing animals, like our neighbours had decided to do. The world of re-wilding was not a concept that we, or many people in the neighbourhood, were familiar with. It was only after talking to people like Paul Sterry that we began to consider an alternative use for the field.

THE WILDING PROJECT

After researching the project and thinking long and hard, we decided that we would like to let nature take its course in the field. Locals tried to discourage us saying that it would look a mess; that we would not be able to do anything with it if we let it go to ruin; that the weeds would contaminate their gardens; and that our financial asset would diminish. We ignored these arguments, simply left our portion of the field to its own devices and let the natural flora and fauna take over. We did not 'seed' the field but relied on the soil's natural seedbank, and colonisation from nearby 'reservoirs' of biodiversity, to work their magic. The result is the mosaic of plant species we see today.

When we embarked on this conservation route, we quickly saw a massive increase in the abundance and variety of insects, birds and other wildlife that descended on our field, almost instantly. We now began to look at the land as an extension of our garden, rather than just as a field at the rear of our property. No longer was it just a financial asset: it became a place of daily enjoyment.

As a result of this awakening, we started to consider and plan how to manage what had become our wilding project, as well as what would give us the most enjoyment. We cut a series of paths through the grass and that immediately allowed us to walk through the field, rather than just around the perimeter as previously. This new perspective – that of being in and part of the land rather than on the edge – immediately allowed us to see and enjoy the variety of wildlife in intimate close-up. Even then, we did not all fully appreciate the true value of the land. That revelation came when the pandemic hit, and we were all locked down. The ability to walk out into the field with the family and the dog every day was priceless. Being surrounded by nature had a huge positive impact on our welfare and mental well-being. Our wilded field became an integral and much-prized part of our home life.

CONTINUING TO EVOLVE

The immense enjoyment that we continue to get from the field in its own right, and from seeing the evolution of the wildlife throughout the seasons, inspires us to do even more. We have recently added a large pond, which acts as a focal point that has attracted new and varied wildlife: everything from dragonflies and feeding Swallows to drinking Barn Owls and Badgers. Plans are also underway to plant a 300-metre-long native mixed hedgerow. As the years go by, the Hughes family – my wife and me, plus our three boys – now spend more and more time in the field. Our intrepid sons regularly swim in the pond and are always interested in the new wildlife they encounter, while for me it is the resident Kestrel that is the highlight of my daily visits.

THE CHALLENGES

Apart from the debate about the wisdom of buying the field in the first place, the biggest challenge for us was to let go of the stereotypical and conventional land-uses we thought the field had to comply with. We made the decision to break the mould and embark on wilding,

A Kestrel, photographed on the Hughes family field, and the beneficiary of abundant small mammal populations that call the meadow home.

when almost everyone around us advised us against it. We also lacked a clear example of what the outcome might look like and found it impossible to visit a project of this kind in the local area. Nor could we talk to anyone who had gone through the experience. Nevertheless, we went ahead with our wilding project. The field now adds so much enjoyment to our everyday lives, and we are delighted to see our neighbours following our lead and wilding areas of their gardens. From experience, we know they will benefit from an abundance of new and interesting wildlife.

ADVICE AND LEGACY

What started out as little more than a financial venture has evolved into an environmental project that has altered the Hughes family's view of the world around them. With every passing day more wildlife appears and through interactions with our field's plants and animals our knowledge and empathy has grown. Along with a growing conviction that we have done the right thing environmentally. So, our advice to others would be do not be put off by the misconception that a 'wilded' field is scruffy and worthless. Try to look at it in a different light because wildlife will thrive in this varied environment. We feel sure that our sons, who have had so much enjoyment from this land, will continue to drive the ongoing evolution of the project in the future. Our wilded field is our legacy to them.

An oak wood on the edge of Dartmoor
by
Mic Cady, Devon

My wife Julia and I moved to a hamlet on the southern edge of Dartmoor five years ago. At the same time, through a lucky combination of factors, and with the patience and kindness of the then-owners, we were able to buy a nearby woodland of about 13 acres. It is located on a very steep, rocky slope that leads down to one of the Dartmoor-fed rivers. So, it is classic riparian woodland, often now described by ecologists as temperate rainforest.

Its most obvious and notable inhabitants are previously coppiced, multi-stemmed oaks. Some are huge, and their individual stems look like mature trees. From the evidence of fallen limbs, these wonderful and ancient trees were last coppiced (probably for charcoal) between 80 and 100 years ago. As well as the oaks there are stands of Ash (also coppiced in the past), species of birch and willow, Holly, Rowan, (near and alongside the river), Hazel, and many hundreds of self-sown Sycamores; the latter range in age and size from two giants (again, formerly coppiced) to thin saplings.

In spring, the wood is blue with Bluebells, from top to bottom and from side to side. As the season progresses, these are followed by ferns of several species. Buzzards nest in our woodland, Ravens are regular visitors, as are many other species of bird, and Roe Deer call our wood home.

So, it is a beautiful place, and a very special one. That is why we bought it – to love it and protect it for as long as we are able.

WORKING IN THE WOOD

We work in the wood from late summer through to mid-January, when the Bluebells push their noses up and work has to stop in order not to damage them. The work takes two forms: coppicing (that is, cutting down to the ground) of species such as Hazel; and felling Sycamores and willows so as to create glades. This work enables the trees that remain to literally stretch their limbs, and the glades become attractive to insects, bats, birds, and other creatures.

We only use hand tools (including large bow saws), because working with power tools would wreck the magic of the wood as well as reducing the trees to mere commodities. We want to respect the wood itself *for* itself. All of the cut material of whatever size is left on the woodland floor, in stacked piles. We never burn any of it *in situ* (as some coppice workers and others do) as all of it can have benefits for wildlife – from homes for voles and mice, to nesting places for Wrens and Robins. We do remove some of the larger pieces of cut wood for our wood-burning stove, but most will slowly decay in place over the years.

The canopy of the woodland comprises a mosaic of tree species, which contribute to the complexity and diversity of the associated wildlife.

By coppicing, we have re-kindled a tradition that began in the wood hundreds of years before – the earliest references we have to the wood are from 1639 and 1730, where it is described as 'coppice wood'. Coppicing is one of the ultimate sustainable activities – so long as the deer don't eat the regrowth, the stubs will produce multiple new stems that can be coppiced again after a number of years have elapsed. And then the cycle can continue once more, and so on pretty much *ad infinitum*. A single biggish Hazel stub can throw up to 30 or more new stems after coppicing.

You don't need to own a wood like ours to produce a sustainable coppiced 'crop' that could become – for example – plant supports: think pea sticks and bean poles. Even a small garden could have a Hazel grown for such a purpose. Much better that than buying bamboo which originates from goodness knows where. Willow is also good, but is best pollarded (that is, cut at waist or shoulder level). A medium-sized pollarded willow can throw up dozens of dead-straight shoots several metres long every year. You could use these shoots to make dead hedges for wildlife, for shade or privacy, or to create new living hedges simply by pushing them into the ground – many will 'take' and thrive after a year or two.

SHADOWS CAST OVER BEAUTY

As I began writing this, a neighbour started clearing a large area of scrub, Bramble, Hazel and scattered mature trees immediately adjacent to our wood. We knew from past experience that this area had been excellent for birds of many species, and we also knew that Hazel Dormice were present. We did our best to persuade him to stop and leave the land for wildlife, but he was determined to make it suitable for sheep grazing.

My wife and I find this incomprehensible, and profoundly depressing in a time of rapid climate change and ecological catastrophe. We are located within Dartmoor National Park, but that has provided no protection against this habitat destruction. And this is very far from the only example of destruction and wilful ignorance on Dartmoor. It makes us wonder what national parks are actually for, and it makes us fear for other areas adjacent to the wood.

It seems the only option for us is to do our very best for the land in our care and its wildlife, for the duration of our lives. Recent events make us wonder how and why so many other people seem to care so little about the natural world. And, as a result, we wonder what that means for all our futures.

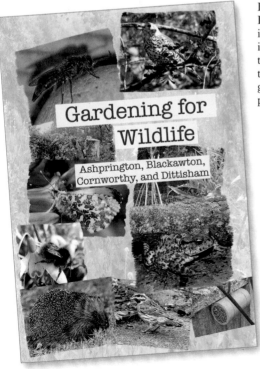

In the South Hams district of Devon, which sits on the fringes of Dartmoor, residents of four parishes have embarked on a project to inform and encourage wildlife recovery and restoration. Their name is **The Habitat Group** and their mission is to improve biodiversity in the local area by developing sustainable habitats, the end goal being the creation of a 'People's National Park' network of nature-friendly gardens and farms. This is a self-help guide they produced, to inspire people and provide practical advice about ways to help wildlife.

The Cirl Bunting is one of many species to benefit from advice offered by The Habitat Group.

Ask Not What Nature Can Do for You, Ask What You Can Do for Nature

Much is made these days about the well-being benefits to people of connecting with nature. However, parodying President John F. Kennedy's inaugural words 'Ask not what your country can do for you – ask what you can do for your country', try turning the narrative on its head and giving it an ecological slant, to make it less about us as individuals and more about environmental concern. If you do, then there is arguably a better chance of securing a sustainable future for the planet along with its habitats, biodiversity, and the health of its human population. Enlightened self-interest or informed environmental empathy, call it what you will.

Translating that aspirational prose into reality is the challenge, but a process in which we can all participate. A cynic might well ask: Why bother? What difference can one person's actions make among a global population of 7.8 billion people and rising? For some, this dispiriting, defeatist argument is enough to make them give up. However, anyone with even a modicum of self-awareness knows there are good choices and bad ones to be made in life. Choose the right paths and we *can* make a difference, big or small and, if nothing else, we can set an example for others to follow and build upon.

There are some for whom nature, wildlife and the environment are anathema, people who are focussed solely on their own lives, and driven by self-interest. I fear there is nothing to be said that will alter their outlooks. At the other end of the spectrum are the informed and enlightened converts who already have a clear idea of what to do. And then there are those in between: people who want to do something to help the environment but don't quite know the route to take; and those that think they are acting in nature's best interest but perhaps are not. This middle ground is where I hope *The Biodiversity Gardener* may have helped by providing inspiration, information and food for thought.

Historical perspective

Turning back the clock, until Galileo Galilei (1564–1642) provided evidence for the heliocentric nature of the Solar System proposed by the likes of Nicolaus Copernicus (1473–1543), conventional wisdom held that the Sun revolved around the Earth. There are parallels between that antiquated world view and many people's blinkered outlook today: the world revolving around themselves. And it is not unique to individuals: what has been termed 'strategic narcissism' can be seen as a manifestation of the same perspective but at a national level. Changing these insular views of the world is at the heart of solving many of the problems that beset the planet and its human inhabitants.

As an unintended consequence of the Covid-19 pandemic, a spotlight was shone on the finest qualities of human nature and endeavour, with humanity's failings being thrown into stark, contrasting relief. By inference, attention was also focussed on how the human race does and should deal with those other self-inflicted crises of our times: habitat destruction, biodiversity loss, pollution (notably plastic), and climate change. Through our use and abuse of the natural world there is good reason to suppose that Covid-19 is a zoonotic disease (one transmitted from animals to humans) and that people unwittingly sparked its genesis. Scaling up, as a species the blame for the planet-wide environmental devastation that has occurred in the last 50 years falls fairly and squarely on our shoulders too. A reasonable conclusion to be drawn is that we continue with our exploitative relationship with wild animals and the natural world at our peril. And our unwillingness to think beyond our own lifespans is putting the future of humanity in jeopardy, as well as that of the planet.

By nature, we are an inventive species and there is an understandable desire to engineer solutions to the manifestations of problems that most directly affect us. However, in the case of Covid-19, by concentrating on vaccinating our way to a safer planet there is a danger we fail to grasp why it happened in the first place, and what we should do to reduce the risk of future pandemics. Turning to climate change, if technology can be developed to capture carbon emissions at source and remove CO_2 from the atmosphere, then the worthy goal of reversing climate change might just be achievable. However, in the absence of that technology, there is a danger that by focussing on carbon and how climatic impacts affect us as humans, we come up with solutions that simply justify continuing our existing, energy-wasteful, biodiversity-destructive lifestyles and we remain blind to the root causes. Furthermore, the race to carbon neutrality, use of carbon credits and the concept of 'offsetting' can sometimes legitimise the continuing abuse and destruction of natural habitats and biodiversity.

The phrase 'No-one's safe until everyone's safe' is as relevant to habitat destruction, biodiversity loss and climate change as it is to global pandemic resolution. We all live on the same planet, a finite world with finite resources. Talking of which, Easter Island is sometimes cited as a case study of a disaster caused by unbridled environmental exploitation in a closed system, one that led to unsustainable ecological degradation and a dismal tally of plant and animal extinctions. Whatever the precise cause of the catastrophe – habitat destruction pure and simple or a plague of introduced Polynesian Rats – the inescapable reality is that Easter Island's ecosystem was wrecked as a consequence of human settlement, and the lives of surviving inhabitants were degraded as a result. Bizarrely, it has been argued that this self-inflicted environmental catastrophe is a success story in human terms, the argument being that people's ingenuity allowed them to survive a disaster of their own making. I don't see it that way.

The early residents of Easter Island had the excuse of ignorance. We do not. Scaling up, the United Kingdom is an island nation that inexorably is heading on the same environmental trajectory as Easter Island. And planet Earth is also a closed system with (energy from the Sun apart) finite resources. By combining increased consumption with a reliance on unsustainable economic growth, you have the ingredients needed for a disaster mirroring Easter Island but on a global scale.

Contrasting visions for the future of Brazil's Amazon. On the left, one that is insanely destructive and ultimately self-destructive, while on the right, another advocated by anyone with even a modicum of environmental respect, not to mention enlightened self-interest. But before we in the UK rush to criticise too harshly, remember that our ancestors cut down almost all our primary forest millennia ago. And wilful habitat destruction continues to this day on our watch – just think about HS2.

Add to that eye-watering human population growth and the problem can only get worse and harder to solve. Perhaps it is time for an evidence-based revision of the advice in Genesis 1:28: 'Be fruitful and multiply and fill the earth and subdue it'.

Human ingenuity and energy efficiency measures could conceivably come to the rescue and allow our species to engineer a solution to its own survival on a dying planet. But at what cost? Probably the wholesale degradation and destruction of the natural world if current economic policies are the driving forces. Along with an insidious erosion of the quality of human life too. As a species, perhaps we need to ask ourselves an existential question: Do we exist merely to consume? Assuming the answer is 'no' (and not 'I shop, therefore I am') then far better surely if human ingenuity was oriented towards planetary survival with a sense of global community? And recognition of our roles both as a problem and as part of the solution.

Stating the obvious, without solving the issues that beset humanity (inequalities, poverty and the rest) at the global level, we will never resolve the planetary environmental problems caused by our species. To do this you have to consider everyone on the planet. It's all very well preaching from a position of relative ease in the wealthy UK. But it's hard to convince somebody in the developing world when their concerns relate to how they can put any food or water on the table as opposed to whether what they eat is organic or which brand of supermarket they choose to make deliveries.

Human actions are behind most of the ills that face the environment, and human nature can sometimes be a fundamental stumbling block when it comes to conservation. Although harmonious cooperation does exist in the sector, there are examples where special interest groups in particular work in splendid isolation from one another. And there are instances where potential allies are at odds, fragile egos and blinkered, narrow-minded outlooks fomenting 'my way or no way' attitudes. When environmental cooperation turns to factional conflict then conservation is the loser. If the fight to save beleaguered wildlife is seen as battle with opposing sides, had those forces driving biodiversity loss initiated a divide-and-rule 'black ops' strategy, it could hardly have been more successful. So, the irony is that the conservation world often divides and fails of its own accord without the need for any external influence. Add to this an inability, present in all of us,

to recognise that often we don't know enough to realise how little we know. Taken as a whole, the result is that human nature can sometimes be nature's worst enemy.

Autumn 2022 saw announcements from a new UK government signalling the desire to dismantle sections of long-standing, recent and agreed future environmental legislation. At the time of writing, it is impossible to unpick true motives and intent from rhetoric, and the final outcome is uncertain. However, an unintended consequence of the conservation consternation caused by the news means this dark cloud might have a silver lining. It appears environmental detractors have unwittingly unleashed the catalyst that finally unites disparate factions for the greater good of nature conservation. They are unified by the sense that this really is an unprecedented attack on nature.

If the conservation sector does not protest effectively enough, and environmental legislation is altered, I

My garden is a tiny island in a rising tide of wildlife impoverishment, and such is the case in many other parts of the world. As an example, take a look at Brufut Woods in The Gambia on Google Earth. The site is a wonderful reserve but a represents a tiny fragment of the forest that once cloaked West Africa. It is surrounded on all sides by increasingly intensive agriculture and encroaching development. Nevertheless, somehow avian gems such as this Northern Red Bishop still survive, amidst the sea of plastic rubbish that surrounds Brufut. For now, at least.

This vision of hell on earth was taken in Kazakhstan a few years ago. As we drove past the belching chimneys my minder, who had a gallows sense of humour, told me to hold my breath because this was where they extracted the country's uranium. I laughed nervously and wondered whether there was some truth in what he was saying, since Kazakhstan is reckoned to hold 12 percent of the world's uranium ore and is the largest producer of the element in its refined form. How many more generations will it take before an obsession with economic growth at any environmental cost mean investment zones in the UK look like this? Surely, even the most hardened of environmental detractors would concede that would be no way to run a country, let alone a planet.

doubt the beneficiaries of change will be wildlife. More likely I fear, it will be those who champion unfettered and unregulated growth: those who want to exploit our portion of planet Earth and regard current environmental legislation as an obstacle that stands in their way. Make no mistake, there are and always will be influential forces lurking in the background who see the environment and those who advocate on its behalf as the enemy. Personally, I am all for growth, growth and more growth. But green growth, literally and metaphorically. Growth in environmental awareness. Growth in biodiversity that leads to a healthier environment. And growth that

results in a sustainable future for the planet's human population. Not short-sighted and short-term economic growth achieved at the expense of the environment.

Returning to Copernicus, among this polymath's many achievements were economic theories. Perhaps what planet Earth needs most right now is a renaissance intellect and communicator suited to our times, and an economic model that reins in our more barbarous tendencies while allowing what's most creative about humanity to flourish. Someone and something to usher in a new Age of Enlightenment, one tailored to the twenty-first century and the needs of our sickly planet.

Synergy

Saving what's left of British wildlife and restoring what's lost will require a range of different approaches, each one of which has its merits. At the grand end of the spectrum are wilding or rewilding landscape-scale projects where there is a realistic prospect of creating genuine climax vegetation wilderness, and where finances are in place to ensure that it remains in that state. Inspirational and instrumental in this approach becoming accepted and adopted is of course the Knepp Estate and Isabella Tree's influential book

Wilding: The Return of Nature to a British Farm (see the References section for details).

For all its virtues, rewilding still requires a vision of the desired ecological outcome and an informed ability to balance the benefits of adopting the approach in a given location against any environmental losses that might occur. The process by which rewilding is achieved also needs to be considered. Take, for example, an area of upland moorland. If undertaken indiscriminately, planting trees has the potential to damage critical bog communities of plants and affect nesting habitats for breeding waders. In that instance, better surely to allow native trees to colonise naturally by reducing grazing pressure and reversing or eliminating the damage done to uplands through drainage and intentional burning. Understanding the local environment and its natural history, along with a vision of the end goal, are the keys to nuanced and successful rewilding projects.

While my biodiversity gardening approach has the best interests of native wildlife at heart, it is not an attempt at rewilding. It has required an awareness and acceptance of the role that historical land-use played in creating the unintentionally wildlife-rich habitats that I knew in my youth, and whose biodiversity I value. In my case, the vision was not to restore the forested climax community that would have dominated the scene in the absence of man. In natural history terms I have attempted to turn back the clock a few centuries and nurture the mosaic of man-influenced habitats that gave rise to local biodiversity in the first place. What my garden has achieved is a celebration of native wildlife. However, more importantly it serves as a biodiversity hotspot from which re-colonisation of the surrounding countryside might occur under the guardianship of more sympathetic future generations of landowners.

There is overlap of course between all these approaches, and tales from Brazil's Atlantic rainforest give cause for hope. Here, under the right stewardship formerly wrecked, deforested land is recovering not only in terms of tree cover but also the abundance and range of wildlife it formerly hosted. The recovery and recolonisation did not arise spontaneously but came from tiny pockets of forest that had escaped the ravages of man.

The role that farming plays in biodiversity loss, and its potential for stemming the tide, cannot be ignored. I do not have the answer to how the latter might be achieved but instinctively I feel that poisoning the land and intentionally minimising wildlife diversity with the emphasis solely on food production is neither beneficial for the environment nor sustainable in the long term. However, while economic forces – a profit motive and a demand on the part of consumers for cheap food – continue to drive the process I cannot foresee change. Long term, all would benefit if feeding the nation and food security were meaningfully integrated with the

An additional tool in the conservation armoury is the small-scale, habitat-oriented approach that I have adopted, one that might loosely fall under the descriptive umbrella of biodiversity gardening.

conservation of those species that can live in a farmed landscape, instead of a situation where agriculture takes priority over the environment. Rather than having an adversarial relationship with nature, perhaps a biologically rich and productive environment should take centre stage, for moral reasons, as plain common sense, and with an eye to the legacy we leave for future generations of wildlife, people included.

Underpinning all of the above is education. It would help obviously if environmental awareness and a grounded understanding of the complexity and inter-relatedness of life on Earth were a compulsory part of our education system. Failing that, it needs informed individuals who can communicate and engage with willing audiences and help shape their attitudes and resolve. And advocates who are able to tackle detractors head-on and unflinchingly.

What's to be done?

Solving the problems that beset planet Earth is a process not an event. In theory no problem is insurmountable, and we can all do our bit to help. Armed with this knowledge, shame on us if we do nothing or the wrong thing. If the statement that heads this chapter, 'Ask not what nature can do for you – ask what you can do for nature', is framed as a question, perhaps a starting point should be 'Treat it with the respect it deserves'. Even if you have no prospect of owning land, you can still do your bit. Perhaps volunteer to help others who do manage land, be they individuals or charities. However, perhaps the most significant thing you can do is to give money to larger organisations that buy land and manage it for wildlife. Personally, in this regard I would only consider bodies that also manage human access. In the context of the UK, the RSPB is the only real contender, while for work abroad that might mean the World Land Trust. With access to land that remains rich in wildlife comes responsibility. Not the right to ruin.

Given my misgivings about governments of any hue, and the factional and sometimes competing strands within conservation, I fear that existing systems and organisations are not fit for purpose when it comes to protection of the environment as a whole. A few more Anders Holch Povlsens wouldn't go amiss, rather than ego-driven billionaires and developing nations seeking immortality through space exploration. So, here's an invitation to anyone reading this with an environmental conscience and a deep pocket. Perhaps what the UK could do with in the short term is a new and entirely independent conservation organisation, whose remit is to advise and advocate on all aspects of the environment and champion its wildlife. One that through evidence can challenge preconceptions, unite factions in the conservation world, speak truth to power when it comes to government policy, and influence change. And perhaps equally importantly, an organisation that can serve as a one-stop shop, citizen's advice bureau equivalent for individuals who want to help the environment and wildlife at the local level; one that offers advice and, more importantly, support for anyone concerned with managing land appropriately for wildlife and safeguarding biodiversity-rich habitats for the future. And let's not forget advocacy when it comes to challenging the planning system and fighting habitat destruction via legal routes. As a suggestion for a name, how about *The Nature Conservancy Council*?

Throughout my lifetime, I have watched the environment of north Hampshire, specifically the borough of Basingstoke, being eroded, with formerly wildlife-rich habitats degraded or destroyed and species driven to local extinction in the name of profit and progress. Unsurprisingly, researching the background to *The Biodiversity Gardener* was often as depressing as it was illuminating. However, I was able to draw some positive things from the processes of allowing my biodiversity garden to flourish and from writing the book. The journey opened my eyes and educated me. I hope readers will benefit from my experiences and that the book encourages others to follow the path I have travelled.

The Biodiversity Gardener is not an attempt to brag about the wildlife in my garden. Instead, the intention is to open the eyes of others to the sheer abundance and variety of life that could and should exist in the English countryside, and the potential for maximising biodiversity on their doorsteps. By keeping a photographic record of my journey, I have tried to convey the sense of wonder and privilege I feel when I encounter the natural world. In addition to raising awareness of the potential lifeline that biodiversity gardens offer for the future of British wildlife, I hope the book will also encourage readers to expand their horizons. And reach the following conclusions. If all that wildlife can be found in one small garden, how much more natural wonder must there be out there in the big, wide world? And if all that wildlife can be fostered in a half-acre plot, how much more could be achieved with a few acres, or a few hundred acres?

For me, the natural world makes life worth living. With all that's going on in the world, sometimes it's the only thing that makes life worth living. Hopefully, *The Biodiversity Gardener* has conveyed a sense of how privileged we all are to live on planet Earth; and how inter-related and inter-dependent all elements of the natural world are, ourselves included. Let's not see ourselves as separate and detached from the environment but instead afford respect and rights to all life on earth – be that plants, animals or our fellow humans. Biodiversity gardening is one small step in the direction of achieving that ambition.

References

FURTHER READING

Beebee, T. J. C. (2022). *Impacts of Human Population on Wildlife – A British Perspective*. Cambridge University Press.

Blackman, R. L. (1974). *Aphids (Invertebrate Types)*. Ginn & Company Ltd, London and Aylesbury.

Bonham-Carter, V. (1971). *The Survival of the English Countryside*. Hodder & Stoughton Ltd, London.

British Wildlife. The magazine for the modern naturalist. NHBS Ltd.

Carson, R. (1962). *Silent Spring*. Houghton Mifflin, Boston and New York.

Cassidy, A. (2019). *Vermin, Victims and Disease*. Palgrave Macmillan, London.

Clark, J. F. M. (2009). *Bugs and the Victorians*. Yale University Press, New Haven and London.

Darwin, C. (1881). *The Formation of Vegetable Mould Through the Action of Worms, with Observations on their Habits*. John Murray, London.

Finberg, H. P. R. (editor). (1972). *The Agrarian History of England and Wales*, volume 1, part 2: A.D. 43–1042 (specifically the chapter on Roman Britain by S. Applebaum). Cambridge University Press.

Fox, R. T., & R. B. Hall. (1979). *The Clay Tobacco Pipes of the Portsmouth Harbour Region 1680–1932*. Self-published.

Goulson, D. (2021). *Silent Earth: Averting the Insect Apocalypse*. Vintage, London.

Goulson, D. (2021). *Gardening for Bumblebees: A Practical Guide to Creating a Paradise for Pollinators*. Vintage.

Goulson, D. (2019). *The Garden Jungle: or Gardening to Save the Planet*. Vintage.

Goulson, D. (2014). *A Buzz in the Meadow*. Picador, New York.

Helm, D. (2019). *Green and Prosperous Land: A Blueprint for Rescuing the British Countryside*. William Collins, London.

Jones, E. L. (2021). *Landscape History and Rural Society in Southern England – An Economic and Environmental Perspective*. Palgrave Macmillan, London.

Maclean, N. (editor) (2010). *Silent Summer*. Cambridge University Press.

Magalotti, L. (1821). *Travels of Cosmo the Third, Grand Duke of Tuscany, Through England During the Reign of King Charles the Second (1669): Translation, From the Italian Manuscript in the Laurentian Library at Florence, to Which is Prefixed, a Memoir of His Life*. Viewable at archive.org and available as a facsimile copy via online searches.

Monbiot, G. (2022). *Regenesis: Feeding the World without Devouring the Planet*. Allen Lane / Penguin, London.

Monbiot, G. (2013). *Feral: Rewilding the Land, the Sea, and Human Life*. Allen Lane / Penguin.

Orwell, G. (1946). *Some Thoughts on the Common Toad*. Tribune, London.

Orwell, G. (1939). *Coming Up for Air*. Victor Gollancz, London.

Owen, J. A. & G. S. Boulger. (1907). *The Country Month by Month*. Duckworth & Co., London.

Shoard, M. (1980). *The Theft of the Countryside*. Temple Smith, London.

Spooner, B., and P. Roberts. (2005). *Fungi*. Collins New Naturalist Library 96. Collins, London.

Stace, C. (2019). *New Flora of the British Isles*, 4th edition. C & M Floristics.

Stokes, E. (Applin, B. & B. Applin, editors). (2008). *The Making of Basingstoke, from Prehistory to the Present Day*. Basingstoke Archaeological and Historical Society.

Thirsk, J. (1997). *Alternative Agriculture – A History from the Black Death to the Present Day*. Oxford University Press.

Thirsk, J. (general editor) & S. Piggot (editor). (1981). *The Agrarian History of England and Wales*, volume I, part I: *Prehistory*. Cambridge University Press.

Thomas, J., and R. Lewington (illustrator). (2010). *The Butterflies of Britain and Ireland*. Revised edition. British Wildlife Publishing, Totnes, Devon.

Tree, I. (2019). *Wilding: The Return of Nature to a British Farm*. Pan MacMillan, London.

Uglow, J. (2004). *A Little History of British Gardening*. Chatto & Windus, London.

Vale, R., and B. Vale. (2009). *Time to Eat the Dog? The Real Guide to Sustainable Living*. Thames & Hudson, London.

Vesey-Fitzgerald, B. (1953). *British Birds and Their Nests* – A Ladybird Senior. Wills & Hepworth Ltd, Loughborough.

Vesey-Fitzgerald, B. (1954). *A Second Book of British Birds and Their Nests* – A Ladybird Senior. Wills & Hepworth Ltd.

Vesey-Fitzgerald, B. (1956). *A Third Book of British Birds and Their Nests* – A Ladybird Senior. Wills & Hepworth Ltd.

Vesey-Fitzgerald, B. S. (1969). *The Vanishing Wild Life of Britain*. MacGibbon & Kee Ltd, London.

Watkins, C. (1990). *Woodland Management and Conservation*. Britain's Ancient Woodland (series). David & Charles, Exeter.

Willes, M. (2014). *The Gardens of the British Working Class*. Yale University Press, New Haven and London.

Wood, Rev. J. G., & T. Wood. (1886). *The Field Naturalist's Handbook* (4th edition). Cassell & Company, Limited: London, Paris, New York and Melbourne.

ACADEMIC AND POPULAR REFERENCES

Albery, A. (1999). 'Agriculture and wildlife conservation: accident or design?' *British Wildlife* 11, no.1: 10–16.

Albery, A. (2011). 'Woodland management in Hampshire 900 to 1815.' *Rural History* 22, no. 2: 159–81.

Alexander, K., T. Green, and J. Butler (2006). 'The value of different tree and shrub species to wildlife.' *British Wildlife* 18, no.1: 18–28.

Broughton, R. K., J. D. Shutt, and A. C. Lees. (2022). 'Rethinking bird feeding – are we putting extra pressure on some struggling woodland birds?' *British Birds* 115, no. 1: 2–6.

Cassidy, A. (2019). 'How the Badger Became Tuberculous.' In: *Vermin, Victims and Disease*. Palgrave Macmillan, Cham.

Compton, S. G. and R. S. Key. (2000). '*Coincya wrightii* (O. E. Schulz) Stace (*Rhynchosinapis wrightii* (O.E. Schulz) Dandy ex A. R. Clapham).' *Journal of Ecology* 88, no. 3: 535–47.

Fuller, R. M. (1987). 'The changing extent of conservation interest of lowland grassland in England and Wales: A review of grassland surveys 1930–1984.' *Biological Conservation* 40, no. 4: 281–300.

Grant, M. (2000). 'The Alien Benedictine Priory of Monk Sherborne, Hampshire from the twelfth to the fifteenth centuries.' *Hampshire Studies: Proceedings of the Hampshire Field Club and Archaeological Society* 55: 46–67.

Groome, G., J. Denton, and P. Smith (2018). 'The impact of dogs on the environment.' *In Practice* 40.

Kahn, P. H., Jr., and T. Weiss (2017). 'The importance of children interacting with Big Nature.' *Children, Youth and Environments* 27, no. 2: 7–24.

Milne, G. (2022). 'What can archaeology & woodland history tell us about growing more trees?' *British Archaeology*, May/June 2022.

Okin, G. S. (2017). 'Environmental impacts of food consumption by dogs and cats.' *PLoS ONE* 12, no. 8: e0181301. https://doi.org/10.1371/journal.pone.0181301

Perkins, R., M. Whitehead, W. Civil and D. Goulson (2020). 'Potential role of veterinary flea products in widespread pesticide contamination of English rivers.' *Science of The Total Environment* 755, part 1: 143560.

Shutt, J., and A. Lees (2022). 'Why do we feed our garden birds?' *Birdwatch*, April 2022.

Southwood, T. R. E. (1961). 'Number of species of insect associated with various trees.' *Journal of Animal Ecology* 30, no. 1: 1–8.

Stanbury, A., M. Eaton, N. Aebischer, D. Balmer, A. Brown, A. Douse, P. Lindley, N. McCulloch, D. Noble, and I. Win (2021). 'The status of our bird populations: the fifth Birds of Conservation Concern in the United Kingdom, Channel Islands and Isle of Man and second IUCN Red List assessment of extinction risk for Great Britain.' *British Birds* 114: 723–47. Available online at https://britishbirds.co.uk/content/status-our-bird-populations.

Woods, M., R. A. McDonald, and S. Harris. (1997). *Domestic Cat Predation on Wildlife*. The Mammal Society.

ONLINE RESOURCES

Amphibians

Toad decline – Froglife article https://www.froglife.org/2018/03/23/amphibian-and-reptile-declines-uk-perspective/

Toad patrolling – Froglife article https://www.froglife.org/what-we-do/toads-on-roads/how-to-become-a-toad-patroller/

Birds

Bird Papillomavirus: Lawson, B., R. A. Robinson, J. R. R. Fernandez, et al. (2018.) 'Spatio-temporal dynamics and aetiology of proliferative leg skin lesions in wild British finches.' *Scientific Reports* 8: 14670. https://www.nature.com/articles/s41598-018-32255-y

Burns, F., M. A. Eaton, D. E. Balmer, A. Banks, et al., (2020). *The State of the UK's Birds 2020*. RSPB, BTO, WWT, DAERA, JNCC, NatureScot, NE and NRW, Sandy, Bedfordshire. (2020). https://www.rspb.org.uk/contentassets/8d123c9a8487449ca36293c6e0e57379/state-of-uk-birds-2020-report-download-16-12-2020.pdf

Trichomonosis: Rijks, J. M., A. A. G. Laumen, R. Slaterus, et al. (2019). 'Trichomonosis in Greenfinches (*Chloris chloris*) in the Netherlands 2009–2017: A Concealed Threat." *Frontiers in Veterinary Science* 6: 425. https://www.frontiersin.org/articles/10.3389/fvets.2019.00425/full

Conservation and biodiversity loss

The State of Nature Conservation Authors: Hayhow, D. B., M. A. Eaton, A. J. Stanbury, et al. (2019). *The State of Nature 2019*. The State of Nature partnership. Available as an online download.

Habitat for wildlife

Green space in Urban areas: 'UK natural capital: ecosystem accounts for urban areas.' Census2021, Office for National Statistics. https://www.ons.gov.uk/economy/environmentalaccounts/bulletins/uknaturalcapital/urbanaccounts#:~:text=Approximately%20520%20thousand%20hectares%20of,to%20residential%20gardens%20(30.1%25).

Overton Biodiversity Society (2006). 'A Study of Local Hedgerows'. https://www.overton-biodiversity.org/resources/docs/obs-hedgerows.pdf

Plantlife advice on roadside verge best practice: https://www.plantlife.org.uk/application/files/3315/7063/5411/Managing_grassland_road_verges_Singles.pdf

Rotherham roadside verges: Forrest, Adele. (2019.) 'The story behind Rotherham's bloomin' lovely 'River of Colour.' *Rotherham Advertiser*. https://www.rotherhamadvertiser.co.uk/leisure/view,feature-the-story-behind-rotherhams-bloomin-lovely-river-of-colour_32425.htm

Trees, shrubs and wildlife: Alexander, K., J. Butler and T. Green. 'The value of tree and shrub species to wildlife.' Latest News, The Arboricultural Association. Last updated 21/07/2021. https://www.trees.org.uk/News-Blog/Latest-News/The-value-of-tree-and-shrub-species-to-wildlife

Warwickshire County Council. 'Scientific evidence for habitat creation and restoration.' https://api.warwickshire.gov.uk/documents/WCCC-863-794

Insects

Fipronil – Buglife online article. (2020.) 'New research reveals widespread contamination of English rivers with potent pesticides commonly used as flea treatments for pets.' https://www.buglife.org.uk/news/new-research-reveals-widespread-contamination-of-english-rivers-with-potent-pesticides-commonly-used-as-flea-treatments-for-pets/

UK Butterfly Monitoring Scheme https://ukbms.org/

Mammals

Hedgehogs and the Outer Hebrides – NatureScot article https://www.nature.scot/professional-advice/land-and-sea-management/managing-wildlife/uist-wader-research

Pets

Martens, P., B. Su, and S. Deblomme (2019). 'The ecological paw print of companion dogs and cats.' *BioScience* 69, no. 6: 467–74. https://doi.org/10.1093/biosci/biz044

Woods, M., R. A. McDonald, and S. Harris (2003). 'Predation of wildlife by domestic cats *Felis catus*.' *Mammal Review* 33, no. 2: 174–88. https://www.uvm.edu/rsenr/wfb175/Cat%20Predation%20Woods%20et%20al.pdf

Plants

Buglife's Ragwort background information: 'Ragwort: Noxious weed or precious wildflower?' https://www.buglife.org.uk/sites/default/files/Ragwort.pdf

Code of Practice on How to Prevent the spread of Ragwort http://www.defra.gov.uk/publications/files/pb9840-cop-ragwort.pdf

Ragwort Facts: 'Ragwort – a UK Scientific Perspective.' https://www.ragwortfacts.com/

Thomas, P. A., M. El-Barghathi, A. Polwart. (2011). 'Biological Flora of the British Isles: *Euonymus europaeus* L.' *Journal of Ecology* 99, 345 (2011). https://besjournals.onlinelibrary.wiley.com/doi/full/10.1111/j.1365-2745.2010.01760.x

Pollution and Waste

FAO and UNEP (2021). *Global Assessment of Soil Pollution: Report*. Food and Agriculture Association of the United Nations, Rome.https://www.fao.org/3/cb4894en/online/cb4894en.html

Food Waste in the UK – House of Lords report https://lordslibrary.parliament.uk/food-waste-in-the-uk/

Monitoring Freshwater: Biggs, J., E. McGoff, N. Ewald, P. Williams, F. Dunn, and P. Nicolet (2016). *Clean Water for Wildlife Technical Manual. Evaluating PackTest nitrate and phosphate test kits to find clean water and assess the extent of pollution*. Freshwater Habitats Trust, Oxford. https://freshwaterhabitats.org.uk/wp-content/uploads/2015/10/CWfWTechnicalDocumentFINAL.pdf

USEFUL ORGANISATIONS AND WEBSITES

Amphibian and Reptile Conservation – a charity committed to conserving amphibians and reptiles and saving the disappearing habitats on which they depend. arc-trust.org

Berkshire, Buckinghamshire and Oxfordshire Wildlife Trust (BBOWT)–planningadvice.bbowt.org.uk/wildlife/planning-advice

Birds on the Brink – a grant-awarding conservation charity that receives funding from the international competition Bird Photographer of the Year. birdsonthebrink.co.uk

Botanical Society of Britain and Ireland (BSBI) – our leading botanical charity, concerned with the study, distribution and conservation of wild plants. bsbi.org

British Dragonfly Society – dedicated to the study, identification and conservation of British dragonflies and damselflies. british-dragonflies.org.uk

British Lichen Society – promoting the study and conservation of lichens and their habitats. britishlichensociety.org

British Mycological Society – an organisation that supports the study of all aspects of fungal science. britmycolsoc.org.uk

British Myriapod and Isopod Group (BMIG) – an organisation that aims to promote awareness and knowledge of centipedes, millipedes, myriapods and isopods. www.bmig.org.uk

British Trust for Ornithology (BTO) – an organisation devoted to the study or birds in the British Isles. bto.org

Buglife – an invertebrate conservation charity, dedicated to the study of invertebrates, and that campaigns and educates on their behalf. buglife.org.uk

Butterfly Conservation – an environmental charity dedicated to conserving butterflies, moths and their environment. butterfly-conservation.org

Conchological Society of Great Britain and Ireland – a society dedicated to the study of British snails and slugs. conchsoc.org

ClientEarth – an environmental charity that uses the law to create powerful change to protect life on Earth. clientearth.org

DEFRA MagicMap – a mapping system with detailed environmental information. Magic.defra.gov.uk/magicmap.aspx

Earthworm Society of Britain – a society that promotes research on and conservation of earthworms and their environment. earthwormsoc.org.uk

Environment Agency – water quality monitoring information. environment.data.gov.uk/water-quality/view/explore

Field Studies Council – an organisation whose aim is to help people learn about the environment so they make informed choices about how best to protect it. field-studies-council.org

Freshwater Habitats Trust – a charity working to conserve freshwater wildlife and habitats. freshwaterhabitats.org.uk

Froglife – a charity committed to the conservation of amphibians and reptiles, and their environment. froglife.org

Hantsmoths – a website devoted to the lepidoptera of Hampshire and the Isle of Wight, with background information and photographs of almost all British species. Similar websites exist for many other counties. hantsmoths.org.uk

iRecord – a website that helps you manage and share wildlife sightings. irecord.org.uk

iSpot – an online community that helps identify and record nature. ispotnature.org

Lacewings and Allies Recording Scheme – a scheme that covers the following orders, with background information and photographs: Neuroptera, Megaloptera, Raphidioptera and Mecoptera of the British Isles. lacewings.myspecies.info

Mammal Society – an organisation dedicated to the study and conservation of British mammals. mammal.org.uk

NatureSpot – a record of the wildlife of Leicestershire and Rutland but much more than that: a wide-ranging natural history resource of images and background information that is relevant to much of lowland England. naturespot.org.uk

Orthopterists' Society – a recording scheme for grasshoppers, bush-crickets, crickets and related insects, with lots of background information. orthsoc.org

People's Trust for Endangered Species (PTES) – an organisation that stands up for wildlife, and in particular endangered species. ptes.org

Plantlife – a wild plant conservation charity, whose remit extends to fungi. plantlife.org.uk

National Biodiversity Network (NBN) – a collaboration that collects and shares biodiversity information via a range of media, including the online NBN Atlas, their data-search website. nbn.org.uk

Natural England – a non-departmental public body in the United Kingdom sponsored by the Department for Environment, Food and Rural Affairs, and the government's advisor for the natural environment in England. naturalengland.org.uk

NatureScot – the public body responsible for Scotland's natural heritage. nature.scot

Royal Society for the Protection of Birds (RSPB) – the most important bird conservation charity in the UK and arguably the most powerful and influential independent conservation body. rspb.org.uk

Soil Association – the UK's leading organic food and farming charity. soilassociation.org

Spider and Harvestman Recording Scheme – including background information on and photographs of the group. srs.britishspiders.org.uk/portal.php

UK Butterflies – a website full of information about British butterflies, including their life cycles. ukbutterflies.co.uk

UK Moths – an online guide to the moths of Great Britain and Ireland. ukmoths.org.uk

Natural Resources Wales – sponsored by the Welsh Government, the body responsible for the environment, including nature conservation, in Wales. naturalresources.wales

The Wildlife Trusts – a federation of independent wildlife conservation charities, organised mainly by county. wildlifetrusts.org

List of species

MAMMALS

Badger *Meles meles* 266, 276, 336, 338
Bank Vole *Myodes glareolus* 117, 268, 270, 271
Brandt's Bat *Myotis brandtii* 275
Brown Hare *Lepus europaeus* 265
Brown Long-eared Bat *Plecotus auritus* 272, 275, 276
Brown Rat *Rattus norvegicus* 253, 268
Common Pipistrelle *Pipistrellus pipistrellus* 275, 276
Common Shrew *Sorex araneus* 264
Cat *Felis catus* 244, 268, 276–278
Dog *Canis (lupus) familiaris* 39, 262, 276–281
Fallow Deer *Dama dama* 262
Fox *Vulpes vulpes* 270, 276
Grey Squirrel *Sciurus carolinensis* 253, 268, 270
Harvest Mouse *Micromys minutus* 55, 267–269
Hazel Dormouse *Muscardinus avellanarius* 91, 104, 202, 250, 251, 253, 267–270, 310, 311, 321, 322, 324, 325, 327, 328, 331, 332
Hedgehog *Erinaceus europaeus* 224, 246, 263, 264, 266, 336
Mole *Talpa europaea* 87, 118, 263, 306
Muntjac *Muntiacus reevesi* 262, 276
Natterer's Bat *Myotis nattereri* 275, 276
Noctule *Nyctalus noctula* 275, 276
Otter *Lutra lutra* 266, 282
Polecat *Mustela putorius* 266
Pygmy Shrew *Sorex minutus* 117, 264
Rabbit *Oryctolagus cuniculus* 83, 265, 276, 278
Roe Deer *Capreolus capreolus* 262, 276, 339
Serotine *Eptesicus serotinus* 275, 276
Short-tailed Vole *Microtus agrestis* 67, 69
Soprano Pipistrelle *Pipistrellus pygmaeus* 275, 276
Stoat *Mustela erminea* 67, 264, 265
Water Shrew *Neomys fodiens* 265
Water Vole *Arvicola amphibius* 25, 230, 268, 277, 322
Weasel *Mustela nivalis* 67, 255, 265
Western Barbastelle *Barbastella barbastellus* 275, 276, 332
Whiskered Bat *Myotis mystacinus* 275
Wood Mouse *Apodemus sylvaticus* 266, 267, 270
Yellow-necked Mouse *Apodemus flavicollis* 266, 267, 270

BIRDS

Barn Owl *Tyto alba* 38, 69, 302, 338
Blackbird *Turdus merula* 99, 121, 230, 259, 261
Blackcap *Sylvia atricapilla* 38, 99, 100, 168, 249, 260
Blue Tit *Cyanites caeruleus* 168, 250–252, 260
Bullfinch *Pyrrhula pyrrhula* 260
Buzzard *Buteo buteo* 69, 339
Carrion Crow *Corvus corone* 259, 261
Chaffinch *Fringilla coelebs* 252, 253, 260
Chiffchaff *Phylloscopus collybita* 13, 100, 120, 260
Cirl Bunting *Emberiza cirlus* 340
Coal Tit *Periparus ater* 38, 260
Collared Dove *Streptopelia decaocto* 261
Corn Bunting *Emberiza calandra* 38, 39, 248
Corncrake *Crex crex* 72
Cuckoo *Cuculus canorus* 248, 259
Dartford Warbler *Sylvia undata* 44
Dunlin *Calidris alpina* 263, 279–281
Dunnock *Prunella modularis* 99, 259, 260
Feral Pigeon *Columba livia* 261
Fieldfare *Turdus pilaris* 38, 248
Goldcrest *Regulus regulus* 38, 120, 202, 260
Goldfinch *Carduelis carduelis* 59, 69, 249, 260
Great Spotted Woodpecker *Dendrocopus major* 38, 109, 207, 249
Great Tit *Parus major* 38, 250–252, 260
Green Woodpecker *Picus viridis* 87, 249
Greenfinch *Chloris chloris* 252, 260
Grey Partridge *Perdix perdix* 9, 19, 85, 248
Grey Wagtail *Motacilla cinerea* 230, 248
House Martin *Delichon urbicum* 247, 253, 260
House Sparrow *Passer domesticus* 248, 253, 255, 256, 260
Jay *Garrulus glandarius* 102, 248, 253, 258, 259, 261, 283
Kestrel *Falco tinunculus* 69, 338
Kingfisher *Alcedo atthis* 44, 230
Lapwing *Vanellus vanellus* 23, 39, 248, 263, 322
Lesser Spotted Woodpecker *Dendrocopus minor* 248, 250
Linnet *Linaria cannabina* 59, 69
Long-tailed Tit *Aegithalos caudatus* 100, 260
Magpie *Pica pica* 259, 261

BUTTERFLIES

TRUE BUGS

TRUE FLIES

INSECT ALSO-RANS

Cockroaches

Earwigs

Lacewings

Snakeflies

Scorpionflies

Mayflies

Caddisflies

Stoneflies

Alderflies

SPIDERS AND ALLIES

CENTIPEDES AND MILLPEDES

Centipedes

Millipedes

plantains *Plantago* spp. 130, 163

Primrose *Primula vulgaris* 162, 287

Purple Loosestrife *Lythrum salicaria* 66

Pyramidal Orchid *Anacamptis pyramidalis* 57

Ragged-robin *Lychnis flos-cuculi* 54

Rhododendron *Rhododendron ponticum* 105, 285

Rigid Hornwort *Ceratophyllum demersum* 113

Rosebay Willowherb *Chamaenerion angustifolium* 162, 171

Rough Hawkbit *Leontodon hispidus* 61

Sea Spurge *Euphorbia paralias* 66

sedges *Carex* spp. 126, 229

Selfheal *Prunella vulgaris* 61, 286

Sheep's Sorrel *Rumex acetosella* 80, 82

Small Scabious *Scabiosa columbaria* 63

Snowdrop *Galanthus nivalis* 108, 284

sorrels *Rumex* spp. 163

Southern Marsh-orchid *Dactylorhiza praetermissa* 54

Spear Thistle *Cirsium vulgare* 64, 287

stitchworts *Stellaria* spp. 163

Summer Snowflake *Leucojum aestivum* 284

Tufted Vetch *Vicia cracca* 61, 119, 174, 287

Variegated Yellow Archangel *Limiastrum galeobdolon* ssp. *argentatum* 284

violets *Viola* spp. 154

Wall Bedstraw *Galium parisense* 197

water-lilies *Nuphar* spp. 229

water-lilies *Nymphaea* spp. 229

water-lilies *Nymphoides* spp. 229

water-starworts *Callitriche* spp. 229, 245

Water-violet *Hottonia palustris* 54

White Dead-nettle *Lamium album* 163

White Water-lily *Nymphaea alba* 229

Wild Basil *Clinopodium vulgare* 57

Wild Cabbage *Brassica oleracea* 151

Wild Carrot *Daucus carota* 61, 163

Wood Anemone *Anemone nemorosa* 98, 99

Wood Dock *Rumex sanguineus* 206

Wood-sorrel *Oxalis acetosella* 98

Wood Vetch *Ervilia sylvatica* 324

Yarrow *Achillea millefolium* 61

Yellow Iris *Iris pseudacorus* 113, 229

Yellow-rattle *Rhinanthus minor* 54, 59, 61, 127

Grasses and sedges

bent grasses *Agrostis* spp. 77

Cock's-foot *Dactylis glomerata* 61, 72, 77–79, 82, 102, 129, 144, 163, 293

Common Bent *Agrostis capillaris* 61

Common Couch *Elymus repens* 77–79, 163

Creeping Soft-grass *Holcus mollis* 61, 78, 79, 82

Crested Dog's-tail *Cynosurus cristatus* 61, 82

Downy Oat-grass *Avenula pubescens* 77

False-brome *Brachypodium sylvaticum* 31, 77–79, 82, 144

fescues *Festuca* spp. 77

Field Wood-rush *Luzula campestris* 54

Glaucous Sedge *Carex flacca* 54

meadow-grasses *Poa* spp. 77, 78

Meadow Foxtail *Alopecurus pratensis* 61, 78, 82

Purple Moor-grass *Molinia caerulea* 79

Red Fescue *Festuca rubra* 61, 78, 82

Rough Meadow-grass *Poa trivialis* 82

Sheep's Fescue *Festuca ovina* 82

Smooth-stalked Meadow-grass *Poa pratensis* 61

Soft-brome *Bromus hordaceus* 82

Sweet Vernal-grass *Anthoxanthum odoratum* 54, 82

Timothy *Phleum pratense* 78, 82

Tor-grass *Brachypodium rupestre* 78, 208

Tufted Hair-grass *Deschampsia cespitosa* 78, 163

Yorkshire-fog *Holcus lanatus* 53, 78, 82, 163

Trees

Alder *Alnus glutinosa* 89, 104, 158, 294

Alder Buckthorn *Frangula alnus* 105, 146, 161

Apple *Malus domestica* 160

Ash *Fraxinus excelsior* 89, 91, 103, 105, 109, 159, 195, 339

Aspen *Populus tremula* 104, 158

Beech *Fagus sylvatica* 105, 158, 171, 192

Black-poplar *Populus nigra* 105

Blackthorn *Prunus spinosa* 98, 100, 104, 159, 170, 287

Buckthorn *Rhamnus cathartica* 105, 146

Bullace *Prunus domestica* 104

Cherry Laurel *Prunus laurocerasus* 105

Cherry Plum *Prunus cerasifera* 104

Common Hawthorn *Crataegus monogyna* 15, 95, 100, 102, 104, 159, 170, 193, 268, 287

Crab Apple *Malus sylvestris* 104

Crack Willow *Salix fragilis* 104, 169

Dogwood *Cornus sanguinea* 105

Downy Birch *Betula pubescens* 104

FUNGI

Lichens